...al,

...tual,
...ssues
...
...ma,

...large chal-
...h stunning
...n the litera-
...the effects
...children),
...vides both
...rchers and
...practitio-
...lance, and
...extremely

...ychiatry
...nd Clinic
...of Medicine

More pre-publication
REVIEWS, COMMENTARIES, EVALUATIONS . . .

"**M**ultiple Victimization of Children* opens a new window of understanding on our conceptualization of child abuse. For too long professionals and the public at large [have] sought to neatly compartmentalize the mistreatment of children and in doing so, [have] done a disservice to the children. Anyone working in the area of child maltreatment intuitively knows most mistreated children suffer live poly-abusive environments but there has been no resource until this book which crystallizes our understandings of this problem. Perhaps one of the greatest contributions of the book is that it will assist direct service providers in better understanding the complexity of their efforts.

Multiple Victimization of Children should not just be read by social workers, psychologists and psychiatrists but by police officers, attorneys and judges."

Paul Mones
Children's Rights Attorney
Author of When a Child Kills

"**F**or those of us who have seen firsthand the tragic effects of abuse and neglect on children, it is gratifying to see researchers begin to recognize that abuse comes in many forms, many combinations and from many different directions. This work helps to lay the groundwork for a holistic approach to understanding and healing the victims of multiple trauma.

The contributors to this work recognize how difficult it can be to discriminate between definitions of psychological and physical maltreatment. They realize that just as child physical abuse is comorbid with interspousal aggression and other types of family disturbance, so must trauma models derive from a multidisciplinary approach.

The research on multiple victimization is still in its. infancy, with theories on the effects of multiple victimization just evolving, but the contributors to this work have provided the necessary theoretical underpinnings to guide the in-depth research and intervention needed if we are to achieve more accurate assessments and treatment of multiply victimized children."

Judge Joette Katz
Associate Justice
Supreme Court of Connecticut,
Hartford

HMTP

The Haworth Maltreatment and Trauma Press
An Imprint of The Haworth Press, Inc.

Multiple Victimization of Children: Conceptual, Developmental, Research, and Treatment Issues

Multiple Victimization of Children: Conceptual, Developmental, Research, and Treatment Issues has been co-published simultaneously as *Journal of Aggression, Maltreatment & Trauma*, Volume 2, Number 1 (#3) 1998.

Multiple Victimization of Children:
Conceptual, Developmental, Research, and Treatment Issues

B. B. Robbie Rossman, PhD
Mindy S. Rosenberg, PhD
Editors

Multiple Victimization of Children: Conceptual, Developmental, Research, and Treatment Issues has been co-published simultaneously as *Journal of Aggression, Maltreatment & Trauma*, Volume 2, Number 1 (#3) 1998.

HMTP

The Haworth Maltreatment & Trauma Press
An Imprint of
The Haworth Press, Inc.
New York • London

Published by

The Haworth Maltreatment & Trauma Press, 10 Alice Street, Binghamton, NY 13904-1580 USA

The Haworth Maltreatment & Trauma Press is an imprint of The Haworth Press, Inc., 10 Alice Street, Binghamton, NY 13904-1580 USA.

Multiple Victimization of Children: Conceptual, Developmental, Research, and Treatment Issues has been co-published simultaneously as *Journal of Aggression, Maltreatment & Trauma,* Volume 2, Number 1 (#3) 1998.

Cover design by Thomas J. Mayshock Jr.

Library of Congress Cataloging-in-Publication Data

Multiple victimization of children : conceptual, developmental, research and treatment issues / B.B. Robbie Rossman, Mindy S. Rosenberg, editors.
     p. cm.
     Issued also as v. 2, no. 1 (#3) 1998 of the Journal of aggression, maltreatment & trauma.
     Includes bibliographical references and index.
     ISBN 0-7890-0361-9 (alk. paper.) – ISBN 0-7890-0382-1 (alk. paper)
     1. Child abuse–Psychological aspects. 2. Abused children–Psychology. 3. Abused children–Rehabilitation. 4. Child development. 5. Psychic trauma in children. I. Rossman, B. B. Robbie. II. Rosenberg, Mindy Susan. III. Journal of aggression, maltreatment & trauma ; v. 2, no. 1(#3).

HV6626.5.M86 1998
618.92′858223–DC21
                                              98-10643
                                                  CIP

INDEXING & ABSTRACTING

Contributions to this publication are selectively indexed or abstracted in print, electronic, online, or CD-ROM version(s) of the reference tools and information services listed below. This list is current as of the copyright date of this publication. See the end of this section for additional notes.

- *Cambridge Scientific Abstracts, Risk Abstracts,* 7200 Wisconsin Avenue #601, Bethesda, MD 20814

- *Child Development Abstracts & Bibliography,* University of Kansas, 213 Bailey Hall, Lawrence, KS 66045

- *CNPIEC Reference Guide: Chinese National Directory of Foreign Periodicals,* P.O. Box 88, Beijing, People's Republic of China

- *Criminal Justice Abstracts,* Willow Tree Press, 15 Washington Street, 4th Floor, Newark, NJ 07102

- *Criminology, Penology and Police Science Abstracts,* Kugler Publications, P. O. Box 11188, 1001 GD Amsterdam, The Netherlands

- *Digest of Neurology and Psychiatry,* The Institute of Living, 400 Washington Street, Hartford, CT 06106

- *Family Studies Database (online and CD/ROM),* National Information Services Corporation, 306 East Baltimore Pike, 2nd Floor, Media, PA 19063

- *Index to Periodical Articles Related to Law,* University of Texas, 727 East 26th Street, Austin, TX 78705

- *INTERNET ACCESS (& additional networks) Bulletin Board for Libraries ("BUBL") coverage of information resources on INTERNET, JANET, and other networks.*
    - <URL:http://bubl.ac.uk/>
    - The new locations will be found under <URL:http://bubl.ac.uk/link/>.
    - Any existing BUBL users who have problems finding information on the new service should contact the BUBL help line by sending e-mail to <bubl@bubl.ac.uk>.
  The Andersonian Library, Curran Building, 101 St. James Road, Glasgow G4 0NS, Scotland

- *Mental Health Abstracts (online through DIALOG),* IFI/Plenum Data Company, 3202 Kirkwood Highway, Wilmington, DE 19808

(continued)

- *PASCAL,* %Institute de L'Information Scientifique et Technique. Cross-disciplinary electronic database covering the fields of science, technology & medicine. Also available on CD-ROM, and can generate customized retrospective searches. For more information: INIST, Customer Desk, 2, allee du Parc de Brabois, F-54514 Vandoeuvre Cedex, France; http//www.inist.fr

- *Psychiatric Rehabilitation Journal,* 930 Commonwealth Avenue, Boston, MA 02215

- *Published International Literature on Traumatic Stress (The PILOTS Database),* National Center for Post-Traumatic Stress Disorder (116D), VA Medical Center, White River Junction, VT 05009

- *Referativnyi Zhurnal* (Abstracts Journal of the All-Russian Institute of Scientific and Technical Information), 20 Usievich Street, Moscow 125219, Russia

SPECIAL BIBLIOGRAPHIC NOTES

related to special journal issues (separates)
and indexing/abstracting

☐ indexing/abstracting services in this list will also cover material in any "separate" that is co-published simultaneously with Haworth's special thematic journal issue or DocuSerial. Indexing/abstracting usually covers material at the article/chapter level.

☐ monographic co-editions are intended for either non-subscribers or libraries which intend to purchase a second copy for their circulating collections.

☐ monographic co-editions are reported to all jobbers/wholesalers/approval plans. The source journal is listed as the "series" to assist the prevention of duplicate purchasing in the same manner utilized for books-in-series.

☐ to facilitate user/access services all indexing/abstracting services are encouraged to utilize the co-indexing entry note indicated at the bottom of the first page of each article/chapter/contribution.

☐ this is intended to assist a library user of any reference tool (whether print, electronic, online, or CD-ROM) to locate the monographic version if the library has purchased this version but not a subscription to the source journal.

☐ individual articles/chapters in any Haworth publication are also available through the Haworth Document Delivery Service (HDDS).

Multiple Victimization of Children: Conceptual, Developmental, Research, and Treatment Issues

CONTENTS

ABOUT THE EDITORS

B. B. Robbie Rossman, PhD, is Senior Clinical Professor on the Child Clinical Faculty in the Psychology Department at the University of Denver, where she teaches, conducts research, and provides clinical supervision. She is a member of various professional societies, including the American Psychological Association, the Society for Research in Child Development, and the American Counseling Association and serves as a reviewer and editorial board member for several professional publications, including the *Journal of Child Sexual Abuse* and the *Family Violence and Sexual Assault Bulletin*. Dr. Rossman's research interests are in the area of children's stress and coping–specifically in children who experience the trauma of witnessing parental violence and/or personal maltreatment. She has authored journal articles and chapters and has presented invited papers on these subjects.

Mindy S. Rosenberg, PhD, is in private practice in Sausalito, California. She has been a faculty member at the University of Denver and Yale University and a Visiting Assistant Professor at the University of California, Berkeley. Dr. Rosenberg's research interests are in the area of child maltreatment, with a focus on children of battered women and the socioemotional sequelae of child physical and psychological abuse. She has authored numerous professional articles and book chapters on this topic and has been invited to lecture and consult on related issues across the country and internationally. Dr. Rosenberg is Co-Editor of *Prevention of Child Maltreatment: Developmental and Ecological Perspectives.*

ABOUT THE CONTRIBUTORS

David Baumgarten, JD, is County Attorney in Gunnison County, Colorado. He has practiced criminal and civil law, and now, as County Attorney, represents the Department of Social Services in cases of alleged child maltreatment.

Bette L. Bottoms, PhD, is Assistant Professor of Psychology at the University of Illinois, Chicago, with research interests on religion-related child abuse, the reliability of children's eyewitness testimony, and jurors' perceptions of children's testimony. She is co-editor (with Gail Goodman) of the book *Child Victims, Child Witnesses* (Guilford, 1993).

Holland Cole-Detke, PhD, obtained her doctorate from the clinical psychology program at the University of Delaware. Her research interests include developmental psychopathology and attachment, with a specific focus on eating disorders and depression.

Jan L. Culbertson, PhD, is Associate Professor, Department of Pediatrics, University of Oklahoma Health Sciences Center, and Director of Child Neuropsychology Services, Child Study Center. She has been active in teaching, clinical practice, editorships, and in leadership roles within the American Psychological Association, including past president of Division 12, Section 1 (Clinical Child Psychology) and Division 37 (Child, Youth, and Family Services).

E. Mark Cummings, PhD, is Professor of Psychology at Notre Dame University. He has published widely on topics pertinent to developmental, child clinical, and family psychology, including the impact of aggression, abuse, and depression in children in families. He is Associate Editor on the Board of Editors for *Child Development* and is on the editorial board of *Developmental Psychology*.

Kathleen R. Diviak, MA, is a doctoral student in psychology at the University of Illinois, Chicago, with research interests in allegations of repressed memories of childhood abuse and women's health issues.

Michael Eltz, PhD, is a post-doctoral Fellow at the University of Colorado Health Sciences Center. His research and clinical interests focus on the role of relational schema in emotion regulation and multidisciplinary treatment for disadvantaged children.

Gail S. Goodman, PhD, Professor of Psychology at the University of California, Davis, has numerous scientific publications on child abuse and children's testimony. She has served as President of the Division of Child, Youth, and Family Services, is current President of the Division of Psychology and Law of the American Psychological Association, and is a founding member of the American Professional Society on the Abuse of Children (APSAC).

K. Lori Hanson, MA, is a doctoral student in psychology at Saint Louis University and does research with children in violent families.

Stuart N. Hart, EdD, is affiliated with the Office for the Study of the Psychological Rights of the Child, and Professor, School of Education, Indiana University at Indianapolis.

Susan Harter, PhD, is Professor of Psychology at the University of Denver. Her research interests include the development of the self system, childhood dysphoria and depression, developmental changes in affect identification and expression, and gender-related relationship styles. She publishes widely in these areas, and is internationally known for this work and her scales of perceived competence which have been translated into several languages.

Clare Haynes-Seman, PhD, is Associate Professor in Pediatrics at the University of Colorado School of Medicine, and Director of the Family Evaluation Team at the Kempe National Center for the Prevention and Treatment of Child Abuse and Neglect. For over a decade, her clinical work has involved developing assessment procedures for evaluating parent-child relationships and psychosocial difficulties that interfere with effective parenting in cases of alleged child maltreatment.

Honore M. Hughes, PhD, is Professor, Department of Psychology, Saint Louis University. Her research first drew attention to children in violent families and she continues those contributions as well as additional writing, editorial work and teaching.

Roger Kobak, PhD, is Associate Professor in the clinical psychology program at the University of Delaware. His research interests and publications have been in the areas of attachment theory, the development of relationships, and identification of risk factors for adolescent psychopathology.

Douglas S. Liebert, PhD, is a clinical and forensic psychologist and marriage, family and child counselor. He is currently Clinical Director of the Family Therapy Institute of Sacramento, Inc., on the clinical faculty at the Professional School of Psychology, Sacramento, and was prior chair of the state ethics committee of the California Association of Marriage and Family Therapists.

Donna B. Marold, PhD, is a licensed clinical psychologist and marriage and family therapist in private practice. She is also a senior attending psychologist at the Center for Trauma and Dissociation at Bethesda Hospital in Denver and a Research Associate at the University of Denver. Her research, treatment and forensic work have focused on the diagnosis and treatment of dissociative disorders in children and adults.

Ann S. Masten, PhD, is Associate Professor of Child Psychology and Associate Director of the Institute of Child Development at the University of Minnesota. Her research has focused on the processes by which children's academic and social competence and mental health are fostered or undermined. She has studied the effects of homelessness, war and other adversities on development.

Caroline C. Murray, EdD, is Lecturer in Psychology in the Department of Psychiatry (Emerita) at Harvard Medical School. She works with the Massachusetts Mental Health Center, Indochinese Psychiatric Clinic and Harvard School of Public Health and World Federation for Mental Health in the Harvard Program in Refugee Trauma.

Frank W. Putnam, MD, is a child psychiatrist and Senior Clinical Investigator, Chief, on the Unit on Dissociative Disorders in the Laboratory of Developmental Psychology, National Institute of Mental Health, who directs research on the psychobiological effects of trauma and maltreatment on children and adults.

Allison Redlich, MA, is a doctoral student in psychology at the University of California, Davis, with research interests in children's allegations of sexual abuse, perpetrators' motivations, and jurors' reactions to child witnesses.

Mindy S. Rosenberg, PhD, is in independent practice as a clinical psychologist and forensic consultant in the area of stress and trauma and its effects on child, adolescent and young adult development. She has authored numerous journal articles and book chapters on child maltreatment including witnessing interparental violence, and has co-edited *Prevention of Child Maltreatment: Developmental and Ecological Perspectives* with Diane Willis and E. Wayne Holden.

B. B. Robbie Rossman, PhD, is Senior Clinical Professor in the Psychology Department at the University of Denver and Adjunct Clinical Instructor with the University of Colorado Health Sciences Center. She is also co-editor for the *Journal of Emotional Abuse* and has authored numerous journal articles and book chapters on her research interests, which include children's reaction to stressful and traumatic experiences, including witnessing interparental violence.

Phillip R. Shaver, PhD, is currently Professor and Chair of the Psychology Department at the University of California, Davis, with research interests in emotions, close relationships, and social influences in therapy settings. He has edited five books in addition to his numerous publications, including *Measures of Personality and Social Psychological Attitudes* and coauthored *In Search of Intimacy.*

Stephen R. Shirk, PhD, is Director of the Child Study Center and Associate Professor of Psychology at the University of Denver. His postdoctoral work focused on family violence and his current research examines the role of relationship schema, and interpersonal processes in child psychopathology and therapy with children and youth.

Linda Son, EdD, is a recent graduate of Harvard University's Graduate School of Education and researcher with the Refugee Trauma Program, focusing on the psychological impact of war trauma on children and adolescents.

Daniel J. Sonkin, PhD, is a licensed marriage, family and child counselor in independent practice in Sausalito, California, and lecturer at the California State University, Sonoma. He is also chair of the state ethics committee of the California Association of Marriage and Family Therapists, and author of several books on domestic violence, including treatment of men who batter and child abuse.

Penelope K. Trickett, PhD, is Research Associate Professor in the Department of Psychology, University of Southern California. Her research is in the area of child victimization, focusing on sexual abuse. She contributes frequently to the literature in this area and has recently co-edited a volume on the impact of violence on children.

Diane J. Willis, PhD, is Professor of Psychology, Department of Pediatrics, University of Oklahoma Health Sciences Center and Director of Psychological Services, Child Study Center. She has held a number of influential leadership positions including past member of the U.S. Advisory Board on Child Abuse and Neglect (1990-94), Chair of the American Psychological Association (APA) Coordinating Committee on Child Abuse and Neglect, past President of the APA Division 12, Sections 1 (Clinical Child Psychology), and 5 (Society of Pediatric Psychology), and Division 37 (Child, Youth, and Family Services), and is author or editor of over thirty books, chapters, and articles.

Margaret O'Dougherty Wright, PhD, is Associate Professor of Clinical Psychology at Miami University. Her research focuses on the impact of stressful child experiences on later adaptation, with a particular interest in the integration of biological, developmental, social and cultural factors in understanding the development of psychopathology.

Foreword

Chaos is in the mind of the beholder, due to ignorance of the multitude of factors and their individual and interactive influences on the conditions we experience. Our lack of effectiveness in understanding and combatting child maltreatment is probably substantially due to the tendencies of theorists, researchers and intervenors to reduce it to "understandable" dimensions and overly invest themselves in the territories they establish. A metaphor I have used occasionally to indicate the significance of psychological maltreatment, slightly modified, aptly fits the general field of child maltreatment work: like the man who lost his car keys in the dark and chooses to search for them under the street light, we will not find the keys to child maltreatment until we investigate the grey and dark areas of multiple factors and relationships. Reporting, theory, research, and intervention for abuse and neglect have tended to be restricted to singular or primary consideration of physical, psychological or sexual maltreatment, as though they did not co-occur. In truth it is probable that the vast majority of cases embody at least two of these forms in interaction. This book helps to correct this fault by clarifying conditions of multiple victimization, and their conceptual and treatment implications. Its contributions should be of practical and heuristic significance to all those ready to deal with the genuine complexities of child maltreatment.

Stuart N. Hart

[Haworth co-indexing entry note]: "Foreword." Hart, Stuart N. Co-published simultaneously in *Journal of Aggression, Maltreatment & Trauma* (The Haworth Maltreatment & Trauma Press, an imprint of The Haworth Press, Inc.) Vol. 2, No. 1 (#3), 1998, p. xix; and: *Multiple Victimization of Children: Conceptual, Developmental, Research, and Treatment Issues* (ed: B. B. Robbie Rossman, and Mindy S. Rosenberg) The Haworth Maltreatment & Trauma Press, an imprint of The Haworth Press, Inc., 1998, p. xix. Single or multiple copies of this article are available for a fee from The Haworth Document Delivery Service [1-800-342-9678, 9:00 a.m. - 5:00 p.m. (EST). E-mail address: getinfo@haworth.com].

Preface

It is a pleasure to introduce this volume. We often view the victimization of children in singular terms such as child physical maltreatment, sexual maltreatment, neglect, or psychological maltreatment. However, it has become increasingly clear that many children suffer from multiple types of maltreatment, sometimes by several perpetrators. This topic, though, has not received much emphasis in the research or intervention literature. The editors, Rossman and Rosenberg, have brought together an excellent group of researchers and clinicians to discuss the state of the art concerning theory, research, and intervention for the children who have been multiply victimized. The expertise of the editors is also apparent, not only by their choices for authors, but also by their individual and combined efforts in researching and treating these children. This is evident in the articles they have written for this collection.

The inclusion of conceptual models from child development, stress, and trauma perspectives has been generally lacking in the field, and the articles in this volume provide important frameworks for enhancing our understanding of the dynamics involved in such victimization. In addition, children and adolescents are often grouped together in research and treatment programs without looking carefully at differential effects of the victimization. The editors and authors do an excellent job of focusing on the impact of such victimization occurring at different ages and the effects on different aspects of personality and perceptions. Intervention is also presented for children at different developmental levels. This is much more helpful than generic or global interventions.

The combination of researchers and clinicians from different perspectives in this book gives the reader a broad view for understanding the dynamics of such victimization and trauma and for intervening with these

[Haworth co-indexing entry note]: "Preface." Geffner, Robert. Co-published simultaneously in *Journal of Aggression, Maltreatment & Trauma* (The Haworth Maltreatment & Trauma Press, an imprint of The Haworth Press, Inc.) Vol. 2, No. 1 (#3), 1998, pp. xxi-xxii; and: *Multiple Victimization of Children: Conceptual, Developmental, Research, and Treatment Issues* (ed: B. B. Robbie Rossman, and Mindy S. Rosenberg) The Haworth Maltreatment & Trauma Press, an imprint of The Haworth Press, Inc., 1998, pp. xxi-xxii. Single or multiple copies of this article are available for a fee from The Haworth Document Delivery Service [1-800-342-9678, 9:00 a.m. - 5:00 p.m. (EST). E-mail address: getinfo@haworth.com].

xxi

children. As the editors note, a paradigm shift is necessary in both the research and treatment of children who have been victims of multiple forms of abuse. The articles in this volume should be a significant contribution to the field, and should help in accomplishing this goal. I am grateful to the editors and the authors for producing such a worthwhile addition to our knowledge, and for including their work as part of this docuserial program.

Robert Geffner, PhD
Senior Editor
Journal of Aggression, Maltreatment & Trauma

INTRODUCTION

The Multiple Victimization of Children: Incidence and Conceptual Issues

B. B. Robbie Rossman
Mindy S. Rosenberg

SUMMARY. Incidence of different types of child abuse is reported and the issue of co-occurrence of different types of abuse and adversity is raised. Three dimensions along which multiple victimization may be considered are proposed. A paradigm shift is recommended wherein professionals concerned with child abuse take into consideration all of the sources of abuse and adversity in a child's life circumstance, remaining cognizant of the child's developmental position, tasks and needs. Confronting this complexity will advance our understanding of child abuse and lead to more productive interventions and policies to support the growth and well-being of children. *[Article copies available for a fee from The Haworth Document Delivery Service: 1-800-342-9678. E-mail address: getinfo@haworth.com]*

Address correspondence to: B. B. Robbie Rossman, PhD, Department of Psychology, 2155 Race Street, University of Denver, Denver, CO 80208.

[Haworth co-indexing entry note]: "The Multiple Victimization of Children: Incidence and Conceptual Issues." Rossman, B. B. Robbie, and Mindy S. Rosenberg. Co-published simultaneously in *Journal of Aggression, Maltreatment & Trauma* (The Haworth Maltreatment & Trauma Press, an imprint of The Haworth Press, Inc.) Vol. 2, No. 1 (#3), 1998, pp. 1-5; and: *Multiple Victimization of Children: Conceptual, Developmental, Research, and Treatment Issues* (ed: B. B. Robbie Rossman, and Mindy S. Rosenberg) The Haworth Maltreatment & Trauma Press, an imprint of The Haworth Press, Inc., 1998, pp. 1-5. Single or multiple copies of this article are available for a fee from The Haworth Document Delivery Service [1-800-342-9678, 9:00 a.m. - 5:00 p.m. (EST). E-mail address: getinfo@haworth.com].

1

In 1994 there were abuse reports received involving more than 2.9 million children in this country (HHS/NCCAN, 1996), with over one million children determined to be victims of child abuse or neglect. Case reports have increased 13.9% since 1990, but abuse rates remained stable at 43 children per 1000 for 1992-1994. Incidence reports are organized in terms of four types of maltreatment (i.e., physical abuse and neglect, sexual abuse, and emotional maltreatment) and research has focused on one type of abuse at a time. Yet, the NCCAN report notes that some states will record a child under several categories if more than one is indicated; and, researchers are beginning to either screen out or gather information about additional types of abuse when targeting one. This emerging awareness that children may be victimized in multiple ways is timely. While clinicians have always needed to respond to the multiple adversities encountered by children, researchers, theorists, educators, legal professionals and policy makers have attended to single types of abuse even when co-occurring with other forms of adversity.

One purpose of this volume is to address the need to focus on the multiple victimization of children. A second purpose is to foster the use of developmental theory and research in understanding the impact of multiple sources of adversity in children's lives. Adversity is experienced differently by different children, and an important source of this heterogeneity is the child's developmental task and strengths and weaknesses when the adversity occurs. As noted by several authors in this volume, there needs to be a paradigm shift wherein development and multiple sources of adversity are taken into consideration in trying to understand the etiology, sequelae, intervention, and needed legal action or policy. In this volume theorists, researchers, and clinicians have made this paradigm shift.

CHILD MALTREATMENT

In the following articles authors have defined the four major types of abuse. However, the reader should be warned that definitions vary from one research project to another and one legal jurisdiction to another. In addition to formal definitions, phenomena such as sibling abuse have raised the issue of the extent to which the perpetrator needs to be in a position of power over the child victim for an act to be considered legally abusive. Commonly, a five-year age difference between abuser and abused has been the way in which a position of power is determined (Finkelhor, 1979). Unfortunately, this criterion may miss important exceptions such as where a 16-year-old sexually abuses a 14-year-old or a nine-year-old batters a six-year-old.

Definitional issues remain complex, legally and psychologically, and we don't currently have a precise scale against which to judge either the finer nuances of abusive behaviors or the immediate or longer-term sequelae. This is not surprising, since even single types of abusive behaviors cannot be studied under controlled conditions where systematic information about abuse severity would be available.

MULTIPLE VICTIMIZATION

Initially, multiple victimization was conceptualized as a situation where a child had experienced more than one type of maltreatment. This definition was troublesome because, for example, psychological maltreatment and physical neglect overlap definitionally, and psychological maltreatment seems inherent in the other forms of abuse. It was also troublesome because it did not include a time dimension. This is important because one might expect different sequelae for a child who had been sexually abused only once, as with some cases of extrafamilial abuse, versus a child who had been repeatedly abused. The latter child has been multiply victimized which may have implications not captured when repetition is only thought of as a dimension of abuse severity. Finally, the concept of multiple victimization needs to encompass instances of abuse that are embedded in other types of adversity such as neighborhood violence or extreme poverty. The concept of embeddedness or multiple risk, while familiar to resilience researchers, has not been treated directly in work on maltreatment. As consideration of multiple victimization increases, the concept will probably be refined to include different or additional dimensions. The three dimensions of type, repetition and embeddedness offered here will hopefully serve as a stimulus for further thinking and scholarship.

THIS VOLUME

This volume is divided into five sections. In the first section, the authors apply three conceptual models to further our understanding of multiple victimization and provide theoretical underpinnings to guide research and intervention. Ann Masten and Margaret Wright describe cumulative risk and protection models relevant for child maltreatment. Mark Cummings presents a stress and coping approach to understanding the problem marital conflict poses for children, emphasizing the study of the specific context of exposure, individual differences in children's coping responses, and the multi-dimensional nature of coping. Frank Putnam then addresses trauma models and their relationship to maltreatment effects, noting that a posttraumatic stress disorder model of victimization could be useful but is currently hindered by definitional constraints and not sufficiently inclusive.

The second section is concerned with the current literature on multiply victimized young children, school-aged children, and adolescents. Authors in this section searched to find examples of empirically based research using multiply victimized children and youth. Unfortunately, they found few studies at any one age group that considered sequelae associated with more than one type of maltreatment. Clare Haynes-Seman and David Baumgarten focus on young children, B. B. Robbie Rossman, Honore Hughes and K. Lori Hanson review the literature on school-aged children, and Rossman and Mindy Rosenberg address the adolescent age group.

In the next section, authors integrate the theoretical and research literature in specific developmental domains known to be affected by child abuse. Because the research literature on multiple victimization is still in its infancy, authors were encouraged to apply their expertise, identify research gaps, and speculate about ways in which development would be affected for these children. Caroline Murray and Linda Son describe effects of trauma and multiple victimization on the development of children's cognition and memory. Susan Harter focuses on the self system and how multiple victimization affects various aspects of the self such as awareness and coherence. Penelope Trickett elaborates on the development of behavior and emotion regulation in maltreated children and families, and Holland Cole-Detke and Roger Kobak describe the effects of multiple abuse on interpersonal relationships from an Attachment perspective.

Treatment approaches and issues are considered in the fourth section. Within the relatively small literature on empirical treatment studies, it was rare to find systematic analysis of treatment approaches that targeted multiply victimized children. Therefore, authors primarily used theoretical ideas to guide their thinking about what treatment might be developed for this population, and reviewed available literature from that perspective. Jan Culbertson and Diane Willis focus on developmental and ecological perspectives in their discussion of treatment approaches for young children and their families. Stephen Shirk and Michael Eltz consider school-age children, and address the process and outcome features of child psychotherapy. Donna Marold uses Eriksonian theory to guide her in working with adolescents and offers clinical examples of issues that arise in therapy with this population.

The last section consists of articles on special topics, including the work of Gail Goodman and colleagues on correlates of multiple victimization in religion-related abuse cases, and Daniel Sonkin and Douglas Liebert's article on specific issues that might create legal and ethical dilemmas for clinicians treating multiply victimized clients. Thus, the volume presents the best current information and thinking about multiple victimization. It hopefully, at the same time, challenges researchers, clinicians, and others working with this population to extend their thinking and work toward more accurate assessment of multiply victimized children and youth, and interventions that can address the complexity of psychological outcomes associated with their experiences.

REFERENCES

Finkelhor, D.A. (1979). *Sexually victimized children*. New York: Norton.

U.S. Department of Health and Human Services, National Center on Child Abuse and Neglect. (1996). *Child maltreatment 1994: Reports from the states to the National Center on Child Abuse and Neglect*. Washington, DC: U.S. Government Printing Office.

INCIDENCE AND CONCEPTUAL ISSUES

Cumulative Risk and Protection Models of Child Maltreatment

Ann S. Masten
Margaret O'Dougherty Wright

SUMMARY. The often misused concepts of risk, vulnerability, protective factors, and resilience are clearly defined and existing models of child risk are presented. Research of risk and protective factors for child maltreatment is then discussed as it reflects on these models. A major conclusion is that child maltreatment exists within a complex context of cumulative risk and protection which needs to be considered in designing research of intervention programs. This article provides one of the clearest presentations and integrations in the literature of the conceptual bases and research findings relevant for

Address correspondence to: Ann S. Masten, PhD, Institute of Child Development, University of Minnesota, 51 East River Road, Minneapolis, MN 55455.

Preparation of this article was facilitated by grants to Dr. Masten from the William T. Grant Foundation and to Dr. Wright from the Ohio Department of Mental Health.

[Haworth co-indexing entry note]: "Cumulative Risk and Protection Models of Child Maltreatment." Masten, Ann S., and Margaret O'Dougherty Wright. Co-published simultaneously in *Journal of Aggression, Maltreatment & Trauma* (The Haworth Maltreatment & Trauma Press, an imprint of The Haworth Press, Inc.) Vol. 2, No. 1 (#3), 1998, pp. 7-30; and: *Multiple Victimization of Children: Conceptual, Developmental, Research, and Treatment Issues* (ed: B. B. Robbie Rossman, and Mindy S. Rosenberg) The Haworth Maltreatment & Trauma Press, an imprint of The Haworth Press, Inc., 1998, pp. 7-30. Single or multiple copies of this article are available for a fee from The Haworth Document Delivery Service [1-800-342-9678, 9:00 a.m. - 5:00 p.m. (EST). E-mail address: getinfo@haworth.com].

7

considering child risk and resilience. *[Article copies available for a fee from The Haworth Document Delivery Service: 1-800-342-9678. E-mail address: getinfo@haworth.com]*

INTRODUCTION

Efforts to understand the etiology and consequences of child maltreatment increasingly reflect the recognition of complexity and context in human development (Cicchetti & Carlson, 1989; National Research Council, 1993). After a quarter century of research, no single risk factor has emerged as the primary catalyst for abusive or neglectful treatment; rather, data have suggested that a complex interplay of multiple risk factors and the absence of protective or buffering influences characterize the pathway to abuse and neglect. Similarly, no single pattern of response to maltreatment has been observed. Instead, outcomes of maltreated children are diverse. Theories about maltreatment, as well as empirical data, point to the importance of models that encompass multiple systems in dynamic interaction as they influence and are influenced by individual development. Such multifactorial models represent, for maltreatment research as well as the field of child development more generally, first steps toward a more comprehensive understanding of individual functioning in the context of the many systems directly or indirectly connected to the child, including family, peers, community, culture and society.

The purpose of this article is to examine cumulative risk and protection approaches for understanding the antecedents and consequences of child victimization in the form of physical and sexual abuse, neglect or psychological maltreatment. First, the conceptual roots and meaning of risk, vulnerability, resources and resilience will be considered, particularly with respect to maltreatment. Next, multifactorial models of maltreatment will be discussed and then the data concerning three aspects of maltreatment will be examined in relation to cumulative risk/protection models: (a) risk for parents maltreating children, (b) risk for a child becoming the victim of maltreatment, and (c) maltreatment as a risk factor for psychosocial development. Finally, implications of these models and findings for intervention and future research will be discussed.

CONCEPTUAL MODELS OF RISK, VULNERABILITY, AND RESILIENCE

Terms such as "risk," "vulnerability," and "protective factor" have been used in varying and often confusing ways in the literature reviewed here. Therefore, a glossary of these terms as utilized in this article is provided in Table 1. The terms are defined with respect to their use in the behavioral sciences and their meaning for *individual* adaptation or development. These terms refer to the *functional significance* of a measurable quality of the individual, his or her environment or relationships for the adjustment or developmental outcome of the individual. The same characteristic theoretically could function both as a vulnerability and a protective factor, depending on the criterion, the context, the child, the age period, etc.

Risk and Cumulative Risk

Risk implies uncertainty, either about whether a hazard will occur or about outcome once a hazard has occurred. In the study of child maltreatment, investigators have attempted to identify the predictors of *occurrence* (risk factors for parents maltreating children or the risk factors for children becoming victims) as well as predictors of *consequences* (i.e., maltreatment as a risk factor for developmental problems or psychopathology).

Historically, psychosocial risk research has followed a pattern that begins a period of cross-sectional, retrospective research that is typically followed by prospective studies revealing greater heterogeneity of outcomes among members of the risk group than retrospective data would suggest (Masten & Garmezy, 1985). For example, retrospective studies of abusive parents indicated high rates of childhood abuse among the parents, leading to a bleak picture of the intergenerational transmission of maltreatment; prospective studies suggest a weaker link and indicate that the majority of those abused as children do not become abusive parents (Kaufman & Zigler, 1989; Widom, 1989b).

Studies focused on the antecedent predictors of troublesome outcomes also typically reveal a multiplicity of risk factors. Consequently, risk status often is calculated on the basis of multiple-risk indicators that combine some of these risk factors, to achieve greater predictive power (Garmezy & Masten, 1994). In child maltreatment, multifactorial risk can be considered in terms of the multiple factors that together predict a greater likelihood of parents or others maltreating children or that predict worse outcomes in maltreated children.

It is also possible that risk factors interact and the effects are magnified when they co-occur or pile-up, such that the overall effect is greater than the sum of the individual risk factors. Prematurity, for example, has worse consequences in the context of poverty (Kopp, 1983; Sameroff & Chandler, 1975). Child maltreatment in the context of psychosocial disadvan-

TABLE 1. A Glossary of Individual Risk and Resilience Terminology

Compensatory factor	A correlate of successful adaptation or development under both favorable and unfavorable conditions that may directly offset or counterbalance the negative effects of risk or adversity.
Cumulative protection	The presence of multiple protective factors in an individual's life, either within or across time.
Cumulative risk	Risk status that is compounded by (a) the presence of multiple risk factors, (b) multiple occurrences of the same risk factor, or (c) the accumulating effects of ongoing risk or adversity.
Protective factor	A correlate of resilience that may reflect preventive or ameliorative influences; a positive moderator of risk or adversity.
Resilience	Successful adaptation or development during or following adverse conditions that challenge or threaten adaptive functioning or healthy development.
Risk	An elevated probability of an undesirable outcome.
Risk factor	A measurable characteristic of individuals that heightens the probability of a worse outcome in the future for groups of individuals who share the risk factor or who have more of the risk variable than a comparison group who do not have the risk factor or have less of the risk variable.
Stress	The state or experience of an imbalance between the demands impinging on an individual and the actual or perceived resources available to meet the challenge, that at some level disrupts the equilibrium of functioning or threatens the organism's adaptive capacity.
Stressors	Events or experiences with the expected potential to trigger stress; stimuli that are believed to cause stress in normative populations.
Vulnerability	Individual susceptibility to undesirable outcomes related to traits or conditions that function to jeopardize adaptation by increasing the probability of exposure to or consequences of risk factors; the diathesis in diathesis/stressor models of psychopathology.
Vulnerability factor	A characteristic that increases the degree of an individual's exposure to or the net negative impact of risk factors or stressors on individual functioning or development; a negative moderator of risk or adversity.

tage or poor parenting could also have much greater consequences than any of these risk factors occurring in isolation.

Both theory and data on cumulative risk suggest that severe and repeated stressors have more damaging consequences (Garmezy & Masten, 1994). For all types of child maltreatment, severity dimensions of the experience as well as chronic or repeated mistreatment have been associated with worse outcomes (National Research Council, 1993).

Certain risk factors may also have more salient effects than others. In the case of delinquency, for example, harsh and inconsistent parenting is more salient than poor parental health as a risk factor (Loeber, 1990). In child maltreatment, the fact that the perpetrator is also the primary caregiver could have more damaging consequences than similar maltreatment by an extra-familial adult.

In risk research, as corroborating evidence mounts for the riskiness of certain experiences or characteristics for particular outcomes, attention to the processes underlying the connections between the risk factors and outcomes increases (Rutter, 1990). Research shifts focus from studies delineating risk to studies testing hypotheses about the mechanisms through which risk factors have their influence. Ironically, cumulative risk indices, while powerful predictors, may obscure the processes underlying risk effects. As the study of risk shifts to process, much more focused studies may be required to test hypothesized mechanisms. Process-oriented research, particularly in the initial stages, may require closer examination of portions of complex multi-system models.

Vulnerability

Risk is sometimes confused with vulnerability, the latter referring to *individual susceptibility* to harm or injury. An individual can belong to a group believed to be at risk for exposure to some hazard or to negative outcome, but an individual can also have a vulnerability that makes exposure to hazard or its negative impact more likely. Some groups of people (e.g., infants) also may be viewed as generally "vulnerable" because each person in the category is relatively defenseless under many threatening conditions.

An analogy may clarify the meaning of vulnerability. Living in certain states increases the risk of exposure to tornadoes, but some homes are more vulnerable to damage when exposed to tornado force winds. Such homes may be structurally weak or unprotected. Moreover, one effect of a tornado may be to weaken the structure of a specific home such that it becomes more vulnerable to future stressors.

Such an analogy, however, only captures part of the story of human vulnerability because people, unlike houses, can behave in ways that influence their own exposure to hazards. For example, individuals can increase their risk by provocative behaviors or choices that place them in very risky situations, such as walking alone at night in a high crime area. Similarly, children inclined to intervene in violent interactions between their parents may be more vulnerable to harm than children who are more cautious and withdraw when conflict escalates.

In child maltreatment research, investigators have examined whether some individuals and families are more vulnerable to the risky conditions that may contribute to maltreating or becoming a victim, and also the degree to which some children are more vulnerable to the experience of maltreatment, so that the impact is greater. Some children, due to their temperament, appearance, or behavior, may be more likely to become victims of maltreatment. Others may be more vulnerable to becoming victims because normal protective mechanisms are not present, as when a parent fails to provide basic safety from dangerous adults. It is also conceivable that culture plays a role in individual vulnerability, for example, girls may be more vulnerable to neglect in cultures where girls are valued less than boys (Skuse & Bentovim, 1994).

Children also vary in their susceptibility to damage from victimization once it occurs; vulnerability may vary by personality, age, appraisals of the experience, and many other individual differences. It is also possible for a child's vulnerability to change as a function of development or experience. Maltreatment may disrupt many normal developmental processes, such as the development of self-concept, interpersonal relationships, or self-regulation of affect or arousal. Thus, one consequence of maltreatment for a child may be increasing vulnerability to subsequent trauma; repeated or chronic victimization could lead to increasingly severe and long-lasting effects on a child through increasing vulnerability.

Resilience

Studies of children at risk due to the presence of one or more risk factors, including various stressors and adversities, have revealed striking variations in outcome, particularly in prospective studies (Masten, 1994). Such variations can be attributed to inadequate risk indices, lower doses of risk, unmeasured risk or vulnerability factors, or other unmeasured properties of individuals, their environments, or their interaction that compensate for adversity or protect development in other ways. In the area of maltreatment, all of these factors may be operative. In addition, some of the damaging effects may not occur until a later developmental stage. Thus, outcome needs to be assessed longitudinally, with multiple assessment periods.

The observation of unexpectedly good development among high-risk children gave rise to the study of resilience, an effort to identify the processes underlying successful adaptation under adverse conditions. Variables associated with better outcomes in the context of risk or adversity have been called "compensatory factors," "protective factors" "buffers," and "resilience factors." In child maltreatment research, there has been increasing interest in the qualities of the child, family, community, and society that either function to prevent or reduce the risk for child maltreatment despite apparently high-risk conditions or that reduce the impact of maltreatment on development in individual children (Cicchetti, Rogosch, Lynch, & Holt, 1993; Crittenden, 1985; National Research Council, 1993).

Compensatory factors are assets or resources that generally predict good outcomes, so that given high-risk conditions, better outcomes would be expected for people with these assets. Often, risk and compensatory factors are different names for the same continuous variables, such as intellectual functioning, that are correlated with outcomes, such as academic achievement. However, some assets/resources may operate only at the positive end (by their presence): a talent or a good community center, for example, may help if you have it but not hurt you if you lack it. Similarly, there are risk factors that may harm you if they occur, such as maltreatment, but that do not help you if they do not occur.

When variables apparently function to *prevent* risks or *ameliorate* their effects, these are often termed protective factors. Just as risk and compensatory factors can refer to the same variables, vulnerability and protective factors may refer to continuous variables, such as the quality of parenting, that may ameliorate or potentiate risk at different points along a continuum. Yet there are presumably protective factors that operate solely by their presence in the context of risk/adversity. Human antibodies and automobile airbags are examples of protective factors that operate only by their presence, and only when triggered. Similarly, a child in danger can trigger protective intervention by dialing 911. Under normal conditions, however, such protective factors may have no function, except perhaps by offering greater "peace of mind."

Complexity

It is difficult for definitions of risk, vulnerability, and protective factors to capture the complexity of human behavior and development. Many influences operate simultaneously in a child's life and living systems continually interact in ways that change risk, vulnerability and protective processes. Moreover, the same child characteristic, for example, may be protective in one situation or for one outcome and a vulnerability or risk factor with respect to another situation or outcome. For example, compliance with adult requests, while adaptive in a classroom setting or healthy home environment, may make a child vulnerable to an exploitive or abusive adult. Moreover, people and situations change over time. With development, a child's growing understanding of the world may increase the awareness and distress associated with interparental conflict at the same time that resources outside the family become more accessible.

Multifactorial Models of Risk and Intervention

A wide variety of risks, resources, vulnerabilities and protective factors have been linked to psychosocial development. Prominent among these are the quality of caregiving, socioeconomic status, intellectual functioning, and stressful or traumatic life experiences, including maltreatment (Masten & Coatsworth, 1995). These variables include attributes and relationships among child, peers, family, community, culture, and society. Thus, multifactorial models predicting an outcome such as antisocial behavior now typically encompass multiple systems in which development unfolds. Concomitantly, models of intervention designed to address cumulative risk for such problems include multiple strategies aimed at preventing or ameliorating risks, boosting assets and resources, and facilitating adaptive transactions between the child and his or her family, peers, school, and community (Masten, 1994; Yoshikawa, 1994).

Multifactorial Risk Models of Maltreatment

The significance of multiple risk factors and multiple systems has been recognized for some time in theoretical approaches to maltreatment and child development. Particularly influential have been the transactional model as delineated by Sameroff and Chandler (1975) and Bronfenbrenner's (1977) ecological model of the embeddedness of individual development in multiple systems. At the heart of both of these models is the idea that individual development must be viewed in the context of complex interactions of multiple systems.

In the maltreatment literature, several sets of investigators have suggested broad multi-system models that incorporate compensatory or protective factors as well as risks. For example, in an influential paper, Garbarino and Sherman (1980) described the "human ecology of child maltreatment."

These investigators were among the first to consider community context in maltreatment, demonstrating that risk for child maltreatment varies by neighborhood, even when matched for SES. The high-risk neighborhood in this study was characterized by more stresses and fewer supports for the families and children.

In another influential paper, Belsky (1984) described multiple system influences on parenting in relation to child maltreatment. His model included child influences, the role of parental personality functioning (related to a parent's own developmental history), and the supports and stressors arising from the contexts of a parent's life, such as their marital relationship, social network, and work experiences.

Cicchetti and colleagues (Cicchetti, 1990; Cicchetti & Rizley, 1981) have conceptualized the causes and consequences of child maltreatment within an organizational-transactional model of development. More than a decade ago, Cicchetti and Rizley (1981) discussed the importance of multiple risk factors for understanding the etiology of child abuse, the importance of differentiating risk patterns in relation to patterns of maltreatment, and the shortage of research on the processes underlying risk. They classified risk factors for maltreatment as "potentiating" (worsening risk) or "compensatory" (decreasing risk), and also as transient or enduring stresses or strains. Vulnerability factors (biological, psychological, or environmental) were defined as enduring potentiators of risk, while protective factors were enduring and risk-lowering. Cicchetti and Lynch (1993) extended this model to the outcomes of child maltreatment, discussing potentiating and compensatory factors for violence at the macrosystem, exosystem, and microsystem levels, as well as their interconnections, in relation to ontogenetic development. Children living in violent communities may have enduring protective factors in the proximal environment of their families, or vice versa. They point out that little is known about the effects of community-level violence on families and children, much less about the effects arising from interactions of community, family, and child. Finally, Cicchetti and collaborators at the Mt. Hope Family Center have demonstrated how a multi-risk multi-system model of child maltreatment, grounded in developmental theory and research, can be applied to the design of multimodal interventions (Cicchetti & Toth, 1987).

In the area of childhood sexual abuse, Finkelhor (1984) has proposed a multifactorial sociocultural model that highlights individual, family, and cultural context variables that might account for an individual overriding inhibitions and engaging in sexually abusive behaviors. These factors are grouped into four predisposing preconditions: (a) a potential offender who is motivated to sexually abuse a child; (b) internal and (c) external inhibitions prohibiting this behavior have been overcome; and (d) a potential victim's resistance must be overcome, either by the offender or other conditions (Finkelhor, 1984). In this model, preconditions could arise from the individual or sociological level. For example, a father may begin to view a child as a source of potential sexual gratification when his emotional needs are unmet and his behavior is disinhibited by heavy alcohol consumption. Societal factors that could potentiate the risk of acting on these impulses might include erotic portrayal of children in the media, child pornography, male socialization practices that sexualize emotional needs and excuse deviant acts committed while intoxicated, and weak criminal sanctions against offenders. Sexual abuse in this framework arises from the interactions of individual motivations and needs and the social environment (Araji & Finkelhor, 1986; Hartman & Burgess, 1989).

Process models that attempt to spell out in detail how maltreatment arises or affects the individuals involved have typically focused on more narrow aspects of multiple systems theory, often involving transactions between the individual and family systems. For example, Egeland, Sroufe, Erickson, and their colleagues at Minnesota (Egeland, Sroufe, & Erickson, 1983; Erickson, Egeland, & Pianta, 1989), as well as Cicchetti and his colleagues at Harvard and at Rochester (Cicchetti & Rizley, 1981; Cicchetti, 1990), have focused closely on the role of attachment and internal working models of the self and relationships in the consequences of maltreatment. Wolfe (1987, 1991) has described a "transitional" process through which abusive behavior develops in family interactions, with sequential stages of escalating risk for abusive behavior. Dodge and his colleagues (Dodge, Bates, & Pettit, 1990) have examined how distortions in social information processing may mediate in part the relation of child maltreatment to subsequent aggression. A number of investigators have examined the role of learning, through such processes as modeling and negative reinforcement, in the development of aggression and the transmission of abusive behavior from one generation to the next (Kaufman & Zigler, 1989; Widom, 1989a,b). Some stress and coping models also have focused on cognitive mediation of challenging experiences and coping responses (see article by Cummings, this volume). Stress-reactivity or negative affectivity could also be possible vulnerability factors for differentially negative consequences of maltreatment in children. Stress-reactivity could also potentiate parental violence under adversity (Wolfe, 1987). Trauma models of maltreatment also address the linkage of severe stressors to individual functioning (see article by Putnam in this volume). In these models the focus has been on the individual symptoms typically resulting from trauma, such as hyperarousal, intrusive thoughts and images, altered states of awareness, and the regulatory systems implicated by such symptoms.

Preventive and protective processes have only recently become the focus of closer scrutiny in child maltreatment studies. Two recent examples illustrate the shift taking place from the identification of such factors to underlying processes, a shift that parallels a general transition in the resilience literature (Masten, 1994). Egeland, Carlson, and Sroufe (1993) drew on longitudinal data from the Mother-Child Project in Minnesota to argue that resilience should be conceptualized as a capacity that develops over time. Their data support the idea that good caregiving mediates high cumulative environmental risk, promoting positive change over time.

In a second article published in the same special volume focused on resilience, Cicchetti et al. (1993) examined resilience in a more differentiated way than usual. A group of maltreated children from very high cumulative-risk backgrounds were compared with nonmaltreated children from the same background on a variety of potential protective personality characteristics and with respect to seven aspects of adaptive functioning. Only a small proportion of these high-risk children had *no* areas of adaptive functioning. Strong ego-control was more prominent among competent maltreated children, suggesting that greater control was adaptive under dangerous living conditions. Moreover, resilience in this article was conceptualized as a dynamic process of development in context, not as a static trait of the individual.

EVIDENCE OF CUMULATIVE RISK AND PROTECTION FROM STUDIES OF MALTREATMENT

The goal of this section is to examine the current status of the evidence pertinent to multifactorial models of risk/protection for maltreatment. The review is very selective, serving only to highlight pertinent data and issues. Other articles of this volume focus in more depth on specific research findings on the etiology and consequences of maltreatment.

Risk for Parents Maltreating

Cumulative risk. There has been extensive study of the predictors of maltreatment in the context of the family (National Research Council, 1993). However, most of these studies have focused on single-risk factors as related to the occurrence of maltreatment. Even studies that demonstrate multiple correlates of maltreatment usually do not examine the joint effects of these risk factors.

The search for distinct profiles of risk for physical or sexual abuse of children by adults has not been successful (National Research Council, 1993), although the search itself reflects a cumulative risk perspective. The lack of a distinct profile of risk for offenders would be expected if many interacting factors are involved; there would be multiple pathways leading to abuse by parents and other adults.

The multiple-risk context in which child maltreatment by parents is embedded, while much discussed in theory and models, also has not been examined extensively in longitudinal research. For example, there has been great interest in the experience of childhood abuse as a risk factor for a parent becoming abusive (Kaufman & Zigler, 1989; National Research Council, 1993; Widom, 1989b). Retrospective data suggested this link and prospective data continue to support it, albeit at a much lower risk level. However, it is not clear to what degree the actual risk mechanisms are related to the many other correlated risk factors associated with child maltreatment rather than maltreatment itself. Experiencing maltreatment as a child is embedded in a multiple-risk context and perpetrating maltreatment as a parent also is embedded in a complex risk/vulnerability matrix. This makes it very difficult to sort out possible causal pathways in empirical studies.

Shared risk. Common risk factors for physical abuse and neglect by parents have emerged in a variety of studies (National Research Council, 1993; Pianta, Egeland, & Erickson, 1989). These include risk factors such as poverty and low maternal education that have been implicated as risks for many other aspects of parental dysfunction (Garmezy & Masten, 1994). Similarly, many of the single-risk factors for sexual abuse are predictors of many other adult problem behaviors (e.g., social isolation, mother dominated by or abused by father, recent job loss, deterioration of the marital relationship [Araji & Finkelhor, 1986]).

Vulnerability. Just as no distinct risk profiles of abusers have been found, no distinct personality profiles that predict general or specific types of parental maltreatment of children have emerged (Kendall-Tackett, Williams, & Finkelhor, 1993; National Research Council, 1993; Wolfe, 1987). In the area of sexual abuse, possible biological vulnerabilities for this disturbed behavior have been explored but not substantiated. Hormone levels and chromosomal make-up have been studied extensively but there is no definitive evidence linking abnormalities in these areas to sexual abuse (Kelly & Lusk, 1992).

The only biological factor thought to potentiate sexual abuse is excessive alcohol or drug consumption, which has been reported in 19 to 70% of sexual abuse cases (National Research Council, 1993). Alcohol may operate through a general disinhibition mechanism, which is consistent with findings that maltreating parents have problems with poor impulse control, antisocial personality, and emotional distress (National Research Council, 1993), which often are associated with substance abuse. These three characteristics could be potentiators of other risk factors that increase the likelihood of abuse. However, these are very general characteristics of adult dysfunction that are probably common in a variety of high-risk, high-adversity families (Garmezy & Masten, 1994). Nonetheless, they may represent vulnerability factors that play an important role in exacerbating risk.

Compensatory and protective factors. A number of studies have examined the correlates of good parenting under high-risk conditions for maltreatment (Belsky, 1984; Crittenden, 1985; Kaufman & Zigler, 1989; Kendall-Tackett et al., 1993; National Research Council, 1993). Results suggest many of the same resilience factors found in a variety of other high-risk or high-adversity situations (Wright & Masten, in press). These include the opportunity for the maltreated child or adolescent to have positive relationships with other competent adults, sometimes in the form of therapy, and currently supportive relationships of parents who were abused as children with adults, including spouses and friends. Social support within the extended family or community which prevents isolation and enhances opportunities for detection and intervention may be crucial.

Risks for Child Victimization

Cumulative risk. Studies focused on predicting child victimization also have emphasized single factors related to child maltreatment rather than cumulative risk or interactions of risk variables (National Research Council, 1993). Yet it is clear that these individual risk factors often co-occur and could have joint effects.

In the area of child sexual abuse, child characteristics may play only a minor role in the initiation of abuse but the presence of certain risk conditions, particularly in combination, may be important in the persistence or escalation of abusive experiences (Ammerman, 1991; Finkelhor, 1984; Meiselman, 1990; National Research Council, 1993; Wolfe, 1985). Often the oldest female child is selected, or a child that has any physical or emotional condition that increases their dependency on the offender (e.g., mental retardation, physical deformities, seizures). Children who have been taught to obey adults without question may not know when or how to resist inappropriate demands. Other general risk factors in the home environment include lack of a close relationship with the mother, lack of supervision, social isolation, sleeping arrangements that allow easy access and a family environment that is chaotic and/or abusive in multiple respects.

Vulnerability factors. Little presently is known about child vulnerabilities that potentiate risk for maltreatment given a risky situation. Evidence suggestive of vulnerability factors includes the following (National Research Council, 1993): (a) one child may be singled out as a victim in a family; (b) some maltreated children placed in foster care are revictimized; (c) certain child characteristics appear to be more related to physical than to sexual abuse in young children (Wolfe, 1985). It has also been suggested in transactional models of maltreatment that child behavior may play a role in triggering or maintaining parental abuse once conditions are ripe for violence (Crittenden, 1985; Erickson et al., 1989; National Research Council, 1993; Wolfe, 1985).

Compensatory and protective factors. Factors that may operate to reduce the risk of maltreatment in a family believed to be at risk for maltreatment were indicated above. The most definitive evidence of these effects eventually may come from evaluations of successful intervention programs that attempt to reduce risk through home visiting, parent-child relationship enhancement, parent education, and other means.

Efforts to reduce the risk of sexual victimization of children usually have taken a different tack, with a broad public health strategy. Preschools and elementary schools, for example, are attempting to teach children personal safety skills appropriate to their developmental level and to provide information about what kinds of activities between adults and children or with other individuals are inappropriate (Macmillan, Macmillan, Offord, Griffith, & Macmillan, 1994).

Prevention of revictimization has not received as much attention as primary prevention, perhaps because less is known about the rates and predictors of revictimization. Revictimization can be conceptualized as a consequence of maltreatment through the operation of vulnerabilities to endangering oneself acquired through abuse experiences or as the consequence of continuity in risky conditions producing abuse. This distinction may be crucial to the design of interventions to reduce the repetition of maltreatment, since the former may be better addressed by focusing on the victim and the latter by focusing on reducing the risky conditions. Revictimization is discussed further in the next section.

Child Maltreatment as a Risk Factor for Subsequent Problems

Cumulative risk. When child maltreatment is considered as a predictor and possible causal factor for later problems in development, cumulative risk could refer to the embeddedness of any single type of maltreatment in a context of many other risk factors or to the co-occurrence of multiple types of maltreatment. It could also refer to the effects of chronic, repeated abuse rather than single instances of maltreatment. Greater attention has been given to the combined effects of multiple risk factors in the study of consequences of child maltreatment than for its etiology.

A number of investigators have pointed out the difficulty of isolating the consequences of maltreatment from the effects of the cumulative risk context in which it occurs. However, there is some evidence that the effects of maltreatment exceed the general risk associated with psychosocial disadvantage or general family dysfunction (Cicchetti et al., 1993; Dodge et al., 1990; Erickson et al., 1989; Kendall-Tackett et al., 1993; Okun, Parker, & Levendosky, 1994). In the area of sexual abuse, the higher functioning of nonabused siblings in the same family suggests there may be traumatic processes in the sexual abuse itself that are separate from the effects of general family dysfunction. Again, a multifactorial model appears more appropriate. Prior vulnerabilities, specific family stressors and general family dysfunction and disadvantage heighten the effect of abuse and maltreatment.

There also is considerable evidence that forms of maltreatment co-occur (National Research Council, 1993; Pianta et al., 1989; see also other articles of this volume). However, it usually is not clear whether or how outcomes are worse when they do co-occur. It is possible that there are "ceiling effects" at extremely high cumulative risk levels.

A more delineated consideration of co-occurrence has been the subject of several recent studies attempting to differentiate the effects of interparental conflict, witnessing the battering of a parenting figure, and physical abuse, which co-occur frequently but also occur separately. Jouriles, Murphy, and O'Leary (1989), for example, examined the effects of marital violence on child problems while controlling for general marital discord. Physical aggression between spouses who had sought marital therapy was found to contribute independently to problems in their 5- to 12-year-old children. However, it was not clear whether or not these children were witnesses only or also the victims of family violence.

Comparing the effects of witnessing family violence versus being the victim versus both has been the subject of several recent studies (described in the article by Rossman, Hughes, & Hanson). Generally, abused witnesses and nonabused witnesses have more problems than children who have not been abused or witnesses to family violence. In some studies, nonabused witnesses fall in the middle on child functioning measures. When the nonabused witnesses appear to fall in the middle, it is conceivable that exposure to more violence results in worse outcomes or that multiple forms of violence are more likely in families where there are more risk factors. When the two "witness" groups do not differ, general risk in both groups may be so high that there is a ceiling effect. Additional research is needed to clarify the cumulative effects of multiple forms of victimization in violent families.

The complexity of cumulative risk effects also is illustrated by the data on incest. Incest is one of the most frequent types of sexual abuse and it often has a high cumulative risk pattern: incest frequently occurs over a long period of time, escalates to more severe and frequent forms of abuse, and occurs with a person that the child depends on or is close to. Assault characteristics (penetration, long duration, higher frequency, overt coercion) and offender characteristics (male, much older than the victim, father, prior positive relationships with the victim) have consistently been related to worse outcomes (Hanson, 1990; Kendall-Tackett et al., 1993). Lack of maternal support at the time of disclosure and the child's participation in courtroom hearings that are lengthy and harshly contested have also been associated with heightened symptomatology and slower recovery.

The physical and sexual abuse of children often extends over months or years. Even after disclosure and intervention by social service agencies or other professionals, many children are revictimized (Daro, 1988; Bentovim, Van Elberg, & Boston, 1988; Gomes-Schwartz et al., 1990). Incest survivors appear to have higher risk for subsequent sexual trauma, sometimes years later (Meiselman, 1990; Koss & Dinero, 1989; Russell, 1986).

There is a paucity of empirical work that has examined why revictimization occurs, either in terms of ongoing cumulative environmental risk or with respect to increases in vulnerability resulting from victimization. The mechanisms that have been proposed suggest that the factors resulting in initial abuse may subsequently create personal vulnerabilities in the victim that heighten her or his risk for continued abuse or later revictimization.

Vulnerability. Heterogeneity of outcomes in maltreated children have been attributed to characteristics of the maltreatment (e.g., type, duration, severity), the context in which it occurs, timing, and individual differences in the victim. Timing and individual characteristics that potentiate risk for negative sequelae suggest vulnerability. Infants, for example, are widely viewed as more vulnerable to the consequences of neglect because they are so dependent on caregiving, and evidence strongly supports this age-related vulnerability (Crittenden, 1985; National Research Council, 1993). Developmental theorists also have suggested that very young children are more vulnerable to disturbances in the attachment relationship with primary caregivers because fundamental working models of relationships and the self are forming during this period (Cicchetti, 1990; Cole & Putnam, 1992). Similarly, trauma researchers have suggested that basic physiological regulatory systems may be permanently affected by severe, repeated trauma in early development, creating a vulnerability to subsequent stress and other developmental consequences, such as earlier menarche in sexually traumatized girls (Putnam & Trickett, 1993). The period of development (infancy, preschool, middle childhood, adolescence) during which abuse occurs may heighten vulnerability for different types of symptomatology. In addition, certain symptoms (e.g., sexual dysfunction, dissociation, fears, aggression, etc.) may be more closely related to age at onset and multiple-risk factors in the maltreating environment. At this time, however, evidence for specific hypotheses pertaining to age at onset and type of psychopathology is insufficient to draw conclusions. Timing of the traumatic experiences should not be examined in isolation from other risk factors but in context and over time. Little research has been carried out in this area because of the complexity of interwoven factors, variety of mechanisms underlying outcome and the difficulty clearly identifying and assessing these interactions (Cole & Putnam, 1992; Kendall-Tackett et al., 1993).

One of the few studies in the maltreatment literature on the interactive effects of multiple-risk factors was conducted by Walker, Downey, and Bergman (1989). They examined the joint effects of parental psychopathology and maltreatment (all neglected and most physically abused as well) in a sample of children recruited at ages 7 to 15. Longitudinal data indicated that having a parent with schizophrenia was associated with increased child problems only in conjunction with the stressor of maltreatment.

Possible vulnerabilities with respect to revictimization have received very little research attention. In the physical maltreatment literature, it has been suggested that children learn maladaptive interactions so well that they may evoke such interactions in other situations (Cicchetti & Lynch, 1993). Similarly, in the sexual abuse literature, it has been suggested that children may develop or learn sexualized behaviors that put them at continued risk of abuse by the original or other perpetrators, fail to learn self-protection skills that reduce the risk of later victimization, learn to accept violence and exploitation as part of close relationships, or have difficulty accurately assessing trustworthiness in relationships (Herman, 1992; Meiselman, 1990; Russell, 1986). Effects arising from the sexually abusive acts and the harmful impact on the child's relationships with family members (betrayal, shame, stigma) may create serious subsequent vulnerabilities. Briere (1992) proposes that traumatic sexualization might result in negative self-evaluation, a chronic perception of danger or injustice, powerlessness and preoccupation with control, dissociative coping processes and other maladaptive efforts to reduce internal painful feelings that place the child at great risk for additional harm.

Compensatory and protective factors. Studies searching for the correlates of good outcomes in maltreated children have found very similar factors as widely observed in the broader resilience literature. These include a good parent-child relationship or bond with another caring, competent adult and higher intellectual functioning (Egeland et al., 1993; National Research Council, 1993; Pianta, Egeland, & Sroufe, 1990), reflecting two of the most important human adaptational systems (Masten et al., 1990). Many of these factors also appear to be associated with lower risk. As an example, maternal support (demonstrated by believing the child's report of abuse and acting in a protective way once abuse is identified) reduces the negative emotional sequelae for the child (Everson, Hunter, Runyan, Edelsohn, & Coulter, 1989). Similarly, a less disturbed home environment (e.g., less overall stress, enmeshment and expression of anger) is associated with fewer child symptoms (Kendall-Tackett et al., 1993). Other possible correlates of better outcomes in the sexual abuse literature include better prior adjustment, positive action taken by others in response to the abuse acts, and a non-self-blaming cognitive interpretation of the abuse by the child (Courtois, 1988; Kendall-Tackett et al., 1993). Other unique protective factors, such as out-of-home placement, have also been studied, but the data are unclear (Egeland et al., 1993; National Research Council, 1993).

The possibility that maltreated children have strengths and weaknesses in their adaptive functioning has only recently been considered, as discussed above (Cicchetti et al., 1993). There appears to be virtually no consideration of the possibility that the same characteristic may function as a potentiator of some outcomes and a protective factor for others, or as a risk factor for one child and a protective factor for another, or as a protective factor at one point in development and a risk at another time. These subtleties of risk and resilience await future study.

CONCLUSIONS AND RECOMMENDATIONS

Complex and dynamic systems models of the etiology and consequences of child maltreatment have been proposed over the past 15 years. Research up to now generally has not matched the integrative quality of these models, often focusing on single systems or risk factors. Nonetheless, the emerging database in child maltreatment is highly congruent with such models.

The following conclusions supported by child maltreatment research strongly suggest cumulative risk/protective processes, multiple causes and pathways to abuse, and diverse consequences related to interaction of qualities in the child, family, community, and culture, and the nature of the maltreatment experience itself.

- Forms of child maltreatment co-occur
- Maltreatment co-occurs with other known risk factors for child problems
- Outcome is better predicted by multiple-risk indicators than by single-risk factors
- No characteristic of perpetrators or victims is necessary or sufficient to account for occurrence or outcome
- Consequences of maltreatment are heterogeneous
- Different risk factors, including types of maltreatment, predict similar child problems
- Within a maltreated group, child outcomes vary in ways that suggest the influence of other risks, vulnerabilities, and protective factors

These findings implicate complex processes in the emergence of maltreatment and its aftermath.

Cumulative risk has multiple meanings in maltreatment theory and research. It can refer to multiple causes or consequences, the embeddedness of risk, co-occurrence of types of maltreatment, the piling-up of negative experiences, the repeated or chronic exposure to abuse, dimensions underlying "profiles" of offenders or victims, and also to the characteristics of the maltreatment itself, such as severity or frequency or who the perpetrator is. In each case, however, cumulative risk perspectives acknowledge the complexities of context and causes in dynamic interaction throughout development.

Implications for research. It is time to move beyond single-risk factor studies of maltreatment and other forms of research compartmentalization (National Research Council, 1993; Rosenberg, 1987). Research needs to be directed at understanding the processes by which developmental, individual, family, community, cultural, and societal influences interact in the etiology and sequelae of child maltreatment. This will require longitudinal, multifactorial research, encompassing more than one system at a time. Development of research programs that focus on the overlap and co-occurrence of different types of victimization, assess the frequency of unreported victimization (within the family, within peer groups, etc.), and examine how family members buffer or exacerbate the effects of victimization are critically needed (Finkelhor & Dziuba-Leatherman, 1994).

Implications for prevention and treatment. Cumulative risk and protection models also have profound implications for prevention and treatment in child maltreatment. Given multifactorial influences on occurrence and consequences, there is no single or simple target for change that will dramatically alter risk. Moreover, the effectiveness of a particular intervention strategy will depend on the characteristics of the child, the context, and the nature of the risk situation. Home visiting programs, shown to be effective for disadvantaged, high-risk families as a preventive intervention for maltreatment, may not be nearly as effective for socioeconomically advantaged families (Macmillan et al., 1994).

Clinical practitioners have implicitly endorsed a cumulative risk and protection model through eclectic, multimodal interventions. Similarly, practitioners who seek to identify the strengths as well as the difficulties in a child's life, identifying assets as well as risk factors and problems in the child, family, community, school, peer group, culture, etc., also are acting on an implicit risk and protection model.

Research-based intervention programs, such as the Mount Hope Family Center programs in Rochester (Cicchetti & Toth, 1987) and prevention programs such as STEEP in Minneapolis (Steps Toward Effective and Enjoyable Parenting; Egeland, & Erickson, 1990) are exemplary in combining clinical wisdom and developmental theory. These programs target multiple systems and interactions, and are well-grounded in the child development knowledge base as well as child maltreatment theory and research. Evaluations of such theory-based, clinically sound interventions offer the best test of processes hypothesized in risk/protection models.

Cultural, community, and societal influences on maltreatment have not been adequately addressed in intervention programs or related research (National Research Council, 1993). Concomitantly, community and national strategies and policies have undoubtedly been neglected in even the relatively comprehensive intervention programs. Understanding how the overall level of violence in the United States, weak criminal sanctions against sexual offenders, common law privacy rights of parents, and other relevant cultural characteristics of the macrosystem may contribute to maltreatment and then figuring out what to do about it, will necessitate long-term interdisciplinary collaborations.

Cumulative risk/resilience approaches offer great promise and great challenges for those who strive to understand the etiology and consequences of child maltreatment. Most importantly, these models provide a framework for designing better programs to reduce risk and improve developmental outcomes of the youngest victims of violence and neglect.

REFERENCES

Ammerman, R.T. (1991). The role of the child in physical abuse: A reappraisal. *Violence and Victims, 6*, 87-100.

Ammerman, R.T., & Hersen, M. (1990). *Children at risk: An evaluation of factors contributing to child abuse and neglect.* New York: Plenum Press.

Araji, S., & Finkelhor, D. (1986). Abusers: A review of the research. In D. Finkelhor (Ed.), *A sourcebook on child sexual abuse* (pp. 89-118). Beverly Hills, CA: Sage.

Belsky, J. (1984). The determinants of parenting: A process model. *Child Development, 55*, 83-96.

Bentovim, A., van Elberg, A., & Boston, P. (1984). The results of treatment. In A. Bentovim, A. Elton, J. Hildebrand, M. Tranter, & E. Vizard (Eds.), *Child sexual abuse within the family: Assessment and treatment* (pp. 252-268). London: Wright.

Briere, J. (1992). *Child abuse trauma: Theory and treatment of the lasting effects.* Newbury Park, CA: Sage.

Bronfenbrenner, U. (1977). *The ecology of human development: Experiments by nature and design.* Cambridge: Harvard University Press.

Cicchetti, D. (1990). The organization and coherence of socioemotional, cognitive, and representational development: Illustrations through a developmental psychopathology perspective on Down Syndrome and child maltreatment. In R. Thompson (Ed.), *Socioemotional development: Nebraska symposium on motivation* (Vol. 36) (pp. 259-366). Lincoln, NE: Cambridge University Press.

Cicchetti, D., & Carlson, V. (Eds.) (1989). *Child maltreatment.* New York: Cambridge University Press.

Cicchetti, D., & Lynch, M. (1993). Toward an ecological/transactional model of community violence and child maltreatment: Consequences for children's development. *Psychiatry, 56*, 96-118.

Cicchetti, D., & Rizley, R. (1981). Developmental perspectives on the etiology, intergenerational transmission, and sequelae of child maltreatment. *New Directions for Child Development, 11*, 31-55.

Cicchetti, D., Rogosch, F.A., Lynch, M., & Holt, K.D. (1993). Resilience in maltreated children: Processes leading to adaptive outcomes. *Development and Psychopathology, 5*, 629-647.

Cicchetti, D., & Toth, S. (1987). The application of a transactional risk model to intervention with multi-risk maltreating families. *Zero to Three*, Vol. VII, 1-8.

Cole, P.M., & Putnam, F.W. (1992). Effect of incest on self and social functioning: A developmental psychopathology perspective. *Journal of Consulting and Clinical Psychology, 60*, 174-184.

Crittenden, P.M. (1985). Maltreated infants: Vulnerability and resilience. *Journal of Child Psychology and Psychiatry, 26*, 85-96.

Daro, D. (1988). *Confronting child abuse: Research for effective program design.* New York: Free Press.

Dodge, K.A., Bates, J.E., & Pettit, G.S. (1990). Mechanisms in the cycle of violence. *Science, 250*, 1678-1683.

Egeland, B., Sroufe, L. Alan, & Erickson, M. (1983). The developmental consequence of different patterns of maltreatment. *Child Abuse and Neglect, 7,* 459-469.

Egeland, B., Carlson, E., & Sroufe, L.A. (1993). Resilience as process. *Development and Psychopathology, 5,* 517-528.

Egeland, B., & Erickson, M.F. (1990). Rising above the past: Strategies for helping new mothers break the cycle of abuse and neglect. *Zero to Three,* 29-35.

Erickson, M.F., Egeland, B., & Pianta, R. (1989). The effects of maltreatment on the development of young children. In D. Cicchetti & V. Carlson (Eds.), *Child maltreatment: Theory and research on the causes and consequences of child abuse and neglect* (pp. 647-684). New York: Cambridge University Press.

Everson, M.D., Hunter, W.M., Runyan, D.K., Edelsohn, G.A., & Coulter, M.L. (1989). Maternal support following disclosure of incest. *American Journal of Orthopsychiatry, 59,* 197-207.

Finkelhor, D. (1984). *Child sexual abuse.* New York: Free Press.

Finkelhor, D., Araji, S., Baron, L., Growne, A., Peters, S.D., & Wyatt, G.E. (1986). *A sourcebook on child sexual abuse.* Newbury Park, CA: Sage.

Finkelhor, D., & Dziuba-Leatherman, J. (1994). Victimization of children. *American Psychologist, 49,* 173-183.

Garbarino, J., & Sherman, D. (1980). High-risk neighborhoods and high-risk families: The human ecology of child maltreatment. *Child Development, 51,* 188-198.

Garmezy, N., & Masten, A.S. (1994). Chronic adversities. In M. Rutter, L. Herzov, & E. Taylor (Eds.), *Child and adolescent psychiatry* (3rd ed). Oxford: Blackwell.

Gomes-Schwartz, B., Horowitz, J.M., & Cardarelli, A. (1990). *Child sexual abuse: The initial effects.* Newbury Park, CA: Sage.

Hanson, R.K. (1990). The psychological impact of sexual assault on women and children: A review. *Annals of Sex Research, 3,* 187-232.

Hartman, C.R., & Burgess, A.W. (1989). Sexual abuse of children. Causes and consequences. In D. Cicchetti & V. Carlson (Eds.), *Child maltreatment: Theory and research on the causes and consequences of child abuse and neglect.* New York: Cambridge University Press.

Herman, J.L. (1992). *Trauma and recovery.* New York: Basic Books.

Jouriles, E.N., Murphy, C.M., O'Leary, K.D. (1989). Interspousal aggression, marital discord, and child problems. *Journal of Consulting and Clinical Psychology, 57,* 453-455.

Kaufman, J., & Zigler, E. (1989). The intergenerational transmission of child abuse. In D. Cicchetti & V. Carlson (Eds.), *Child maltreatment: Theory and research on the causes and consequences of child abuse and neglect* (pp. 129-150). New York: Cambridge University Press.

Kelly, R.J., & Lusk, R. (1992). Theories of pedophilia. In W. O'Donohue & J.H. Geer (Eds.), *The sexual abuse of children: Theory and research, Volume 1.* Hillsdale, NJ: Lawrence Erlbaum Press.

Kendall-Tackett, K.A., Williams, L.M., & Finkelhor, D. (1993). Impact of sexual abuse on children: A review and synthesis of recent empirical studies. *Psychological Bulletin, 113*, 164-180.

Kopp, C.B. (1983). Risk factors in development. In P.H. Mussen (Ed.), *Handbook of child psychology* (4th ed.). Vol. 2: M.M. Haith & J.J. Campos (Eds.), *Infancy and developmental psychobiology* (pp. 1081-1188). New York: Wiley.

Koss, M.P., & Dinero, T.E. (1989). Discriminant analysis of risk factors for sexual victimization among a national sample of college women. *Journal of Consulting and Clinical Psychology, 57*, 242-250.

Loeber, R. (1990). Development and risk factors of juvenile antisocial behavior and delinquency. *Clinical Psychology Review, 10*, 1-41.

Macmillan, H.L., MacMillan, J.H., Offord, D.R., Griffith, L., & MacMillan, A. (1994). Primary prevention of child sexual abuse: A critical review. Part II. *Journal of Child Psychology and Psychiatry, 35*, 857-876.

Masten, A.S. (1994). Resilience in individual development: Successful adaptation despite risk and adversity. In M.C. Wang & E. Gordon (Eds.), *Educational resilience in inner city America: Challenges and prospects* (pp. 3-25). Hillsdale, NJ: Lawrence Erlbaum.

Masten, A.S., Best, K.M., & Garmezy, N. (1990). Resilience and development: Contributions from the study of children who overcome adversity. *Development and Psychopathology, 2*, 425-444.

Masten, A.S., & Coatsworth, J.D. (1995). Competence, resilience, and psychopathology. In D. Cicchetti & D. Cohen (Ed.), *Developmental psychopathology. Vol. 2. Risk, disorder, and adaptation* (pp. 715-752). New York: Wiley.

Masten, A.S., & Garmezy, N. (1985). Risk, vulnerability, and protective factors in developmental psychopathology. In B.B. Lahey & A.E. Kazdin (Eds.), *Advances in clinical child psychology* (Vol. 8) (pp. 1-52). New York: Plenum Press.

Meiselman, K.C. (1990). *Resolving the trauma of incest*. San Francisco: Jossey-Bass Publishers.

National Research Council, Panel on Research on Child Abuse and Neglect, Commission on Behavioral and Social Sciences and Education (1993). *Understanding child abuse and neglect*. Washington, DC: National Academy Press.

Okun, A., Parker, J.G., & Levendosky, A.A. (1994). Distinct and interactive contributions of physical abuse, socioeconomic disadvantage, and negative life events to children's social, cognitive, and affective adjustment. *Development and Psychopathology, 6*, 77-98.

Pianta, R.C., Egeland, B., & Erickson, M.F. (1989). The antecedents of maltreatment: Results of the Mother-Child Interaction Project. In D. Cicchetti & V. Carlson (Eds.), *Child maltreatment* (pp. 203-253). New York: Cambridge University Press.

Pianta, R.C., Egeland, B., & Sroufe, L.A. (1990). Maternal stress and children's development: Prediction of school outcomes and identification of protective factors. In J. Rolf, A.S. Masten, D. Cicchetti, K.H. Nuechterlein, & S. Weintraub (Eds.), *Risk and protective factors in the development of psychopathology* (pp. 215-235). New York: Cambridge University Press.

Putnam, F.W., & Trickett, P.K. (1993). Child sexual abuse: A model of chronic trauma. *Psychiatry, 56,* 82-95.

Rolf, J., Masten, A.S., Cicchetti, D., Nuechterlein, K.H., & Weintraub, S. (1990). *Risk and protective factors in the development of psychopathology.* New York: Cambridge University Press.

Rosenberg, M. (1987). New directions for research on the psychological maltreatment of children. *American Psychologist, 42,* 166-171.

Russell, D.E.H. (1986). *The secret trauma: Incest in the lives of girls and women.* New York: Basic Books.

Rutter, M. (1990). Psychosocial resilience and protective mechanisms. In J. Rolf, A.S. Masten, D. Cicchetti, K.H. Nuechterlein, & S. Weintraub (Eds.), *Risk and protective factors in the development of psychopathology* (pp. 181-214). New York: Cambridge University Press.

Sameroff, A.J., & Chandler, M.J. (1975). Reproductive risk and the continuum of caretaking casualty. *Review of Child Development Research, 4,* 187-244.

Skuse, D., & Bentovim, A. (1994). Physical and emotional maltreatment. In M. Rutter, L. Herzov, & E. Taylor (Eds.), *Child and adolescent psychiatry* (34rd Edition. Oxford: Blackwell.

Walker, E., Downey, G., & Bergman, A. (1989). The effects of parental psychopathology and maltreatment on child behavior: A test of the diathesis-stress model. *Child Development, 60,* 15-24.

Widom, C.S. (1989a). The cycle of violence. *Science, 244,* 160-166.

Widom, C.S. (1989b). Does violence beget violence? A critical examination of the literature. *Psychological Bulletin, 106,* 3-28.

Wolfe, D.A. (1985). Child abusive parents: An empirical review and analysis. *Psychological Bulletin, 97,* 462-482.

Wolfe, D.A. (1987). *Child abuse: Implications for child development and psychopathology.* Newbury Park: Sage.

Wolfe, D.A. (1991). *Preventing physical and emotional abuse of children.* New York: Guilford Press.

Wright, M. O'D., & Masten, A.S. (in press). Vulnerability and resilience in young children. In S.I. Greenspan, J.D. Osofsky, & K. Pruett (Eds.), *Handbook of child and adolescent psychiatry: Infant and early childhood: Theory and issues.* New York: Basic Books.

Yoshikawa, H. (1994). Prevention as cumulative protection: Effects of early family support and education on chronic delinquency and its risks. *Psychological Bulletin, 115,* 28-54.

Stress and Coping Approaches and Research: The Impact of Marital Conflict on Children

E. Mark Cummings

SUMMARY. The stress and coping approach offers a useful heuristic for conceptualizing complex social processes at a microsocial level. Its application to the study of the impact of marital conflict on children has advanced understanding of constructive versus destructive marital conflict processes and the comorbidity of marital conflict and other family risk factors (e.g., parental depression and alcoholism, child abuse and maltreatment, divorce). An updated stress and coping model is outlined that emphasizes the role of children's feelings of emotional security, the primacy of emotionality in guiding responding, but also the importance of children's coping efficacy and appraisal. Children's distress and behavioral dysregulation increase when marital conflict is frequent and destructive, suggesting that sensitization to anger may contribute to maladaptive coping processes and the development over time of problems in adjustment. *[Article copies available for a fee from The Haworth Document Delivery Service: 1-800-342-9678. E-mail address: getinfo@haworth.com]*

Research has established, consistent with clinical observation, that certain adverse family environments (e.g., marital conflict, the physical abuse

---

Address correspondence to: E. Mark Cummings, PhD, Department of Psychology, University of Notre Dame, Notre Dame, IN 46556-5636.

[Haworth co-indexing entry note]: "Stress and Coping Approaches and Research: The Impact of Marital Conflict on Children." Cummings, E. Mark. Co-published simultaneously in *Journal of Aggression, Maltreatment & Trauma* (The Haworth Maltreatment & Trauma Press, an imprint of The Haworth Press, Inc.) Vol. 2, No. 1 (#3), 1998, pp. 31-50; and: *Multiple Victimization of Children: Conceptual, Developmental, Research, and Treatment Issues* (ed: B. B. Robbie Rossman, and Mindy S. Rosenberg) The Haworth Maltreatment & Trauma Press, an imprint of The Haworth Press, Inc., 1998, pp. 31-50. Single or multiple copies of this article are available for a fee from The Haworth Document Delivery Service [1-800-342-9678, 9:00 a.m. - 5:00 p.m. (EST). E-mail address: getinfo@haworth.com].

31

of children, parental depression) are associated with children's increased risk for the development of psychopathology. Field methods of examining correlations between global assessments of family functioning and global indices of child outcomes have proven useful for this stage of identifying risk environments for children. However, it is clear that reliance on such methodologies has reached a point of diminishing returns and it is questionable whether continued repetitive reliance on such approaches can yield substantial new advances that inform scientific understanding and practical application (e.g., clinical practice). A diversity of new and creative approaches and methodologies for the study of family adversity and child development are needed for a next generation of investigation (Cummings & Davies, 1994a).

Specifically, the study of child maltreatment and adversity needs to move beyond simply documenting global associations between child and family characteristics to a next stage of carefully differentiating between and among processes of effect in complex family environments. One set of issues revolves around the fact that family environments are multi-dimensional and interdependent, making it critical to precisely define and distinguish between family environments that hold adversity for children. Another set of concerns relates to the fact that correlations between family variables do not substantiate conclusions about cause-and-effect. Thus, correlations between two variables may be due to a third variable that is not assessed and therefore not acknowledged in a model of family relations. The next generation of family research needs to be increasingly concerned with identifying (a) causal relations, (b) directions of effect, and (c) multiple pathways of effect (Cummings, 1995; Fincham & Osborne, 1993).

The "stress and coping" tradition of research and theory provides a valuable avenue for addressing questions pertinent to this next stage of research on families. Thus, the stress and coping approach offers a useful heuristic for conceptualizing complex social processes at a microsocial level. Lazarus and Folkman, who pioneered this approach, define stress as "a particular relationship between the person and the environment that is appraised by the person as taxing or exceeding his or her resources and endangering his or her well-being" (Lazarus & Folkman, 1984, p. 19). Coping is conceptualized as a dynamic process, that is, "the changing thoughts and acts that the individual uses to manage the external and/or internal demands of a specific person-environment transaction that is appraised as stressful" (Folkman, 1991, p. 5).

When coping is viewed from a contextual perspective, emphasis is placed on the *specific* thoughts and acts that the individual uses to cope with *specific* contexts, as guided by personal appraisals of situations, especially perceived ability to cope, that is, coping efficacy. Individual differences also figure prominently, including personal dispositions, family history, age, and sex. Interactions between the individual and specific environmental contexts find expression in multidimensional coping processes and strategies that develop into stable patterns leading over time to either adjustment or maladjustment in functioning (see also Sroufe & Rutter, 1984).

Further, family adversity does not lead directly to diagnoses of psychopathology in children. The development of psychopathology in family contexts reflects a series of microsocial processes that occur interactively over a period of time, reflecting gradual adaptations by children to family circumstances. Coping patterns that come to occur in specific social contexts mediate relations between family background and experiences, on the one hand, and child development outcomes, on the other.

Thus, negative outcomes in children develop over time as a result of person-environment interactions that gradually shape how children respond and react to socioemotional events and interactions. The "products" of child maltreatment and other adversities within the family are specific, maladaptive emotional, social, and/or cognitive response patterns and dispositions. Adjustment problems in children associated with adverse family environments are more informatively understood in terms of coping processes, as opposed to simply diagnostic classification. Thus, a stress and coping approach to the study of the impact of adverse family environments on children outlines a theory and methodology for articulating the active response processes of individual children in specific family contexts that may lead to, and underlie, diagnostic classifications.

A STRESS AND COPING MODEL FOR THE IMPACT OF MARITAL CONFLICT ON CHILDREN

Inspired by this general model, several years ago we proposed a framework for approaching the study of the impact of marital conflict on children (Cummings & Cummings, 1988). Marital conflict is an often overlooked form of child adversity that co-occurs with other, more commonly recognized forms, including child maltreatment. For example, interspousal aggression is strongly associated with parental aggression towards children (Gelles, 1987; Jouriles, Barling & O'Leary, 1987). Approximately 40% of the children who are victims of parental physical abuse are also witnesses to spousal violence (Straus, Gelles & Steinmetz, 1980).

Our initial model, which was intended as a guide for research, is presented in Figure 1. This model posited that children's family background of experiences, their own personal characteristics, and the context and stimulus characteristics of anger expressions each influenced their stress and coping responses, which could be conceptualized in terms of specific cognitive, emotional, social, or physiological responses, or, more broadly, as coping strategies or styles. Over time these response patterns were seen as contributing to adaptive functioning, or, alternatively, maladaptive outcomes reflecting adjustment problems.

This model placed emphasis on the importance of studying specific contexts of exposure to marital conflict, individual differences between children in coping responses, including their histories of exposure to marital conflict, and the multidimensional nature of coping processes. This model was followed by a long series of process-oriented empirical investigations, mostly relying upon analogue (e.g., Cummings, 1987) and pro-

FIGURE 1. Children's Processes of Stress and Coping with Marital Conflict.

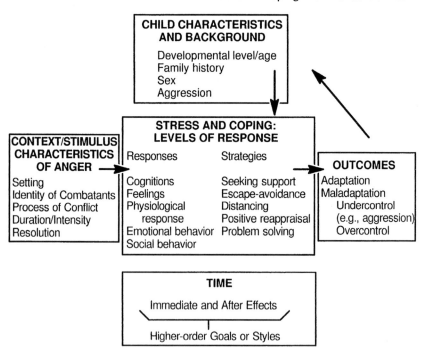

From Cummings and Cummings (1988).

cess-oriented field methodologies (Grych, Seid & Fincham, 1992) to more precisely specify causal relations at a microsocial level. These new findings have been extensively reviewed, and their implications for marital and family functioning considered (Cummings & Davies, 1994a). Our initial framework was followed by a model by Grych and Fincham (1990) that further advanced conceptualizations of the role of children's appraisal processes in coping with marital conflict. Theoretical models have been expanded further to consider the impact of marital conflict on children through changes in the family system's functioning, especially parent-child relations (Cummings & Davies, 1994b). We have also presented a theory of the role of children's sense of emotional security in organizing and directing children's coping processes and adjustment in reaction to marital conflict (Davies & Cummings, 1994a).

The model in Figure 1 thus provides bases for conceptualizing multiple pathways of effect associated with marital conflict from a stress and coping perspective. In addition, this model can be elaborated to incorporate the impact of other forms of child adversity, including but not limited to marital conflict. For example, one can consider the context/stimulus characteristics of family adversity more generally (e.g., marital conflict, child maltreatment, parental depression or alcoholism), rather than limiting the model to marital anger expression as a family context. Also, the conceptualization of family history can be broadened to include histories of adversity in addition to marital conflict. Similarly, children's emotional security is posited to derive from parental behavior towards children (e.g., hostility or abuse, emotional unresponsiveness or neglect) as well as from marital conflict history. Recent work has moved towards broadening theoretical models of family adversity and further development of conceptualizations of emotional security and other processes that account for the effects of these experiences on children's development (Cummings & Davies, 1994a; Cummings & Davies, 1995).

In sum, the marital relationship is just one of several family systems that have significant impact on children's development within families. There may be multiple and co-occurring forms of adversity associated with contexts of destructive marital conflict. Further, given the centrality of marital conflict to important forms of negative emotional and behavioral processes in families, marital conflict may be very important, even central, to an understanding of co-occurring forms of adversity in families.

Before beginning, two cautionary points should be made. First, stress is a normal part of life and children developing in supportive, nurturant environments can handle reasonable amounts of stress. Children are not necessarily "victims" because they are exposed to adversity within the family. It is important not to over-pathologize risk environments. Further, children's healthy, adaptive development requires that they experience challenge and adversity in order to learn to cope effectively with life's everyday realities. On the other hand, too much adversity and stress can undermine children's social and emotional functioning, leading to problems in adjustment.

Second, the notion of "victimization" should not be interpreted to mean that children are passive recipients of environmental experience or that they have no impact on family functioning. Individual children can be remarkably resilient and competent in the face of even the most adverse environmental circumstances (Garmezy & Masten, 1991). Also, while parents bear a primary responsibility for child outcomes, the bidirectionality of effects should be acknowledged. For example, certain child temperaments place strains on parental resources, caregiving abilities, and the marital relationship (Mangeldorf, Gunnar, Kestenbaum, Land & Andreas, 1990).

COMORBIDITY BETWEEN MARITAL CONFLICT AND OTHER RISK ENVIRONMENTS

Marital discord and children's psychological problems have long been linked, with early reports of such relations in the 1930s and 1940s (e.g., Baruch & Wilcox, 1944; Towle, 1931). Associations between marital conflict and adjustment problems in children are now well-established. These relations are relatively modest in non-clinic samples, but typically more robust in clinic samples, particularly when marital violence occurs (Fincham & Osborne, 1993; Grych & Fincham, 1990). These differences in the impact of marital conflict in discordant versus harmonious families suggest that the expression of marital conflict may be quite different in these different family environments, with effects on children varying as a function of particular patterns of conflict expression.

Destructive versus Constructive Conflict Processes

Thus, an implication is that it is critical to distinguish specific contexts of marital conflict. Marital conflict that increases children's risk for adjustment problems is likely to be comorbid with particularly problematic marital conflict styles (e.g., interspousal physical abuse, chronic lack of resolution of conflicts). A general failure until recently to adequately differentiate contexts of marital conflict has likely clouded actual relationships between marital conflict and children's adjustment problems (Fincham & Osborne, 1993). Thus, when only conflict averages are reported, the impact of *destructive marital conflict* on children may be underestimated, whereas relatively constructive forms of expression of differences between partners may, in fact, have little, or no, negative effects on children.

Destructive marital conflict may enhance the negative impact of other forms of family adversity, for example, by increasing the general arousal or tension level in children and families, by reducing the availability of parental support for children, and by fostering aggressiveness between siblings (Cummings & Davies, 1994a). Marital conflict processes may have effects in some ways similar to physical abuse on children when both represent destructive conflict processes. For example, both may introduce stresses that greatly increase children's problems in their regulation of emotionality and behavior, fostering the development of problems in adjustment. Further, a combination of two or more psychosocial stressors may potentiate or multiply children's risk for developing psychological problems; that is, two or more simultaneous family stressors may have far larger effects than the sum of the stressors (Rutter, 1981).

Notably, angry expressions of marital differences reliably elicit overt distress, anger and aggression from bystanding children (Cummings, Zahn-Waxler & Radke-Yarrow, 1981). On the other hand, quite different reactions are observed in children in response to constructive discussions of marital differences. A recent study examined children's reactions to marital disputes characterized by high rates of positive (e.g., smiling) and low rates of negative (e.g., disapproving looks) behavior. In this specific context of marital conflict children rarely expressed anger or distress, typically evidencing positive behavior (e.g., smiling, play) (Easterbrooks, Cummings & Emde, 1994). With the understandable concern about the negative effects of marital discord, it is important to put the occurrence of conflict within families in perspective. Conflicts are a normal part of life and may sometimes be necessary for working out important issues concerning marital and family functioning. The exploration of the possibly beneficial effects of exposure to constructive conflict within positive family environments is just beginning.

Marital Conflict and Other Family Risk Factors

Another important interpretative consideration is that marital discord seldom occurs alone but may covary with other types of family disturbance, such as divorce, parental depression, physical abuse, alcoholism. In fact, marital conflict is found to be a predictor of children's negative outcomes in homes that are characterized as disturbed for other reasons.

Thus, parental conflict is a better forecaster of children's functioning than changes in family structure, such as marital status (Amato & Keith, 1991). Marital conflict also appears to play a significant role in the transmission of psychological problems from depressed parent to child (for an extensive review of family systems associated with parental depression and their effects on children, see Cummings & Davies, 1994b), or in the negative impact of parental alcoholism (West & Prinz, 1987). On the other hand, some effects attributed to marital conflict may be due to other family disturbances with which it is comorbid.

Thus, family risk factors often are not independent, a notion implicit in this volume's concept of "multiple victimization." In particular, child physical abuse is often found to be comorbid with other types of family disturbances. As noted above, child physical abuse and interspousal aggression are highly associated (Jouriles, Barling & O'Leary, 1987). Furthermore, high levels of marital conflict have been associated with internalizing and externalizing symptomatology for abused children (Trickett & Susman, 1989).

The combined effects of child abuse and marital conflict are not yet well understood. Some work suggests that children who are *exposed* to spousal abuse exhibit adjustment problems similar to those of children who are direct *victims* of parental violence (Jaffe, Wolfe, Wilson & Zak, 1986). Recent analogue studies extend this line of inquiry, suggesting that abused children are especially sensitive and reactive to a variety of forms of anger expression by others, including interadult or "background" anger.

One study investigated the behavioral responses of physically abused and nonabused boys to background anger and found that physically abused boys were more aroused and angered by background anger than other children and more prone to intervene (Cummings, Hennessy, Rabideau & Cicchetti, 1994). Another study found that physically abused children reported more fear than non-abused children in response to videotaped segments of interadult anger. Moreover, abused children were particularly sensitive to whether or not anger between adults was resolved (Hennessy, Rabideau, Cicchetti & Cummings, 1994). One hypothesis for the apparent hypersensitivity of physically abused children to conflict between adults, and whether conflict is adequately resolved, is that physically abused children are fearful, based upon experience, that interadult conflict will proliferate to include them as victims. Another possibility is that physically abused children are emotionally sensitized to all forms of anger expression as a result of much higher levels of exposure than among other children (Cummings & Davies, 1994a).

In sum, with regard to the issue of multiple victimization, the evidence suggests that marital conflict may take many forms and often co-occurs with other family disturbance. Consistent with a stress and coping approach, contexts of marital conflict expression should be well-defined, but also inclusive, so that the impact of broader family contexts are taken into account. Thus, violence, hostility, and abuse within families impacts upon children as stressors in terms of the entire range of family systems that are affected, for example, parent-child abuse, interparental aggression and anger, intersibling aggression and anger. These subsystems are likely to be interdependent, with aggressivity in one subsystem affecting the likelihood of aggressivity in another. Further, each of these subsystems may have a significant impact upon children's development of maladaptive coping styles and patterns (e.g., hyperarousal and proneness to hostility in everyday social contexts, excessive fearfulness and withdrawal in interactions with peers and adults).

EFFECTS OF EXPOSURE TO MARITAL CONFLICT
ON CHILDREN

In our research since the early 1980s we have stressed the careful definition of person-environment interactions surrounding marital conflict, emphasizing the need to differentiate contexts of marital conflict and anger expression. Anger and conflict expression has often been treated as if it were a single or unitary phenomenon. In fact, anger and conflict expressions vary on a variety of dimensions and domains. As we have noted, differences in marital conflict styles are important not only for their distinct effects on children, but also because marital conflict may act as a sort of microcosm for co-occurring forms of adversity or multiple pathways of adversity.

With regard to marital conflict styles, distressed partners may seldom actually talk about the issues troubling them, but nonetheless their feelings may still surface in the form of looks, gestures, and the things left unsaid rather than said. If couples fight a lot, does that necessarily mean that they are unhappy? Some couples have frequent disagreements and disputes but in general feel comfortable with the process of open disagreement and often things end up on a positive note. In other cases marital disputes are highly verbal and emotionally heated, with fights sometimes escalating to include physical violence. Do children respond to whether the parents are fighting a lot, or do they take into account the whole picture, including the end result of the fight?

Children's Reactions During Exposure to Background Anger

Analogue studies have been essential to tease apart these relations, given that marital conflict and resolution seldom takes "pure" forms in the home, even if it were possible to observe them reliably, and, further, are confounded with the broader family context, including the possibility of comorbidity with other family risk factors. Analogue and field studies have productively complemented each other over the past few years in explicating the impact of exposure to specific forms of anger expression on children (see review in Cummings & Davies, 1994a). It has now been conclusively shown that exposure to marital conflict is a significant stressor for children (Emery, Fincham & Cummings, 1992). In fact, significant distress and anger in response to marital conflicts in the home have been reported in children as young as 1 year of age (Cummings et al., 1981), and even children's heart rate, blood pressure, and other physiological responses may be affected (El-Sheikh, Cummings & Goetsch, 1989). Further, exposure to background anger elevates children's interpersonal aggressiveness (Cummings, Iannotti & Zahn-Waxler, 1985). Children's distress may also motivate them to become involved in the parents' disputes as mediators or comforters, a tendency that is observed to be greatest among children from homes marked by interparental violence (J. S. Cummings, Pellegrini, Notarius & Cummings 1989; O'Brien, Margolin, John & Krueger, 1991).

Effects of Different Ways of Fighting

Research shows that children react quite differently to different ways adults fight. The greatest stress appears to be induced when conflicts get physical and topics of dispute concern the children.

Interspousal aggression. Marital conflict is particularly likely to be linked with dysregulated styles of coping with conflict (e.g., elevated emotionality, E.M. Cummings, Vogel, Cummings & El-Sheikh, 1989) and adjustment problems (Fantuzzo et al., 1991; Holden & Ritchie, 1991) when children are exposed to interparental violence. In the home physical aggression between parents elicits more distress from children than verbal anger (Cummings et al., 1981).

Nonverbal anger. Research using experimental methodologies suggests that children are quite sensitive to nonverbal anger between adults. In fact, negative emotional responses are as great as for verbal conflicts (E.M. Cummings et al., 1989). However, there is a virtual absence of field research on this question, largely due to the lack of development of methods sensitive to the occurrence of nonverbal anger; this is a notable gap in the study of the impact on children of marital conflict or other forms of adversity (e.g., maltreatment).

Child-related conflicts. A recent study (Grych & Fincham, 1993) reported that, in relation to non-child-related conflicts, children reacted to child-related conflicts with greater shame, self-blame, and fear. Another reported that marital fights over child-rearing were better predictors of child behavior problems than either global marital distress or conflicts in areas not related to child-rearing (Snyder, Klein, Gdowski, Faulstich & LaCombe, 1988). Also, child-rearing disagreements have been found to predict children's emotional difficulties, even after controlling for global marital adjustment and exposure to marital conflict (Jouriles et al., 1991). With regard to a family-wide model for adversity and abuse, one implication is that physical abuse or neglect attributed by parents to the children's own behavior or characteristics may also be maximally stressful, since such attributions are likely to increase children's feelings of shame, self-blame, and fear.

Resolution Reduces the Stress Associated with Exposure to Conflict

Children's coping behaviors are also affected by constructive conflict processes. The observation by children of the resolution of adults' conflicts much reduces their distress reactions and aggressiveness resulting from exposure to marital conflict (Cummings, 1987). They detect resolution when it occurs "behind closed doors," with a substantial reduction in the apparent stress of exposure to interadult conflict. Further, they benefit from a later explanation of how an unseen resolution occurred (Cummings, Simpson & Wilson, 1993).

EFFECTS OF MARITAL CONFLICT ON THE FAMILY SYSTEM

Another pathway through which marital conflict may "victimize" children is by causing problems in the functioning of the family system, in particular parent-child relations (Emery et al., 1992; see extensive reviews in Cummings & Davies, 1994a; Davies & Cummings, 1994). Marital conflict or other forms of adversity (e.g., maltreatment) may be both a cause and a product of discord within the larger family system (Rutter, 1979). There are multiple pathways through which destructive marital conflict styles may negatively impact parenting practices and/or parent-child attachments, thereby increasing children's experiences of stress and distress within the family, undermining emotional relationships, and contributing to the emergence of dysfunctional coping styles that contribute to child maladjustment.

Changes in Parenting Practices

The stress, frustration, and hopelessness of marital conflict can carry over into the parents' interactions with their children (Belsky, 1984). For example, Belsky, Youngblade, Rovine and Volling (1991) reported that increases in marital conflict and discord across infancy and early childhood were associated with parental negativity and control. Spousal conflict and negativity have been associated with aversive parent-child interactions (Floyd & Zmich, 1991) and inconsistent discipline (Stoneman, Brody & Burke, 1989). Negative changes in parent-child relations due to marital conflict may be an important pathway through which family conflict contributes to psychopathology in children (Christensen & Margolin, 1988; Fauber, Forehand, Thomas & Wierson, 1990).

Parent-Child Attachment

A primary effect of marital conflict on children can be to undermine the quality of the emotional bond or attachment between parents and children, thereby leaving children at increased risk for feelings of emotional insecurity and adjustment problems (Davies & Cummings, 1994). By preoccupying and disturbing the parents, interparental conflict may decrease their sensitivity, psychological availability, and the appropriateness of their behavior towards children. Several studies indicate relations between marital conflict and insecure parent-child attachment (Cox & Owen, 1993; Howes & Markman, 1989; Isabella & Belsky, 1985). On the other hand, the negative impact of marital conflict on children may be reduced if parents can maintain secure attachments with children despite their marital difficulties (Emery, 1982), an unlikely outcome in the presence of other forms of child abuse.

Changes in Sibling Relationships

Increased agonistic behavior between siblings may result from marital conflict (Brody, Stoneman & Burke, 1987; Brody, Stoneman, McCoy & Forehand, 1992). However, siblings may also help each other cope. Jenkins, Smith and Graham (1989) reported that seeking contact with a sibling was a frequently described strategy for coping with interparental conflict among 9-12 year olds. There is also evidence that siblings try to buffer each other from the impact of adults' angry behavior (Cummings & Smith, 1993). In relation to peer dyads, positive affect between female siblings and prosocial behavior between male siblings increased in association with exposure to simulated parental conflicts.

AN UPDATED STRESS AND COPING MODEL

Research has now considered many of the elements outlined in our 1988 framework for a stress and coping approach (Cummings & Cummings, 1988; see Figure 1). The original model has also been expanded to include the impact of marital conflict on children's coping styles through effects on parenting, attachment, and other aspects of the family system (Cummings & Davies, 1994a). Can theory be articulated further with regard to the coping processes that account for children's adjustment outcomes?

Children's appraisals of their relative emotional security in the face of marital conflict may hold the key to an integration of current evidence (Davies & Cummings, 1995). Folkman (1991) has emphasized the importance of appraisal processes to an individual's coping with stressful events:

> The behavioral flow begins with a person's cognitive appraisal of a person-environment relationship. The appraisal includes an evaluation of the personal significance of the encounter (primary appraisal) and an evaluation of the options for coping (secondary appraisal). In primary appraisal the person asks, "What do I have at stake in this encounter?" and in secondary appraisal the question is "What can I do?".... Together, primary appraisal and secondary appraisal shape emotion quality and intensity and influence coping response. (p. 5)

Specifically with regard to children's coping with marital conflict, Grych and Fincham (1990) argue that in primary processing of marital conflict the child "extracts information regarding its negativity, threat, and self-relevance" (p. 281). In secondary processing the child tries to "discover why the conflict is occurring (causal attribution), who is responsible for it (responsibility attribution), and whether they have adequate skills for successfully coping with the conflict (efficacy expectation)" (p. 282). Presumably, similar primary and secondary processing takes place in situations in which child maltreatment has co-occurred with marital conflict.

Such additional adversity may make the child's appraisal task more complex, difficult, and subject to distortion (e.g., children's attribution of responsibility for family adversity to themselves rather than the parents).

Our formulation extends these notions and makes additional propositions. First, we contend that children do not simply evaluate conflict in a general way but appraise it with regard to a *particular* higher-order goal or concern (see Figure 1), that is, their feelings of emotional security. Substantial evidence demonstrates that emotional security is a guiding concern for children within families (Davies & Cummings, 1994).

Second, we argue that traditional conceptualizations of stress and coping are too cognitive, assuming that cognitive analysis is primary and emotion is secondary. Consistent with a functionalist perspective (Bretherton, Fritz, Zahn-Waxler & Ridgeway, 1986), emotions constitute internal monitoring and guidance systems for coping with marital conflict, with the function of appraising interparental disputes and motivating behavioral responding. Emotions are *not* reduced to cognitions but play a primary role in children's coping with marital conflict. For example, children induced to feel sad or angry prior to exposure to interadult anger exhibit more distress behavior, appraise the adults as more angry, and report more dysregulation than children induced to feel "just okay" (Davies & Cummings, 1995).

Third, we propose that children's perceptions of coping efficacy are fundamental to their adjustment and revolve around the extent to which they appraise emotional security or insecurity in particular family contexts of marital conflict. Rossman and Rosenberg (1992) have shown that children's beliefs about their control over parental conflict may act as compensatory moderators of stress, predicting lower rates of behavior problems. Analogue studies of particular contexts of marital conflict also suggest the significance of the emotional security implications of conflict. Accordingly, interadult aggression and child-related conflict predict elevated stress reactions, whereas multiple contexts of conflict resolution (e.g, observed, explained or resolution "behind closed doors") result in reduced child distress.

Demonstrating the significance of coping efficacy and appraisal, in a recent study we found that appraisals of coping efficacy and the threat posed by marital conflict predicted adjustment in boys whereas self-blame was linked with internalizing problems for girls (Cummings, Davies & Simpson, 1994). The appraised destructiveness of conflict was significantly related to perceived threat in boys and self-blame in girls. Further, boys appeared more attuned, or, alternatively, less shielded from marital conflict, as reflected by higher correlations with mothers' reports of marital conflict for boys than for girls. The particular significance of boys' appraisals was suggested by the fact that their perceptions were better predictors of adjustment outcomes than mothers' reports.

Is there evidence in children's actual processes of coping with adults' angry behavior for an emotional security hypothesis? We think that findings of sensitization to background anger as a result of repeated or intense exposure to marital conflict provides additional, compelling support. According to attachment theory formulations (Bowlby, 1973), emotional insecurity predicts greater distress and behavioral dysregulation in the face of stressful events (see recent formulations by Cassidy, 1993; Kobak & Barbagli, 1993). Therefore, if emotional security is the operative process in children's coping with marital conflict, children's distress and behavioral dysregulation in the face of background anger should increase when marital conflict is frequent and destructive, that is, sensitization should be observed in children's reactions. An alternative, cognitively-based theory is that children exposed to a great deal of marital conflict will "get used to it," that is, habituate.

The evidence strongly supports the predictions of sensitization that follow from an emotional security hypothesis. Greater marital conflict has repeatedly been linked with children's *greater reactivity* to exposure to background anger. That is, positive links have repeatedly been found between destructive marital conflict (e.g., interparental aggression, lack of resolution) and children's behavioral, emotional, and even physiological reactivity to background anger (Cummings & Davies, 1994a). Here, the findings of analogue and field studies complement each other in providing clear support for the same pattern of relations.

But what of the notion that people "get used to" events that they observe a lot? While it remains plausible, albeit not shown empirically, that children exposed to much marital conflict do not find its expression as "novel" as do children exposed to few parental fights, emotional and behavioral reactions do not reflect habituation. Further, increased emotional and behavioral dysregulation is likely to contribute to maladaptive coping processes and children's development over time of problems in adjustment (Cummings & Davies, 1994a).

In sum, recent findings support the utility of a stress and coping approach for understanding children's coping with marital conflict. In particular, a theory that emphasizes the importance of children's appraisals and coping efficacy with regard to issues of emotional security may hold the key to a process-oriented conceptualization of the impact of marital conflict and other forms of adversity (e.g., maltreatment) on children.

CONCLUSION

Theory and research on the impact of marital conflict on children has thus been significantly advanced by conceptual models based upon the stress and coping approach. This approach also holds promise for understanding sequelae of other forms of family adversity (e.g., maltreatment) and the co-occurrence of multiple forms of adversity. In addition, marital conflict has been related in its effects to other forms of "victimization" of children, and has demonstrated impacts on children through multiple pathways. This approach thus offers conceptualizations that might be productively applied to advancing process-oriented understanding of the impact of other dysfunctional family circumstances on children.

REFERENCES

Amato, P.R., & Keith, B. (1991). Parental divorce and the well-being of children: A meta-analysis. *Psychological Bulletin, 110,* 26-46.

Baruch, D.W., & Wilcox, J.A. (1944). A study of sex differences in preschool children's adjustment coexistent with interparental tensions. *Journal of Genetic Psychology, 64,* 281-303.

Belsky, J. (1984). The determinants of parenting: A process model. *Child Development, 55,* 83-96.

Belsky, J., Youngblade, L., Rovine, M., & Volling, B. (1991). Patterns of marital change and parent-child interaction. *Journal of Marriage and the Family, 53,* 487-498.

Bowlby, J. (1973). *Attachment and loss: Vol. 2. Separation.* New York: Basic Books.

Bretherton, I., Fritz, J., Zahn-Waxler, C., & Ridgeway, D. (1986). Learning to talk about emotions: A functionalist perspective. *Child Development, 57,* 529-548.

Brody, G.H., Stoneman, Z., & Burke, M. (1987). Family system and individual child correlates of sibling behavior. *American Journal of Orthopsychiatry, 57,* 561-569.

Brody, G.H., Stoneman, Z., McCoy, J.K., & Forehand, R. (1992). Contemporaneous and longitudinal associations of sibling conflict with family relationship assessments and family discussions about sibling problems. *Child Development, 63,* 391-400.

Cassidy, J. (1993, March). Emotion regulation within attachment relationships. In J. Cassidy & L. Berlin (Chairs), *Attachment and emotions.* Symposium conducted at the meeting of the Society for Research in Child Development, New Orleans, LA.

Christensen, A., & Margolin, G. (1988). Conflict and alliance in distressed and nondistressed families. In R.A. Hinde & J. Stevenson-Hinde (Eds.), *Relationships within families* (pp. 263-282). New York: Oxford University Press.

Cox, M.J., & Owen, M.T. (1993, March). Marital conflict and conflict negotiation: Effects on infant-mother and infant-father relationships. In M. Cox & J. Brooks-Gunn (Chairs), *Conflict in families: Causes and consequences*. Symposium conducted at the meeting of the Society for Research in Child Development, New Orleans, LA.

Cummings, E.M. (1987). Coping with background anger in early childhood. *Child Development, 58*, 976-984.

Cummings, E.M. (1995). The usefulness of experiments for the study of the family. *Journal of Family Psychology, 9*, 175-185.

Cummings, E.M., & Cummings, J.L. (1988). A process-oriented approach to children's coping with adults' angry behavior. *Developmental Review, 8*, 296-321.

Cummings, E.M., & Davies, P.T. (1994a). *Children and marital conflict: The impact of family dispute and resolution*. New York: Guilford.

Cummings, E.M., & Davies, P.T. (1994b). Maternal depression and child development. *Journal of Child Psychology and Psychiatry, 35*, 73-112.

Cummings, E.M., & Davies, P.T. (1995). The impact of parents on their children: An emotional security hypothesis. *Annals of Child Development, 10*, 167-208.

Cummings, E.M., Davies, P.T., & Simpson, K. (1994). Marital conflict, gender, and children's appraisals and coping efficacy as mediators of child adjustment. *Journal of Family Psychology, 8*, 141-149.

Cummings, E.M., Hennessy, K.D., Rabideau, G.J., & Cicchetti, D. (1994). Coping with anger involving a family member in physically abused and non-abused boys. *Development and Psychopathology, 6*, 31-41.

Cummings, E.M., Iannotti, R.J., & Zahn-Waxler, C. (1985). The influence of conflict between adults on the emotions and aggression of young children. *Developmental Psychology, 21*, 495-507.

Cummings, E.M., Simpson, K.S., & Wilson, A. (1993). Children's responses to interadult anger as a function of information about resolution. *Developmental Psychology, 29*, 978-985.

Cummings, E.M., & Smith, D. (1993). The impact of anger between adults on siblings' emotions and social behavior. *Journal of Child Psychology and Psychiatry, 34*, 1425-1433.

Cummings, E.M., Vogel, E., Cummings, J.S., & El-Sheikh, M. (1989). Children's responses to different forms of expression of anger between adults. *Child Development, 60*, 1392-1404.

Cummings, E.M., Zahn-Waxler, C., & Radke-Yarrow, M. (1981). Young children's responses to expressions of anger and affection by others in the family. *Child Development, 52*, 1274-1282.

Cummings, J.S., Pellegrini, D., Notarius, C., & Cummings, E.M. (1989). Children's responses to angry adult behavior as a function of marital distress and history of interparent hostility. *Child Development, 60*, 1035-1043.

Davies, P.T., & Cummings, E.M. (1994). Marital conflict and child adjustment: An emotional security hypothesis. *Psychological Bulletin, 116*, 387-411.

Davies, P.T., & Cummings, E.M. (1995). Children's emotions as organizers of their reactions to interadult anger: A functionalist perspective. *Developmental Psychology, 31*, 677-684.

Easterbrooks, A., Cummings, E.M., & Emde, R.N. (1994). Young children's responses to constructive marital disputes. *Journal of Family Psychology, 8*, 160-169.

El-Sheikh, M., Cummings, E.M., & Goetsch, V. (1989). Coping with adults' angry behavior: Behavioral, physiological, and self-reported responding in preschoolers. *Developmental Psychology, 25*, 490-498.

Emery, R.E. (1982). Interparental conflict and the children of discord and divorce. *Psychological Bulletin, 92*, 310-330.

Emery, R.E., Fincham, F.D., & Cummings, E.M. (1992). Parenting in context: Systemic thinking about parental conflict and its influence on children. *Journal of Consulting and Clinical Psychology, 60*, 909-912.

Fantuzzo, J.W., DePaola, L.M., Lambert, L., Martino, T., Anderson, G., & Sutton, S. (1991). Effects of interparental violence on the psychological adjustment and competencies of young children. *Journal of Clinical and Consulting Psychology, 59*, 258-265.

Fauber, R., Forehand, R., Thomas, A.M., & Wierson, M. (1990). A mediational model of the impact of marital conflict on adolescent adjustment in intact and divorced families: The role of disrupted parenting. *Child Development, 61*, 1112-1123.

Fincham, F., & Osborne, L. (1993). Marital conflict and children: Retrospect and prospect. *Clinical Psychology Review, 13*, 75-88.

Floyd, F., & Zmich, D. (1991). Marriage and the parenting partnership: Perceptions and interactions of parents with mentally retarded and typically developing children. *Child Development, 62*, 1434-1448.

Folkman, S. (1991). Coping across the lifespan: Theoretical issues. In E.M. Cummings, A. Greene, & K. Karraker (Eds.), *Lifespan developmental psychology: Perspectives on stress and coping* (pp. 3-20). Hillsdale, NJ: Lawrence Erlbaum Associates.

Garmezy, N., & Masten, A. (1991). The protective role of competence indicators in children at risk. In E.M. Cummings, A. Greene, & K. Karraker (Eds.), *Lifespan developmental psychology: Perspectives on stress and coping* (pp. 151-176). Hillsdale, NJ: Erlbaum.

Gelles, R.J. (1987). *Family violence.* (2nd ed.). Newbury Park, CA: Sage.

Grych, J.H., & Fincham, F.D. (1990). Marital conflict and children's adjustment: A cognitive-contextual framework. *Psychological Bulletin, 108*, 267-290.

Grych, J.H., & Fincham, F.D. (1993). Children's appraisals of marital conflict: Initial investigations of the cognitive-contextual framework. *Child Development, 64*, 215-230.

Grych, J., Seid, M., & Fincham, F. (1992). Assessing marital conflict from the child's perspective: The children's perception of interparental conflict scale. *Child Development, 63*, 558-572.

Hennessy, K., Rabideau, G., Cicchetti, D., & Cummings, E.M. (1994). Responses of physically abused children to different forms of interadult anger. *Child Development, 65,* 815-828.

Holden, G.W., & Ritchie, K.L. (1991). Linking extreme marital discord, child rearing, and child behavior problems: Evidence from battered women. *Child Development, 62,* 311-327.

Howes, P., & Markman, H.J. (1989). Marital quality and child functioning: A longitudinal investigation. *Child Development, 60,* 1044-1051.

Isabella, R.A., & Belsky, J. (1985). Marital change during the transitions to parenthood and security of infant-parent attachment. *Journal of Family Issues, 6,* 505-522.

Jaffe, P., Wolfe, D., Wilson, S., & Zak, L. (1986). Similarities in behavioral and social maladjustment among child victims and witnesses to family violence. *American Journal of Orthopsychiatry, 56,* 142-146.

Jenkins, M., Smith, M, & Graham, P. (1989). Coping with parental quarrels. *Journal of the American Academy of Child and Adolescent Psychiatry, 28,* 182-189.

Jouriles, E., Barling, J., & O'Leary, K. (1987). Predicting child behavior problems in maritally violent families. *Journal of Abnormal Child Psychology, 15,* 165-173.

Jouriles, E.N., Murphy, C.M., Farris, A.M., Smith, D.A., Richters, J.E., & Waters, E. (1991). Marital adjustment, parental disagreements about child rearing, and behavior problems in boys: Increasing the specificity of the marital assessment. *Child Development, 62,* 1424-1433.

Kobak, R.R., & Barbagli, J. (1993, March). Maternal attachment strategies and emotion regulation with adolescent offspring. In J. Cassidy & L. Berlin (Chairs), *Attachment and emotions.* Symposium conducted at the meeting of the Society for Research in Child Development. New Orleans, LA.

Lazarus, R.S., & Folkman, S. (1984). *Stress, coping, and appraisal.* New York: Springer.

Mangelsdorf, S., Gunnar, M., Kestenbaum, R., Lang, S., & Andreas, D. (1990). Infant proneness-to-distress temperament, maternal personality, and mother-infant attachment: Associations and goodness of fit. *Child Development, 61,* 820-831.

O'Brien, M., Margolin, G., John, R.S., & Krueger, L. (1991). Mothers' and sons' cognitive and emotional reactions to simulated marital and family conflict. *Journal of Consulting and Clinical Psychology, 59,* 692-703.

Rossman, B.B.R., & Rosenberg, M.S. (1992). Family stress and functioning in children: The moderating effects of children's beliefs about their control over parental conflict. *Journal of Child Psychology and Psychiatry, 33,* 699-715.

Rutter, M. (1979). Maternal deprivation, 1972-1978: New findings, new concepts, new approaches. *Child Development, 50,* 283-305.

Rutter, M. (1981). Stress, coping, and development: Some issues and some questions. *Journal of Child Psychology and Psychiatry, 22,* 323-356.

Snyder, D.K., Klein, M.A., Gdowski, C.L., Faulstich, C., & LaCombe, J. (1988). Generalized dysfunction in clinic and nonclinic families: A comparative analysis. *Journal of Abnormal Child Psychology, 16,* 97-109.

Sroufe, L.A., & Rutter, M. (1984). The domain of developmental psychopathology. *Child Development, 55,* 17-29.

Stoneman, Z., Brody, G., & Burke, M. (1989). Sibling temperaments and maternal and paternal perceptions of marital, family, and personal functioning. *Journal of Marriage and the Family, 51,* 99-113.

Straus, M.A., Gelles, R., & Steinmetz, S. (1980). *Behind closed doors: Violence in the American family.* New York: Anchor Press.

Towle, C. (1931). The evaluation and management of marital status in foster homes. *American Journal of Orthopsychiatry, 1,* 271-284.

Trickett, P.K., & Susman, E.J. (1989). Perceived similarities and disagreements about child-rearing practices in abusive and nonabusive families: Intergenerational and concurrent family processes. In D. Cicchetti & V. Carlson (Eds.), *Child maltreatment: Theory and research on the causes and consequences of child abuse and neglect* (pp. 280-301). New York: Cambridge University Press.

West, M.O., & Prinz, R.J. (1987). Parental alcoholism and childhood psychopathology. *Psychological Bulletin, 102,* 204-218.

Trauma Models of the Effects
of Childhood Maltreatment

Frank W. Putnam

SUMMARY. Trauma models of child maltreatment effects are addressed, with emphasis on the *Diagnostic and Statistical Manual of Mental Disorders'* diagnosis of posttraumatic stress disorder and the degree to which it fails to account for many salient symptoms and behaviors associated with maltreatment and victimization in children and adults. Research is presented to support the idea that posttraumatic stress disorder is best conceptualized as a dimensional outcome rather than a categorical all-or-none diagnosis. The PTSD model(s) needs to be either expanded to correct deficiencies or to be integrated into a larger model of the effects of trauma and victimization. *[Article copies available for a fee from The Haworth Document Delivery Service: 1-800-342-9678. E-mail address: getinfo@haworth.com]*

Childhood maltreatment is a significant risk factor for the development of mental health problems in childhood, adolescence and adulthood (Armsworth & Holaday, 1993; Coons, Bowman, Pellow, & Schneider, 1989; Finkelhor, 1990; Spaccarelli, 1994; Wyatt & Powell, 1988). However, considerable variability occurs in both short-term and long-term outcomes. Attempts to account for the heterogeneity of maltreatment effects have

---

Address correspondence to: Frank W. Putman, PhD, Building 15K, National Institute of Mental Health, Laboratory of Developmental Psychology, 9000 Rockville Pike, Bethesda, MD 20892-2668.

[Haworth co-indexing entry note]: "Trauma Models of the Effects of Childhood Maltreatment." Putnam, Frank W. Co-published simultaneously in *Journal of Aggression, Maltreatment & Trauma* (The Haworth Maltreatment & Trauma Press, an imprint of The Haworth Press, Inc.) Vol. 2, No. 1 (#3), 1998, pp. 51-66; and: *Multiple Victimization of Children: Conceptual, Developmental, Research, and Treatment Issues* (ed: B. B. Robbie Rossman, and Mindy S. Rosenberg) The Haworth Maltreatment & Trauma Press, an imprint of The Haworth Press, Inc., 1998, pp. 51-66. Single or multiple copies of this article are available for a fee from The Haworth Document Delivery Service [1-800-342-9678, 9:00 a.m. - 5:00 p.m. (EST). E-mail address: getinfo@haworth.com].

51

generated a variety of different classes of theoretical models (Spaccarelli, 1994). One group of models, "trauma-related" models, seeks to account for short and longer range effects in terms of the psychological and biological sequelae of stress and trauma associated with maltreatment. Trauma-related models of the effects of childhood maltreatment reflect extensions of prior theory and research with adult trauma-related models, particularly those derived from combat-related posttraumatic stress disorder (PTSD).

There are a number of trauma models reflecting the different theoretical perspectives that have been brought to bear on this subject. Psychoanalytic theory from Horowitz (1979, 1986), Krystal (1978) and others was extremely important in setting the stage for an appreciation of psychological and cognitive effects of trauma and for providing the first generation of psychometric tools, such as the Impact of Events Scale to assess trauma effects (Horowitz, 1979; Horowitz, 1986; Krystal, 1978). Cognitive and cognitive-behavioral trauma models by Janoff-Bulman (1983, 1985) and others made important early contributions (Janoff-Bulman, 1985; Janoff-Bulman & Frieze, 1983). The existential-humanistic writings of Lifton (1976, 1988) have also exerted considerable influence on conceptualizations of the meaning of traumatic experiences (Lifton, 1988; Lifton & Olson, 1976).

Finkelhor's (1988) traumagenic dynamics model, offered as an alternative to the PTSD model described subsequently, focuses on four key aspects of sexual abuse: (1) traumatic sexualization; (2) powerlessness; (3) stigmatization; and (4) betrayal. The strength of this model is that it addresses key aspects of the traumatic experience of sexual abuse that are ignored by most models and "explains" common outcomes such as depression. A criticism of the model is that it is not easily operationalized and is difficult to verify empirically (Spaccarelli, 1994). Nonetheless, the traumagenic dynamics model is an important conceptualization of the effects of sexual abuse and readers are encouraged to familiarize themselves with Finkelhor's ideas (Finkelhor, 1988).

Most operationalized trauma-related models are now closely tied to the *Diagnostic and Statistical Manual of Mental Disorders* (DSM) diagnosis of posttraumatic stress disorder and primarily seek to account for a specific set of "posttraumatic" psychological and biological symptoms and behaviors. Central to current trauma models are a set of neurobiological theories of the effects of trauma on the nervous system (Kolb, 1987; Pitman, 1988; van der Kolk, Greenberg, Boyd, & Krystal, 1985). The mesh between these theories, the diagnosis of PTSD and current research on the biological sequelae of trauma is less than perfect, but there is substantial empirical support for the basic concepts (Charney, Deutch,

Krystal, Southwich, & Davis, 1993). This review will focus on PTSD-based trauma models and their applicability to children and adolescents.

THE DSM DIAGNOSIS OF POSTTRAUMATIC STRESS DISORDER

Posttraumatic stress disorder first became an official psychiatric diagnosis in the 1980 third edition of the *Diagnostic and Statistical Manual of Mental Disorders* (American Psychiatric Association, 1980). Despite a substantial body of research supporting the diagnosis, some skepticism remains about its validity. A few still view PTSD as a manifestation of malingering or a form of personality disorder (Davidson & Foa, 1991). PTSD is included under the anxiety disorders in the DSM, a grouping that is the subject of continued debate.

The essential feature of PTSD is the development and persistence of a specific set of symptoms following exposure to a severe traumatic stressor (American Psychiatric Association, 1994). The question of exactly what constitutes a significant traumatic event remains the subject of considerable debate. The DSM-IV (1994) broadened prior definitions by defining a traumatic event as one in which the individual experiences, witnesses or is confronted with an event or events that involve actual or threatened death, or threat to physical integrity of self or others, and which produces an emotional experience involving intense fear, helplessness or horror. It is noted that children may express these emotions through agitated or disorganized behavior. Considerable disagreement remains as to how to craft a definition that is sufficiently comprehensive to capture an individual's personal experience of trauma without becoming meaninglessly over-inclusive.

There is better agreement about the types of symptoms associated with a traumatic experience. Traditionally these have been divided into three categories: (1) reexperiencing symptoms; (2) avoidant symptoms; and (3) symptoms associated with increased arousal. Reexperiencing symptoms include recurrent and distressing recollections of the traumatic event such as images, thoughts or perceptions of the trauma. In young children this may be manifest by repetitive play involving elements or themes related to the traumatic event. Recurrent dreams, a vivid sense of reliving the traumatic experience, illusions, hallucinations and dissociative flashbacks related to the trauma are also common reexperiencing symptoms. In young children, specific traumatic reenactments may occur. Also included in the reexperiencing symptom category are manifestations of intense psychological and physiological distress that are related to exposure to cues or stimuli reminiscent of the traumatic experience.

Avoidant symptoms involve efforts to avoid thoughts, feelings, activities, places, people or other stimuli that evoke recollections of the traumatic event. Included in this category are functional amnesias for the traumatic experience and emotional numbing, affect constriction and feelings of detachment or estrangement from self and others. A foreshortened sense of the future, common in traumatized adults, is generally classified as an avoidant symptom. Symptoms of increased arousal include problems falling and/or staying asleep, irritability and explosive outbursts of anger, problems with concentration and attention, hypervigilance and an exaggerated startle response.

Recently it has been recognized that dissociative symptoms, manifest by a disruption in the normally integrative functions of consciousness, memory, identity and perception, are commonly associated with significant trauma (Putnam, 1985). There is considerable confusion in the DSM-IV about which diagnostic category to assign trauma-related dissociative symptoms to, and thus these symptoms are included with PTSD (dissociative amnesia), Acute Stress Disorder (derealization, depersonalization, dissociative amnesia) and also under the dissociative disorders (American Psychiatric Association, 1994). Significant dissociative symptoms immediately subsequent to a traumatic experience ("peritraumatic dissociation") appear to play an important role in the subsequent development of PTSD. Several studies have found that peritraumatic dissociation is a strong predictor of the subsequent development of posttraumatic stress disorder (Koopman, Classen, & Spiegel, 1994; Marmar, Weiss, Schlenger, Fairbank, Jordan, Kulka, & Hough, 1994).

APPLICATION OF THE DSM PTSD DIAGNOSIS TO CHILDREN AND ADOLESCENTS

The original PTSD trauma model was largely derived from clinical experience with combat-related trauma, primarily Vietnam veterans. Some have questioned its applicability to other forms of trauma and other populations, particularly children (Armsworth & Holaday, 1993; Finkelhor, 1990; Hillary & Schare, 1993). The scant pre-1980s literature on the effects of trauma on children took a psychoanalytic approach, primarily focusing on symptoms of regression and dependency, although dissociation was commented on by some investigators (Bloch, Silber, & Perry, 1956; Freud & Burlingham, 1943; Friedman & Linn, 1957; Mercier & Desperet, 1943). The seminal volume, *Post-Traumatic Stress Disorder in*

Children, edited by Spencer Eth and Robert Pynoos (1985), was the first systematic application of the DSM-based PTSD trauma model to children. Following this lead, a number of investigators began to apply the PTSD model to investigations of traumatized children. Studies have demonstrated that PTSD can be diagnosed in children following exposure to warfare (Arroyo & Eth, 1985; Jensen & Shaw, 1993), urban violence (Pynoos, Frederick, Nader, Arroyo, Steinberg, Eth, Nunex, & Fairbanks, 1987), disasters (Yule & Williams, 1990), severe injury (Stoddard, Norman, Murphy, & Beardslee, 1989) and witnessing the rape or murder of parents (Malmquist, 1986; Pynoos & Nader, 1988a).

The applicability of the DSM-based PTSD trauma model to maltreated children has proven more problematic (McNally, 1993). A number of studies and reviews support the idea that PTSD can be frequently diagnosed in adults who were physically and sexually abused in childhood (Coons, Bowman, Pellow, & Schneider, 1989; Donaldson & Gardner, 1985; Greenwald & Leitenberg, 1990; Rowan & Foy, 1993; Rowan, Foy, Rodriguez, & Ryan, 1994). However, investigators rigorously applying the DSM PTSD criteria to abused children have reported widely varying results (McNally, 1991; McNally, 1993). For example, Sirles, Smith, and Kusama (1989) found that none of their 207 incest victims met full diagnostic criteria for PTSD. On the other hand, Kiser, Ackerman, Brown, Edwards, McColgan, Pugh, and Pruitt (1988) reported that 9 out of 10 of their sexual abuse sample fulfilled PTSD criteria. The balance of studies to date suggest that although PTSD may be diagnosed in a substantial minority, the majority of maltreated children do not fully qualify for a DSM diagnosis of posttraumatic stress disorder (McNally, 1993). Several reviewers have cautioned that the DSM diagnosis of PTSD is not widely applicable to maltreated children (Armsworth & Holaday, 1993; Finkelhor, 1990).

Among the problems complicating the diagnosis of PTSD in children and adolescents is a lack of agreement about how to establish this diagnosis in children (Hillary & Schare, 1993). In research studies, DSM diagnoses are traditionally based on structured or semi-structured diagnostic interviews. PTSD diagnostic modules have been grafted on to a number of standard child and adolescent structured interviews such as the Diagnostic Interview Schedule (DIS) and the Diagnostic Interview for Children and Adolescents. However, there is evidence that the sensitivity of these interviews for PTSD may be very low (McNally, 1991).

McLeer and colleagues developed a structured interview for PTSD, and in a series of studies found that 42.7-48% of their samples of sexually abused children and adolescents met full DSM criteria (McLeer,

Deblinger, Atkins, Foa, & Ralphe, 1988; McLeer, Callagahan, Henry, & Wallen, 1994; McLeer, Deblinger, Henry, & Orvaschel, 1992). Wolfe, Gentile, and Wolfe (1989) developed the Children's Impact of Traumatic Events Scale (CITES), a structured interview, to assess abuse trauma. However, it does not render a full DSM diagnosis of PTSD because it fails to assess several symptoms. Perhaps the best structured PTSD interview for children is the Post-Traumatic Stress Disorder Reaction Index (PTSD-RI) which has been primarly applied to children exposed to disaster and violence (McNally, 1991). The PTSD-RI is highly correlated with confirmed PTSD caseness (McNally, 1991). The other widely used structured interview for PTSD is the Children's Posttraumatic Stress Disorder Inventory (CPTSDI) developed by Saigh (1991). Unfortunately, neither the PTSD-RI nor the CPTSDI have been included in maltreatment studies published to date.

Another source of error for the DSM diagnosis-based PTSD model of trauma in children is the failure to substitute developmentally relevant PTSD symptoms for the adult symptoms (Davidson & Foa, 1991; Lyons, 1987; McNally, 1991). There was a minor redress of this deficiency in the DSM-IV, but most critiques note that there are significant age-specific problems with the current DSM PTSD criteria (American Psychiatric Association, 1994). For example, there is virtually no evidence that traumatized children manifest a foreshortened sense of future in the same way that has been described in adults (McNally, 1991). Pynoos and Nader (1988) suggest that what occurs in children is a "change in future orientation" manifest by profound shifts in attitudes about personal safety and interpersonal relationships (Pynoos & Nader, 1988b). Similarly, reexperiencing symptoms may be very different in children, adolescents and adults. The DSM-IV includes the concept of "traumatic play" as a reexperiencing symptom in young children, but does not specify what constitutes traumatic play–a concept clinically illustrated by ambiguous and somewhat contradictory anecdotes scattered throughout the literature. In short, the larger conceptual failure of the DSM to include an alternative set of developmentally relevant symptoms for those diagnoses shared by children and adults also plagues the application of the adult-derived diagnosis of PTSD to children and adolescents.

Researchers of adult combat-related PTSD have established that subjects meeting DSM criteria often show significantly greater psychophysiological reactivity to trauma-related stimuli than combat-matched, non-PTSD veterans (Charney, Deutch, Krystal, Southwich, & Davis, 1993; Pitman, Orr, Forgue et al., 1987; Pitman, Orr, & Steketee, 1989). However, discriminate function analyses employing these markers for diagnostic purposes have not demonstrated acceptable sensitivity or specificity (Pitman et al., 1987). Current research with adults sexually abused in childhood shows even poorer specificity than combat subjects (Roger Pitman, personal communication, March, 1994). Recent studies of biological markers of stress and trauma in sexually abused girls demonstrate significant hormonal, neurotransmitter and immune system dysregulation in children who do not fulfill DSM criteria for PTSD (De Bellis, Burke, Trickett, & Putnam, in press; De Bellis, Chrousos, Dorn, Burke, Helmers, Kling, Trickett, & Putnam, 1994a; De Bellis, Lefter, Trickett, & Putnam, 1994b). Thus, although biological reactivity and hyperarousal are included in the syndromal criteria, established biological markers of stress and hyperarousal do not appear to be very specific for PTSD as defined by DSM criteria.

PREMORBID FACTORS CONTRIBUTING TO THE DEVELOPMENT OF PTSD

The question of who "gets" PTSD and who does not is poorly understood for both adults and children. The issue of predisposing personality factors has been a contentious subject in the clinical literature from the first reports of "shell shock" and "combat fatigue" which preceded the creation of the PTSD diagnosis. Studies investigating measures administered prior to the development of PTSD find some support for characterological premorbid factors. For example, Schnurr, Friedman, and Rosenberg (1993) analyzed MMPIs administered in college prior to military service and found that combat veterans who subsequently developed PTSD had higher scores for hypochondriasis, psychopathy and paranoia.

Although predisposing genetic factors are often suggested, only one study has evaluated genetic contributions to the development of PTSD (True, Rice, Eisen, Heath, Goldberg, Lyons, & Nowak, 1993). Studying 4042 Vietnam era veteran twin pairs, True et al. (1993) found that a surprisingly high percentage of the PTSD symptom variance could be accounted for genetically and virtually none was explained by shared family environment. They reported that after controlling for combat exposure, 13-30% of reexperiencing symptoms, 30-34% of avoidant symptoms and 28-32% of arousal symptoms were accounted for by genetic factors.

A history of childhood maltreatment appears also to be a potential predisposing factor for the development of combat-related PTSD. Using case-control methodology, Bremner, Southwick, Johnson, Yehuda, and Charney (1993) found that 29% of veterans with PTSD reported childhood physical or sexual abuse compared with 7% of non-PTSD combat-matched controls. Engel and colleagues (1993) extended this line of research to a large sample of Desert Storm veterans where they noted a significant gender interaction (Engel, Engel, Campbell, McFall, Russo, & Katon, 1993). Women were more likely to report pre-combat abuse, and women with histories of pre-combat abuse had significantly greater PTSD symptoms after controlling for prior psychiatric history and level of combat exposure. These two preliminary studies suggest that histories of prior trauma may increase likelihood of developing PTSD to new traumatic stressors.

PTSD AS A DIMENSIONAL OUTCOME

Although caseness for PTSD is difficult to establish in many maltreated children, the extant data suggest that, at least in children, PTSD may be better conceptualized as a dimensional process rather than a categorical all-or-none outcome. Several studies report that many maltreated children exhibit partial forms of PTSD (Armsworth & Holaday, 1993; Deblinger, McLeer, Atkins, Ralphe, & Foa, 1989; Famularo, Kinscherff, & Fenton, 1991; Hillary & Schare, 1993; Mannarino, Cohen, & Berman, 1994; McNally, 1991; Wolfe, Sas, & Wekerle, 1994; Wolfe et al., 1989). A similar dimensional, partial PTSD response is noted in children to other forms of trauma (Earls, Smith, Reich, & Jung, 1988; Jensen & Shaw, 1993; Malmquist, 1986; McNally, 1993; Yule & Williams, 1990). McNally's review suggests that maltreated children are more likely to manifest reexperiencing and avoidant symptoms than hyperarousal symptoms (McNally, 1993). However, elevated catecholamine levels indicative of autonomic nervous system hyperarousal have been reported in sexually abused girls compared with matched controls and Wolfe et al. (1994) found that two-thirds of their sample met the DSM hyperarousal criterion, a finding supported by De Bellis et al. (1994b).

Wolfe et al. (1994) explored the relation between PTSD symptomatology and selected victim and event characteristics in 90 abused children and adolescents (mean age = 12.4 years). They found that 80% of the sample met the reexperiencing symptom criterion, 64.4% met the avoidant symptom criterion and 66.7% met the hyperarousal criterion. Overall, 48.9% fulfilled all the DSM criteria for a diagnosis of PTSD. The PTSD group contained significantly more females and older children and was more likely to have been abused for a year or longer. Non-PTSD children were more likely to have suffered isolated instances of abuse. Abuse-related variables of duration, severity, coercion and relationship to abuser accounted for 26.9% of the PTSD variance after controlling for IQ, age, gender, receptive language ability and the nature of the abuse. Guilt and self-blame accounted for an additional 10.1% of the variance.

These results are similar to data reported for PTSD associated with combat and other types of trauma. Typically, approximately 15-35% of the PTSD symptom variance is accounted for by indices of trauma severity. However, our analyses of the interrelationship of trauma variables in sexually abused girls suggests that many indices of child sexual abuse trauma are strongly confounded with each other (De Bellis & Putnam, 1994). For example, duration and age of onset are confounded with relationship to perpetrator in our sample. Biological father-daughter incest starts significantly earlier and continues significantly longer than stepfather-stepdaughter incest. The complex interrelationships of abuse variables and family environmental factors are likely to constrain the amount of variance explained by any single index of stress or trauma. Future research needs to include more multivariate approaches and to control for these confounds.

PROBLEMS WITH THE PTSD TRAUMA MODELS FOR MALTREATED CHILDREN AND ADOLESCENTS

Perhaps most problematic is the fact that neither the categorical nor dimensional PTSD trauma model addresses many of the symptoms and behaviors in maltreated children that most trouble clinicians, parents, foster parents and teachers.

Depression, aggression, hypersexuality, suicide, self-mutilation (and risk taking), dissociation, problems with affect regulation, somatization, impulsivity, hyperactivity and attentional problems, low self-esteem and other disturbances of self-image are among the more common symptoms reported in maltreated children (Armsworth & Holaday, 1993; Mannarino et al., 1994; Mannarino, Cohen, & Gregor, 1989; McLeer et al., 1994; Merry & Andrews, 1994; Oates, O'Toole, Lynch, Stern, & Cooney, 1994; Wyatt & Powell, 1988). As noted above, serious biological sequelae are being increasingly recognized in maltreated children who do not fulfill diagnostic criteria for PTSD (De Bellis & Putnam, 1994).

High rates of major psychiatric comorbidity seem to be the rule for maltreated children who exceed the threshold of meeting diagnostic criteria for one Axis I diagnosis. This is paralleled in adults with PTSD by high rates of comorbidity with major depression, substance abuse and anxiety (Davidson & Foa, 1991). In adults, significant amounts of character pathology and Axis II personality disorders are also commonly associated with chronic PTSD (Southwick, Yehuda, & Giller, 1993). The PTSD trauma models offer little or no guidance about this association. Finkelhor's (1988) traumagenic dynamics model and Spaccarelli's (1994) stress, appraisal and coping transactional model are considerably more informative on this issue.

One potential benefit of the PTSD model of trauma should be that therapists could take advantage of proven adult treatments to guide treatment of PTSD symptoms in children and adolescents. Unfortunately, despite the increased clinical utilization of the PTSD diagnosis, there are very few controlled clinical trials in adults. A recent review by Solomon, Gerrity, and Muff (1992) found only 11 randomized, empirical clinical trials out of over 250 published PTSD treatment reports. Thus, at present the PTSD model is not especially therapeutically informative. A few studies have been conducted with children meeting DSM PTSD criteria. Deblinger, McLeer, and Henry (1990) reported some success with a short-term cognitive behavioral treatment program for sexually abused girls with PTSD. Drawing upon uncontrolled pharmacotherapy studies with adult PTSD, Famularo, Kinscherff, and Fenton (1988) conducted on-off-on clinical trials with propranolol in maltreated children with PTSD. He reports improvements similar to those reported for adults with PTSD. However, most attempts at treatment for maltreated children are more focused on non-PTSD symptoms such as depression and anxiety or behaviors such as aggression and hypersexuality than on PTSD symptoms. Children and adolescents have yet to reap any significant benefits from treatment studies of adults with PTSD.

CONCLUSION

Trauma models of the effects of maltreatment and multiple victimization are derived from a rich legacy of multidisciplinary approaches. Currently most operationalized trauma models are closely tied to the DSM diagnosis of posttraumatic stress disorder. In this model, traumatic events are defined as those experiences that seriously endanger life and limb and produce emotional experiences of fear, helplessness and horror. Posttraumatic stress disorder occurs when an individual develops a specific set of persistent symptoms involving reexperiences of the trauma, avoidance of trauma-related stimuli and increased arousal.

PTSD can be diagnosed in children and adolescents who have experienced an array of traumatic events. However, the majority of maltreated children and adolescents do not meet full DSM criteria for PTSD and therefore cannot be adequately characterized clinically or for research purposes by relying exclusively on this approach. Critiques of the use of the categorical PTSD model in children note that many of the criteria are developmentally inappropriate and/or are difficult to adequately evaluate in children and adolescents. Many of the clinically most relevant symptoms and behavior problems noted in victimized children, such as depression, aggression, self-mutilation, etc., are not included under the PTSD diagnosis. Several studies suggest that in children, PTSD is best conceptualized as a dimensional outcome rather than a categorical all-or-none diagnosis.

The PTSD trauma model is an important conceptualization of trauma effects. It links a set of symptoms found in traumatized children and adolescents with those in adults and it is strongly supported by sophisticated neurobiological research on trauma-related biological alterations of the central and autonomic nervous system, and the hypothalamic-pituitary-adrenal axis. Potentially, the PTSD model can help to inform more objective evaluations of difficult questions such as whether or not maltreatment occurred in a young child and to offer guidance in treatment. However, categorical and dimensional PTSD trauma models fail to account for many of the symptoms and behaviors that comprise the salient outcomes associated with maltreatment and victimization in children and adults. The PTSD model(s) needs to be either expanded to correct these deficiencies or to be integrated into a larger model of the effects of trauma and victimization.

REFERENCES

American Psychiatric Association (1980). *Diagnostic and statistical manual of mental disorders (3rd edition).* Washington, DC: American Psychiatric Association, Inc.

American Psychiatric Association (1994). *Diagnostic and statistical manual for mental disorders (4th edition).* Washington, DC: American Psychiatric Press, Inc.

Armsworth, M. W., & Holaday, M. (1993). The effects of psychological trauma on children and adolescents. *Journal of Counseling and Development, 72,* 49-56.

Arroyo, W., & Eth, S. (1985). Children traumatized by Central American warfare. In S. Eth & R. Pynoos (Eds.), *Post-Traumatic Stress Disorder in Children* (pp. 101-120). Washington, DC: American Psychiatric Press.

Bloch, D. A., Silber, E., & Perry, S. E. (1956). Some factors in the emotional reaction of children to disaster. *American Journal of Psychiatry, 113,* 416-422.

Bremner, D. J., Southwick, S. M., Johnson, D. R., Yehuda, R., & Charney, D. S. (1993). Childhood physical abuse and combat-related posttraumatic stress disorder in Vietnam veterans. *American Journal of Psychiatry, 150,* 235-239.

Charney, D. S., Deutch, A. Y., Krystal, J. H., Southwich, S. M., & Davis, M. (1993). Psychobiological mechanisms of posttraumatic stress disorder. *Archives of General Psychiatry, 50,* 294-305.

Coons, P. M., Bowman, E. S., Pellow, T. A., & Schneider, P. (1989). Posttraumatic aspects of the treatment of victims of sexual abuse and incest. *Psychiatric Clinics of North America, 12,* 325-335.

Davidson, J. R., & Foa, E. B. (1991). Diagnostic issues in posttraumatic stress disorder: Considerations for the DSM-IV. *Journal of Abnormal Psychology, 100,* 346-355.

De Bellis, M. D., Burke, L., Trickett, P. K., & Putnam, F. W. (In press). Antinuclear antibodies and thyroid function in sexually abused girls. *Journal of Traumatic Stress.*

De Bellis, M. D., Chrousos, G. P., Dorn, L. D., Burke, L., Helmers, K., King, M. A., Trickett, P. K., & Putnam, F. W. (1994a). Hypothalamic-pituitary-adrenal axis dysregulation in sexually abused girls. *Journal of Clinical Endocrinology and Metabolism, 78,* 249-255.

De Bellis, M. D., Lefter, L., Trickett, P. K., & Putnam, F. W. (1994b). Urinary catecholamine excretion in sexually abused girls. *Journal of the American Academy of Child and Adolescent Psychiatry, 33,* 320-327.

De Bellis, M. D., & Putnam, F. W. (1994). The psychobiology of childhood maltreatment. *Child and Adolescent Psychiatric Clinics of North America, 3,* 1-16.

Deblinger, E., McLeer, S. V., Atkins, M. S., Ralphe, D., & Foa, E. (1989). Posttraumatic stress in sexually abused, physically abused, and nonabused children. *Child Abuse & Neglect, 13,* 403-408.

Deblinger, E., McLeer, S. V., & Henry, D. (1990). Cognitive behavioral treatment for sexually abused children suffering posttraumatic stress: Preliminary findings. *Journal of the American Academy of Child and Adolescent Psychiatry, 29,* 747-752.

Donaldson, M., & Gardner, J. (1985). Traumatic stress among women after childhood incest. In C. Figley (Ed.), *Trauma and its wake* (pp. 358-377). New York: Brunner/Mazel.

Earls, F., Smith, E., Reich, W., & Jung, K. G. (1988). Investigating psychopathological consequences of a disaster in children: A pilot study incorporating a structured diagnostic interview. *Journal of the American Academy of Child and Adolescent Psychiatry, 27,* 90-95.

Engel, C. C., Engel, A. L., Campbell, S. J., McFall, M. E., Russo, J., & Katon, W. (1993). Posttraumatic stress disorder symptoms and precombat sexual and physical abuse in Desert Storm veterans. *Journal of Nervous and Mental Disease, 181,* 683-688.

Eth, S., & Pynoos, R. (Ed.). (1985). *Post-Traumatic Stress Disorder in Children.* Washington, DC: American Psychiatric Press, Inc.

Famularo, R., Kinscherff, R., & Fenton, T. (1988). Propranolol treatment of childhood posttraumatic stress disorder, acute type. *American Journal of Diseases of Children, 142,* 1244-1247.

Famularo, R., Kinscherff, R., & Fenton, T. (1991). Posttraumatic stress disorder among children clinically diagnosed as borderline personality disorder. *Journal of Nervous and Mental Disease, 179,* 4281-4301.

Finkelhor, D. (1988). The trauma of sexual abuse: Two models. In G. E. Wyatt & G. J. Powell (Eds.), *Lasting effects of child sexual abuse* (pp. 61-82). Newbury Park, CA: Sage.

Finkelhor, D. (1990). Early and long-term effects of child sexual abuse: An update. *Professional Psychology: Research and Practice, 21,* 325-330.

Freud, A., & Burlingham, D. T. (1943). *War and children.* New York: Medical War Books, Ernst Willard.

Friedman, P., & Linn, L. (1957). Some psychiatric notes on the Andrea Doria disaster. *American Journal of Psychiatry, 114,* 426-432.

Greenwald, E., & Leitenberg, H. (1990). Posttraumatic stress disorder in a non-clinical and nonstudent sample of adult women sexually abused as children. *Journal of Interpersonal Violence, 5,* 217-228.

Hillary, B. E., & Schare, M. L. (1993). Sexually and physically abused adolescents: An empirical search for PTSD. *Journal of Clinical Psychology, 49,* 161-165.

Horowitz, M. (1979). Psychological response to serious life events. In V. Hamilton & D. M. Warburton (Eds.), *Human stress and cognition: An informational processing approach* (pp. 237-265). New York: Wiley.

Horowitz, M. (1986). *Stress response syndromes.* Northwale, NJ: Jason Aronson.

Janoff-Bulman, R. (1985). The aftermath of victimization: Rebuilding shattered assumptions. In C. R. Figley (Ed.), *Trauma and its wake: The study and treatment of post-traumatic stress disorder* (pp. 15-35). New York: Brunner/Mazel.

Janoff-Bulman, R., & Frieze, I. H. (1983). A theoretical perspective for understanding reactions to victimization. *Journal of Social Issues, 39,* 1-17.

Jensen, P. S., & Shaw, J. (1993). Children as victims of war: Current knowledge and future research needs. *Journal of the American Academy of Child and Adolescent Psychiatry, 32,* 697-708.

Kiser, L. J., Ackerman, B. J., Brown, E., Edwards, N. B., McColgan, E., Pugh, R., & Pruitt, D. B. (1988). Post-traumatic stress in young children: A reaction to purported sexual abuse. *Journal of the American Academy of Child and Adolescent Psychiatry, 27,* 645-649.

Kolb, L. C. (1987). A neuropsychological hypothesis explaining the posttraumatic stress disorder. *American Journal of Psychiatry, 144,* 989-995.

Koopman, C., Classen, C., & Spiegel, D. (1994). Predictors of posttraumatic stress symptoms among survivors of the Oakland/Berkeley, California firestorm. *American Journal of Psychiatry, 151,* 888-894.

Krystal, H. (1978). Trauma and affect. *Psychoanalytic Study of the Child, 33,* 81-116.

Lifton, R. J. (1988). Understanding the traumatized self: Imagery symbolization and transformation. In J. P. Wilson, Z. Harel, & B. Kahana (Eds.), *Human adaptation to extreme stress from the Holocaust to Vietnam* (pp. 7-32). New York: Plenum Press.

Lifton, R. J., & Olson, E. (1976). The human meaning of total disaster. *Psychiatry, 39,* 1-18.

Lyons, J. A. (1987). Posttraumatic stress disorder in children and adolescents: A review of the literature. *Developmental and Behavioral Pediatrics, 8,* 349-356.

Malmquist, C. P. (1986). Children who witness parental murder: Posttraumatic aspects. *Journal of the American Academy of Child and Adolescent Psychiatry, 25,* 320-325.

Mannarino, A. P., Cohen, J. A., & Berman, S. R. (1994). The relationship between preabuse factors and psychological symptomatology in sexually abused girls. *Child Abuse & Neglect, 18,* 63-71.

Mannarino, A. P., Cohen, J. A., & Gregor, M. (1989). Emotional and behavioral difficulties in sexually abused girls. *Journal of Interpersonal Violence, 4,* 437-451.

Marmar, C. R., Weiss, D. S., Schlenger, W. E., Fairbank, J. A., Jordan, B. K., Kulka, R. A., & Hough, R. L. (1994). Peritraumatic dissociation and posttraumatic stress in male Vietnam theater veterans. *American Journal of Psychiatry, 151,* 902-907.

McLeer, S., Deblinger, V., Atkins, M. S., Foa, E. B., & Ralphe, D. L. (1988). Posttraumatic stress disorder in sexually abused children. *Journal of the American Academy of Child and Adolescent Psychiatry, 27,* 650-654.

McLeer, S. V., Callagahan, M., Henry, D., & Wallen, J. (1994). Psychiatric disorders in sexually abused children. *Journal of the American Academy of Child and Adolescent Psychiatry, 33,* 313-319.

McLeer, S. V., Deblinger, E., Henry, D., & Orvaschel, H. (1992). Sexually abused children at high risk for post-traumatic stress disorder. *Journal of the American Academy of Child and Adolescent Psychiatry, 31,* 875-879.

McNally, R. J. (1991). Assessment of posttraumatic stress disorder in children. *Psychological Assessment, 3,* 531-537.

McNally, R. J. (1993). Stressors that produce posttraumatic stress disorder in children. In J. R. Davidson & E. B. Foa (Eds.), *Posttraumatic stress disorder: DSM-IV and beyond* (pp. 57-74). Washington, DC: American Psychiatric Press, Inc.

Mercier, M. H., & Desperet, J. L. (1943). Psychological effects of the war on French children. *Psychosomatic Medicine, 5,* 266-272.

Merry, S. N., & Andrews, L. K. (1994). Psychiatric status of sexually abused children 12 months after disclosure of abuse. *Journal of the American Academy of Child and Adolescent Psychiatry, 33,* 939-944.

Oates, R. K., O'Toole, B. I., Lynch, D. L., Stern, A., & Cooney, G. (1994). Stability and change in outcomes for sexually abused children. *Journal of the American Academy of Child and Adolescent Psychiatry, 33,* 945-953.

Pitman, R. K. (1988). Post-traumatic stress disorder, conditioning and network theory. *Psychiatric Annals, 18,* 182-189.

Pitman, R. K., Orr, S. P., Forgue, D. F., deJong, J., and others. (1987). Psychophysiologic assessment of post-traumatic stress disorder imagery in Vietnam combat veterans. *Archives of General Psychiatry, 44,* 970-975.

Pitman, R. K., Orr, S. P., & Steketee, G. S. (1989). Psychophysiological investigations of posttraumatic stress disorder imagery. *Psychopharmacology Bulletin, 25,* 426-431.

Putnam, F. W. (1985). Dissociation as a response to extreme trauma. In R. P. Kluft (Eds.), *Childhood antecedents of multiple personality* (pp. 65-98). Washington: American Psychiatric Press, Inc.

Pynoos, R., Frederick, C., Nader, K., Arroyo, W., Steinberg, A., Eth, S., Nunex, F., & Fairbanks, L. (1987). Life threat and posttraumatic stress in school-age children. *Archives of General Psychiatry, 44,* 1057-1063.

Pynoos, R. S., & Nader, K. (1988a). Children who witness the sexual assaults of their mothers. *Journal of the American Academy of Child and Adolescent Psychiatry, 27,* 567-572.

Pynoos, R. S., & Nader, K. (1988b). Psychological first aid and treatment approach to children exposed to community violence: Research implications. *Journal of Traumatic Stress, 1,* 455-473.

Rowan, A., & Foy, D. W. (1993). Posttraumatic stress disorder in child sexual abuse survivors: A literature review. *Journal of Traumatic Stress, 6,* 3-20.

Rowan, A. B., Foy, D. W., Rodriguez, N., & Ryan, S. (1994). Posttraumatic stress disorder in a clinical sample of adults sexually abused as children. *Child Abuse & Neglect, 18,* 51-61.

Saigh, P. A. (1991). The development and validation of the Children's Posttraumatic Stress Disorder Inventory. *International Journal of Special Education, 4,* 75-84.

Schnurr, P. P., Friedman, M. J., & Rosenberg, S. D. (1993). Premilitary MMPI scores as predictors of combat-related PTSD symptoms. *American Journal of Psychiatry, 150,* 479-483.

Sirles, E. A., Smith, J. A., & Kusama, H. (1989). Psychiatric status of intrafamilial child sexual abuse victims. *Journal of the American Academy of Child and Adolescent Psychiatry, 28,* 225-229.

Solomon, S. D., Gerrity, E. T., & Muff, A. M. (1992). Efficacy of treatments for posttraumatic stress disorder: An empirical review. *Journal of the American Medical Association, 268,* 633-638.

Southwick, S. M., Yehuda, R., & Giller, E. L. (1993). Personality disorders in treatment-seeking combat veterans with posttraumatic stress disorder. *American Journal of Psychiatry, 150,* 1020-1023.

Spaccarelli, S. (1994). Stress, appraisal, and coping in child sexual abuse: A theoretical and empirical review. *Psychological Bulletin, 116,* 340-362.

Stoddard, F. J., Norman, D. K., Murphy, J. M., & Beardslee, W. R. (1989). Psychiatric outcome of burned children and adolescents. *Journal of the American Academy of Child and Adolescent Psychiatry, 28,* 589-595.

True, W., Rice, L., Eisen, S. A., Heath, A. C., Goldberg, J., Lyons, M. J., & Nowak, J. (1993). A twin study of genetic and environmental contributions to the liability for posttraumatic stress symptoms. *Archives of General Psychiatry, 50,* 257-264.

van der Kolk, B. A., Greenberg, M., Boyd, H., & Krystal, J. H. (1985). Inescapable shock, neurotransmitters and addiction to trauma: Towards a psychobiology of post traumatic stress disorder. *Biological Psychiatry, 22,* 314-325.

Wolfe, D. A., Sas, L., & Wekerle, C. (1994). Factors associated with the development of posttraumatic stress disorder among child victims of sexual abuse. *Child Abuse & Neglect, 18,* 37-50.

Wolfe, V. V., Gentile, C., & Wolfe, D. A. (1989). The impact of sexual abuse on children: A PTSD formulation. *Behavior Therapy, 20,* 215-228.

Wyatt, G. E., & Powell, G. J. (Ed.). (1988). *Lasting effects of child sexual abuse.* Newbury Park, CA: Sage.

Yule, W., & Williams, R. M. (1990). Post-traumatic stress reactions in children. *Journal of Traumatic Stress, 3,* 279-295.

OVERVIEW OF THE LITERATURE

The Victimization of Young Children

Clare Haynes-Seman
David Baumgarten

SUMMARY. The prevalence of maltreatment of infants and young children means that the development of many is compromised during their first five years of life. A developmental framework is provided as a context within which to examine expected consequences of maltreatment for infants and young children. Clinical and empirical research is reviewed that informs professionals about early disturbances in parent-child relationships, that prospectively documents outcomes for children of at-risk mothers, and that cross-sectionally examines the impact of specific forms of maltreatment on particular developmental outcomes. *[Article copies available for a fee from The Haworth Document Delivery Service: 1-800-342-9678. E-mail address: getinfo@haworth.com]*

Prevalence of maltreatment of infants and young children means that a significant number of young children are compromised in their negotiation

Address correspondence to: Clare Haynes-Seman, PhD, Kempe National Center for the Prevention and Treatment of Child Abuse and Neglect, 1205 Oneida Street, Denver, CO 80262.

[Haworth co-indexing entry note]: "The Victimization of Young Children." Haynes-Seman, Clare, and David Baumgarten. Co-published simultaneously in *Journal of Aggression, Maltreatment & Trauma* (The Haworth Maltreatment & Trauma Press, an imprint of The Haworth Press, Inc.) Vol. 2, No. 1 (#3), 1998, pp. 67-86; and: *Multiple Victimization of Children: Conceptual, Developmental, Research, and Treatment Issues* (ed: B. B. Robbie Rossman, and Mindy S. Rosenberg) The Haworth Maltreatment & Trauma Press, an imprint of The Haworth Press, Inc., 1998, pp. 67-86. Single or multiple copies of this article are available for a fee from The Haworth Document Delivery Service [1-800-342-9678, 9:00 a.m. - 5:00 p.m. (EST). E-mail address: getinfo@haworth.com].

of developmental issues of the first five years of life. A normal developmental framework is presented for understanding what children need to develop healthy attachments and a good sense of self and others, and to provide a context for examination of the expected consequences of maltreatment for the infant and young child. Following a brief discussion of some of the methodological issues that confront researchers in this area, clinical and empirical research is examined that informs professionals about early disturbances in parent-child relationships, that prospectively documents outcomes for children of at-risk mothers, and that cross-sectionally examines the impact of specific forms of maltreatment on particular developmental outcomes.

PREVALENCE OF VICTIMIZATION OF CHILDREN

Maltreatment of children continues to be a significant problem in the United States. Statistics compiled by the National Committee to Prevent Child Abuse (1994) indicate that 2,989,000 children were reported to Child Protection Services in 1993 as alleged victims of child abuse. Child maltreatment reports showed an average of 6% increase each year from 1988 to 1993. The majority of the reports of maltreatment and the highest substantiation rate involve neglect. No age breakdown for reporting and substantiation are available from the Committee; however, young children are at high risk for death from maltreatment. From 1991 through 1993, 86% of the children who died from maltreatment were under the age of five. Forty-six percent were under the age of one at the time of their death. The rate of fatalities for children under five was 5.7 per 100,000 in 1993. In the same year the rate for children under one was 14.5 per 100,000. To ameliorate the consequences of maltreatment for survivors, professionals need to understand more fully the impact of victimization when it occurs at specific developmental ages and why victimization at a particular developmental age may have more severe consequences than at other ages.

For those infants and young children who survive neglect and abuse by caregivers, early experiences of maltreatment may be expected to have a significant impact on development. The issues encountered by the child and caregivers in the first five years of life provide the foundation for the development of a healthy sense of self and capacity for productive relationships (Erikson, 1950). How do abuse experiences affect the negotiation of childhood issues of basic trust versus distrust; autonomy versus self-doubt and shame; and initiative versus guilt (Erikson, 1950; Cicchetti, 1987)?

A DEVELOPMENTAL ISSUES FRAMEWORK

Age and developmental level are crucial factors in a child's response to maltreatment by a parent or caregiver. To understand the unhealthy impact of maltreatment on infants, toddlers, and young children it is important to examine factors that lead to healthy attachment relationships and to the successful negotiation of the developmental issues of the first five years of life. Infants and young children have three basic needs: these are the need for nurturance, stimulation, and protection. Nurturance includes both physical and emotional nurturance. Physical nurturance refers to being assured of adequate food, sleep, hygiene, medical and dental care. Emotional nurturance is a prerequisite for self-esteem and includes being valued, loved, cared for and nurtured by persons upon whom the child relies for care. Stimulation includes both social company, involvement in play and exploratory activities, and opportunities for interactions with peers. Infants and young children need assurance of safety in their environments and rely on parents or parent-figures to protect and buffer them from danger and to permit them freedom to explore and experience their environment in safety.

A child who experiences the emotional investment of parents who value him or her develops healthy attachment relationships with nurturing parents. The child's cognitive, physical, emotional and social development flourishes within his or her biological constraints. Early attachment relationships are models for all future relationships. These early patterns become a part of the child's personality and are carried into and influence future relationships (Bowlby, 1988).

Erikson (1950) describes the tasks of the first five years of life that must be completed in order for the child to develop a healthy personality. A child who is emotionally nurtured and loved by his or her parents learns to trust that his or her needs will be met, thus establishing trust rather than mistrust. This moves the child toward the second issue of autonomy versus shame and doubt. Sensitive and responsive caregiving enables the toddler to develop confidence in his or her ability to express needs and wishes that may be in opposition to those of the parents without fear of loss of their love. The outcome of this stage becomes decisive for the balance between cooperation and willfulness. When the child's signals meet with predictable responses that relieve tension and lead to a sense of well-being, the child learns that what s/he does makes a difference, and develops feelings of efficacy. At age four and five, the child has developed motor and language skills, and is now ready to "find out what he can do with it" (Erikson, 1950, p. 75). Experiences that lead to the development of trust and autonomy become the basis for the child's development of a sense of initiative versus guilt and a healthy confidence in others and their intentions toward the child.

The child's age and developmental level are important factors in the child's response to victimization. When abuse or neglect in the earliest months and years of life interfere with the development of basic trust, the child's future development is compromised (Buxbaum, 1983; Fraiberg, 1987). A young child hurt by caregivers associates physical closeness with pain, increase in tension, or anxiety rather than with comfort and satisfaction. Not only does the young child have minimal defenses to protect him or herself, but he or she is deprived of experiences that lead to healthy attachment relationships and promote the child's development of a good sense of self, trust in persons, and the sense that the world is good and reliable.

Children under age five, perhaps because of their physical vulnerability, are most likely to suffer from fatal child abuse (National Committee to Prevent Child Abuse, 1994; Belsky, 1992). "Shaken Baby Syndrome" even when not fatal (Alexander, Crabbe, Sato, Smith & Bennett, 1990) may cause severe brain damage with a bleak forecast for multiple aspects of development, including cognitive, motor, emotional and social. Infants who do not receive adequate nutrition in the first months of life to support adequate weight gain show cognitive, physical, and social-emotional deficits related to experience and lack of nutrition (Haynes, Cutler, Gray & Kempe, 1984; Drotar, 1988). A parent's using the baby as a sexual object and incorporating sexual games into normal social play leads to "traumatic sexualization" (Finkelhor & Browne, 1985). The child links sexual stimulation with pleasurable activities and parental attention (Haynes-Seman & Krugman, 1989). Infants and toddlers abused by their parents interpret social overtures as threats and react with verbal and physical aggression (George & Main, 1979). When infants or young children are abused by caregivers, the prognosis for normal physical growth and psychological development is further compromised.

The repeated number of incidents have an additive effect. Experience with chronic violence does not inoculate children against negative outcomes; instead, it tends to increase their susceptibility to developmental harm and post-traumatic stress (Pynoos & Nader, 1988). Stress can exceed the child's ability to absorb it and cope with it. This is particularly true with infants and young children who have limited cognitive, physical, or social-emotional strategies for coping with trauma. Brief traumas have only limited effects on children but repeated trauma may lead to anger, despair, and severe psychic numbing which in turn results in major personality changes (Terr, 1990). Cumulative forms of abuse have a synergistic effect. Most children can cope with low levels of risk, one or two risk factors. It is the accumulation of risks that jeopardizes development (Sameroff, Seifer, Barocas, Zax & Greenspan, 1987). Feelings of helplessness may be a realistic response under conditions where the stresses are unpredictable and uncontrollable (Peterson, Luborsky & Seligman, 1983). There is a loss of resilience. The child's developmental level is a factor in resilience; that is, younger children are less able to cope with stress than older children.

Not only must we consider current damage to the child but we must also consider loss of potential to the child as a functioning member of society. The victim may become the abuser. Many abusive parents were themselves hurt and uncared for by their parents.

METHODOLOGICAL ISSUES

Most empirical research related to maltreatment of infants and young children is cross-sectional. There is a lack of consensus about an operational definition of the various forms of maltreatment (Panel on Research in Child Abuse and Neglect, 1993; Garbarino, 1991), as well as a lack of attention to age at onset, duration, severity, interval from maltreatment experiences and current assessment, and the presence of confounding or mediating factors (Houck & King, 1989) that might account for poor outcomes or for resiliency and lack of symptomatology in some victims. Prospective studies are needed that examine factors that are presumed to be associated with at-risk parenting, different patterns of parenting attitudes and behaviors, and outcomes for children at different developmental levels and in different domains of functioning. Confounding factors such as intelligence, social class, as well as mediating factors such as changes in family circumstances, and/or change in the child's living situation or experiences with primary caregivers, and the ages at which these changes occur, all need to be factored into studies that examine the outcomes of maltreatment on the child. The failure to use comparison groups and to specify the conditions of assessment have been remediated in research of the last decade. Instruments developed on nonmaltreated samples such as the Strange Situation Paradigm (Ainsworth & Wittig, 1969), and the play narratives to assess moral development in young children developed by Emde (Buchsbaum & Emde, 1990) can be applied to maltreated and comparison samples to provide insight into how abuse and neglect influence important aspects of development in the first five years of life.

CLINICAL AND EMPIRICAL RESEARCH

Early Disturbances in Parent-Child Relationships

Early disturbances in the parent-child relationship may lead to the development of pathologic behaviors that are observable in interactions between the child and the abusive or neglectful caregiver. Fraiberg (1987) describes pathological defenses used by abused and neglected infants and toddlers between 3 and 36 months of age to ward off persons upon whom they were dependent for care who were associated with pain or disappointment. These defenses include: selective and discriminate avoidance of the abusive caregiver; freezing and becoming immobilized often deteriorating into a panic state when their fragile ego defenses were overwhelmed by a situation; transformation of painful affects into affects of pleasure, especially in sadomasochistic games that involve teasing or withholding of resources; and, turning aggression against self when needs are not met while exhibiting a high threshold for pain. If the abusive interactions continue, these pathological defenses may become permanent maladaptive defense mechanisms.

Gaensbauer and Sands (1979) observed distorted affective communications in abused or neglected infants 3 to 36 months of age in a modified Strange Situation Paradigm. The maltreated infants showed: "affective withdrawal" during social interactions; a lack of pleasure in interaction as evidenced by a failure to respond to attempts to elicit a smile or in a failure to spontaneously initiate pleasurable interactions; inconsistency and unpredictability in affective communications characterized by abrupt changes in mood that seem unrelated to the situation; indiscriminate attachment behaviors; ambiguity or ambivalence in affective expression making it difficult to read the child's cues; and, persistence of negative affect messages such as distress, anger, and sadness that cannot be ameliorated by responses of the caregiver. Although the authors indicate that these "disturbances in affective communication probably grow out of dysynchronous, unsatisfying interactions with caretakers very early in the child's life" (p. 248), they argue that the infant becomes an active participant in the process. They conclude that this then becomes the "greatest tragedy of child abuse–parent and child locked in a destructive pattern which neither of them knows how to alter" (p. 248).

Studies that differentiate abused and neglected infants have found clearcut differences in behavioral patterns in the first years. In two separate studies, Crittendon (1985) compared maltreated infants and adequately reared lower socioeconomic class infants and toddlers who ranged in age from 1 to 19 months and 2 to 24 months, respectively. The results of both studies showed abnormal behavioral patterns for abused and neglected toddlers. Abused toddlers were more difficult and openly angry while neglected children were more passive and helpless under stress. All maltreated children showed anxious attachments, with abused, neglected children displaying attachments that were both avoidant and resistant. This would be a combination of the insecure, avoidant "A" pattern and insecure, ambivalent "C" pattern (Ainsworth & Wittig, 1969). An exciting aspect of Crittendon's work was finding that if mothers of maltreated children improved their behaviors, the infants became more cooperative and their developmental quotients improved. The maltreated infants adapted their interactive behavior quickly in response to a more sensitive interactional partner.

The consequences of early nonorganic failure to thrive (NOFTT) are similar to those observed in neglected infants and toddlers. As with other abuse, NOFTT has been defined differently in different studies, but most studies defined it as poor growth without organic explanation and is often attributed to a disturbance in the mother-child relationship that may be related to the mother's distress expressed in anxiety, depression, or hostility. In a study of 34 NOFTT infants between 8 and 26 months of age and their mothers and 34 matched dyads, Hutheson, Black, and Starr (1993) found no differences on measures of parenting stress, informal support, life events, and negative affectivity in the NOFTT and comparison dyads. However, mothers of the NOFTT toddlers were more hostile, intrusive, and less flexible, and there was more tension in their interaction with their infants. Dietrich, Starr and Weisfeld (1983) compared abuse alone with abuse and NOFTT infants, and found more interactional problems in the combined than in the abuse alone group. Studies that have compared NOFTT mothers with controls have found that NOFTT mothers are less accepting of their babies as well as less warm and positive in their interactions with them (e.g., Drotar, Eckerle, Satola, Pallotta & Wyatt, 1990; Haynes et al., 1984). NOFTT infants were described as less responsive and vocal, exhibiting gaze abnormalities, and preferring distal to proximal interactions (Powell, Low & Speers, 1987).

A Prospective Study of At-Risk Parents

Egeland, Sroufe, and Erickson (1983) (Egeland & Vaughn, 1981) at the University of Minnesota have conducted one of the few prospective studies of early parent-child attachment and subsequent psychological outcomes. Their sample consisted of 267 mother-infant dyads at risk for parenting because of poverty, limited education, youth of the mother, and generally chaotic living conditions. They used the nonmaltreating mothers in their sample as a control group. They identified four maltreating groups: physically abusive; hostile/verbally abusive; psychologically unavailable; and neglectful. Because physical abuse frequently accompanied other forms of maltreatment, each of the other groups were divided into "with" or "without" physical abuse. Behaviors of the physically abusive mothers ranged from frequent and intense spanking to unprovoked attacks resulting in serious injury to the child. Mothers in the hostile/verbally abusive group chronically found fault with their children and criticized them in a harsh manner. Mothers in the psychologically unavailable group were unresponsive and passively rejecting of their children. Mothers in the neglect group were irresponsible or incompetent in daily child care activities, failing to provide physical care or to protect their children from household dangers.

The researchers used the Strange Situation Paradigm to assess differences in attachment patterns. Ainsworth and Wittig (1969) initially defined three attachment patterns: insecure, avoidant (A Group); secure, healthy (B Group); and, insecure, ambivalent (C Group). The "insecure, avoidant" and the "insecure, ambivalent" have subsequently been labelled: "anxious avoidant" and "anxious resistant." In the Minnesota study, differences in attachment relationship began to emerge at 12 months and were clearly evident at 18 months. All of the maltreated children were classified as "anxiously attached" at 18 months. Carlson, Cicchetti, Barnett, and Braunwald (1989) also found that maltreated 12-month olds compared to matched controls were more likely to be rated insecurely attached (A/C attachment pattern), and that there was a preponderance of an insecure-disorganized/disoriented attachment when they used the D attachment pattern (Main & Solomon, 1986).

Evidence of the impact on subsequent developmental issues of autonomy versus self-doubt, and initiative versus guilt were also apparent in the Minnesota study (Egeland et al., 1983). At two years of age, toddlers in the maltreated group all expressed more anger, frustration, and noncompliance than controls in the tool-use problem solving task. At 42 months the children were observed during a "barrier box" task and in teaching tasks with their mothers. A subsample of the children was also observed in their preschool or day care settings. Although the outcomes for the maltreated children were varied, all of the children had difficulty coping with a frustrating situation, such as the barrier box, and the quality of their interactions with their mothers in the teaching task were poor. In areas of social competence, the children in the maltreated groups were below their nonmaltreated age-mates. The physically abused children were the most distractible in the barrier task and least persistent and enthusiastic in the teaching tasks. They were least compliant with mother and other adults, and expressed negative emotions in all situations. They lacked self-esteem, initiative, and creativity in the barrier box task and showed behaviors associated with socioemotional disorders. The verbally abused children expressed the most anger and were the most avoidant of their mothers. In the teaching task they were noncompliant, low in self-esteem, and showed a lack of persistence and enthusiasm. Children of the psychologically unavailable mothers, while highly dependent on teachers for help, support, and nurturance in the preschool, were angry and noncompliant with their mothers. They exhibited little creativity, persistence, or enthusiasm in the barrier box task. The neglected children were distractible, impulsive, low in ego control, and were the least flexible and creative in the barrier task. In the teaching tasks, they were avoidant of their mothers, and in general lacked the self-esteem and agency to cope effectively with their environment.

A subsequent report by Erickson, Sroufe, and Egeland (1985) based on observations of the children in preschool settings confirmed differences in the anxiously attached and securely attached children both in peer interactions and in interactions with teachers. The anxiously attached children were highly dependent, noncompliant, and poorly skilled in social interactions with peers. These children presented varied behavioral problems, and were described by teachers as hostile, impulsive, giving up easily, and withdrawn. Comparison of the anxious-avoidant (A) attachment pattern characteristic of physically abused children and the anxious resistant (C) attachment pattern characteristic of neglected children confirmed earlier predictions of members of the research team. Children in the anxious-avoidant group received high hostility and noncompliance scores on the rating scale while anxious-resistant children received low agency ratings and high scores on the distractibility factors.

The authors found that changes in the quality of care and support led to differences in behavioral outcomes for children classified as securely attached or anxiously attached in the first two years of life. For example, for those securely attached children who exhibited behavior problems there was a pattern of inadequate maternal care and loss of support. For those anxiously attached children who did not exhibit behavioral problems when they reached preschool, the mothers had become more sensitive and responsive to the needs of their children. Egeland, Jacobvitz, and Sroufe (1988) also found that mediating factors influenced whether mothers abused as children were able to break the cycle with their children. Factors that enabled abused mothers to avoid abusing their children included emotional support from a nonabusive adult, involvement in therapy, or a supportive relationship with another adult. In contrast, mothers who repeated their own histories of abuse with their children showed heightened stress, greater psychological distress (e.g., anxiety, depression, dependency), and dissociated their childhood experiences from their current view of themselves as parents.

Cross-Sectional Research on Impact of Maltreatment on Preschool Children

Maltreatment by a parent or caregiver in the first years of life negatively impacts subsequent peer interactions. More than two decades ago, Galdston (1971) described differences in peer interactions of abused children under 4 years of age observed in a nursery school setting. He noted little interaction among the children except for unpredictable displays of aggression among the boys. In general, the abused children were "listless, apathetic, and uninterested in other children, toys or adults" (p. 339). Research has continued to find differences in aggressive and anti-social behavior of young abused children with agemates. George and Main (1979) compared social interactions of 10 physically abused and 10 matched controls between 1 and 3 years of age in a day care setting. The physically abused toddlers assaulted other toddlers twice as often as controls, and half of the physically abused toddlers and none of the controls assaulted or threatened to assault caregivers. The physically abused toddlers avoided other toddlers four times as often as the comparison toddlers, and caregivers three times as often as comparison toddlers. All of the physically abused toddlers responded to friendly overtures with approach-avoidance behavior.

Research indicates that the capacity for empathy may also be impaired in abused toddlers. Main and George (1985) looked at responses of 10 abused and 10 disadvantaged toddlers to distress in agemates in a day care setting. Their findings showed that the abused toddlers exhibited angry or other aversive responses to distress of other toddlers. No abused toddler responded to the distress of another toddler with concern, empathy, or sadness whereas the disadvantaged toddlers showed concern, empathy, or sadness to one third of the distress incidents they witnessed. Eight of the abused toddlers and only one of the controls responded with fear, physical attack or angry behavior to the crying of other children. Three abused toddlers were observed to alternately comfort and attack the distressed child.

Several other studies support the findings of increased aggression and anti-social behavior with decreased prosocial behavior in maltreated preschoolers compared to their peers (Howes & Espinosa, 1985; Howes &

Eldredge, 1985; Alessandri, 1991). Abused children were less competent in social interactions with peers (Howes & Espinosa, 1985), showed less prosocial behavior and were less friendly with peers than nonmaltreated agemates, and were more likely to respond to aggression with aggression or resistance than nonmaltreated controls who responded to aggression with distress (Howes & Eldredge, 1985). Alessandri (1991) found that physical aggression and antisocial behavior were more prevalent in abused preschool children who also engaged in more sensori-motor (repetitive) than symbolic play activities, engaged in less parallel and group play, showed less sustained involvement with materials, and were less competent in interactions with peers than nonmaltreated controls. Dodge, Bates, and Pettit (1990) found that preschool children classified as physically harmed were rated as more aggressive by teachers and peers than unharmed children. They also showed more difficulties in social information processing, in terms of being inattentive to social cues, attributing hostile intent to others, and showing limited problem-solving ability.

The degree to which cognitive development relates to peer relations and adaptive functioning in the preschool setting may need to be considered in comparing maltreated and nonmaltreated children. In a study of 60 abused, neglected, and nonmaltreated preschoolers, Frodi and Smetana (1984) found that the ability to discriminate emotion in others did not differentiate the abused and nonabused children when they controlled for IQ. Nonmaltreated children with higher IQs were significantly better in discriminating people's emotions than maltreated or nonmaltreated with lower IQs. In another study of young children's judgements of moral and social transgression, Smetana, Kelly and Twentyman (1984) found that when they controlled for IQ, abused and neglected children did not differ on most measures of moral and social judgement. The abused and neglected children did, however, differ from each other. A comparison of abused, neglected, and a comparison group of children 38 to 68 months of age on responses to moral stimuli items related to familiar transgressions in a day care setting revealed an interesting pattern of results. Abused children were more likely than neglected children to see psychological distress to be universally wrong. Abused and comparison but not neglected children considered all transgressions deserve punishment when committed by others. Neglected children were more likely than abused children to consider unfair distribution of resources to be universally wrong. As the authors point out, this study clearly indicates the need to distinguish neglected and abused children rather than lumping them together when examining outcome. They conclude that neglect may have a more negative impact on social-cognitive development than abuse. Their findings also suggest that moral and social judgment are constructed from experiences.

Hoffman-Plotkin and Twentyman (1984) found that abused and neglected preschool children displayed significant cognitive and social deficits compared to nonmaltreated agemates. In a sample of 42 preschool children with histories of abuse, neglect, and no prior history of maltreatment, the abused and neglected children had lower scores on all measures of cognitive functioning than the comparison children. Behavioral observations and teacher and parent ratings showed differences in the abused and neglected children in the direction expected. The neglected children had the least number of interactions with other children. The abused were more aggressive on behavioral observations and were rated as more aggressive, less mature, and less ready to learn by teachers and parents.

Not surprisingly, researchers who have examined the relationship between maltreatment and language development have found a negative impact on language development. Studies that compare neglected, abused, and neglected and abused preschool children find that the impact of neglect on language development is significantly worse than abuse alone or abuse and neglect (Allen & Oliver, 1982; Fox, Long & Langlois, 1988). Allen and Oliver (1982) conclude that lack of stimulation as occurs in neglect alone impairs language development. They account for reports that abuse negatively impacted language development as follows:

> The absence of a significant association for abuse casts considerable doubt on the previously advanced theories in this area, and this coupled with the significant findings for neglect suggests that what the previous investigators have been reporting was a "hidden neglect," rather than abuse, effect. The significant single-order correlation between abuse and neglect also supports this hypothesis. The lack of a significant association between the interaction of abuse and neglect and language delay also supports the hypothesis that neglect alone is more problematic for language development than abuse and neglect together. (p. 304)

Studies that have examined differences in language expression of maltreated and nonmaltreated preschool children find extensive differences in use of language and in content. Gersten, Coster, Schneider-Rosen, Carlson, and Cicchetti (1986) found that maltreated insecurely attached toddlers used more social exchanges and fillers to mark conversational turns. These exchanges were relatively content free. In another study Coster, Gersten, Beegly, and Cicchetti (1989) observed that maltreated and nonmaltreated toddlers showed differences in expression but not in comprehension.

Abused toddlers used language as fillers with few requests for information, few references to persons or events beyond the immediate environment, or utterances to describe their own activities and internal states.

Drotar and Sturm (1992) documented differences in personality development, problem solving, and behavior problems in preschool children with early histories of NOFTT. They compared 48 preschool children with early histories of NOFTT with 47 matched physically healthy children. The NOFTT children showed more behavioral problems, and less ability to contain impulses, delay gratification or change behavior in response to novel situations. These results are similar to the findings of the Minnesota researchers for the neglected children, suggesting that NOFTT is a form of emotional neglect. Drotar and Sturm suggest that these early difficulties may influence social and emotional development and learning. Clearly, competence at one level influences competence at the next (Cicchetti, 1987).

Psychological maltreatment, although generally considered to be present in all forms of maltreatment, has not received a great deal of attention. Whereas other forms of maltreatment have been defined according to parental behaviors or consequences for the child that are contrary to community standards, there is a lack of agreement about the definition of psychological maltreatment (Garbarino, 1991). In its broadest legal definition, psychological maltreatment has been labelled as "emotional abuse." The definition proposed by the state of Nevada has been accepted by many other states: "A substantial injury to the intellectual or psychological capacity of a child as evidenced by an observable and substantial impairment of his ability to function within his normal range of performance or behavior" (Carson & Davidson, 1987, p. 187). Although difficult to document, psychological maltreatment is present in most cases of abuse (physical and sexual) and neglect and often accounts for the severity of outcome. For example, Claussen and Crittendon (1991) compared 175 maltreated children under 6 years of age reported to Children Protection Services to a normative sample of 215 children recruited from community families. Psychological maltreatment was present in almost all cases of physical maltreatment, and was more significant in accounting for detrimental outcomes than the severity of the injury.

Almost two decades ago, Kempe (1978) described sexual abuse as "another hidden pediatric problem." Increasing awareness led to increased diagnosis. He reported that during the years 1967 to 1972 the number of children from birth to age 5 diagnosed as sexual abuse victims "increased from 5% to 25% of the total while the incidence during the latency age period from 5 to 10 . . . remained stable at 25%" (p. 383). He recognized that "Incestuous relationships may begin at the toddler age and continue into adult life" (p. 386). Several studies suggest an increased prevalence of sexual abuse in preschool children (e.g., Campis, Hebden-Curtis & Demaso, 1993). Sexual abuse of young children may be more common than retrospective studies of adult populations indicate (Finkelhor, 1986). Finkelhor (1986, 1993) suggests that this underrepresentation may reflect loss of memory or repression that occurs for children without a cognitive framework in which to interpret their experiences.

Finkelhor and Browne (1985) describe the "traumatic sexualization" of young children who are drawn into sexually inappropriate games by caregivers long before they understand that such activities are inappropriate (Haynes-Seman & Krugman, 1989; Haynes-Seman & Baumgarten, 1994). By the time the child learns that these activities are not acceptable, he or she may have become a participant in the abuse. Yates (1982) describes how children who experience early sexual abuse become eroticized and participants in the abuse. When placed in a protective environment, they use sexual overtures to engage others, both adults and age-mates. Even in cases where the abuser is not a family member but someone to whom the parents have entrusted the care of the child, young children experience a sense of betrayal, powerlessness in stopping the abuse due to their dependency on the abuser, and stigmatization and perhaps guilt for being a participant in the abuse (Ehrensaft, 1992).

Several studies have compared sexually abused preschool children with school-age children. These studies show that preschool children are more likely to present with behavioral and physical indicators than are school age children according to parental report (Campis et al., 1993). Often it may be the presence of physical or behavioral symptoms that prompt parents or caregivers to suspect sexual abuse. For young children, verbal statements that alert others to the possibility of sexual abuse typically are accidental and in response to a precipitating event unrelated to the abuse itself (e.g., Campis et al., 1993). Behavioral symptoms include nightmares, disruptive behavior, aggressive behavior, clinginess and fearfulness, specific sexual behavior with dolls, putting objects in the vagina and/or anus, excessive masturbation, seductive behavior, requests for sexual stimulation, and age-inappropriate sexual play or knowledge.

Other studies have compared sexually abused children with nonsexually abused same age children. In a study of 81 sexually abused 4- to 8-year-olds and a comparison group of 90 children matched for age, gender, and race, Hibbard and Hartman (1992) found that the sexually abused children were more symptomatic than the comparison children according to parental assessment using the Achenbach Child Behavior Checklist. Sexually abused children were described more often as depressed and unhappy, exhibiting more mood swings, demanding attention, physically attacking people, doing poorly in school, exhibiting strange behavior, having trouble sleeping, being secretive, and worrying more. The authors emphasize that many nonabused children also exhibited these behaviors according to parental assessment. They did not find differences in reports of night-mares, enuresis, withdrawal, fears, or a number of other items that have been described as indicators of sexual abuse. Young sexually abused children tend to depict genitals more often in their drawings than do nonsexually abused children (Hibbard, Roghmann & Hoekelman, 1987). They also exhibit sexual behavior at greater levels than do nonsexually abused children (Friedrich et al., 1992).

Multiple Forms of Maltreatment

As the review of research studies indicates, most researchers tend to isolate forms of maltreatment and to look at the effects of what is presumed to be the major presenting problem on different facets of development or relationships. Psychological maltreatment is often a "hidden" problem in all forms of maltreatment. When a child is referred because of physical abuse, the abuse becomes the overriding issue for professionals who may ignore other forms of maltreatment that are also present and perhaps more emotionally damaging than the severity of the physical injury. Multiple forms of maltreatment may mask the impact of specific forms of maltreatment, as was demonstrated in the documentation of greater language delays for children who were neglected than for those who were abused or even those who were both abused and neglected (Allen & Oliver, 1982; Fox et al., 1988); or, may increase the negative impact as documented with NOFTT infants who were also abused (Dietrich et al., 1983) or with physically abused children who also experienced psychological maltreatment (Claussen & Crittendon, 1991). Maltreatment at one developmental period may increase vulnerability to other forms of maltreatment later. Neglected children may be more vulnerable to later sexual abuse because, very often, the physical neglect is also accompanied by emotional neglect that makes the child vulnerable to the attention of a pedophile or abusive parent (Steele, 1991); or NOFTT infants may become the victims of fatal physical injury (Koel, 1969).

CONCLUSION

When parents and intimate family members, who are supposed to value, love, and protect the child, abuse or neglect the child, they betray the child's trust and inflict psychological and physical pain and otherwise traumatize the child. Neglect or failure to feed may be combined with physical assault, assault on the child's psyche, or using the child to meet sexual or emotional needs. The very young child has minimal resources to cope with trauma. He or she cannot escape abuse or feed himself; has no sense of right or wrong, or what is appropriate or inappropriate; has defenses that are primitive against any unwanted or painful stimulation. In the words of Anna Freud, the child is really at the "mercy" of the caregiver.

Every child needs nurturance, social company, and protection in order to thrive in all aspects of development (Winnicott, 1988). When the parents provide empathic care, and adequately meet the needs of the child in each of these areas, the child develops a good sense of self, others, and the world. A healthy attachment relationship develops between infant and each parent which then becomes the model for all future relationships of intimacy (Ainsworth & Wittig, 1969; Bowlby, 1988). In an unhealthy attachment relationship, instead of a happy, curious little person who is eager to explore the world of persons and objects confident that he or she will be protected by parents who love and value him, the child becomes depressed and may show little or no interest in interacting with parents, other children, or even with toys. The parents are in a real sense the mediators of the world for the child. In their failure to do this, they commit the child to struggle to function adaptively with each new developmental challenge. What would give the child the capacity for loving and caring is not passed on, and, if the problems are not resolved, these children begin and go through life without ever experiencing the joy of life or the pain of loss (Fraiberg, 1987).

Breaking the cycle of abuse through early intervention with at-risk parents, that includes psychotherapy when indicated, may help ameliorate the problem of abuse of infants and young children by parents and caregivers. Lidz (1963) joins other professionals (e.g., Buxbaum, 1983; Kohut, 1977) who have recognized that only when one is free from the "battles of childhood" is one free to "shape the future":

> The potential for adaptability cannot achieve realization if persons, individually or collectively, must be engaged in fighting old battles of childhood, seeking finally to gain what had been denied them then, rather than meeting new situations; seeking to hurt others because of the hurts of childhood, or, throughout adult life, seeking to reshape or repossess the past–the most futile of all human endeavors–rather than to shape the future. (Lidz, 1963, p. 29)

REFERENCES

Ainsworth, M.D.S., & Wittig, B.A. (1969). Attachment and exploratory behavior of one-year-olds in a strange situation. In B.M. Foss (Ed.), *Determinants of infant behaviour, Vol. IV* (pp. 111-136). London: Methuen.

Alessandri, S.M. (1991). Play and social behavior in maltreated preschoolers. *Development and Psychopathology, 3*, 191-205.

Alexander, R., Crabbe, L., Sato, Y., Smith, W., & Bennett, T. (1990). Serial abuse in children who are shaken. *American Journal of Diseases of Children, 144*, 58-60.

Allen, R.E., & Oliver, J.M. (1982). The effects of child maltreatment on language development. *Child Abuse & Neglect, 6*, 299-306.

Belsky, J. (1992). Child maltreatment: An ecological-contextual analysis. Paper for Panel on Research on Child Abuse and Neglect. Washington, DC: National Research Council.

Bowlby, J. (1988). Developmental psychiatry comes of age. *American Journal of Psychiatry, 145*, 1-10.

Buchsbaum, H.K., & Emde, R.N. (1990). Play narratives in 36-month-old children: Early moral development and family relationships. *The Psychoanalytic Study of the Child, 45*, 129-155.

Buxbaum, E. (1983). Vulnerable mother-vulnerable babies. In J.D. Call, E. Galenson, & R.L. Tyson (Eds.), *Frontiers of infant psychiatry* (pp. 86-94). New York: Basic Books.

Campis, Hebden-Curtis, J., & Demaso, D.R. (1993). Developmental differences in detection and disclosure of sexual abuse. *Journal of the American Academy of Child and Adolescent Psychiatry, 32*, 920-924.

Carlson, V., Cicchetti, D., Barnett, D., & Braunwald, K. (1989). Disorganized/disoriented attachment relationships in maltreated infants. *Developmental Psychology, 25*, 525-531.

Carson, J., & Davidson, H. (1987). Emotional abuse and the law. In M.R. Brassard, R. Germain, & S.N. Hart (Eds.), *Psychological maltreatment of children and youth* (pp. 185-202). New York: Pergamon.

Cicchetti, D. (1987). Developmental psychopathology in infancy: Illustrations from the study of maltreated youngsters. *Journal of Consulting Clinical Psychology, 55*, 837-845.

Claussen, A.I.E., & Crittendon, P.M. (1991). Physical and psychological maltreatment. *Child Abuse & Neglect, 15*, 5-18.

Coster, W.J., Gersten, M., Beegly, M., & Cicchetti, D. (1989). Communication functioning in maltreated toddlers. *Developmental Psychology, 25*, 1020-1029.

Crittendon, P.M. (1985). Maltreated infants: Vulnerability and resilience. *Journal of Child Psychology and Psychiatry, 26(1)*, 85-96.

Dietrich, K.N., Starr, R.H., Jr., & Weisfeld, G.E. (1983). Infant maltreatment: Caretaker-infant interaction and developmental consequences at different levels of parenting failure. *Pediatrics, 72*, 532-540.

Dodge, K.A., Bates, J.E., & Pettit, G.S. (1990). Mechanisms in the cycle of violence. *Science, 250*, 1678-1682.

Drotar, D. (1988). Failure to thrive. In D.K. Routh (Ed.), *Handbook of pediatric psychology* (pp. 71-107). New York: Guilford Press.

Drotar, D., Eckerle, D., Satola, J., Pallotta, J., & Wyatt, B. (1990). Maternal interactional behavior with nonorganic failure to thrive infants: A case comparison study. *Child Abuse & Neglect, 14*, 41-51.

Drotar, D., & Sturm, L. (1992). Personality development, problem solving, and behavior problems among preschool children with early histories of nonorganic failure to thrive: A controlled study. *Journal of Developmental & Behavioral Pediatrics, 13(4)*, 266-273.

Egeland, B., & Sroufe, A. (1981). Attachment and early maltreatment. *Child Development, 52*, 44-52.

Egeland, B., Sroufe, A., & Erickson, M. (1983). The developmental consequences of different patterns of maltreatment. *Child Abuse & Neglect, 7*, 459-469.

Egeland, B., & Vaughn, B. (1981). Failure of "bond formation" as a cause of abuse, neglect, and maltreatment. *American Journal of Orthopsychiatry, 51(1)*, 78-84.

Egeland, B., Jacobvitz, D., & Sroufe, L.A. (1988). Breaking the cycle of abuse. *Child Development, 59*, 1080-1088.

Ehrensaft, D. (1992). Preschool child sex abuse: The aftermath of the Presidio case. *American Journal of Orthopsychiatry, 62(2)*, 234-244.

Erickson, M., Sroufe, A., & Egeland, B. (1985). The relationship between quality of attachment and behavior problems in preschool in a high-risk sample. In I. Bretherton & E. Waters (Eds.), *Monographs of the Society for Research in Child Development, 50*, 147-166.

Erikson, E.H. (1950). *Childhood and society.* New York: W.W. Norton.

Finkelhor, D. (1993). Epidemiological factors in the clinical identification of child sexual abuse. *Child Abuse & Neglect, 17*, 67-70.

Finkelhor, D., & Associates (1986). *Sourcebook on child sexual abuse.* Newbury Park, CA: Sage.

Finkelhor, D., & Browne, A. (1985). The traumatic impact of child sexual abuse: A conceptualization. *American Journal of Orthopsychiatry, 55(4)*, 530-541.

Fox, L., Long, S., & Langlois, A. (1988). Patterns of language comprehension. Deficit in abused and neglected children. *Journal of Speech and Hearing Disorders, 53*, 239-244.

Fraiberg, S. (1987). The origins of human bonds. In L. Fraiberg (Ed.), *Selected writings of Selma Fraiberg* (pp. 3-26). Columbus, OH: Ohio State University Press.

Fraiberg, S. (1987). Pathological defenses in infancy. In L. Fraiberg (Ed.), *Selected writings of Selma Fraiberg* (pp. 183-202). Columbus, OH: Ohio State University Press.

Friedrich, W.N., Grambsch, P., Damon, L., Hewitt, S.K., Koverola, C., Lang, R.A., Wolfe, V., & Broughton, D. (1992). Child sexual behavior inventory: Normative and clinical comparison. *Psychological Assessment, 4(3)*, 303-311.

Frodi, A.M., & Smetana, J. (1984). Abused, neglected, and nonmaltreated pre-schoolers' ability to discriminate emotions in others: The effects of IQ. *Child Abuse & Neglect, 8,* 459-465.

Gaensbauer, T.J., & Sands, K. (1979). Distorted affective communications in abused/neglected infants and their potential impact on caretakers. *Journal of the American Academy of Child Psychiatry, 18,* 236-250.

Galdston, R. (1971). Violence begins at home: The parent's center project for the study and prevention of child abuse. *Journal of the American Academy of Child Psychiatry, 10,* 336-350.

Garbarino, J. (1991). Not all bad outcomes are the result of child abuse. Special Issue: Defining psychological maltreatment. *Development & Psychopathology, 3(1),* 45-50.

George, C., & Main, M. (1979) Social interactions of young abused children: Approach, avoidance, and aggression. *Child Development, 10,* 305-318.

Gersten, M., Coster, W., Schneider-Rosen, K., Carlson, V., & Cicchetti, D. (1986). The socio-economic bases of communicative functioning: Quality of attachment, language development and early maltreatment. In M.E. Lamb, A.L. Browne, & B. Rozoff (Eds.), *Advances in Developmental Psychology, Vol. 4* (pp. 105-151). Hillsdale, NJ: Erlbaum.

Haynes, C.F., Cutler, C., Gray, J., & Kempe, R.S. (1984). Hospitalized cases of nonorganic failure to thrive: The scope of the problem and short-term lay health visitor intervention. *Child Abuse & Neglect, 8,* 119-242.

Haynes-Seman, C., & Baumgarten, D. (1994). *Children speak for themselves: Using the Kempe Interactional Assessment to evaluate allegations of parent-child sexual abuse.* New York: Brunner/Mazel.

Haynes-Seman, C., & Krugman, R.D. (1989). Sexualized attention: Normal interaction or precursor to sexual abuse? *American Journal of Orthopsychiatry, 59,* 238-245.

Hibbard, R.A., & Hartman, G.L. (1992). Behavioral problems in alleged sexual abuse victims. *Child Abuse & Neglect, 16,* 755-762.

Hibbard, R.A., Roghmann, K., & Hoekelman, R.A. (1987). Genitalia in children's drawings: An association with sexual abuse. *Pediatrics, 779,* 129-137.

Hoffman-Plotkin, D., & Twentyman, C. (1984). A multimodal assessment of behavioral and cognitive deficits in abused and neglected preschoolers. *Child Development, 55,* 794-802.

Houck, G.M., & King, M.C. (1989). Child maltreatment: Family characteristics and developmental consequences. Special issue: Family violence. *Issues in Mental Health Nursing, 10(3-4),* 193-208.

Howes, C., & Espinosa, M.P. (1985). The consequences of child abuse for the formation of relationships with peers. *Child Abuse & Neglect, 9,* 397-404.

Howes, C., & Eldredge, R. (1985). Response of abused, neglected, and nonmaltreated children to the behaviors of their peers. *Journal of Applied Developmental Psychology, 6,* 261-270.

Hutheson, J.J., Black, M.M., & Starr, R.H., Jr. (1993). Developmental differences in interactional characteristics of mothers and their children with failure to thrive. *Journal of Pediatric Psychology, 18(4)*, 453-466.

Kempe, C.H. (1978). Sexual abuse, another hidden pediatric problem. The 1977 C. Anderson Aldrich Lecture. *Pediatrics, 62*, 382-389.

Koel, B.S. (1969). Failure to thrive and fatal injury as a continuum. *American Journal of Diseases of Children, 118*, 565-67.

Kohut, H. (1977). *The restoration of the self.* New York: International Universities Press.

Lidz, T. (1963). *The family and human adaptation.* New York: International Universities Press.

Main, M., & George, C. (1985). Responses of abused and disadvantaged toddlers to distress in agemates: A study in the day care setting. *Developmental Psychology, 21*, 407-412.

Main, M., & Solomon, J. (1986). Discovery of an insecure-disorganized/disoriented attachment pattern. In T.B. Brazelton & M.W. Yogman (Eds.), *Affective development in infancy* (pp. 95-124). Norwood, NJ: Ablex.

National Committee to Prevent Child Abuse (1994). *Current trends in child abuse reporting and fatalities: The results of the 1993 annual fifty state survey.* Chicago, IL: Author.

Panel on Research on Child Abuse and Neglect, Commission on Behavioral and Social Science and Education, National Research Council (1993). *Understanding child abuse and neglect.* Washington, DC: National Academy Press.

Peterson, C., Luborsky, L., & Seligman, L. (1983). Attributions and depressive mood shifts: A case study among the symptom-context method. *Journal of Abnormal Psychology, 92*, 96-103.

Powell, G.F., Low, J.F., & Speers, M.A. (1987). Behavior as a diagnostic aid in failure to thrive. *Journal of Developmental and Behavioral Pediatrics, 8*, 18-24.

Pynoos, R., & Nader, K. (1988). Psychological first aide and treatment approach to children exposed to community violence: Research implications. *Journal of Traumatic Stress Studies, 1*, 445-473.

Sameroff, A., Seifer, R., Barocas, R., Zax, M., & Greenspan, S. (1987). Intelligence quotient scores of 4-year-old children: Social environmental risk factors. *Pediatrics, 79*, 343-390.

Smetana, J., Kelly, M., & Twentyman, C. (1984). Abused, neglected, and nonmaltreated children's judgments of moral and social transgression. *Child Development, 55*, 277-287.

Steele, B.F. (1991). The psychopathology of incest participants. In S. Kramer & S. Akhtar (Eds.), *The trauma of transgression: Psychotherapy of incest victims* (pp. 14-56). Northvale, NJ: Jason Aronson.

Terr, L. (1990). *Too scared to cry.* New York: Harper Collins.

Winnicott, D.W. (1988). *Babies and their mothers. Classics in child development.* Reading, MA: Addison-Wesley.

Yates, A. (1982). Children eroticized by incest. *American Journal of Psychiatry, 129*, 482-485.

The Victimization of School-Age Children

B. B. Robbie Rossman
Honore M. Hughes
K. Lori Hanson

SUMMARY. Definitional and methodological issues related to physical neglect and abuse, sexual abuse and psychological maltreatment are raised, followed by discussion of sequelae for each type of abuse that is relevant for developing an understanding of the multiply victimized child. Some research of multiply victimized children is presented along with case examples. While evidence is mixed, it appears that multiple victimization places children at greater risk for maladaptation. More fine-grained assessment and conceptual analysis are needed to identify which and how many types of psychological abuse tend to co-occur with physical and sexual maltreatment. *[Article copies available for a fee from The Haworth Document Delivery Service: 1-800-342-9678. E-mail address: getinfo@haworth.com]*

In this article we present information relevant for developing an understanding of the multiply victimized school-age child by addressing methodological issues and reviewing literature in the areas of physical neglect and abuse, and sexual and psychological maltreatment. This provides the context for a discussion of the co-occurrence of multiple forms of abuse.

Address correspondence to: B. B. Robbie Rossman, PhD, Department of Psychology, University of Denver, Denver, CO 80208.

[Haworth co-indexing entry note]: "The Victimization of School-Age Children." Rossman, B. B. Robbie, Honore M. Hughes, and K. Lori Hanson. Co-published simultaneously in *Journal of Aggression, Maltreatment & Trauma* (The Haworth Maltreatment & Trauma Press, an imprint of The Haworth Press, Inc.) Vol. 2, No. 1 (#3), 1998, pp. 87-106; and: *Multiple Victimization of Children: Conceptual, Developmental, Research, and Treatment Issues* (ed: B. B. Robbie Rossman, and Mindy S. Rosenberg) The Haworth Maltreatment & Trauma Press, an imprint of The Haworth Press, Inc., 1998, pp. 87-106. Single or multiple copies of this article are available for a fee from The Haworth Document Delivery Service [1-800-342-9678, 9:00 a.m. - 5:00 p.m. (EST). E-mail address: getinfo@haworth.com].

METHODOLOGICAL ISSUES

Four types of child maltreatment are usually included in studies of victimization or "caretaking casualties" (Zuravin, 1991): physical abuse, physical neglect, sexual abuse, and emotional abuse. One difficulty with research in these areas is that typically these four categories of maltreatment have been investigated in isolation by independent groups of researchers. In addition, each researcher uses an idiosyncratic definition of the maltreatment, there tends to be overlap in definitions across types of abuse, and rarely are other forms of abuse assessed (Zuravin, 1991).

Haugaard (1992) notes that these definitional differences have arisen naturally due to societal confusion about what is appropriate to expect from parents regarding their interactions with their children. However, some criteria have been proposed for arriving at a shared definition, including the standards of the community, the intent of the adult, and the result to the child. In addition, for child sexual abuse, the ability of the child to consent to the interaction, and the type of sexual act have been added as criteria. Nonetheless, Haugaard emphasized the difficulties associated with each of the proposed criteria, especially related to the value judgments made by people implementing them. The use of idiosyncratic definitions is troublesome for prevalence surveys as are societal values that promote under-reporting. Finkelhor (1984) points out that with sexual abuse, only 20-30% of the incidents come to the attention of the authorities. Haugaard feels that expecting shared, exact definitions is probably unrealistic, but researchers need to provide clear definitions for their research context.

Additional problems plague abuse researchers as summarized by Briere (1992). One of the most bothersome is investigators' overdependence on retrospective designs which are limited by reliance on the memories of participants, and which cannot address issues of causality.

A continuing puzzle for abuse researchers has been the failure to identify clear syndromes or symptom patterns uniquely associated with different types of maltreatment. It may be that these do not exist. However, two further methodological issues may render a unique symptom picture hard to detect. These include failure to attend to the interaction of the child's developmental level with age of abuse onset, cessation or symptom assessment, or the role of moderating or mediating variables in the expression of symptomatology. Some of these variables include: maltreatment characteristics (type, duration, severity of abuse); individual factors (child's age, gender, coping abilities); family factors (conflict, stress, supportiveness); and, environmental factors (place or social context of abuse) (Conte, 1990; Hansen, Cane, & Christopher, 1990; Hughes & Fantuzzo, 1994). In addition, the amount of time away from an abusive situation may impact a child's current symptomatology, but most studies include only descriptions of the child's current age and abuse status. Symptoms experienced by a child may be rather transient (short-term), lasting (long-term), may be expressed differently at different ages, or may lie dormant and surface at a later time. For reviews of long-term consequences of physical and sexual abuse, see Malinosky-Rummell and Hansen (1993) and Beitchman et al. (1992), respectively.

Even when age is considered, division into age groups can be arbitrary and inconsistent, making it difficult to compare groups of children. On the other hand, the sensible grouping of children by developmental level can be quite helpful. For example, the nature of the middle-childhood developmental tasks of building cognitive, emotional and social competence and establishing successful peer relationships is important to consider when reviewing the consequences of abuse during this period (Erikson, 1950; Mueller & Silverman, 1989). Victimization of a child may inhibit, distort or totally discontinue a child's progress on these tasks. All of the above issues make interpretation of findings and comparison across studies difficult.

PHYSICAL NEGLECT
AND PSYCHOLOGICAL MALTREATMENT

Definition and Prevalence

In 1994, based on states with comparable reporting categories, neglect (53%) and emotional maltreatment (5%) were estimated to account for 58% of the over one million substantiated or indicated victims (National Center for Child Abuse and Neglect [NCAAN], 1996). These estimates suggest that neglect and psychological abuse represent a serious risk for children in this country.

Neglect is defined as a situation where a caretaker fails to provide aspects of care thought necessary for the normal development of a person's intellectual, physical, and emotional capacities (Giovannoni, 1989). Originally the separation of neglect from physical abuse reflected the difference between an act of omission (neglect) and an act of commission (abuse). Currently, this distinction is not maintained in some jurisdictions where "severe neglect" includes a situation "where any person having the custody of a child willfully causes or permits the person or health of a child to be placed in a situation such that his/her person or health is endangered . . . including the intentional failure to provide adequate food, clothing, or shelter" (Deering's California Penal Code, 1983, p. 685) as compared with "general neglect" where negligent failure is assumed.

As definitions of neglect are elaborated and move beyond the provision of food, shelter and physical safety, distinctions between neglect and psychological maltreatment become less clear. Psychological maltreatment refers to a "repeated pattern of caregiver behavior or extreme incident(s) that convey to children that they are worthless, flawed, unloved, unwanted, endangered, or only of value in meeting another's needs" (American Professional Society on the Abuse of Children [APSAC], 1995, p. 2). It captures the affective and cognitive aspects of child maltreatment, including acts of omission or commission that are judged by the community and professionals to be immediately or ultimately psychologically damaging, behaviorally, cognitively, affectively, or physically. Indeed, Hart and Brassard (1990) argue that psychological maltreatment may be a key factor in accounting for negative sequelae of all types of abuse.

Moreover, categories of psychologically maltreating behaviors (i.e., spurning, terrorizing, isolating, corrupting/exploiting, and denying emotional responsiveness, APSAC, 1995) overlap significantly with the established categories of neglect (i.e., emotional abuse, emotional neglect, and physical neglect, NCAAN, 1996). Thus, it is difficult to discriminate between definitions of physical neglect and psychological maltreatment, since several types of caregiver behaviors appear capable of being physically as well as psychologically damaging (withholding of food or medical treatment). It is also difficult to imagine physical damage to a child that did not have psychological ramifications. Therefore, the literature on neglect is informative with regard to psychological maltreatment and vice versa.

Another difficulty in reviewing the existing literature on neglect and psychological abuse stems from the research tradition of studying physical abuse and neglect together (e.g., Widom, 1989), making studies of neglect or psychological abuse alone rare. Only studies where neglect or psychological abuse have been specifically identified are reviewed here, but some studies that included older and younger children have been included.

Symptomatology of Victims

The Mother-Child Interaction Project at the University of Minnesota (Erickson, Egeland, & Pianta, 1989) was one of the earliest and only studies to discriminate prospectively among types of maternal maltreating behaviors: physical abuse, hostile/verbal abuse (similar to emotional abuse), psychological unavailability (similar to emotional neglect), and, physical neglect. Also unique in assessing multiple domains of functioning, this study examined development of children in these categories from 12 months through six years. While there was significant overlap among maltreatment classifications, results reported still held when children with mixed abuse backgrounds were eliminated from each classification. Relative to nonmaltreated comparison children, their findings for neglect and psychological maltreatment were as follows. At two years of age the emotionally abused children were characterized by lower IQ scores and greater negative affect, anger, and noncompliance. At this age, physically neglected children had much lower IQ scores, self-esteem, and affect positivity, as well as greater noncompliance, dependence on, and avoidance of adults. By six years of age, they were regarded as having the most severe problems, showing lower cognitive scores, greater dependence, more trouble comprehending school work, and higher internalizing and externalizing problem scores. Children in the emotional neglect group appeared to be starting out well, but by two years showed lower IQ scores, greater affective negativity, deficits in impulse control, self-abusive behaviors, noncompliance, and high dependence on preschool teachers. They seemed to have shown the greatest decline by preschool. Of these groups, the physically neglected group appeared to be the most disadvantaged cognitively, and the emotional neglect group was showing the greatest aggressive and disruptive behavior. However, by preschool all maltreatment groups were showing heightened anxiety (e.g., inability to attend), anger, social deficits and trouble functioning independently in school.

Several other studies have also focused on aspects of cognitive and social development with physically neglected children. Consistent with other work, Fox, Long and Langlois (1988) found that 3-8 year-old severely neglected children had significantly lower IQ scores and language comprehension than controls (but not significantly lower than physically abused children). They felt several factors could account for the poor outcome of neglected children: chronic illness, malnutrition, or failure to thrive; and, the extent to which not talking is both valued in maltreating families and is safer.

Evidence about social development has been mixed, with some studies showing differences for neglected children and others not. When IQ was controlled, 3-5 year-old neglected children were not different from nonmaltreated children in social sensitivity, including abilities to identify feelings and their causes (Frodi & Smetana, 1984). Smetana and Kelly (1989) found that the moral and societal knowledge of 3-5 year-old neglected children did not differ in many respects from controls, though neglected children did feel more punishment was deserved when a transgression was committed by self. In addition, while Kelly (1986) observed that all children aggressed in response to perceived harmful behavior and acted unfairly in response to perceived violation of their rights, only 20% of neglected children judged their actual transgressions as wrong.

Hoffman-Plotkin and Twentyman (1984) showed that neglected 3-6 year-old children were characterized by greater withdrawal from social interaction, whereas physically abused children were more aggressive, with both showing less prosocial behavior than controls. Howes and Espinosa (1985) found young neglected children to show less positive affect and social behavior, less complex play, and initiation of fewer social interactions than nonmaltreated peers. These findings of social negativity and withdrawal of neglected children could reflect both children's modeling of the neglecting parent and their carrying out behaviors consistent with internal working models of self and other that may serve to reduce anxiety related to social interaction (Mueller & Silverman, 1989). However, these reactions may interfere with the development of social skills and the expectation of social support.

Finally, neglected children tend to show problems with behavioral adjustment. Crittenden and Claussen (1991; Claussen & Crittenden, 1991) assessed the relationship between adjustment for 10-17 year-olds and severity of maltreatment in five categories: physical injury (abuse), emotional abuse, cognitive neglect, social/emotional neglect, and physical neglect. Cognitive and social/emotional neglect and emotional abuse were considered to be psychological maltreatment. Looking at mother and self-reported behavior problems, significant relationships were noted only for emotional abuse, however, relationships were observed for most behavior problem scales (viz., with conduct disorder, attentional problems, anxiety-withdrawal, psychotic behavior, and motor excess, but not with socialized aggression). Caseworkers' reports of behavior problems revealed significant relationships between: physical neglect and socialized aggression; social/emotional neglect and anxiety/withdrawal and psychotic behavior; cognitive neglect and anxiety/withdrawal; and, emotional abuse and conduct disorder, attentional problems, anxiety/withdrawal, and psychotic behavior. Thus, severity of emotional abuse was most consistently related to behavior problems, while physical neglect was less related to adjustment than has been noted for younger children. The authors note that for older children physical neglect may constitute a smaller problem because they are less dependent on caretakers and have more outside resources. In contrast, emotional abuse may be particularly damaging for children in this age range since identity formation is a major developmental task.

Hart, Brassard and Karlson (1987) summarize sequelae of psychological maltreatment as including attachment disorders, cognitive deficits, poor academic achievement and peer relationships, behavior problems, anxiety disorders, and antisocial behavior. Thus, physical neglect and psychological maltreatment appear associated with a number of cognitive, social, behavioral, and emotional deficits for school-age children.

PHYSICAL ABUSE

Definition and Prevalence

The development of a definition of physical abuse is problematic due to the difficulties associated with distinguishing acceptable forms of physical punishment from abuse. According to Kelly (1983) and Wolfe (1988), physical abuse has been defined as an "act of commission" by the parent and is characterized by the presence of nonaccidental injury. Physical abuse often occurs in infrequent episodes, accompanied by frustration on the part of the parent. Examples include excessive corporal punishment, as well as excessively close confinement, such as locking in a closet or tying a child to a bed. In addition, acts such as burning and beating, sensory overload, and prevention of sleep would be considered abusive. While injury has been a crucial factor in identifying abuse for legal purposes, increasing emphasis has been placed upon the circumstances and nature of the act, as opposed to the consequences to the child (Wolfe, 1988).

Several sources provide estimates of occurrence of physical abuse. Despite the methodological weaknesses inherent in these reports (e.g., differential reporting criteria across the U.S., lack of reliability data), their figures indicated that physical abuse accounted for 26% of the over 2.1 million substantiated/indicated reports in 1994 (NCAAN, 1996).

Symptomatology of Victims

The most obvious consequences for a child who has been physically abused are physical injuries. These injuries can range from minor bruises and lacerations to more serious problems such as loss of consciousness, interrupted breathing, broken bones, third degree burns, or even death (e.g., Hansen et al., 1990). These injuries may also lead to long-term physical disabilities, which will likely influence other areas of development.

Victims of physical abuse are also negatively affected in cognitive areas (e.g., Hansen et al., 1990; Youngblade & Belsky, 1990). Physically abused children score lower than average on standardized measures of intelligence and display lower school adjustment than nonabused children. Youngblade and Belsky (1990) note that these cognitive differences persisted regardless of socioeconomic status (SES) for groups of 4-8 year-old children participating in the Harvard Child Maltreatment Project. In addition, there is a higher incidence rate of developmental delays in physically abused children, including language disorders, mental retardation, and fine motor delays (Hansen et al., 1990). Hansen and colleagues (1990) further note that it is not clear whether cognitive skills are actually lower due to physical abuse, or whether the differences are more a result of the children's chaotic lifestyles. In addition, physically abused children tend to have lower school attendance and are more often placed in special education classrooms.

Behaviorally, the most frequent and noticeable characteristic of physically abused children is their aggressive behavior (Hansen et al., 1990; Hughes & Fantuzzo, 1994; Youngblade & Belsky, 1990). In both observational and parent/teacher-report studies, physically abused children displayed more aggressive behavior toward family members (including parents and siblings), peers, therapists, and other caregivers. This aggression may be exhibited through threatening demands and/or physically negative behaviors. It is thought that the child's expression of such behaviors might be due to a modeling effect. These children also show a higher rate of other problems (e.g., temper tantrums, hyperactivity, noncompliance, and delinquency) and regressive behaviors (e.g., enuresis, encopresis, and dependency).

Physically abused children appear to suffer consequences in the area of social skills and peer relationships as well (e.g., Cane & Hansen, 1989), though this may vary depending on the source of report. Smetana and Kelly (1989) discuss a study by Barahal, Waterman, and Martin which found that physically abused 6-8 year-olds were less socially sensitive than nonabused children, and that abused children's ability to comprehend and imitate social roles was inferior. In contrast, Hansen and colleagues (1990) report, according to parent and teacher-ratings, no differences in the social skills and competency of abused and nonabused children.

However, related to deficits in peer relationships, problems have been noted by several authors (Hansen et al., 1990; Mueller & Silverman, 1989; Youngblade & Belsky, 1990). Physically abused children are reported to engage in fewer social interactions and pro-social behaviors. Mueller and Silverman (1989) describe two clinical impressions of the physically abused child which would have an impact on peer relationships: the aggressive, provocative child and the excessively withdrawn, avoidant child. They further recount a study by Jacobson and Straker comparing severely physically abused to nonabused children, which concluded from observations that abused children interacted less, with less enjoyment, and in a less sustained and imaginative fashion.

Moreover, the abused children in the Harvard Child Maltreatment Project displayed higher dependency, had less curiosity regarding social interactions, were less trusting and showed less empathy than nonabused peers (Youngblade & Belsky, 1990). Hansen et al. (1990) found that physically abused children express fewer positive emotions or concern toward peers and adults. In addition, since physically abused children display more aggressive behavior and fantasy aggression in their play, other children may not wish to participate in such behavior, and it may be difficult for abused children to enter new peer groups.

Physically abused children are also affected emotionally by the abuse they sustain, as well as by the associated consequences discussed to this point. They experience a higher incidence rate of internalizing behavior problems (e.g., depression, anxiety, and somatic complaints), and lower self-esteem, as rated by themselves and their mothers (Hansen et al., 1990). In addition, they may exhibit a higher rate of self-mutilation and suicide attempts if threatened with separation or abandonment from caretakers (Youngblade & Belsky, 1990). These children may feel hopeless and experience less pleasure in things such as play, and internalizing and externalizing problems are not mutually exclusive. Thus, physically maltreated school-age children also appear to experience multiple deficits.

SEXUAL ABUSE

Definition and Prevalence

Sexual abuse is equally as difficult to define and develop occurrence criteria for as physical abuse. One definition which has been in use for some time is that proposed by NCAAN (1988): "contact and interactions between a child and an adult when the child is being used for the sexual stimulation of the perpetrator or another person."

Estimates of sexual abuse are very difficult to obtain. In a review of prevalence rates, Finkelhor (1986) pointed out that there is considerable variation in the prevalence rates derived from North American studies, with rates ranging from 6% to 62% for females, and from 3% to 31% for males. He attributes the large range in estimates to differences among studies, including variations in definitions, samples, and methods of obtaining the information. Excluding noncontact sexual abuse, his best estimate of sexual abuse for girls is that 22% to 38% of all females have been sexually abused at some point in their life before the age of 18. He also estimates that boys are abused at a 1: 2.5 ratio to girls. The NCAAN (1996) survey estimates that 14% of substantiated/indicated cases are due to sexual abuse.

Symptomatology of Victims

Within the past five to ten years, there has been an increase in the number of empirical studies focusing specifically on the consequences of sexual abuse, and Kendall-Tackett, Williams, and Finkelhor (1993) provide an excellent review of the existing literature. By examining research across different ages, these authors found that symptoms do not appear uniformly across all age groups. As a result, they have hypothesized that there are possible developmental patterns of symptoms in victims of sexual abuse (see also Gomes-Schwartz, Horowitz, & Cararelli, 1991).

There are various physical consequences of sexual abuse (Conte, 1990). Aside from the pain caused from specific types of abuse, victims often experience gynecological problems, urinary tract infections, and genital complaints. There are higher reported rates of muscle tension, headaches, stomachaches, vomiting, and gastrointestinal difficulties. Disturbances in eating and sleeping habits may occur as well. Some psychosomatic complaints have been noted in sexually abused children, including hysterical symptoms and seizures. Kendall-Tackett et al. (1993) report that the onset of puberty in sexually abused girls may be advanced by as much as a year.

Negative cognitive effects of sexual abuse on children seem to develop in an indirect manner, such as affecting school performance through lack of concentration (Conte, 1990; Kendall-Tackett et al., 1993). Concentration problems may result from the child's preoccupation or day dreaming, a possible Post-Traumatic Stress Disorder (PTSD) symptom. In addition, a decline in school performance can lead to school avoidance for some children.

Most behavior problems occur at higher rates in sexually abused children than in nonabused children. However, when compared to a clinical sample, sexually abused children show fewer behavior problems, except on sexualized behaviors, fears, and PTSD symptoms, where they show comparable or greater levels of problems (Conte, 1990; Gomes-Schwartz et al., 1985; Kendall-Tackett et al., 1993). In the review by Kendall-Tackett and colleagues, the highest effect sizes across studies were for the externalizing problems of sexualized and aggressive behavior. Inappropriate sexual behavior has been the symptom most commonly noted in studies of sexually abused children, although it is not diagnostic of sexual abuse. The authors note that this behavior is more common in preschool and adolescent children, and seems to occur less in school-aged children. These inappropriate sexual behaviors may include: sexual play with dolls, open masturbation, putting objects into the vagina or anus, requesting sexual stimulation from adults or other children, or other seductive actions, language, or dress (Conte, 1990; Kendall-Tackett et al., 1993). Additional externalizing behaviors noted include aggression and hostility, hyperactivity, and excessive risk-taking behaviors (Gomes-Schwartz et al., 1985).

Socially, children who have been sexually abused display lower levels of social competence and greater isolation from others (Kendall-Tackett et al., 1993). From their experience of sexual abuse, children may learn basic betrayal and mistrust of others. Moreover, they also learn some antisocial interaction patterns, such as how to use power to coerce smaller persons, keep secrets from adults, and use others for one's own needs (Conte, 1990).

Internalizing behaviors also occur at higher rates in sexually abused children. Several PTSD symptoms, such as nightmares, anxiety, and fears are particularly common (Conte, 1990). Depression is often noted through such behaviors as decreased involvement and interests, negative self-perceptions, suicidal attempts, self-mutilation, and feelings of shame and guilt (Kendall-Tackett et al., 1993). Somatic complaints may occur as well, as noted previously. In addition, Gomes-Schwartz et al. (1990) reported that school-age youngsters in their study were characterized by either internalized fears or externalized anger.

Other problem behaviors have also been reported. Kendall-Tackett and colleagues (1993) describe a set of regressive behaviors which include enuresis, encopresis, tantrums, and whining. Sexual abuse victims also often behave in more passive and compliant ways than other children (Conte, 1990).

While approximately 20-40% of children show significant symptomatology, Kendall-Tackett et al. (1993) make note of the significant percentages of sexually abused children who show no symptoms. They believe that this occurrence is likely due to several factors: assessment of inappropriate symptoms, use of insensitive measurement instruments, the fact that symptoms are suppressed or not yet manifested, or, the child is truly less affected.

MULTIPLE VICTIMIZATION

As noted in the introduction to this volume, there is a noteworthy discrepancy between research which has tended to study single types of abuse, and clinical experience which suggests that many children are multiply victimized. This co-occurrence among maltreatment types should not be surprising. By definition alone, sexual and physical abuse would also involve psychological maltreatment. It would be very difficult to beat or neglect a child without sending a message of rejection. Thus, the literature reviewed for single types of abuse is likely to be relevant for considering the effects of multiple victimization. However, studies are beginning to emerge that more explicitly identify the co-occurrence of different types of maltreatment.

Clinical wisdom and risk factor research (e.g., Sameroff & Seifer, 1983) have led to the inference that multiple stressors have a greater adverse impact on children than single stressors. In addition, Quinton and Rutter (1976) noted that the impact of chronic risk factors was not additive, but that they potentiated each other. Sameroff, Seifer, and Zax (1982) also indicated that the relationship between number of risk factors and decrements in functioning was not linear, but supported a transactional model wherein each risk factor has its own impact which in turn influences other risk factors. Thus, multiple types of maltreatment experiences would be expected to be associated with more adverse outcomes than single types. While this expectation seems sensible, it is based, in part, on the assumption of "all other things being equal." This means that the dosage size for each type of abuse and frequency of administration, plus subjective or objective consequences for the child of each type of abuse are considered equal. Clinically, we know that this may not be the case. Nonetheless, the prediction that more adversity is worse seems more logical than assumptions that greater adversity makes no difference or is better.

Regarding multiple victimization, Erickson et al. (1989) reported on the co-occurrence of several types of maltreatment. They provided observations for physical abuse, physical neglect, and emotional neglect alone, as well as for the last two categories when combined with physical abuse. Support for the speculation that co-occurrence groups would show greater maladjustment than single abuse groups was mixed. Three results, each at different ages, were supportive: physically abused and neglected children had greater negative affectivity and were more dependent on mothers for help than either single abuse group or controls; and, the physically abused and emotionally neglected groups had greater behavioral problems than single abuse groups or controls.

To the best of our knowledge, the only types of investigations of school-age children that have reported outcomes separately for single and multiple abuse victims are those of children who have witnessed parental violence (psychological maltreatment) and children who have both witnessed and been personally abused. These include studies where child witnessing was combined with physical abuse for some children, two by Hughes and collaborators, one by Sternberg and collaborators, and one by Cicchetti and Cummings and associates; and, two studies by Rossman and associates where witnessing was combined with physical neglect or abuse or sexual abuse for some children (a mixed abuse group).

Hughes (1988) studied externalizing problems, anxiety, self-esteem, and depressive symptoms for 3-12 year-old physically abused witnesses, nonabused witnesses, and nonabused, nonwitness comparison children. Maternally-reported externalizing problems were significantly more frequent for abused witnesses than other groups, and problem intensity was higher for abused witnesses than comparison children, with nonabused witnesses falling between the other groups. Self-reported anxiety scores for both witness groups were significantly higher than for comparison children. Self-reported self-esteem was significantly higher for 6-8 year-old comparison children than for either witness group, and for 9-12 year-old comparison children than for abused witnesses, with nonabused witnesses falling in between. No group differences in self-reported depression for 7-12 year-old children were observed.

In a second study (Hughes, Parkinson, & Vargo, 1989), abused witnesses were found to evidence significantly higher maternally-reported internalizing and externalizing behavior problems than comparison children, with nonabused witnesses falling between these groups. All groups differed significantly when total behavior problems were considered. This pattern of differences for total behavior problems was also observed within different age groups (4-5, 6-8, and 9-12 year-olds). In addition, these same differences between groups held when the children's scores were examined by gender. However, higher percentages of girls than boys in all groups received scores indicating clinically significant levels of total problems.

Sternberg et al. (1993) studied depression and behavior problems in 8-12 year-old children falling into four groups: physically abused, nonabused witnesses to parental violence, physically abused witnesses to parental violence, and nonabused, nonwitness children. For maternally-reported behavior problems, externalizing problems differed among groups such that both witness groups were similar and significantly higher than either the abused nonwitness or comparison groups which did not differ. Mothers of girls in all maltreated groups reported more externalizing problems for girls than did mothers of boys. When child-report measures were considered, all maltreatment groups were similar in reporting greater depressive symptoms than comparison children.

Hennessy, Rabideau, Cicchetti, and Cummings (1994) investigated the responses of 6-11 year-old children to different forms of interparental anger presented via videotape. All children had witnessed some interparental violence, and some children had also been physically abused. Children were asked how the actors felt and how they personally felt watching the interaction. Interactions varied depending on whether they were friendly or angry, whether anger was portrayed nonverbally, verbally, or physically, and whether or not angry interactions were resolved. Abused child witnesses reported greater fear than nonabused witnesses in response to all forms of adult anger, and to unresolved but not resolved anger. In addition, boys responded with greater anger than girls to all forms of angry interactions, whereas girls responded with greater fear than boys.

Rossman et al. (1991) conducted a study of 4.5-5.5 year-old children falling into either comparison, witness or mixed-abuse witness groups. Analyses revealed that, relative to controls, self-perceptions of competence for both witness groups were significantly lower, and maternally-reported problem behaviors were significantly higher, being highest for abused witnesses. In a second study of 4-9 year-olds in the same groups, Rossman et al. (1993) found that maternal ratings of school/preschool performance and social competence were significantly higher and PTSD symptoms lower for comparison children than witness groups, though the witness groups did not differ. Maternally-reported internalizing and externalizing problems were significantly higher for nonabused witness children, but did not differ between comparison and abused witness children. After analyses to rule out alternative explanations of this unexpected result, the authors speculated that the mothers' observational context may have played a role. The abused witnesses had all been abused at home and may have been suppressing behavior in the abusive setting to avoid further maltreatment. However, in a different context, the abused witnesses were seen as more distressed, since a significantly higher proportion of these children than comparison children had been referred for psychological services by an outside agency.

Overall, there were anomalous findings in all studies that have examined multiple abuse groups (e.g., findings that multiple abuse groups were not significantly different from single abuse groups), with some hints that for older children, psychological abuse may be as detrimental as being multiply abused. While the results were mixed, the weight of the evidence seems to suggest that experiencing several types of chronic maltreatment places a child at greater risk for cognitive, emotional, social, and/or behavioral dysfunction. There are some indications that the varied patterns of findings may be due to methodological differences and age or gender factors. However, the picture is far from clear, and more research is needed that concurrently assesses all of the types of maltreatment children experience as well as additional important mediating variables.

CASE EXAMPLES

In closing we present a tale of two girls, Lauren, age six, and Tammy, age eight (names fictitious), to illustrate sequelae of multiple victimization as well as the possible role played by protective factors. At the time we worked with these girls, neither had a biological father in the picture. Tammy's father had committed suicide several years earlier after years of substance abuse and violent behavior including beating Tammy's mother, emotional abuse of the family, and physically abusing Tammy once. Tammy's mother showed many of the sequelae of her own battering including depression, poor self-concept and self-confidence, concerns about control over her own anger, and questions about how to deal with Tammy's declining academic performance and aggressive and noncompliant behaviors at home and school.

Lauren was in a public-school day treatment program for behaviorally and emotionally disturbed children. Prior to leaving the family when Lauren was three, her biological father had physically abused both Lauren and her mother. Lauren's mother had a degenerative neural disease, problems with alcohol, and physically neglected and abused Lauren. Her mother received medical and psychiatric treatment. Lauren often came to school in a disheveled state with dirty clothes, uncombed hair, and needing a bath. Lauren's behavioral problems included vacillation between withdrawal and aggression directed toward adults, withdrawal from peers and aggression at their social overtures, and an extreme fear of touch which made the occasional needed use of physical restraint terrifying for her. In addition, learning deficits were present, though she appeared to be only slightly below normal intelligence. Both girls were multiply victimized and both received weekly individual treatment sessions, Tammy in an outpatient clinic, and Lauren in the school setting.

Tammy's treatment quickly moved into a fantasy mode, with collateral work with her mother around parenting and her own issues. Tammy's fantasy play was repetitive, with all stories involving disastrous things happening to children and adults. The stories unfolded without affect and with magical rescues. Intervention in the play consisted of suggesting that the victims show emotion and obtain "realistic" treatment for their injuries to help Tammy link affect to her reenactments and to provide her with realistic options for staying safe. Gradually Tammy began incorporating these features in her fantasy, the stories became less frequent, and her aggression decreased while academic performance improved.

Lauren began treatment alternating between aggressing against the therapist versus trying to hide, behavioral reenactments of the abuse she was not yet able to portray in fantasy. The therapist set limits on aggression, encouraged verbalizing feelings, and provided large empty boxes into which she could retreat. The therapist reflected her feelings and reinforced her need to stay safe. Gradually Lauren was able to spend parts of sessions out of hiding, rolling a nerf ball to the therapist. As Lauren appeared more capable of interaction, the therapist introduced the idea of shaking hands. It was important that she tolerate physical contact so she could use others to calm. After two years of treatment Lauren was able to sit close to the therapist, tolerate a hand on her shoulder, and insisted on "high fives" to end sessions.

Implications

The complexity of these cases of multiple maltreatment is familiar to most clinicians. However, researchers, without more inclusive clinical background, might be likely to consider them comparable in age, gender and intelligence, and put Tammy in a parental violence exposure group and Lauren in a physical abuse group. This categorization would obscure important differences between them: onset and severity of abuse; deficits prior to treatment; and, level of maternal support. These kinds of factors, often unassessed in research, may contribute to the lack of clarity about the sequelae of single and multiple maltreatment experiences.

CONCLUSION

The research on single or multiple victimization of school-age children reviewed is complex, and unique syndromes have not been identified. However, some commonalities in reactions can be noted. While not definitive signs of abuse, the most apparent symptoms of physical neglect were withdrawing behaviors, of physical abuse were aggressive behaviors, and of sexual abuse were precocious sexual behaviors. In addition, there appeared to be a tendency for multiple victimization that included some type of psychological maltreatment to be more damaging than singular abuse that had not, consistent with Hart and Brassard's (1990) argument that psychological abuse may be a key factor in accounting for negative sequelae of all types of abuse. Conceptual and empirical analysis is needed of what and how many types of psychological abuse typically co-occur with other forms of abuse.

Researchers focusing on any type of maltreatment need to include measures to assess the severity and chronicity of other forms of maltreatment, as well as the occurrence of other types of traumatic experiences such as medical trauma, neighborhood violence, or loss. More extensive assessment can help us build more representative base rates of co-occurrence, and better address questions about the existence of unique abuse syndromes, the relationship between number and type of risks and functioning, and the influence of potential protective and vulnerability factors.

REFERENCES

American Professional Society on the Abuse of Children. (1995). Guidelines for psychosocial evaluation of suspected psychological maltreatment in children and adolescents. Chicago: Author.

Beitchman, J.H., Zucker, K.J., Hood, J.E., daCosta, G.A., Akman, D., & Cassavia, E. (1992). A review of the long-term effects of child sexual abuse. *Child Abuse and Neglect, 16*, 101-118.

Brier, J. (1992). Methodological issues in the study of sexual abuse effects. *Journal of Consulting and Clinical Psychology, 60*, 196-203.

Claussen, A.E., & Crittenden, P.M. (1991). Physical and psychological maltreatment: Relationship among types of maltreatment. *Child Abuse and Neglect, 15*, 5-18.

Conaway, L.P., & Hansen, D.J. (1989). Social behavior of physically abused and neglected children: A critical review with implications for research and intervention. *Clinical Psychology Review, 9*, 627-652.

Conte, J.R. (1990). Victims of child sexual abuse. In R.T. Ammerman & M. Hersen (Eds.), *Treatment of family violence: A sourcebook* (pp. 50-76). New York: Wiley.

Crittenden, P.M., & Claussen, A.E. (1991). Physical and psychological maltreatment in adolescence. (Available from author at University of New Hampshire, Center for Family Studies.)

Erikson, E.H. (1950). *Childhood and society.* New York: Norton.

Erickson, M.F., Egland, B., & Pianta, R. (1989). The effects of maltreatment on the development of young children. In D. Cicchetti & V. Carlson (Eds.), *Child maltreatment: Theory and research on the causes and consequences of child abuse and neglect* (pp. 647-684). New York: Cambridge University Press.

Finkelhor, D.A. (1984). *Child sexual abuse: New theories and research.* New York: Free Press.

Finkelhor, D.A. (1986). *Child sexual abuse: A sourcebook*. Newbury Park, CA: Sage.

Fox, L., Long, S.H., & Langlois, A. (1988). Patterns of language comprehension deficit in abused and neglected children. *Journal of Speech and Hearing Disorders, 53*, 239-244.

Frodi, A., & Smetana, J. (1984). Abused, neglected, and normal preschoolers' ability to discriminate emotions in others: The effects of IQ. *Child Abuse and Neglect, 8*, 459-465.

Giovannoni, J. (1989). Definitional issues in child maltreatment. In D. Cicchetti & V. Carlson (Eds.), *Child maltreatment: Theory and research on the causes and consequences of child abuse and neglect* (pp. 3-37). New York: Cambridge University Press.

Gomes-Schwartz, B., Horowitz, J.M., & Sauzier, M. (1985). Severity of emotional distress among sexually abused preschool, school-age, and adolescent children. *Hospital and Community Psychiatry, 36*, 503-508.

Green, B.L. (1990). Defining trauma: Terminology and generic stressor dimensions. *Journal of Applied Social Psychology, 1990*, 1632-1642.

Hansen, D.J., Conaway, L.P., & Christopher, J.S. (1990). Victims of child physical abuse. In R.T. Ammerman & M. Hersen (Eds.), *Treatment of family violence: A sourcebook* (pp. 17-49). New York: Wiley.

Hart, S.N., & Brassard, M.R. (1990). Psychological maltreatment of children. In R.T. Ammerman & M. Hersen (Eds.), *Treatment of family violence: A sourcebook* (pp. 77-112). New York: Wiley.

Haugaard, J.J. (1992). Epidemiology and family violence involving children. In R.T. Ammerman & M. Hersen (Eds.), *Assessment of family violence* (pp. 889-107). New York: Wiley.

Hennessy, K.D., Rabideau, G.J., Cicchetti, D., & Cummings, E.M. (1994). Responses of physically abused and nonabused children to different forms of interadult anger. *Child Development, 65*, 815-828.

Hoffman-Plotkin, D., & Twentyman, C. (1984). A multimodal assessment of behavioral and cognitive deficits in abused and neglected preschoolers. *Child Development, 55*, 794-802.

Howes, C., & Espinosa, M.P. (1985). The consequences of child abuse for the formation of relationships with peers. *Child Abuse and Neglect, 9*, 397-404.

Hughes, H.M. (1988). Psychological and behavioral correlates of family violence in child witnesses and victims. *American Journal of Orthopsychiatry, 58*, 77-90.

Hughes, H.M., Parkinson, D., & Vargo, M. (1989). Witnessing spouse abuse and experiencing physical abuse: A "double whammy"? *Journal of Family Violence, 4*, 197-209.

Hughes, H.M., & Fantuzzo, J.W. (1994). Family violence–Child. In M. Hersen, R.T. Ammerman, & L.A. Sisson (Eds.), *Handbook of aggressive and destructive behavior in psychiatric patients* (pp. 483-499). New York: Plenum.

Kelly, J.A. (1983). *Treating child-abusive families: Intervention based on skills-training principles*. New York: Plenum.

Kelly, M. (1986). *Relations between moral judgment and moral actions in abused, neglected, and nonmaltreated children.* Unpublished doctoral dissertation, University of Rochester.

Kendall-Tackett, K.A., Williams, L.M., & Finkelhor, D. (1993). Impact of sexual abuse on children: A review and synthesis of recent empirical studies. *Psychological Bulletin, 113,* 164-180.

Malinosky-Rummell, R., & Hansen, D.J. (1993). Long-term consequences of childhood physical abuse. *Psychological Bulletin, 114,* 68-79.

Mueller, E., & Silverman, N. (1989). Peer relations in maltreated children. In D. Cicchetti & V. Carlson (Eds.), *Child maltreatment: Theory and research on the causes and consequences of child abuse and neglect* (pp. 529-578). New York: Cambridge University Press.

National Center on Child Abuse and Neglect, U.S. Department of Health and Human Services. (1996). *Child maltreatment 1994: Reports from the states to the National Center on Child Abuse and Neglect.* Washington, DC: U.S. Government Printing Office.

National Center on Child Abuse and Neglect, U.S. Department of Health and Human Services. (1988). *Study findings: Study of national incidence and prevalence on child abuse and neglect: 1988.* Washington, DC: U.S. Government Printing Office.

Quinton, D., & Rutter, M. (1976). Early hospital admissions and later disturbances of behavior: An attempted replication of Douglas' findings. *Developmental Medicine and Child Neurology, 18,* 447-459.

Rossman, B.B.R., Heaton, M., Moss, T., Malik, N., Lintz, C., & Romero, J. (1991). *Functioning in abused and nonabused preschool witnesses to family violence.* Paper presented at the meeting of the American Psychological Association, San Francisco, CA.

Rossman, B.B.R., Bingham, R.D., Cimbora, D.M., Dickerson, L.K., Dexter, R.M., Balog, S., & Mallah, K. (1993). *Relationship of trauma severity to trauma symptoms for child witnesses.* Paper presented at the meeting of the American Psychological Association, Toronto, Ontario, Canada.

Sameroff, A.J., & Seifer, R. (1983). Familial risk and child competence. *Child Development, 54,* 1254-1268.

Sameroff, A.J., Seifer, R., & Zax, M. (1982). Early development of children at risk for emotional disorder. *Monographs of the Society for Research in Child Development, 47 (Serial No. 199).*

Sauzier, M., Salt, S., & Calhoun, R. (1990). The effects of child sexual abuse. In B. Gomes-Schwartz, J.M. Horowitz, & A. Cardarelli (Eds.), *Child sexual abuse: The initial effects* (pp. 75-108). Newbury Park, CA: Sage.

Smetana, J.G., & Kelly, M. (1989). Social cognition in maltreated children. In D. Cicchetti & V. Carlson (Eds.), *Child maltreatment: Theory and research on the causes and consequences of child abuse and neglect* (pp. 620-646). New York: Cambridge University Press.

Smetana, J.G., Kelly, M., & Twentyman, C.T. (1984). Abused, neglected, and nonmaltreated children's conceptions of moral and conventional transgressions. *Child Development, 55,* 277-287.

State of California-Health & Welfare Agency, Department of Social Services. (1983). *Manual of policies and procedures.* Sacramento, CA: Author.

Sternberg, K.J., Lamb, M.E., Greenbaum, C., Cicchetti, D., Dawud, S., Cortes, R.M., Krispin, O., & Lorey, F. (1993). Effects of domestic violence on children's behavior problems and depression. *Developmental Psychology, 29,* 44-52.

Widom, C.S. (1989). Child abuse, neglect, and adult behavior: Research design and findings on criminality, violence, and child abuse. *American Journal of Orthopsychiatry, 59,* 355-367.

Wolfe, D.A. (1988). Child abuse and neglect. In E.J. Mash & L.G. Terdal (Eds.), *Behavioral assessment of childhood disorders* (2nd ed., pp. 627-669). New York: Guilford.

Youngblade, L.M., & Belsky, J. (1990). Social and emotional consequences of child maltreatment. In R.T. Ammerman & M. Hersen (Eds.), *Children at risk: An evaluation of factors contributing to child abuse and neglect* (pp. 109-146). New York: Plenum.

Zuravin, S.J. (1991). Research definitions of child abuse and neglect: Current problems. In R.H. Starr & D.A. Wolfe (Eds.), *The effects of abuse and neglect* (pp. 100-128). New York: Guilford.

Maltreated Adolescents:
Victims Caught Between Childhood and Adulthood

B. B. Robbie Rossman
Mindy S. Rosenberg

SUMMARY. The authors review literature on the developmental tasks of adolescence and the unique problems faced by adolescent victims of maltreatment. The developmental domains addressed include cognition, identity, behavior and affect regulation, family and peer relationships, and sexuality. Research on the co-occurrence of multiple types of victimization is discussed. The relationship between multiple victimization and violent crime, with a focus on parricide, is examined. The authors call for greater attention to the assessment and study of multiple forms of maltreatment and its outcomes in adolescence, since adolescence is one of the least researched developmental periods in terms of single or multiple victimization. *[Article copies available for a fee from The Haworth Document Delivery Service: 1-800-342-9678. E-mail address: getinfo@haworth.com]*

In this article, we will review the abuse literature in terms of the developmental tasks of adolescence and unique problems faced by adolescent abuse victims in their position between childhood and adulthood. The

Address correspondence to: B. B. Robbie Rossman, PhD, Department of Psychology, 2155 Race Street, University of Denver, Denver, CO 80208.

[Haworth co-indexing entry note]: "Maltreated Adolescents: Victims Caught Between Childhood and Adulthood." Rossman, B. B. Robbie, and Mindy S. Rosenberg. Co-published simultaneously in *Journal of Aggression, Maltreatment & Trauma* (The Haworth Maltreatment & Trauma Press, an imprint of The Haworth Press, Inc.) Vol. 2, No. 1 (#3), 1998, pp. 107-129; and: *Multiple Victimization of Children: Conceptual, Developmental, Research, and Treatment Issues* (ed: B. B. Robbie Rossman, and Mindy S. Rosenberg) The Haworth Maltreatment & Trauma Press, an imprint of The Haworth Press, Inc., 1998, pp. 107-129. Single or multiple copies of this article are available for a fee from The Haworth Document Delivery Service [1-800-342-9678, 9:00 a.m. - 5:00 p.m. (EST). E-mail address: getinfo@haworth.com].

107

scant information on multiple victimization is also presented. Consistent with current work on adolescence, both preadolescence, 10-12 years (the average age of menarche now being 11 years), and older teens, aged 13-17, are considered. It is fair to say that adolescence is one of the least researched developmental periods in terms of single or multiple victimization.

According to recent texts on development (e.g., Berk, 1993) and those who write about adolescent development (e.g., Elkind, 1970), adolescent tasks include adaptation to puberty and sexual intimacy, movement into formal cognitive operations, development of a more stable and enduring sense of self and identity, meeting social and cultural expectations for behavior and affect regulation, and establishing a new sense of mastery and independence that allows movement away from the family toward greater engagement with peers. As most parents of adolescents will attest, adolescence represents a complex period in development where parents are once again expected, as are the teens, to readjust expectations for styles of behavior and relating. These transitions are difficult and often require the definition of a new power structure in the family. Families that are flexible, value communication and democratic decision making between parents and youth may tend to have an easier time adjusting to these changes. Families where parents subscribe to authoritarian childrearing styles, where power and control are not easily negotiated, and where marital violence, alcoholism and maltreatment are the norm will have much greater difficulty making such transitions.

When child maltreatment is disclosed in adolescence, it may be the first time that dysfunctional family patterns escalated into abuse, it may be an extension of behavior that evolved over time since childhood, or it may be a change in form such as sexual abuse replacing prior physical abuse. Garbarino (1989) notes that teen abuse victims are in many respects more like wives than like the less powerful younger children or the abused elderly. Teens and wives both have some power, and may be perceived as threatening to perpetrators concerned about maintenance of control and dominance. Teens' power increases through their growing physical strength, ability to think, argue, behave independently, and perhaps seek revenge for abuse suffered.

One of the most disturbing problems recently associated with child maltreatment is delinquency and the commission of violent crimes by youth and young adults. Lewis, Mallouh, and Webb (1989) estimate that 20% of abused children become delinquent, while only 5% of nonabused children follow this trajectory. The best predictor of chronic teen antisocial acts by age 18 is the occurrence of earlier antisocial acts prior to age 15, with most juvenile offenses being accounted for by a relatively small number of offenders (Yoshikawa, 1994). Rivera and Widom (1990) found that abused and neglected children are at significantly greater risk for perpetrating violent crime in adulthood than a matched group of nonmaltreated children. Youth killing parents (parricide) is relatively rare statistically, yet when many of these cases are fully investigated, there is typically evidence of chronic, severe maltreatment, often taking the form of multiple victimization (Mones, 1991).

There are important methodological/conceptual issues that need to be addressed in evaluating the impact of abuse on adolescents. For example, it appears important to discriminate between those who have been part of an abusive system since early childhood, and those where abuse emerged in adolescence due to a family's inability to negotiate the transition to adolescence. However, these distinctions are typically not reported and would be difficult to determine unless various forms of maltreatment had been assessed. For example, psychological maltreatment may precede physical or sexual abuse incidents that are first reported in adolescence.

Other methodological issues involve incidence and the types of cases studied. It is believed that adolescent victimization is even less likely to be reported than abuse of younger children, that sexual and psychological maltreatment are more common than physical abuse in adolescence, and that adolescent girls are more frequent targets of abuse than are adolescent boys (Garbarino, 1989). However, as Garbarino points out, much of what is known about adolescent abuse and neglect comes from protective service and hospital samples of reported cases, which means that data are biased toward reported cases. Other instances of adolescent abuse are likely to go unreported or are misinterpreted as cases of adolescent acting out behavior, school adjustment problems, or indications of dysfunctional families without further investigation of what constitutes the family problems.

Recognizing these limitations on reporting, incidence data from the Fifty State Survey conducted by the National Center on Child Abuse and Neglect (NCCAN, 1990) showed that, for the 46 states reporting age of victims, 283,108 of the 845,955 cases reported, or 33.47%, involved individuals aged 10-17 years; 162,343, or 19.19%, involved 13-17 year-olds. Since NCCAN does not provide information about type of abuse or gender of victim relative to age, it is not possible to evaluate earlier estimates about gender or abuse type. Based on earlier surveys, there were more girls than boys abused in adolescence (Straus, 1988). However, it is also estimated that adolescent males are even less likely than females to report abuse, particularly sexual abuse (Kaplan & Becker, 1992), making gender differences in incidence difficult to evaluate. What is clear is that a substantial number of adolescents experience abuse. We turn now to consideration of the relationship between victimization and the accomplishment of adolescent developmental tasks with special focus on violent behavior.

ADOLESCENT DEVELOPMENTAL TASKS

Movement into Formal Operational Thought

In general, we know little about the impact of trauma on cognition during any age period, except the difficulties with attention, concentration, intrusions, and dissociation discussed below, which are part of trauma symptomatology (Terr, 1991). The literature does not speak directly to the impact of abuse on the adolescent's acquisition of abstract thought or its cognitive/emotional correlates, the "personal fable" or sense of uniqueness of the adolescent, and the "imaginary audience" or adolescents' assumption that those around them are as keenly aware of their characteristics and failings as are they (Elkind, 1970).

What the literature does suggest is that for younger abused children, there appear to be delays in verbal abilities (e.g., Hoffman-Plotkin & Twentyman, 1984; Fox, Long, & Langlois, 1988). School-age and early adolescent witnesses to parental violence show poorer achievement performance, particularly in mathematics and reading (Peplar & Moore, 1989). Fish-Murray, Koby, and van der Kolk (1987) studied accommodation skills and moral reasoning for physically abused and severely neglected children in the school-age to early adolescent range. These children showed poorer accommodation skills (i.e., ability to modify existing schemas to integrate new information) in most domains (e.g., logical or social) than similar nonabused children, with the scientific domain being the most spared. In terms of moral reasoning, their stories suggested that the most powerful male adult figures usually determined what was acceptable behavior or "right." From a Piagetian perspective, these authors argue that affect and cognition are complementary and simultaneous, and abused children interpret the meaning of their pain and fear according to their cognitive structural level. When their system is overloaded with unassimilated emotion, the children lose the flexibility to move through different alternatives to form or select new ones, and activate earlier, well-known schemas instead. Therefore, healthy adaptation to trauma and avoidance of cognitive delays and distortions depend partially on the flexibility of children's cognitive structures, particularly under emotional stress (Fish-Murray, 1990; see Harter's article, this volume). This supposition has two implications: that abuse may interfere with an adolescent's movement into and ability to carry out formal or abstract cognitive operations and form more sophisticated schemas; and that the age of abuse onset may be critical in determining the amount of interference. If a child has been able to progress cognitively in a normal fashion into adolescent abstract thought, subsequent abuse may delay further cognitive elaboration at that level but leave the adolescent better able to cognitively handle the experience of abuse. However, earlier abuse onset would leave the adolescent with much delayed cognitive functioning, and more difficulty processing trauma.

In their review of sexual abuse research, Kendall-Tackett, Williams, and Finkelhor (1993) noted that 23% of the adolescents showed school and/or learning problems. In addition, in their review of the physical maltreatment literature, Malinosky-Rummell and Hansen (1993) reported that physically abused adolescents tend to show both intellectual and academic delays compared to nonabused samples, with neglected boys showing lower IQ scores than abused boys, and both neglected and abused girls showing low scores. Both of these reviews should reflect a mix of adolescents who had been abused since childhood and more recently. However, Pfouts, Schopler and Henley (1981) observed that 40% of adolescents in their study who had witnessed abuse or been abused were truant from school. This suggests that no matter what the age of onset, almost half of these adolescents would be engaging in behavior that would further delay their academic growth.

Findings related to the trauma symptomatology are also relevant for cognitive development. For example, dissociation can be thought of as cognitive/memory distortion, and posttraumatic difficulties with concentration and intrusions should impact cognitive functioning. On the other hand, PTSD symptomatology also can involve emotional irritability, social withdrawal, and depressed affect. Although we have chosen to discuss trauma symptom findings in connection with cognition, they also have implications for other areas of adolescent development.

Kiser, Heston, Millsap and Pruitt (1991) found that approximately half of a clinical population of physically and/or sexually abused children and adolescents demonstrated PTSD symptoms, whereas victims who did not show a PTSD reaction pattern were more likely to exhibit anxiety, depression, externalizing behaviors and greater overall problems. Interestingly, the PTSD reaction pattern was found to be associated with more severe physical abuse, more perpetrators per victim of sexual abuse, and longer duration of sexual abuse. Of victims who had been both physically and sexually abused, 70.8% showed the PTSD reaction pattern; of those physically abused for longer than five years, 90% showed the PTSD reaction pattern; and 66% of severely sexually abused children and adolescents evidenced the PTSD reaction pattern.

Maltreatment has also been linked to dissociative symptomatology (Putnam, 1990). Dissociation has been defined in the Diagnostic and Statistical Manual of Mental Disorders–4th edition (DSM-IV) as a "disruption in the usually integrated functions of consciousness, memory, identity, or perception of the environment" (American Psychiatric Association, 1994, p. 477). Sanders and Giolas (1991) interviewed adolescent inpatients aged 13-17, administered Putnam's Dissociative Experiences Scale, and reviewed hospital records of abuse. They found dissociation scores correlated positively and significantly with self-reported physical, sexual, and psychological maltreatreatment, neglect, and a negative home atmosphere. Based on these and previous findings (Sanders, McRoberts, & Tollerson, 1989) showing a link between childhood stress and later dissociation in college students, the authors argue that dissociation may be a more common reaction to extremely negative experiences than might be assumed.

Symptom abatement is also an important issue in understanding trauma symptomatology associated with abuse. Kendall-Tackett et al. (1993; also see Gomes-Schwartz, Horowitz, Cardarelli, & Sauzier, 1990) reviewed several short-term (12-18 months) follow-up studies of sexual abuse victims of different ages. They noted that distress symptoms in particular tended to be lower at follow-up for about half of the victims, but that 10-24% of the victims showed more severe symptoms, including children without initial symptomatology. In the Gomes-Schwartz et al. (1990) study, signs of anxiety that are also symptomatic of PTSD, such as sleep disturbance and fear of the traumatic stimulus (i.e., offender), seemed most likely to abate, while signs of aggressiveness appeared to remain or get worse. While age, gender, and socioeconomic status (SES) were not found to predict recovery, children and preteens with the most severe initial symptoms tended to show the greatest gains. However, Kendall-Tackett et al. (1993) are quick to point out that the meaning of symptom abatement is not clear, in that it does not necessarily indicate trauma resolution. With development, symptoms could take a different form, they could be masked, or the youth could compensate.

The findings seem particularly relevant for adolescents who have experienced abuse since childhood. There may be substantial variability in the form or intensity of symptomatology adolescents experience related to earlier-onset abuse. If symptomatology does abate during nonabusive periods, the most noticeable impact of maltreatment on cognitive functioning or in other domains may be reduced, but longstanding effects may emerge at other times. Nonetheless, it appears likely that abuse interferes with the accomplishment of adolescent cognitive tasks. This may occur through the disruption of cognition created by trauma symptoms, and/or through the interaction of emotional distress with cognition that leaves the adolescent with fewer alternatives in reacting to stressful circumstances.

Development of Identity

As noted by Elkind (1970), expected adolescent cognitive developments leading to the imaginary audience and personal fable of uniqueness interact with social and emotional growth to create for the adolescent a keen, lonely, and often uncomfortable focus on self. If the adolescent has experienced physical, sexual, or psychological abuse, this self-reflection should be even more painful. Research supports a linkage between abuse and painful contemplation of self. Kendall-Tackett et al. (1993) report that 53% of adolescent sexual abuse victims engage in substance abuse as a self-destructive behavior, 71% carry out self-injurious behaviors, 46% are depressed, 33% have poor self-concept, and 41% have made suicide attempts. For physical abuse, there also appears to be a link with depression, substance abuse and self-injurious behaviors, but the link to suicide was less certain using concurrent rather than retrospective data (Malinowsky-Rummell & Hansen, 1993). Other evidence suggests that the co-occurrence of both physical and sexual abuse made suicidal behavior more likely than the single occurrence of either type of abuse (Carmen, Rieker, & Mills, 1984; Mills, Rieker, & Carmen, 1984). One implication of these findings is that abuse is linked with a sense of pain, worthlessness, and hopelessness regarding the self.

The theme of negative self-focus is echoed in other research concerning adolescent identity development and abuse. Using projective techniques (i.e., Thematic Apperception Test–TAT), Stoval and Craig (1990) studied the mental representations of 8-12 year-old girls who had been physically or sexually abused; co-occurrence was not investigated. Both abuse groups had significantly more negative self-representations than a distressed but nonabused group, with imagery of internally damaged objects being more common in the two abuse groups. Also utilizing projective techniques (Rorschach), Zwiney and Nash (1988) assessed girls 11-13 years who had been sexually abused prior to or after age nine to examine differences between early and late onset of abuse. The early onset girls showed greater distortion in cognition, primitive body concerns, damaged self-image, anxiety and helplessness, and depression than the later onset girls. The early and later onset girls did not differ in rate of abuse, number of perpetrators or type of sexual encounters, but early onset victims were more likely to have fathers or stepfathers as perpetrators and to experience longer duration of abuse (42 months versus about 13 months on average). Calverley and Fischer (1993) assessed the self-representations of briefly hospitalized 12-17 year-old girls who had been sexually abused compared with similar girls who were depressed with no known abuse history. Both groups contained some girls who had been physically abused, but these instances of co-occurrence were not considered separately. In the sexually abused group they observed more core negative self-attributions, more good-bad splitting of the self depending on the target of the relationship described, and greater contradiction in true self-descriptions.

Multiple victimization has also been shown to distort the types of expectations adolescents have about their life and place in the world. Ney, Fung, and Wickett (1994) identified the "worst combinations of child abuse and neglect" in terms of their impact on children's and adolescents' perceptions and expectations of their present and future life. Children and adolescents who experienced a combination of physical neglect, physical abuse and verbal abuse were more likely to endorse negatively the following items: lack of enjoyment of living, lack of life purpose, expectation of poor (i.e., unfortunate) future for oneself, poor chance of a happy marriage, poor chance of having children, and poor chance of being a good parent. Those who were more severely abused expected to die violently, and those with extensive maltreatment overall expected a shortened life.

Both physical and sexual victimization appear likely to create special problems for adolescents in establishing a more complex and integrated identity that includes the belief in a valuable and acceptable self. Instead, the abused adolescent may be left with a great deal of pain upon self-reflection and a fragmented, damaged, and negative sense of self. Unfortunately, it is the adolescent's damaged self that influences subsequent decisions such as those concerned with self-injury, substance abuse or suicide, and the damaged self, if left untreated, accompanies the adolescent into adulthood.

Meeting Social and Cultural Expectations for Behavior and Affect Regulation

While adolescents are expected to "sow some wild oats" in their search for identity and attempts to renegotiate independence-dependence issues, as they grow older they are increasingly expected to be able to abide by family, social, and cultural norms in terms of how they express and regulate affect and behavior. This task appears to be more difficult for abused adolescents. Kendall-Tackett et al. (1993) report that 27% of sexually abused adolescents in studies they reviewed committed illegal acts, 45% tried to run away, 38% were sexually promiscuous, and 8% were seen as delinquent. Malinowsky-Rummell and Hansen (1993) note substantial links between physical abuse and aggressive behaviors, including peer and dating violence, but that evidence for a relationship between nonviolent crimes and physical abuse is mixed. The review of follow-up studies by Lewis, Mallouh, and Webb (1989) suggested that about 20% of maltreated children fall into the delinquent category, whereas the base rate in the population is about 5%. Working with a sample of high-risk adolescents, where some had been abused and some had not, Garbarino, Schellenbach, Sebes, and associates (1986) reported higher rates of problem behaviors overall, but that internalizing and particularly externalizing problem behaviors were elevated significantly among maltreated adolescents. In addition, retrospective studies of individuals who are violent as adults, either within or outside the family or intimate relationships, suggest that physical maltreatment is represented disproportionately in their backgrounds. Evidence seems strong to suggest that adolescent maltreatment may accompany concurrent or later suicide and depression, in addition to deviant, aggressive, and illegal acts that reflect the undercontrol of behavior and emotion and/or disregard of societal standards.

Greater Independence from Family and Engagement with Peers

A major task for adolescents and their families is the renegotiation of dependence-independence issues. Adolescents need to establish a greater sense of self-sufficiency and independence from parents and become engaged with peers. Elkind (1970) points out that this transition is useful in decreasing the egocentrism of the personal fable of uniqueness because feelings and beliefs are shared among peers and the adolescent discovers that they are not alone in experiencing life somewhat differently from their parents.

The renegotiation of independence-dependence appears to play a substantial role in adolescent-onset physical abuse. Pelcovitz, Kaplan, Samit, Krieger, and Cornelius (1984) analyzed family dynamics for 22 adolescent maltreatment families. Families where abuse began in adolescence were characterized as either authoritarian, wherein adolescent limit testing was met with strong physical force, or overindulgent, where the adolescent had been a source of emotional support for parents and the adolescent's limit testing and increasing orientation away from the family were met with physical force. These adolescent-onset families were different from childhood-onset families in being less chaotic, with fewer problems, and had a lower incidence of parents who were themselves abused in childhood (Garbarino & Gilliam, 1980; Pelcovitz et al., 1984). As noted above, the adolescent's sense of distress when trying to move toward a position of greater independence may be reflected in lower self-esteem and suicidal behaviors, and/or in acting out behaviors such as delinquency. In either case, maltreatment may interfere with the establishment of independence and formation of healthy peer relationships. It could push the adolescent toward peer engagement and a rejection of parental ties or perhaps contribute to withdrawal from both the family and peer interaction.

There is a general finding that sexually and physically maltreated adolescents tend to show poorer social competencies than those who are not maltreated, although the evidence is mixed (Kendall-Tackett et al., 1993; Malinowsky-Rummell & Hansen, 1993). Physical maltreatment seems more likely to be associated with aggressive social interactions and relationships, and sexual maltreatment with sexualized behaviors. These behavior patterns might decrease the adolescent's ability to engage with peers and practice a maturing balance of dependence, independence, and nonviolence in relationships. Issues of peer relationships interact strongly with a teen's need to adjust to the changes of puberty and the prospect of sexual intimacy.

Adjusting to Puberty and the Possibility of Sexual Intimacy

Issues surrounding the meaning and establishment of sexually intimate relationships appear to be affected by physical abuse in terms of the tendency to carry out these relationships in the role of perpetrator, or victim or both, and to be influenced by sexual abuse in terms of sexually precocious and overly sexualized relationship behaviors (Kendall-Tackett et al., 1993; Malinowsky-Rummell & Hansen, 1993). These patterns might interfere with the establishment of simple peer friendship intimacy based on shared feelings, beliefs, and activities. Adolescents who show violence in dating relationships have higher rates of physical abuse than would be expected based on population incidence rates (Roscoe & Callahan, 1985), and high school students who report dating violence report higher rates of physical maltreatment than students not involved in date violence (Reuterman & Burcky, 1989). Victims of physical abuse also show a higher incidence of adolescent and adult criminality, including crimes of sexual violence such as rape (Widom, 1989; Yoshikawa, 1994).

Sexual abuse has implications for the unfolding of adolescent sexuality. Relatively less is known about male victims of sexual abuse (Kaplan & Becker, 1992), who are thought to represent between 3-30% of child sexual abuse victims (Peters, Wyatt, & Finkelhor, 1986). While some authors have felt that the impact of sexual abuse for males may be similar to that for females (Groth & Burgess, 1980), others have argued that some issues may be different for male victims since males are socialized to be aggressive rather than passive (Briere, 1989). Male victims are thought to struggle with two major issues: confusion about sexual identity; and feelings of powerlessness that can be acted out later in sexual aggression (Porter, 1986). Concerns about sexual identity and homosexuality are expected to become more intense during adolescence for male victims (Schetky, 1988).

Far more has been written about female victims. For example, inappropriate sexual behavior including teenage prostitution and early pregnancy are commonly reported outcomes of childhood and adolescent sexual abuse (Trickett & Putnam, 1993). The stress of early sexual abuse and/or exposure to male pheromones (e.g., as demonstrated in animal studies, Vandenbergh, Whisett, & Lombardi, 1975) is thought to be a potential factor in creating earlier sexual maturation among abused girls, but the reverse direction of causality, where earlier sexual maturation makes abuse more likely, is equally probable (Trickett & Putnam, 1993). Surbey (1990) found stressful family conditions to be associated with earlier menarche, and Belsky, Steinberg and Draper (1990) report a connection between stress and early maturation. Thus, in addition to feelings of powerlessness and incompetence associated with sexual victimization, there may be biological mechanisms triggered by abuse that make normal development of appropriate sexual behavior more difficult for female abuse victims.

CO-INCIDENCE OF ABUSE IN ADOLESCENCE

Claussen and Crittenden (1991) conducted a study of the co-occurrence of multiple types of victimization for late school-age and adolescent victims (10-17 years) whose families had been brought to the attention of social services. They assessed severity of maltreatment in five categories using a child-outcome based methodology plus parental behaviors and caseworkers' ratings: physical abuse; emotional abuse; and cognitive, social/emotional, and physical neglect. Severity of maltreatment correlated significantly for physical and emotional abuse, emotional abuse and all types of neglect, and among all types of neglect, but not for physical abuse with types of neglect. Mother- and self-reported behavior problems related primarily to severity of emotional abuse, but many types of child problems were interrelated including conduct disorder, attentional problems, anxiety/withdrawal, psychotic behavior, and motor excess, but not socialized aggression. Depression correlated positively with physical abuse but not other forms of maltreatment. Using caseworkers' reports, abuse severity and child behavior problems correlated positively in the following ways: physical neglect and socialized aggression; social/emotional neglect with anxiety/withdrawal and psychotic behavior; cognitive neglect with anxiety/withdrawal; emotional abuse with conduct disorder, attentional problems, anxiety/withdrawal, and psychotic behavior; and, physical abuse with anxiety/withdrawal and motor excess. It is of interest that physical neglect demonstrated fewer relationships with problems than would be expected based on research of younger children (e.g., Erickson, Egland, & Pianta, 1989), but that emotional maltreatment consistently related to problem behaviors. It may be that adolescents are more self-sufficient with regard to physical needs, such that their neglect is less critical. Similarly, adolescents may be especially reactive to the assaults on self and identity reflected in emotional abuse, since identity consolidation represents an especially important developmental task during that period.

Another potential avenue for examining the effects of multiply abusive experiences for adolescents is through the literature on children who have experienced both personal abuse and the psychological maltreatment (terrorizing, Hart & Brassard, 1990) of being exposed to interparental violence (cf. Hughes, 1988; Hughes, Parkinson, & Vargo, 1989; Sternberg, Lamb, Greenbaum, Cicchetti, Dawud, Cortes, Krispin, & Lorey, 1993). Given Claussen and Crittenden's (1991) work and research on resiliency (e.g., Rutter, 1983; Sameroff & Seifer, 1983; Walker, Downey, & Bergman, 1989), one would expect more than one type of victimization or stressor would be associated with more severe dysfunction. Hughes (1988) worked with children 3-12 years who were residing in a battered women's shelter, and found that physically abused child witnesses to parental violence were rated by mothers as having greater externalizing problems than either nonabused witnesses or a comparison group. Anxiety scores were higher and self-esteem scores lower for abused witnesses than comparison children, but not different from nonabused witnesses. Hughes et al. (1989), studying the same groups, reported the internalizing and externalizing behavior problems of abused witnesses to be significantly elevated relative to a nonmaltreated comparison sample, with scores of nonabused witnesses falling in between. Total behavior problem scores showed all groups to be significantly different. This pattern of findings held for different age groups including the 9-12 year-olds. Sternberg et al. (1993) conducted assessments of 8-12 year-old children living with their families who had been physically abused, exposed to parental violence, both physically abused and exposed, and neither abused nor exposed to parental violence. For maternally-reported behavior problems, both witness groups were rated as showing more externalizing behavior problems than either nonwitness group; girls were seen as having greater problems than boys in all but the comparison group. When looking at children's self-report, all maltreatment groups reported higher depression than the comparison group, and physically abused witnesses and nonwitnesses reported greater internalizing and externalizing behavior problems than comparison children, with nonabused witnesses falling in between. Though findings of the few co-incidence studies are somewhat mixed depending on informant and information assessed, there is support for the expectation of an association between multiple victimization and greater distress or dysfunction. It should be pointed out that studies reviewed for singular types of adolescent maltreatment probably speak to the issue of multiple victimization as well. It is difficult to imagine an instance of sexual or physical abuse or neglect that does not also involve some form of psychological maltreatment. However, there is a clear need for further investigation of the multiple victimization of adolescents, which includes retrospective measures of all types of abuse and neglect and prospective follow-up studies.

MULTIPLE VICTIMIZATION AND VIOLENT CRIME: THE EXAMPLE OF PARRICIDE

Within the last ten to fifteen years, the literature on delinquency has noted a relationship between child abuse and neglect in the family histories of juvenile offenders and the commission of crime, particularly violent crime. Most of the research studies have used retrospective methodology to identify the magnitude of association between childhood maltreatment and subsequent violent behavior (e.g., Fagan & Wexler, 1987; Hartstone & Hansen, 1984; Lewis, Shanok, Grant, & Ritvo, 1984; Lewis, Shanok, Pincus, & Glaser, 1979; McCord, 1983). For example, in Lewis et al. (1979), 75% of violent, incarcerated male delinquents and 33% of less violent incarcerated male delinquents experienced severe child abuse in the families. Other studies also confirm that relatively high percentages of delinquent youth experienced some form of maltreatment in their childhood (see Lewis, Mallouh, & Webb, 1989). Although rare, there are prospective longitudinal studies that provide estimates of abused and neglected children who later became involved with the juvenile authorities. For example, Alfaro (1978, 1981) conducted a longitudinal study of 3637 children with maltreatment histories from eight New York counties where 19% of the children were later known to the juvenile justice system for delinquent or status offender behavior (i.e., ungovernable). For abused boys, 8% to 32% were later adjudicated delinquent, while figures for abused girls ranged from 2% to 24%. In addition, Widom (1992) followed 908 cases of substantiated childhood abuse or neglect and a comparison group of 667 demographically similar children not recorded as abused or neglected for 15 to 20 years. Being abused or neglected as a child increased the probability of arrest as a juvenile by 53%, as an adult by 38%, and for violent crime by 38%.

Clearly, a history of maltreatment is not the sole factor in determining whether children grow into violent offenders. Although research has begun to differentiate children who are more resilient in the face of adversity from those who grow up under similar circumstances but do evidence later mental health problems (e.g., see Roff, Masten, Cicchetti, Nuechterlein, & Weintraub, 1990; Werner & Smith, 1992), there are no research studies identifying factors that distinguish maltreated children who become subsequent violent offenders from maltreated children who do not. Lewis et al. (1989) speculate that certain kinds of abuse might contribute to later violence, or additional factors could interact with abuse, that develop into aggressive behavior.

Clinical accounts suggest that exposure to multiple, chronic, and severe forms of victimization without adequate formal or informal intervention might play an integral role in the development of violent criminal behavior, particularly for male children and adolescents. Recent research is beginning to classify different forms of maltreatment and the long-term effects of such multiple victimization on offenders. For example, Ford and Linney (1995) found that in contrast to violent nonsexual offenders and status offenders, juvenile child molesters reported significantly more intrafamily violence and experienced higher rates of physical and sexual abuse. Earliest memories were characterized by victimization themes from abuse and engagement in destructive activities such as destroying property to self-injurious behavior and animal cruelty. All offender groups had deficits in ability to express their needs interpersonally and to engage in critical self-examination.

Parricide. Recent media attention has focused on another population of youth who have also been brutally victimized by their parents. However, these youth turned their fear and rage against perpetrators of abuse rather than strangers, intimates, or the community at large. The Menendez brothers' case provides an example. They were arrested, tried, and convicted for killing their parents. Parricide, the killing of one's parent, is considered one of the rarest forms of intrafamily homicide, with the exception of the category brothers killing sisters. Since 1976, there have been more than

300 parricides each year, and this figure has not been adjusted for unsolved murders. For example, out of 21,500 homicides committed in 1989, 344 were parricides; 194 were patricides and 150 matricides. About 90% of all cases were committed by sons, with the most frequent scenario being sons killing fathers and the rarest being daughters killing mothers (Mones, 1991).

Systematic research on this particular population of youth is relatively scarce. However, there is some literature including descriptive studies, legal cases, clinical accounts and social histories that provide narrative information about these youth, which can later be used to generate hypotheses and further statistical analysis. For example, after reviewing the literature and working on such legal cases in a university forensic clinic, Post (1982) described several factors that contribute to parricide. The typical youth who commits parricide has included a history of repeated, severe maltreatment including multiple forms of abuse and/or neglect since childhood, and had been threatened with a gun or had watched other family members be threatened. Abuse had frequently intensified during the adolescent years, partly as a result of parents feeling their control threatened by youths' increased autonomy. Adolescents tended to become more intolerable of abuse as they moved into puberty, while parents became even more provocative. Rapid changes of emotion, greater need for physical privacy and heightened concern for physical integrity all contributed to the youth's explosive potential. Contrary to children and youth who expressed their rage outside the family, youth who committed parricide tended not to have a delinquent, aggressive, or impulsive behavioral history. Drugs and alcohol were rarely implicated. Emotions were usually suppressed at home, where parents, particularly abusive fathers, didn't tolerate expression of anger, sadness, or other forms of distress. Weapons were readily accessible in the home and youth tended to be desensitized to guns, whether as a result of previous threats with guns and/or youth being taught by a parent how to use guns to hunt or "protect themselves." Family members frequently denied the potential lethality of the family situation, which placed greater responsibility on the youth to solve the problem. Community agencies, schools, and police may or may not have been aware of the family's violence, but if they were, their actions did nothing to prevent its continuation (e.g., taking a father's gun collection away for a short period of time but then returning it; returning a youth to live with the violent father after a placement is completed; investigating alleged abuse by interviewing the youth in the presence of his parents).

Usually within the six months preceding the parricide, there were identifiable events (e.g., parent's increased brutality, sham executions, specific threats to kill with means to do so) that were discrepant from the typical pattern of threat and abuse that may have heightened the youth's expectation of danger. The internal pressure of complex and confusing emotions coupled with new information about the unpredictability and viciousness of the parent's behavior could exceed the youth's coping abilities and resources. Youth in these circumstances had constricted problem solving abilities and were unable to perceive alternative actions to killing the perpetrator. Many families where parricide has occurred were socially isolated, or friends were unaware of the extent or existence of ongoing violence.

The following case example of Keith C. illustrates the complexity of psychological issues that an adolescent faces when struggling with the effects of multiple victimization without protective factors or adequate intervention. His case is fairly typical of adolescents who commit these crimes and differs from delinquent youth who offend outside of the family. The co-author of this article (M. Rosenberg) was one of the mental health professionals who testified in court about Keith's psychological background and the issues that led up to his father's murder. The names and defining characteristics of the case have been changed but the central events are accurate as corroborated by relevant documents (i.e., social service file, academic and mental health records, psychological and vocational evaluations), police reports, and independent interviews with the adolescent, family members, and significant others (e.g., childhood friends, teachers).

Case example of Keith C. Keith C. was arrested for the murder of his father when he was 16 years old. Keith's immediate family consisted of his mother, a sister, two younger brothers and his father (Mr. C). Both parents had serious alcohol problems and his mother eventually separated from his father when Keith was 9 years old. The family was known to protective services since Keith was young, with reports of marital violence and physical abuse towards Keith documented in the file. At various times, the police confiscated Mr. C's rather extensive gun arsenal after he used them to threaten family members and neighbors, but ultimately returned the guns to him. After his parents separated, Keith and the younger children lived with their mother and visited their father on weekends, but eventually Keith lived with his father while the others stayed with their mother. During the weekend visits, Keith's father sexually molested him, and this behavior persisted until Keith was approximately 14 years old. Brutal physical abuse alternated with sexual abuse, and Keith's father made increasingly serious threats to kill with loaded guns (psychological maltreatment in the form of terrorizing behavior). Mr. C involved his son in behavior that endangered his life such as driving the car drunk at high speeds or forcing Keith to drive when he was very young. Other forms of psychological maltreatment included Mr. C isolating his son from developing normal social relationships with peers and monitoring Keith's every move to and from school. Keith experienced rejection and degradation when he was singled out as his father's scapegoat and made to feel inferior as his father blatantly preferred the other children over Keith. Keith was exposed to both corrupting and exploitive behavior by Mr. C's chronic alcoholism, sexual abuse, and formidable demands for his son to act as his caretaker (e.g., made Keith skip school to run errands for him such as buy him cigarettes and other grocery items).

Academically, Keith's skills were compromised: he had difficulty concentrating on school work, performed significantly lower than expected given his intellectual ability, and frequently "spaced out" (i.e., dissociated) in class and missed critical material. He complained of intrusive images of sexual and physical abuse, and there were times when the teacher found him crying in class for "no apparent reason." Some teachers labeled Keith's inattentiveness as "laziness" and he was disciplined for his failure to participate in class. One teacher referred him for therapy, but his father demanded that he keep the sexual abuse a secret and was allowed only to talk about his father's drinking problem. Mr. C threatened to kidnap and kill his siblings if Keith revealed anything about the sexual or physical abuse in the home.

Keith's interpersonal relationships and sense of self-worth and identity suffered tremendously from the years of abuse. The legacy of child maltreatment on Keith's social relationships was his fear of trusting others, expectation of being mistreated by others, and limited knowledge about normal interactions where conflict and intimacy demand assertive communication. It was not surprising that Keith had trouble articulating a coherent identity and was confused about his sexual identity. Rather than given the opportunity to grow up and separate from his father, he was taken hostage psychologically by his father, which made it far more difficult for him to develop an independent sense of self.

As Mr. C's violence, alcohol abuse, and threats to kill his son increased during the months prior to the homicide, Keith's cognitive abilities were overloaded with fear, anxiety, and emotional pain so that he was unable to think flexibly. His capacity to problem solve, use community supports, or think others could be helpful was seriously immobilized. From Keith's perspective, the police and protective services were called multiple times and did nothing to protect him from the likelihood of his own death. When his father told Keith that he would kill him by a certain date, Keith decided to act on his own behalf and the tragedy of his father's death unfolded.

Adolescents such as Keith, who experience chronic, severe, and multiple forms of victimization but who do not commit delinquent acts outside the family may be ignored until it is too late. Terrorizing behaviors such as those listed in the previous example include both situations where children and youth are forced to watch terrifying acts and are forced to participate or somehow experience a terrifying situation directly. The latter component extends Hart and Brassard's (1990) definition of terrorizing forms of psychological maltreatment. What is striking about this particular case and not uncommon to others, is that child protective services and the police were involved at various times, but were unable to intervene effectively to change the course of events. Keith also saw a psychotherapist, but the terrorizing hold Mr. C had over him coupled with Keith's mistrust of interpersonal relationships interfered with the therapy. In many cases such as Keith's, the power of the parent (e.g., threats to kill, demonstration of frightening strength or violence against other people or animals) is frequently underestimated and not well delineated. Consequently, it is not addressed adequately in research or clinical practice and deserves greater attention. Terrorizing behavior and its psychological effects are important to consider in working with adolescents, since the physical abuse may subside at this stage but the psychological maltreatment may increase so that the parent(s) can maintain control and dominance over the youth and family.

CONCLUSION

While issues of adolescent multiple victimization have been inadequately addressed in the literature, existing evidence suggests that physical and sexual maltreatment have sequelae that reflect interference with, or distortion of, adolescent development in the domains of cognition, self and identity, behavior and affect regulation, and interpersonal relationships and sexuality. Research on psychological maltreatment is still in its early stages and rarely emerges in the adolescent victimization literature. Identification of different forms of maltreatment (including psychological abuse and emotional neglect), singly and in combination, and their link to psychological outcome is beginning to be incorporated into research, and can offer a richer and more complex understanding of adolescents' victimization experiences.

Based on available literature, there appears to be an overlap in the types of symptom patterns associated with physical and sexual abuse, but there is also diversity in symptom picture between and within types of abuse. Given this diversity, it seems unlikely that a unique and mutually exclusive pattern of dysfunction will be identified for specific combinations of maltreatment. Kendall-Tackett et al. (1993) echo this view regarding sexual abuse. There appears to be a tendency for sexually inappropriate behaviors and sexual problems to be more common among sexual abuse victims, but interpersonal aggression and violence can occur with both physical and sexual maltreatment. The probability for adolescents to engage in violent behavior, including murder and parricide, seems linked more frequently, but not exclusively, to the occurrence of brutal physical maltreatment, terrorizing, and other forms of psychological maltreatment that are sometimes accompanied by sexual abuse. Clearly, multiple forms of victimization are part of the picture and need further attention in research and clinical practice. By identifying the domains and pathways by which multiple victimization has affected adolescent development, we can further our understanding of the types of interventions that might help this population. In addition, incorporating information about risk and protective factors is crucial to discover why certain maltreated adolescents commit intrafamilial and extrafamilial acts, while others may evidence different types of problems, and still others are able to transform their victimization experiences and adequately meet the challenges of adult life.

REFERENCES

American Psychiatric Association. (1994). *Diagnostic and statistical manual of mental disorders* (4th ed.). Washington, DC: Author.

Belsky, J., Steinberg, L., & Draper, P. (1990). *Childhood experience, interpersonal development, and reproductive strategy: An evolutionary theory of socialization.* Unpublished manuscript, Pennsylvania State University, University Park.

Berk, L.E. (1993). *Infants, children, and adolescents.* Boston, MA: Allyn and Bacon.

Briere, J. (1989). *Therapy for adults molested as children.* New York: Springer.

Calverley, R.M., & Fischer, K.W. (1993). *The development of negative core self-representations in maltreated children and adolescents.* Paper presented at the meeting of the Society for Research in Child Development, New Orleans, LA.

Carmen, E.H., Rieker, P.P., & Mills, T. (1984). Victims of violence and psychiatric illness. *American Journal of Psychiatry, 141,* 378-383.

Claussen, A.E., & Crittenden, P.M. (1991). Physical and psychological maltreatment: Relationship among types of maltreatment. *Child Abuse and Neglect, 15,* 5-18.

Elkind, D. (1970). *Children and adolescents: Interpretive essays on Jean Piaget*. New York: Oxford University Press.

Erickson, M.F., Egland, B., & Pianta, R. (1989). The effects of maltreatment on the development of young children. In D. Cicchetti & V. Carlson (Eds.), *Child maltreatment: Theory and research on the causes and consequences of child abuse and neglect* (pp. 685-706). New York: Cambridge University Press.

Fagan, J., & Wexler, S. (1987). Family origins of violent delinquents. *Criminology, 25*, 643-669.

Fish-Murray, C.C. (1993). Childhood trauma and subsequent suicidal behavior. In A.A. Leenaars (Ed.), *Suicidology: Essays in honor of Edwin Shneidman* (pp. 73-92). Northvale, NJ: Jason Aronson, Inc.

Fish-Murray, C.C., Koby, E.V., & van der Kolk, B.A. (1987). Evolving ideas: The effect of abuse on children's thought. In B.A. van der Kolk (Ed.), *Psychological trauma* (pp. 89-110). Washington, DC: American Psychiatric Association.

Ford, M.E., & Linney, J.A. (1995). Comparative analysis of juvenile sexual offenders, violent nonsexual offenders and status offenders. *Journal of Interpersonal Violence, 10*, 56-70.

Fox, L., Long, S.H., & Langlois, A. (1988). Patterns of language comprehension deficit in abused and neglected children. *Journal of Speech and Hearing Disorders, 53*, 239–244.

Garbarino, J. (1989). Troubled youth, troubled families: the dynamics of adolescent maltreatment. In D. Cicchetti & V. Carson (Eds.), *Child maltreatment: Theory and research on the causes and consequences of child abuse and neglect* (pp. 685-706). New York: Cambridge University Press.

Garbarino, J., & Gilliam, G. (1980). *Understanding abusive families*. Lexington, MA: Lexington Books.

Garbarino, J., Schellenbach, C., Sebes, J., and Associates. (1986). *Troubled youth, troubled families*. New York: Aldine Publishing Co.

Gomes-Schwartz, B., Horowitz, J.M., Cardarelli, A.P., & Sauzier, M. (1990). The aftermath of child sexual abuse: 18 months later. In B. Gomes-Schwartz, J.M. Horowitz, & A.P. Cardarelli (Eds.), *Child sexual abuse: The initial effects* (pp. 132-152). Newbury Park, CA: Sage.

Groth, N., & Burgess, A. (1980). Male rape: Offenders and victims. *American Journal of Psychiatry, 137*, 806-810.

Hart, S.N., & Brassard, M.R. (1990). Psychological maltreatment of children. In R.T. Ammerman & M. Hersen (Eds.), *Treatment of family violence: A sourcebook* (pp. 77-112). New York: John Wiley & Sons.

Hartstone, E., & Hansen, K. (1984). The violent juvenile offender: An empirical portrait. In R. Mathias, P. DeMuro, & R.S. Allison (Eds.), *Violent juvenile offender: An anthology* (pp. 82-112). San Francisco, CA: National Council on Crime and Delinquency.

Hoffman-Plotkin, D., & Twentyman, C. (1984). A multimodal assessment of behavioral and cognitive deficits in abused and neglected preschoolers. *Child Development, 55*, 794-802.

Hughes, H.M. (1988). Psychological and behavioral correlates of family violence in child witnesses and victims. *American Journal of Orthopsychiatry, 58,* 77-90.

Hughes, H.M., Parkinson, D., & Vargo, M. (1989). Witnessing spouse abuse and experiencing physical abuse: A "double whammy?" *Journal of Family Violence, 4,* 197-209.

Kaplan, M.S., & Becker, J.V. (1992). Adolescent perpetrators of incest. In R.T. Ammerman & M. Hersen (Eds.), *Assessment of family violence: A clinical and legal sourcebook* (pp. 332-347). New York: Wiley.

Kendall-Tackett, K.A., Williams, L.M., & Finkelhor, D. (1993). Impact of sexual abuse on children: A review and synthesis of recent empirical studies. *Psychological Bulletin, 113,* 164-180.

Kiser, L.J., Heston, J., Millsap, P.A., & Pruitt, D.B. (1991). Physical and sexual abuse in childhood: Relationship with post-traumatic stress disorder. *Journal of the American Academy of Child and Adolescent Psychiatry, 30,* 776-782.

Lewis, D.O., Mallouh, C., & Webb, V. (1989). Child abuse, delinquency, and violent criminality. In D. Cicchetti & V. Carson (Eds.), *Child maltreatment: Theory and research on the causes and consequences of child abuse and neglect* (pp. 707-721). New York: Cambridge University Press.

Lewis, D.O., Shanok, S., Grant, M., & Ritvo, E. (1984). Homicidally aggressive young children: Neuropsychiatric and experimental correlates. In R. Mathias, P. DeMuro, & R.S. Allison (Eds.), *Violent juvenile offender: An anthology* (pp. 71-82). San Francisco, CA: National Council on Crime and Delinquency.

Lewis, D.O., Shanok, S., Pincus, J., & Glaser, G. (1979). Violent juvenile delinquents: Psychiatric, neurological, and abuse factors. *Journal of the American Academy of Child Psychology, 18,* 307-319.

Malinosky-Rummell, R.I. & Hansen, D.J. (1993). Long-term consequences of childhood physical abuse. *Psychological Bulletin, 114,* 68-79.

McCord, J. (1983). A forty-year perspective on effects of child abuse and neglect. *Child Abuse and Neglect, 7,* 265-270.

Mills, T., Rieker, P.P., & Carmen, E.H. (1984). Hospitalization experiences of victims of abuse. *Victimology: An International Journal, 9,* 439-449.

Mones, P.A. (1991). *When a child kills: Abused children who kill their parents.* New York: Pocket Books.

National Center on Child Abuse and Neglect. (1990). *National child abuse and neglect data tables: 1990.* Washington, DC: National Center on Child Abuse and Neglect.

Ney, P., Fung, T., & Wickett, A. (1994). The worst combinations of child abuse and neglect. *Child Abuse and Neglect, 18,* 705-714.

Pelcovitz, D., Kaplan, S., Samit, C., Krieger, R., & Cornelius, P. (1984). Adolescent abuse: Family structure and implications for treatment. *Journal of Child Psychiatry, 23,* 85-90.

Peplar, D.J., & Moore, T.E. (1989). *Children exposed to family violence: Home environments and cognitive functioning.* Paper presented at the meeting of the Society for Research in Child Development, Kansas City, MO.

Peters, S.D., Wyatt, G.E., & Finkelhor, D. (1986). Prevalence. In D. Finkelhor (Ed.), *A sourcebook on child sexual abuse* (pp. 15-59). Beverly Hills, CA: Sage.

Pfouts, J.H., Schopler, J.H., & Henley, H.C. (1981). Deviant behaviors of child victims and bystanders in violent families. In R.J. Hunner & Y.E. Walker (Eds.), *Exploring the relationship between child abuse and delinquency* (pp. 79-99). Montclair, NJ: Allanheld, Osmun.

Porter, E. (1986). *Treating the young male victim of sexual assault: Issues and intervention strategies.* Syracuse, NY: Safer Society Press.

Post, S. (1982). Adolescent parricide in abusive families. *Child Welfare, 61,* 445-455.

Putnam, F.W. (1990). The disturbance of "self" in victims of child sexual abuse. In R.P. Kluft (Ed.), *Incest-related syndromes of adult psychopathology* (pp. 113-132). Washington, DC: American Psychiatric Press.

Reuterman, N.A., & Burcky, W.D. (1989). Dating violence in high school: A profile of the victims. *Psychology: A Journal of Human Behavior, 26,* 1-9.

Rivera, B., & Widom, C.S. (1990). Childhood victimization and violent offending. *Violence and Victims, 5,* 19-35.

Rogeness, G.A., Amrung, S.A., Macedo, C.A., Harris, W.R., & Fisher, C. (1986). Psychopathology in abused or neglected children. *Journal of the American Academy of Child Psychiatry, 25,* 659-665.

Rolf, J., Masten, A.S., Cicchetti, D., Neuchterlein, K.H., & Weintraub, S. (1990). Psychopathology in abused or neglected children. *Journal of the American Academy of Child Psychiatry, 25,* 659-665.

Roscoe, B., & Callahan, J.E. (1985). Adolescents' self-report of violence in families and dating relations. *Adolescence, 20,* 545-553.

Rutter, M. (1983). Stress, coping, and development: Some issues and some questions. In N. Garmezy & M. Rutter (Eds.), *Stress, coping, and development in children* (pp. 1-42). New York: McGraw-Hill.

Sameroff, A.J., & Seifer, R. (1983). Familial risk and child competence. *Child Development, 54,* 1254-1268.

Sanders, B., & Giolas, M.H. (1991). Dissociation and childhood trauma in psychologically disturbed adolescents. *American Journal of Psychiatry, 148,* 50-54.

Sanders, B., McRoberts, G., & Tollefson, C. (1989). Childhood stress and dissociation in a college population. *Dissociation: Progress in the Dissociative Disorders, 2,* 17-23.

Schetky, D. (1988). The clinical evaluation of child sexual abuse. In D. Schetky & A. Green (Eds)., *Child sexual abuse* (pp. 23-47). New York: Brunner-Mazel.

Sternberg, K.J., Lamb, M.E., Greenbaum, C., Cicchetti, D., Dawud, S., Cortes, R. M., Krispin, O., & Lorey, F. (1993). Effects of domestic violence on children's behavior problems and depression. *Developmental Psychology, 29,* 44-52.

Stoval, G., & Craig, R.J. (1990). Mental representations of physically and sexually abused latency-aged females. *Child Abuse and Neglect, 14,* 233-242.

Straus, M.B. (1988). Abused adolescents. In M.B. Straus (Ed.), *Abuse and victimization across the life span* (pp. 107-123). Baltimore, MD: Johns Hopkins University Press.

Surbey, M.K. (1990). Family composition, stress, and human menarche. In F.B. Bercovitch & T.R. Zeigler (Eds.), *The socioendocrinology of primate reproduction* (pp. 11-32). New York: Alan R. Liss.

Terr, L.C. (1991). Childhood traumas: An outline and overview. *American Journal of Psychiatry, 148*, 10-20.

Trickett, P.K., & Putnam, F.W. (1993). Impact of child sexual abuse on females: Toward a developmental psychobiological integration. *Psychological Science, 4*, 81-87.

Vandenbergh, J.G., Whitsett, J.M., & Lonbardi, J.R. (1975). Partial isolation of a pheromone accelerating puberty in female mice. *Journal of Reproduction and Fertility, 43*, 515-523.

Walker, E., Downey, G., & Bergman, A. (1989). The effects of parental psychopathology and maltreatment on child behavior: A test of the diathesis-stress model. *Child Development, 60*, 15-24.

Werner, E.E., & Smith, R.S. (1992). *Overcoming the odds: High risk children from birth to adulthood.* Ithaca, NY: Cornell University Press.

Widom, C.S. (1989). Child abuse, neglect, and adult behavior: Research design and findings on criminality, violence, and child abuse. *American Journal of Orthopsychiatry, 59*, 355-367.

Widom, C.S. (1992, October). The cycle of violence. *National Institute of Justice: Research in brief* (Document # NCJ 136607).

Yoshikawa, H. (1994). Prevention as cumulative protection: Effects of early family support and education on chronic delinquency and its risks. *Psychological Bulletin, 115*, 28-54.

Zwiney, D.A., & Nash, M.R. (1988). Sexual abuse in early versus late childhood: Differing patterns of pathology as revealed on the Rorschach. *Psychotherapy, 25*, 99-106.

The Effect of Multiple Victimization on Children's Cognition: Variations in Response

Caroline C. Murray
Linda Son

SUMMARY. Children's experience of multiple forms of abuse is regarded as traumatic, with the effect of trauma on attention and perception being the closest to a universal response to multiple victimization that may be discovered. Unique responses are a function of cultural and familial expectations, developmental level, and individual differences. Children's attributions of meaning and subsequent behaviors depend heavily on the interplay between experience, thought and action. Professionals working with multiply victimized children need to understand children's understandings and cognitive capacities in order to devise the most effective interventions. *[Article copies available for a fee from The Haworth Document Delivery Service: 1-800-342-9678. E-mail address: getinfo@haworth.com]*

Address correspondence to: Caroline C. Murray, EdD, 11 Lincoln Avenue, Nantucket, MA 02554.

[Haworth co-indexing entry note]: "The Effect of Multiple Victimization on Children's Cognition: Variations in Response." Murray, Caroline C., and Linda Son. Co-published simultaneously in *Journal of Aggression, Maltreatment & Trauma* (The Haworth Maltreatment & Trauma Press, an imprint of The Haworth Press, Inc.) Vol. 2, No. 1 (#3), 1998, pp. 131-146; and: *Multiple Victimization of Children: Conceptual, Developmental, Research, and Treatment Issues* (ed: B. B. Robbie Rossman, and Mindy S. Rosenberg) The Haworth Maltreatment & Trauma Press, an imprint of The Haworth Press, Inc., 1998, pp. 131-146. Single or multiple copies of this article are available for a fee from The Haworth Document Delivery Service [1-800-342-9678, 9:00 a.m. - 5:00 p.m. (EST). E-mail address: getinfo@haworth.com].

131

Research of the past twenty years suggests that children vary widely in their responses to multiple victimization. In scanning over 50 studies of children in war or refugee situations, there is little consensus on main effects. A study of Cambodian children at a refugee camp, Site 2, in Thailand demonstrated a lack of fit between the children's behaviors and the current definition of post traumatic stress disorder (PTSD) (American Psychiatric Association, 1987; Son, 1994).

Our understanding of the cognitive system, based on data from neurology and biology, provides guidelines for recognizing and accounting for these variations. Although each individual survives or dies, adapts or disintegrates because of the interaction of multiple systems, it is the cognitive system that is the most essential and economical for therapists and theorists to know and use when working with traumatized children. The cognitive system defines and controls emotions and gives meaning to each person's life. It shapes curiosity and complexity as well as limiting growth (Marler, 1991) and provides the basis for communication between therapists and children.

Multiple cognitive factors and consequent multiple reactions overdetermine symptoms, causing confusion and inaccuracies in diagnosis and mistakes in treatment. Survival and adaptation following continued victimization involve three kinds of responses: universal responses determined by phylogenetic brain development; unique responses of the individual's evolution in his/her family and cultural group; and the peculiarly individual responses of each person. In this article cognitive reactions to victimization both universal and unique are examined with implications for treatment.

THE COGNITIVE SYSTEM

The cognitive system includes subsystems of operations, attention, perception, memory, assimilation and accommodation, all developing in different domains at varying rates (Gardner, 1983). For instance, abused children may have difficulty in understanding themselves and others, but achieve high level functioning in domains of mathematics or science (Fish-Murray, Koby, & van der Kolk, 1987).

Cognitive theory is based on neurology and biology. Edelman's (1992) work on neuronal group selection (TNGS) explains how universal as well as unique responses bridge physiology and psychology. TNGS describes the coordination of different regions of the brain over time allowing individuals to build new and increasingly complex schemas and cognitive maps. Evolution provides the neuroanatomy constraining selection and allows each individual to adapt during his/her lifetime. Biochemical processes also effect neuronal structures over time allowing secondary repertoires to evolve from primary sets. This continuous development results in a growing complexity of categorical logic. It does not occur in a straight line or cumulative fashion, but develops like a spiral, coming back on itself over and over as it increases in complexity. This does not necessarily mean an increase in goodness or in adaptability.

Cognitive Operations

Most thinking and responding occurs routinely and unconsciously and in a lawful fashion (LeDoux, 1992). Emergency reactions are essentially reflexive as well as being unconscious. Even if one could consciously review all alternative actions in a time of crisis this would not be adaptive because too much information slows decision-making. Eventually, conscious thought does buffer and control the rate and kind of information flow, but conscious thought processes remain relatively slow, using approximate serial thinking to keep subject matter separate and clear (Mandler, 1992).

When confronted with danger and a desperate sense of urgency, one tends to fall back, unconsciously, on overlearned, long-established neuronal groupings and use immature repertoires and classification systems as a guide. These primitive groupings, given the spiral nature of development, are over used, well-practised and serve readily in an emergency (Edelman, 1992). Most adults and children who regress to primary repertoires after shocking experiences can return to their more recently achieved complex and flexible thinking. Some individuals, however, such as those with borderline personality disorder, appear to return habitually to the simpler and less adaptive levels of response (Noam, 1986). The therapist should be able to recognize the level of logic in the primitive and secondary classification systems of the traumatized person in order to shape a challenging therapy.

Cognitive operations organize data, transform action into thought and solve problems. They appear on a lawful, universal timetable associated with the myelinization of the brain (Piaget, 1969). Only the most significant will be reviewed in this article in the developmental section. They are identity, negation, seriation, reversibility, conservation, class exclusion and inclusion, and those used in propositional logic.

Attention and Perception

The child begins dealing with trauma by attending to it. The therapist reaches the child only when he/she gets the child's attention, so it is important to understand significant aspects of attending. When attending, many areas of the brain selectively receive, judge, and filter multiple inputs from a variety of stimuli for assimilation. This is the first and necessary step for categorizing, finding directionality, imitating and forming concepts. How one pays attention is an enduring part of the individual's lifestyle, governing and determining the amount of information available (Kagan, 1989). Like other cognitive functions, attention has both universal and unique aspects. Increased arousal responses in the autonomic nervous system (ANS) accompanying attention to trauma are probably the most universal aspects of the syndrome of PTSD.

Attention occurs when there is perceptual or cognitive discrepancy or a blocking of ongoing activity setting off the ANS. The combination of ANS reaction and evaluative processes produces emotions. The greater the discrepancy, the greater the activation and emotion. Increased emotional reactions narrow the attentional field, thus limiting access to important information (Mandler, 1992). Abuse usually arouses more than one emotion (loyalty to the abuser, fear, etc.). This distorts attention and perception of ongoing events, making it hard to categorize events clearly for comparison and judgment. In traumatic situations, the visual system and right hemisphere dominate in processing stimuli (Squire & Butters, 1986). Evolution has ensured that taking "a good hard look" and registering the location in the hippocampus enhances survival (Gallistel, Brown, Carey, Gellman, & Keil, 1991), making safety of place one of the first requirements of therapy.

Major individual differences in attention response are shaped by cultural and social class expectations, stage of development, sex, motivation, past experiences, habits, arousal level, states of mind, excitory and inhibitory processes and their speed of habituation (Revelle & Loftus, 1992). Children are thought to have domain preferences that prompt them to attend to preferred symbol systems (Gardner, 1983).

Perceptual conceptualization occurs through existing and ever changing neural maps and parallel processing systems (Edelman, 1992). Frightening and threatening changes in the environment can shape perception and lead a child to erroneous evaluation of events (Murray, 1933).

Memory

Of all the cognitive functions, memory is now receiving the most attention from researchers, therapists and the public. It is certainly key to understanding trauma. Memory and logic are virtually inseparable. What we remember depends on available category systems for coding and the use of age-appropriate logic that puts categories into varying relationships.

It is primarily the differences in memory processes that lead to variance in response to trauma and complicate therapists' treatment plans.

Multiple memory systems code, store and retrieve information on what has happened and is happening, making it possible to predict what will happen, thus shaping drive, will and personality. Memory, shaped by attentional and perceptual systems, is dependent on codes, such as syntactical rules which change with development (Nasby & Yando, 1980). Memory also involves many systems and circuits in the brain that reflect genetic heredity, immune responses and reflexes, as well as routine learning, and conscious and unconscious remembering. Memory, like attention and perception, has universal and individually unique aspects. What all memory systems have in common are evolution and selection which become the key to survival (Edelman, 1992). Memories are encoded primarily by the limbic system, thus ensuring that emotions are a component of memory. Stress and its emotional involvement limit encoding of events, diminishing elaboration (Heuer & Reisberg, 1992). In addition, the hippocampus and the brain stem may be damaged by repeated trauma (Edelman, 1992), thus distorting normal memory processes.

Memories of trauma represent only a narrow range of the total event (Johnson, 1991). What seem to be detailed and complete memories of abuse are really "gist" memories made by logical comparison and reconstruction of personalized memories (Heuer & Reisberg, 1992). Many studies now detail the strengths and deficiencies of children's memories (Christianson, 1992).

After experiencing trauma, forgetting is as important as remembering. Irrelevant memories can and should be ignored by victim and therapist. Irrelevancies can go unrehearsed and fortunately never be thought of again (Luria, 1968). Forgetting is not to be confused with dissociation (amnesia, depersonalization, derealization, identity confusion and alteration). LeDoux (1992, 1994) speculates that traumatic events are encoded primarily through the amygdala rather than the hippocampus, noting that the amygdala has fewer connections with the neocortex than with the hypothalamus. Thus when danger threatens, the thalamo-amygdala system probably establishes emotional memories unchecked by descending influences from the neocortex (LeDoux, 1992). This suggests two different kinds of memory and learning following aversive events: habituation and sensitization (Johnson, 1991). Extreme fears may become conditioned in the early phylogenetic brain, reappearing as repetitive memory phenomena in nightmares, flashbacks and reenactments. This unconscious freezing of trauma memories through neuronal circuitry to the more primitive brain structures would interfere with a person's ability to assign useful categories of meaning using higher cortical functions. Some traumatic memories can therefore be encoded and assimilated but not be available for accommodation by the neocortex. Unaccommodated memories can thus be more successfully treated with deconditioning than with associative techniques.

Differences in memory function have been related to both individual difference factors and states of mind. Some of the individual difference factors include: temperament (Kagan, 1989); stability of heart rate; ethnicity (Kagan, 1983); circadian rhythms (National Institute of Mental Health, 1970); handedness and domain preferences (Fish-Murray et al., 1987); and, gender (Goodman, Brown, Bottoms, & Aman, 1990). However, varying states of mind such as anxiety also determine the nature of memories. The central nervous system of anxious children is more rapidly activated, and anxious children remember threats better than nonanxious ones (Mandler, 1992). A depressed child will expect a worst-case scenario after trauma and if elated will be optimistic about escaping terror. Mood affects motivation and motivation is key to memory consolidation.

Assimilation and Accommodation

Assimilation and accommodation in equilibration keep the child on an adaptive path (Piaget, 1969). The child is constantly trying to keep the cognitive system as a whole equilibrated and autoregulated. This search for organization and the need to find the most adaptive procedures are continuous throughout life. Trauma upsets this equilibration forcing the child to regain his/her mental balance as he/she rapidly reorganizes conceptual schemes and builds corrective categories to deal with the novelty. This period of delay of response is often seen as denial or avoidance but in reality may be a necessary and healthy way of coping as the individual hastily practices and builds new repertoires for survival.

Regaining balance has salubrious effects. Children practicing skills that helped them through trauma can inoculate themselves against further disequilibration. They enjoy the excitement of mastery. Children do not like to be afraid and want to be competent. They act bravely in many terrible situations and challenge each other to cope. Fortunately they do not have the logical ability to grasp the full range of possibilities and alternatives that terrorize adults and consequently they often are not as afraid of the same things as adults.

Assimilation is the conservative process that allows the brain to fit elements presented by the environment into thought structures already in place (Piaget, 1970). Assimilation is achieved primarily by repetition and is seen in repetitive play and retelling of the trauma story. These repetitions are essential and an adaptive grounding of new experiences in already evolved category systems and they should not be seen as pathological.

Imitation is a central part of accommodating and developing adaptive schemas. This often makes traumatized children appear like chameleons. Imitation and emulation appear regularly in studies of traumatized children. Milgram (1990), for example, found that children in Israeli war zones reflected the ideological and ecological features of their communities. Their relatively high levels of anxiety were a function of the expectancy and standards set by military personnel and mental health professionals. Follow-up studies of children forty years after they were released from Hitler's concentration camps found that the children grew up as well-functioning adults in society, but this chameleon effect was an outstanding feature in their behavior (Krell, 1985; Moskovitz, 1985).

The function of accommodation is often dominant and lasting for some time in a child's behavior after disaster, especially in preschool and school-age children. A major normal fear of childhood is being socially unacceptable, being embarrassed. Add to this the fears generated by disasters and it is not surprising to find that frightened children conform to and copy whomever is in control. We should take advantage of the chameleon effect in helping children to adapt, purposively providing them with sound and consistent mentors and play situations that offer toys representing helping figures, such as ambulance drivers, doctors and nurses.

CHANGES IN COGNITION AT DIFFERENT DEVELOPMENTAL LEVELS

As children grow, they become increasingly individualistic in responses and thinking, making it difficult to find uniformity of response. However, knowing the possible and probable operations and structural organization of logic at successive developmental levels makes a good starting point in understanding and treating traumatized children.

Infants

Therapists should pay attention to the actions of victimized infants and toddlers or to those who have regressed to this stage. It is only through interaction with their world that infants are able to construct their own unique reality, their idea of self and causality (Gruber & Voneche, 1977). The key cognitive operation available to the very young is the ability to identify people, objects and goals (Gallistel et al., 1991). Contrast, such as changes in color and shape, catches the infant's attention before surprise, such as abrupt shifts in the environmental surround. Eventually motivation and intentionality guide attention (Kagan, 1984).

Infants' memories are labile and lack differentiation. Encoded memories appear as reenactments, not recall. Memories of abuse seem to be sensorimotor, encoded and remembered through proprioceptor, visual, auditory and olfactory circuits. Pain is a salient feature in ensuring memory at this stage. The hippocampus, a major processor of factual memory, is not usually fully mature until about 18 to 36 months (LeDoux, 1994). Without a fully functioning hippocampus sustained factual memories are not possible, since it is the hippocampus that processes facts, not procedures. Infants are habituating action memories such as crawling, but are not remembering facts of their infancy. Discontinuities in other cognitive functions and brain capabilities in infancy make it just about impossible to remember facts from that time of life. As White and Pillemer (1979) put it, we have universal amnesia for infancy, and consequently neither child nor therapist can expect to retrieve many facts about infant abuse.

Assimilation, such as practicing actions repetitively, begins at birth and occupies the child more than accommodating. Accommodation, using new facts to shift learned patterns of thought, does not prevail as an equilibrating force until the left hemisphere gains dominance at two years (Fox & Bell, 1992).

Since infants shape their world through actions, they react to trauma with action-like somatic symptoms such as clinging, fighting, throwing up, bowel blocks, food refusals, and periods of intense crying and disturbed sleep (Murray, 1993). The weakening of the operation of identity, resulting in confused attachment behavior, can prove difficult. The child tends to become shallow, indiscriminate and diffuse in his/her attachments (Bowlby, 1988). The child can be soothed by being held closely and patted. In working with traumatized infants and especially those regressed to the infantile level, the therapist could use controlled role playing, as well as helping the patient identify people and places that provide safety. Realigning children with familiar caretakers is essential (Bowlby, 1988). Repetitive play and story telling around dominant themes help the child assimilate experiences.

Preschool

Two key operations direct thinking about trauma in two-six year-old range: negation and seriation. Negation, or understanding opposites, starts the child on the path of dialectic thinking. Enjoying and playing with opposition, however, may lead to errors in memory if the child rehearses memories that are the opposite of what actually happened. Seriation begins as a rudimentary way of sorting events but becomes an increasingly sophisticated method for comparing and contrasting and establishing classes and their relationships (Piaget, 1969). After age two, because of this ability to appreciate opposites and gradations of experience, children can tell/show you what happened when they were traumatized; and equally important, they can tell/show you what didn't happen (Farrar & Goodman, 1990).

Toddlers are also improving their use of the operation of identity. Although they are better at identifying familiar people than strangers, their ability to identify perpetrators improves over time. Sixty-one per cent of 36 four-year olds made false identifications, but by age seven only 38% of them made false identifications (Goodman et al., 1990).

Unusual aspects of events now catch a toddler's attention (Hudson & Fivush, 1990). The child attends to discrepancies that threaten his/her own safety, possible abandonment, and interruption of his/her essential needs like feeding, comfort, or play (Goodman et al., 1990). At this age, children remember the reality of their own surroundings but don't pay much attention to or remember well when asked for details in situations that are irrelevant to their daily life (Farrar & Goodman, 1990).

Children are now not only recognizing past experiences but also retrieving prior schemata, making inferences, and being aware of possibilities for action because of increased memory storage. They are now applying old memories to new situations. Visual impressions dominate in encoding memories and establishing classes. This often leads to major errors in inference. Toddlers are remarkably good at answering general questions and resist strongly-worded suggestions associated with abuse (Goodman et al., 1990). At four they can correctly answer questions about physical safety (Farrar & Goodman, 1990). Children remember what is important to them at the time the events took place (Yuille & Tollestrup, 1992), telling their trauma stories in serial strings ("and then . . . and then . . . ") with little sense of causality or purpose. What occurs simultaneously in space and time, however, is often seen to have a causal relationship.

Rudimentary analytic thinking begins at this age as the left hemisphere gains power and as assimilation and accommodation become more equilibrated (Piaget, 1962). Problems abound, however, including literal interpretations, mistaken hypotheses, inferences, and animistic thinking. A further review of age-appropriate logic is provided by Murray (1993). Toddlers are also acquiring a wide range of classification systems which they remember visually. They have a growing facility in using language tags for more efficient memory. Their classes, however, remain rigidly separated and unchangeable, resulting in inflexible and erroneous thinking. This difficulty in understanding exclusion and inclusion of classes continues until about eight or nine.

The therapist's understanding and use of appropriate language for this age child is critical in treatment. These toddlers have trouble distinguishing the difference between "all" and "some" or "one" and "more." They will tell you that if they have been bombed at dawn, all bombing will occur only at dawn; if one man hurt them, all men will hurt them. Since they do not understand superordinate classes or abstract ideas, four-year-olds will say, "I hate you" but really mean, "I do not like what you are doing." They have trouble understanding passive sentences and clauses. Metaphors also confuse them (Fox, 1985). Like the day care provider, the therapist who works with toddlers or regressed adults should speak in short declarative sentences.

Multiple traumas leave preschool children regressed to earlier levels of logical development producing somatic, action-like expressions of fears such as bed wetting, thumb sucking, temper tantrums and poor impulse control. Their newly acquired verbal competence also declines (Cicchetti & Beeghly, 1987). It is useful to help these children with reality testing and improving their logic by practising extension of classes.

School-Age

The operation of reversibility marks the major shift in thinking in school-age children enabling them to conserve, that is to understand that an object, including themselves, remains the same even if its outward appearances change (Piaget, 1962). Children using this new understanding of reciprocity have a sense of symmetry and an understanding of syllogism (Gruber & Voneche, 1977). Actions are now well internalized into schemas of logic in the multiple memory systems with a general increase in recall of relevant information but little or no increase in recall of incidental information (Farrar & Goodman, 1990), even when the incidental information is terrifying.

School-age children now experiment with and enjoy extending class inclusions and exclusions. They like to make collections to maximize and practise this skill. They realize that as many as four or five factors can influence an outcome, so they experiment with excluding one factor at a time to judge its influence (Gruber & Voneche, 1977). They need to be encouraged to use this exclusionary sense to find the probable cause of their traumas.

Children now must of necessity be burdened with guilt for they know they could have handled the trauma event in other ways. Using exclusion also gives children a better feel for reality and thus promotes resilience. It enables them to hold onto the perspective of another person or possible "enemy." This presents a new set of tools for children to use when making complex moral decisions.

In addition, children now seem to prefer certain domains for remembering and communicating (Gardner, 1983). It is useful therapeutically to be aware of this and test for differential rates of development in and among domains (Fish-Murray et al., 1987). Children can now compare and contrast with ease and make interesting novel value judgments. Although they begin to play with possibility and extension of the real, they still make many false inductions from class over-inclusion (Murray, 1993). Early school-age children understand practical space and can identify places where they were traumatized. They could walk you there, if it were possible, but could not yet draw you a satisfactory map (Gruber & Voneche, 1977).

Another characteristic of this age group is the abundance of gender differences. Each sex "hates" the other as they work on refining sex roles. This is the era of gangs and cliques where children learn acceptable boundaries, rules and the range of power and control of their immediate peer groups. Gangs have been with us throughout history and are not inherently evil or bad. Assimilating and accommodating, playing and copying, gangs reflect the culture about them, whether they are tough inner city street gangs or a group of suburban boys practicing the appropriate protection of their turf and lifestyle. Group therapy, probably best in single-sex groups, can bring about the feel and security of a gang and help stabilize the child.

In Western countries children of this age who have experienced multiple victimization tend to withdraw from parents, teachers and peers (Murray, 1993). They become depressed, irritable and restless, have trouble concentrating, and become disruptive. School performance declines. Imaginative play is inhibited, thus lessening their adaptive assimilative functions. They are swamped by action fantasies, relying on old memories of rescue and revenge. They are terrified that events might reoccur. They tend to take risks as if their predictive memory system had momentarily shut down. The more extreme the catastrophe, the greater is their expectation of physical punishment, thus regressing to a toddler's expectation of justice.

A diminished interest in significant activities is a factor in defining childhood PTSD. At the Site 2 refugee camp, the traumatized Cambodian children's behavior contrasts markedly with Western responses to trauma. For example, 12-13 year olds were dedicated to attending school regularly

(99%), and boys were not hyperactive and aggressive like those in the West. These data show the marked importance of cultural expectancy and indicate that many trauma responses thought to be universal are not (Son, 1994).

Focusing on the key image of the trauma and using culturally appropriate symbols in the preferred domains, help the child to use increasingly conscious analysis. To facilitate this process, therapists should try to determine the presence and sophistication of each child's conservation abilities in the various domains using classical Piagetian methods. The work of Noam (1986) demonstrates the importance of understanding different cognitive levels of logic in borderline patients. In addition, the child's predictive memory can be trained to help him/her prepare for continuing and probable future traumatic events.

Adolescence

When the adolescent brain is fully matured, formal operational thought becomes possible. The adolescent can then deal with trauma in qualitatively new ways. Propositional thinking is possible, letting the young acquire the ability to maintain several possibilities simultaneously. Adolescents can abstract and distance themselves from the present, running back and forth through time and history but still remaining grounded. They are more realistic and less impulsive in thinking and behavior than younger school children. Adolescents are now preoccupied with building theories and plans on their own, yet adapting themselves to fit into their society's expectations. They play with "as if" logic and understand the part that chance plays in traumatic situations. They can now use both hypothetical and deductive logic to make sense out of remembered traumas. Among the many other changes that come with adolescence is the ability to distinguish between the contingent and the necessary and to comprehend relativity. Adolescents are beginning to subordinate the real for the possible. There is a great interest in ideals and values. Complying with the social contract often becomes more compelling than conforming to peer pressure. At this age, they revel in reflection as they sort out their dangerous world (Gruber & Voneche, 1977). Moreover, adolescents of both sexes tend to remember relationships more than trauma events or historical narratives (Pillemer, Goldsmith, Panter, & White, 1988). Ideal love combined with passion tends to swamp them, especially if associated with powerful accommodation forces of imitation that lead them into love of the perpetrator.

Teachers and therapists, noting these major qualitative changes in cognition in adolescents, can usefully provide opportunities for more accommodation (reality testing) than assimilation (continual playing with ideal solutions without reality checks) (Murray, 1993). Teens need to express their lofty ideals and passions in pragmatic ways if they are to survive in a warring world. Adolescents need mentors to emulate. This helps them achieve an appropriate sense of control and mastery.

CONCLUSION

Of all the systems that operate and interact following victimization, the cognitive system of children (encompassing various operations and the functions of attention, perception, memory, assimilation and accommodation) is the most important and must be understood if we are to help traumatized children. The child's attribution of meaning and consequent behavior depend on this cognitive system that develops and changes qualitatively over time through the interplay of thought and action. Little concordance appears among research studies on the commonalties of children's cognitive response to trauma. This may be a result of differing research strategies. In addition, the neurological and biological mechanisms underlying the cognitive response are inordinately complex leading to confusion in defining these commonalties. There is an obvious need for rethinking and closely examining what victimization does to children cognitively, using more inductive, epidemiological studies with a systems approach (Lykes, 1993). A meta analysis of research to date would be useful.

The brain's automatic unconscious responses to terror, especially in the functions of attention and perception, are a happy consequence of evolution and probably the closest we will get to categorizing universal responses to multiple victimization. The unique responses will continue to be a function of cultural and familial expectations, developmental level, and individual differences in response.

The therapist's initial understanding of the level of logic and preferred domains used by the traumatized child will allow the therapist to achieve therapeutic results quickly and efficiently. Children grow bored if tasks are too easy or "juvenile," and want to become competent in the next degree of complexity. With the therapist's help, a child can use alternate ways of learning, remembering and adjusting to events.

Children will always think differently than adults, interpreting trauma at their own appropriate level of logic. Logic, at whatever level, qualitatively changing with new experiences, keeps children steady and developing their own unique personalities. All possible efforts should be made to encourage their ability to consciously challenge their old ways of thinking about their feelings to enhance their fitness in their changing environments.

REFERENCES

American Psychiatric Association. (1987). *Diagnostic and statistical manual of mental disorders* (3rd ed.). Washington, DC: Author.

Bowlby, J. (1988). *A secure base. Parent and child attachment and healthy human development.* New York: Basic Books.

Christianson, S.A. (Ed.) (1992). *The handbook of emotion and memory: Research and theory.* Hillside, NJ: Lawrence Erlbaum.

Cicchetti, D., & Beeghly, M. (1987). Symbolic development in maltreated youngsters: An organizational perspective. In D. Cicchetti & M. Beeghly (Eds.), *Symbolic development in atypical children* (pp. 47-68). San Francisco, CA: Jossey-Bass.

Edelman, G.M. (1992). *Bright air, brilliant fire. On the matter of the mind.* New York: Basic Books.

Farrar, M.J., & Goodman, G.S. (1990). Developmental differences in the relation between scripts and episodic memory. In R.F. Fivush & J.A. Hudson (Eds), *Knowing and remembering in young children* (pp. 30-64). New York: Cambridge University Press.

Fish-Murray, C.C., Koby, E.V., & van der Kolk, B.A. (1987). Evolving ideas: The effect of abuse on children's thought. In B.A. van der Kolk (Ed.), *Psychological trauma* (pp. 89-110). Washington, DC: American Psychiatric Press.

Fox, N.A., & Bell, M.A. (1992). Electrophysiological indices of frontal lobe development: Relations to cognition and affective behavior in human infants over the first year of life. In A. Diamond (Ed.), *The development and neural bases of higher cognitive functions* (pp. 677-704). New York: New York Academy of Sciences.

Fox, S.S. (1985). *Good grief: Helping groups of children when a friend dies.* Boston, MA: NE Association for the Education of Young Children.

Gallistel, C.R., Brown, A.L., Carey, S., Gelman, R., & Keil, C.K. (1991). Lessons from animal learning for the study of cognitive development. In S. Carey & C.R. Gelman (Eds), *The epigenesis of mind. Essays on biology and cognition* (pp. 3-36). Hillsdale, NJ: Erlbaum.

Gardner, H. (1983). *Frames of mind. The theory of multiple intelligences.* New York: Basic Books.

Goodman, G.S., Rudy, L., Bottoms, B.L., & Aman, C. (1990). Children's concerns and memory: Issues of ecological validity in the study of children's eyewitness testimony. In R. Fivush & J.A. Hudson (Eds.), *Knowing and remembering in young children* (pp. 249-284). New York: Cambridge University Press.

Gruber H.E., & Voneche, J.J. (1977). *The essential Piaget.* New York: Basic Books.

Heuer, F., & Reisberg, D. (1992). Emotion, arousal, and memory for detail. In S.A. Christianson (Ed.), *The handbook of emotion and memory: Research and theory* (pp. 151-180). Hillsdale, NJ: Lawrence Erlbaum.

Hudson, J.A., & Fivush, R. (1990). Introduction: What young children remember and why. In R. Fivush & J.A. Hudson (Eds.), *Knowing and remembering in young children* (pp. 1-8). New York: Cambridge University Press.

Johnson, G. (1991). *In the palaces of memory: How we build the worlds inside our head*. New York: Alfred A. Knopf.

Kagan, J. (1983). Stress and coping in early development. In N. Garmezy & M. Rutter (Eds.), *Stress, coping and development in children* (pp. 191-216). New York: McGraw Hill.

Kagan, J. (1984). *The nature of the child*. New York: Basic Books.

Kagan, J. (1989). *Unstable ideas. Temperament, cognition, and self*. Cambridge, MA: Harvard University Press.

Krell, R. (1985). Child survivors of the Holocaust forty years later. *Journal of Child Psychiatry, 24*, 378-380.

Le Doux, J.E. (1992). Emotion as memory: Anatomical systems underlying indelible neural traces. In S. A. Christianson (Ed.), *The handbook of emotion and memory: Research and theory* (pp. 269-288). Hillsdale, NJ: Erlbaum.

Le Doux, J.E. (1994). Emotion, memory and the brain. *Scientific American, June*, 50-57.

Luria, A.R. (1968). *The mind of a mnemonist. A little book about a vast memory*. New York: Basic Books.

Lykes, M.B. (1993). *Terror, silence and voice: Accompanying child survivors of war in Central America*. Paper presented at the XXIV Congress of InterAmerican Psychological Association, Santiago, Chile.

Mandler, G. (1992). Memory, arousal, and mood. A theoretical integration. In S.A. Christianson (Ed.), *The handbook of emotion and memory: Research and theory* (pp. 93-110). Hillsdale, NJ: Lawrence Erlbaum.

Marler, P. (1991). The instinct to learn. In S. Carey & R. Gelman (Eds.), *The epigenesis of mind. Essays on biology and cognition* (pp. 37-66). Hillsdale, NJ: Erlbaum.

Milgram, N. (1990). *Childhood PTSD in Israel: A cross cultural frame of reference*. Paper presented at the meeting of the American Psychological Association, Boston, MA.

Moskovitz, S. (1985). Longitudinal follow-up of child survivors of the Holocaust. *Journal of Child Psychiatry, 24*, 401-407.

Murray, C.C. (1993). Childhood trauma and subsequent suicidal behavior. In A.A. Leenars (Ed.), *Suicidology* (pp. 73-92). Northvale, NJ: Jason Aronson.

Murray, H.A. (1933). The effect of fear upon estimates of the maliciousness of other personalities. *Journal of Social Psychology, 4*, 310-329.

Nasby, W., & Yando, R. (1980). Clinical and developmental implications of memory and affect in children. In R.L. Selman & R. Yano (Eds.), *Clinical-Developmental psychology* (pp. 21-44). San Francisco: Jossey-Bass.

National Institute of Mental Health. (1970). *Biological rhythms in psychiatry and medicine*. Chevy-Chase, MD: Author.

Noam, G.G. (1986). The theory of biography and transformation and the borderline personality disorders. Part II: A developmental typology. *McLean Hospital Journal, 11*, 79-104.

Piaget, J. (1962). *Play, dreams and imitation in childhood*. New York: Norton.

Piaget, J. (1969). *The psychology of the child*. New York: Basic Books.

Piaget, J. (1970). *Structuralism*. New York: Basic Books.

Pillemer, D.B., Goldsmith, L.R., Panter, A.T., & White, S.H. (1988). Very long term memories in the first year of college. *Journal of Experimental Psychology, Learning, Memory, and Cognition, 14*, 109-715.

Revelle, W., & Loftus, D.A. (1992). Implications of arousal effects for the study of affect and memory. In S.A. Christianson (Ed.), *The handbook of emotion and memory: Research and theory* (pp. 113-149). Hillsdale, NJ: Erlbaum.

Son, L. (1994). *Understanding the psychological impact of war trauma and the refugee camp experience on Cambodian refugee children residing in site two*. Unpublished doctoral dissertation, Harvard University, Cambridge, MA.

Squire, L.R., & Butters, N. (1986). *Neuropsychology of memory*. New York: Guilford Press.

White, S.H., & Pillemer, D.B. (1979). Childhood amnesia and the development of a socially acceptable memory system. In J. Kihlstrom & F. Evans (Eds.), *Functional disorders of memory* (pp. 29-73). Hillsdale, NJ: Erlbaum.

Yuille, J.C., & Tollestrup, P.A. (1992). A model of diverse effects of emotion on eyewitness memory. In S.A. Christianson (Ed.), *The handbook of emotion and memory: Research and theory* (pp. 201-215). Hillsdale, NJ: Erlbaum.

The Effects of Child Abuse on the Self-System

Susan Harter

SUMMARY. Normal development of aspects of the self-system in terms of the I- and Me-self are discussed. These concepts are then applied to research findings from abused children and youth where damage to the self is noted in terms of its negativity, fractionation, and lack of coherence, natural consequences of dealing with severe and prolonged maltreatment. Comments are also made concerning the nature of parenting in maltreating homes that enhances this damage. *[Article copies available for a fee from The Haworth Document Delivery Service: 1-800-342-9678. E-mail address: getinfo@haworth.com]*

The self has emerged as a central construct within many disciplines, including developmental psychology, clinical psychology, child and adult psychiatry, social psychology, cognitive psychology, and educational psychology. We have come to realize that self-representations are powerful predictors of behavior, and therefore it behooves us to address the

Address correspondence to: Susan Harter, PhD, Department of Psychology, University of Denver, Denver, CO 80208.

Preparation of this article was facilitated by a grant from NICHD. This article also owes much to Donna Marold who shared her expertise, insights, and clinical sensitivity about the numerous sequelae and dynamics of childhood abuse.

[Haworth co-indexing entry note]: "The Effects of Child Abuse on the Self-System." Harter, Susan. Co-published simultaneously in *Journal of Aggression, Maltreatment & Trauma* (The Haworth Maltreatment & Trauma Press, an imprint of The Haworth Press, Inc.) Vol. 2, No. 1 (#3), 1998, pp. 147-169; and: *Multiple Victimization of Children: Conceptual, Developmental, Research, and Treatment Issues* (ed: B. B. Robbie Rossman, and Mindy S. Rosenberg) The Haworth Maltreatment & Trauma Press, an imprint of The Haworth Press, Inc., 1998, pp. 147-169. Single or multiple copies of this article are available for a fee from The Haworth Document Delivery Service [1-800-342-9678, 9:00 a.m. - 5:00 p.m. (EST). E-mail address: getinfo@haworth.com].

antecedents of self-representations. What causal mechanisms lead certain individuals to exude an integrated sense of self, accompanied by high self-esteem, whereas others display a fragmented self-system further marred by self-deprecatory ideation? Normative studies have contributed to our knowledge of these processes. However, recent work in the area of child abuse has further enhanced our understanding, revealing how repeated and severe trauma to children impacts the development of self, crippling its very structure, content, and function. I will first briefly identify several of the most salient themes in the developmental literature on the self, and then address how child abuse has a major, deleterious effect on each aspect of the self-system (as summarized in Table 1).

TABLE 1. Deleterious Effects of Child Abuse on the Self-System

A. Disturbances in I-self functions
   1. Reduced self-awareness, introspection, attention to internal states, needs, thoughts, emotions.
   2. Impaired sense of agency, volition, control over one's actions.
   3. Disruptions in sense of self-continuity, the sense that one is the same person over time.
   4. Lack of a sense of self-coherence, the sense that oneself is integrated or unified.

B. Disturbances in the Me-self
   1. Negative domain-specific self-evaluations in areas deemed highly important; large discrepancy between ideal and real selves.
   2. Low global self-esteem due to feelings of inadequacy in domains of importance and lack of parent and peer support.
   3. Profound sense of inner badness, malevolent core self.
   4. Excessive self-blame, believe that abuse is one's fault and therefore deserved.

C. Negative self-affects
   1. Severe guilt and shame over participation in abuse.
   2. Depressive affect, anger towards the self.

D. Intropunitive behaviors
   1. Suicidal ideation, suicide attempts as escape from the self.
   2. Self-destructive behaviors, self-injury, self-mutilation.

E. Excessive false-self behavior
   1. Suppression, loss of one's true or authentic self.
   2. Development of a socially-acceptable self that conforms to demands and desires of others.

THE DISTINCTION BETWEEN THE I-SELF
AND THE ME-SELF

Historical theorists (James, 1892; Mead, 1934) as well as contemporary scholars (Damon & Hart, 1988; Harter, 1983, in press) have concluded that two conceptually distinct but experientially intertwined aspects of the self can be meaningfully identified, the I-self and the Me-self. The I-self is the knower, the observer, the self as active agent; it is the self as subject, since it organizes and interprets one's experience. The Me-self, in contrast, is the self as object, since it represents the empirical aggregate of what is objectively known about the self, namely, one's self-concept.

Several components of the I-self have been identified (James, 1892; Stern, 1985), components which have their developmental roots in infancy, emerging in interactions with caregivers. These include (a) self-awareness, an appreciation for one's internal states, needs, thoughts, and emotions; (b) self-agency, the sense of the authorship of one's own actions; (c) self-continuity, the sense that one remains the same person over time; and (d) self-coherence, a stable sense of self as a single, coherent, bounded entity. Each of these I-self functions undergoes disruption given repeated, severe trauma in childhood.

The Me-self is more than isolated self-concepts. Rather, it evolves into a *theory* that is constructed to organize one's thinking about one's relationship to the social world (Epstein, 1980; Kelly, 1955; Sarbin, 1962). Such scholars employ the term "theory" quite literally, arguing that the sense of self as a personal epistemology possesses the formal characteristics of a hypothetico-deductive system. Thus, one's self-theory can be evaluated by those criteria which any good theory must meet, for example, whether it is empirically valid, internally consistent, and coherently organized. It is the I-self, as the knower, that actively *constructs* such a Me-self theory.

From a developmental perspective, however, the self-theory constructed by children cannot meet these criteria, given a number of cognitive limitations (Fischer, 1980; Harter, in press; Piaget, 1963). Thus, self-attributes are not internally consistent, coherently organized postulates. Rather, the young child engages in unidimensional, all-or-none thinking in which attributes of both self and others are framed as incompatible opposites; one must be all good (or all bad), all nice (or all mean) (Fischer, 1980; Harter & Whitesell, 1989). Fischer and colleagues (Fischer & Pipp, 1984; Fischer & Ayoub, 1993) have pointed to the natural fractionation of the mind, what they term "affective splitting," which represents a normative form of dissociation that characterizes children's thinking about self and others.

A related normative feature of children's self-descriptions is their *positivity bias*. Most young children describe themselves as paragons of virtue, namely "all good," typically providing a litany of positive attributes and abilities. With development, one comes to appreciate that one can possess both positive and negative attributes; however, for most individuals the positivity bias continues to dominate (Calverley, Fischer, & Ayoub, 1994; Harter, 1986a; Harter & Monsour, 1992). As we shall observe, children with histories of severe abuse reverse these dynamics, adopting a negativity bias. Thus, they come to view the *self* as "all bad." In contrast, *others* (e.g., parents), may be viewed as "all good." However, the underlying cognitive structure is the same, namely all-or-none, unidimensional, thinking.

THE CAUSES OF ONE'S LEVEL OF SELF-ESTEEM

The ability to make evaluative judgments about the self as good or bad extends to one's sense of overall worth as a person, namely, self-esteem. Low self-esteem, in turn, is associated with a number of negative correlates including depression, self-destructive forms of behavior, as well as antiso-cial or aggressive behaviors toward others (Harter, in press). Thus, it be-comes critical to appreciate the antecedents of self-esteem. Two theoretical-ly-derived antecedents have been amply documented. For James (1892), self-esteem was the product of the ratio of one's perceived successes or failures to one's aspirations. If one's perceived successes equalled or ex-ceeded one's aspirations, high self-esteem would result. Conversely, if as-pirations exceeded successes, that is, if one were unsuccessful in domains deemed important, one would experience low self-esteem. Considerable empirical evidence supports this formulation (Harter, 1990, 1993, in press) including findings revealing that the discrepancy between perceptions of one's *real* self and one's *ideal* self is associated with low self-esteem and other indices of maladjustment, including depression (Baumeister, 1990). In our treatment of the effects of abuse on self-esteem, we shall see that many such victims have developed ideal self-images that are virtually unattain-able. Such harsh and perfectionistic self-standards, combined with percep-tions of incompetence and inadequacy, take their toll on self-esteem.

The second major antecedent, namely, the internalized opinions of sig-nificant others, is derived from the formulations of symbolic interactionists (e.g., Cooley, 1902; Mead, 1934) and attachment theorists (see Bowlby, 1969; Bretherton, 1991). From this perspective, self-esteem is created through the incorporation of the attitudes and evaluations that others, nota-bly parents in early childhood, hold toward the self (Coopersmith, 1967; Harter, 1990, in press). Young children's conclusions about what they are like rest heavily on the perceived judgments of external authority, notably parents (Rosenberg, 1979). That knowledge of the self resides in those with superior wisdom is consistent with Piaget's (1932) observations. Although parental opinions continue to impact self-esteem through adolescence, peer approval becomes increasingly critical as one moves into later childhood and beyond (Harter, 1990; Oosterwegel & Oppenheimer, 1993). Children subjected to severe and repeated parental maltreatment do not receive the support necessary to develop a sense of the self as worthy. Rather, the practices of abusing parents contribute to a profound sense of inner badness. Moreover, an abusive history may preclude the development of positive peer relationships, topics to which we shall return.

The Development of Self-Affects

The incorporation of parental attitudes toward the self extends to the emotional reactions of parents, particularly affects such as pride and shame. Findings reveal that a critical ingredient in the development of the child's ability to feel proud or ashamed of the self is the initial experience of parental pride over one's accomplishments or shame over one's transgressions (Harter & Whitesell, 1989; Stipek, 1983). Thus, the parent who implicitly or explicitly shames the child, either by setting impossible standards or by treating the child's behavior with condemnation, a common pattern among abusive parents, will provoke the internalization of a self-shaming schema which will lead to the experience of excessive and debilitating shame for the child, another issue to be examined.

MULTIPLE SELVES VERSUS THE INTEGRATED SELF

James (1892) initially observed that the need to develop numerous social selves to meet the demands of different situations may usher in the "conflict of the different Me's," namely a "discordant splitting" between multiple social selves. Others (e.g., Allport, 1961; Epstein, 1980; Maslow, 1971) have emphasized that one of the most basic needs of the individual is to maintain the unity and coherence of the conceptual system that defines the self. Developmental analyses reveal that there is an increasing proliferation of role-related selves during adolescence (Hart, 1988; Harter & Monsour, 1992). Initially, adolescents recognize the attributes in different roles may conflict, however, they do not yet have the cognitive skills to integrate apparent contradictions (Fischer, 1980; Harter & Monsour, 1992). However, with the development of more advanced cognitive skills, older adolescents can formulate more generalized abstractions about the self, allowing them to integrate, interpret, and normalize diverse self-attributes across roles or contexts. However, as we will come to appreciate, trauma in the form of severe and repeated abuse serves to exacerbate the fragmentation of multiple selves, rendering them unpredictably inaccessible to consciousness, and preventing their integration.

False Self Behavior

The proliferation of multiple selves during adolescence naturally introduces concern over which "is the real me" (Harter, Marold, Whitesell, & Cobbs, in press; Selman, 1980). In addition to this normative concern, there are marked individual differences in the level of false self behavior (feeling phony, putting on an act, changing yourself to be who someone else wants you to be) during adolescence (Harter et al., in press). Within the clinical literature, the origins of false self behavior occur in early childhood, within the context of the family (Bleiberg, 1984; Winnicott, 1965). False self behavior results from caregivers who do not validate the child's true self, thus leading one to become alienated from his/her core self (Harter et al., in press). Moreover, intrusive and demanding parents cause the developing child to develop a false self based upon compliance. Thus, the toddler becomes prematurely attuned to the demands of parents, and as a result loses touch with his/her own desires and needs. One's true self goes into hiding, as the child comes to suppress its expression, and sequelae include depression and hopelessness. This pattern may be particularly noteworthy for children who are victims of abuse, the dynamics of which will be discussed.

FORMS OF ABUSE AND THE NATURE OF PARENTING

Although *sexual* abuse has received the major attention, Briere (1992) observes that it is difficult to conceive of sexual molestation as the only form of abuse experienced by the child. The child who is sexually abused is also highly likely to experience psychological abuse (e.g., betrayal, threats, stigmatization) as well as physical maltreatment. In addition to physical damage from sexual abuse, the child will invariably be subjected to other violent contact (e.g., physical beatings to ensure compliance).

Westen (1993) concurs, noting that we have paid far less attention to the continuous, pathogenic experiences that are associated with sexual abuse, namely neglect, indifference, and empathic failures on the part of parents. He cogently observes that these other forms of maltreatment do not as readily elicit the horror or indignation we feel about sexual molestation. However, those who have carefully described their populations note that the majority of maltreated children suffer from more than one form of abuse, including sexual molestation, physical abuse, neglect, and emotional abuse (Cicchetti, Beeghley, Carlson, & Toth, 1990). In addition, the child may also be a witness to domestic violence. Given this constellation of abusing practices, it is difficult to isolate the effects of one from another, as well as from other dysfunctional features of family interactions (Wolfe, 1989).

There is considerable agreement that many aspects of the abusive family environment are clearly dysfunctional. Thus, effects attributed to abuse are most appropriately interpreted within the context of a pathological family system (Briere, 1992; Bukowski, 1992; Cicchetti, 1989; Erickson, Egeland, & Pianta, 1989; Finkelhor, 1984; Herman, 1992; Westen, 1993; Wolfe, 1989). Cicchetti conceives of child maltreatment as "relational psychopathology," namely dysfunction in the parent-child-environment transactional system (Crittenden, 1988; Crittenden & Ainsworth, 1989). Erikson et al. (1989) concur, citing the difficulty of separating "maltreatment" from "family dysfunction," particularly if one adopts Newberger's (1973) view of maltreatment as an inability of the parents to nurture their offspring.

Thus, many of the effects heretofore attributed to sexual or physical abuse alone, particularly effects on the self-system, must now be viewed from the perspective of coexisting *psychological* or emotional abuse, as well. Briere (1992) summarizes the major forms of parental or caretaker psychological abuse, drawing upon the work of several investigators (e.g., Hart, Germain, & Brassard, 1987). These include (a) rejection, causing the child to feel unworthy or unacceptable; (b) degradation, criticism, humiliation, stigmatization, deprivation of dignity, leading to feelings of inferiority; (c) terrorization, in which the child is verbally assaulted, frightened, and threatened with physical or psychological harm; (d) isolation, in which the child is deprived of social contacts outside of the family; (e) corruption, in which the child is encouraged to engage in antisocial behaviors; (f) lack of emotional responsiveness, in which the child is deprived of loving, sensitive caregiving, or is ignored and neglected; and (g) unreliable or inconsistent parenting with contradictory parental demands. Many of these features represent extreme forms of what Baumrind (1971) has labelled "authoritarian" parenting practices (Bukowski, 1992).

Complementing this perspective are contributions from attachment theory. There is considerable consensus that the vast majority of maltreated children form insecure attachments with their primary caregivers (Cicchetti et al., 1990; Crittenden & Ainsworth, 1989; Erikson et al., 1989; Westen, 1993). The foundation of attachment theory rests on the premise that if the caregiver has fairly consistently responded to the infant's needs and signals, and has respected the infant's need for independent exploration of the environment, the child will develop an internal working model of self as valued, competent, and self-reliant. Conversely, if the parent is insensitive to the infant's needs and signals, inconsistent, and rejecting of the infant's bid for comfort and exploration, the child will develop an internal working model of the self as unworthy, ineffective, and incompetent (Bowlby, 1969; Bretherton, 1991; Crittenden & Ainsworth, 1989). Clearly, the parental practices that have been associated with child abuse represent precisely the kind of treatment that would lead children to develop insecure attachments as well as an internal model of self as inadequate and unworthy.

Of particular interest is the specific type of insecure attachment that children of abuse appear to manifest. A high percentage of such children display the *disorganized/disoriented* (D) style recently identified by Main and Solomon (1990; Cicchetti, 1989; Crittenden & Ainsworth, 1989). Such children vacillate between approaching and avoiding the caregiver. There are also signs of disorientation, such as stereotyped rocking and dazed facial expressions. It has been hypothesized that a history of severe negative and inconsistent parent-child interactions would produce such an attachment style. Crittenden (1985) takes exception to the interpretation that such children are disorganized and disoriented, suggesting that such children are actually displaying a combination of avoidant and ambivalent attachment styles, organized around the attempt to resolve the conflict between the child's need for proximity to the caregiver and expectations of aversive treatment.

Dissociative Reactions to Severe and Prolonged Abuse

As experts have pointed out (see Briere, 1992; Cicchetti, 1989; Herman, 1992; McCann & Pearlman, 1992; Putnam, 1993; Terr, 1991; Westen, 1993), abuse presents formidable challenges, because it thwarts so many basic, developmental needs. The child must attempt to cope with a situation that is unsafe, as well as try to find a way to preserve trust in those who have violated that trust. He/she must find a way to remain connected to caregivers whose behavior has seriously threatened a sense of secure attachment and connection. The child must try to exert some sense of control in an unpredictable situation in which he/she feels helpless. The major strategy for coping with these formidable obstacles is to activate an immature system of psychological defenses, which rely heavily on *dissociative* reactions.

Dissociative processes are generally conceptualized as the most adaptive defensive response to overwhelming trauma (Herman, 1992; Putnam, 1993; Terr, 1991). Terr makes reference to Type II trauma, which involves chronic exposure to external events that are severely damaging to the self (in contrast to Type I trauma which involves a single event). If such abuse occurs in childhood, it conspires with the natural penchant for dissociation, splitting, or fragmentation. Dissociation in childhood, what Fischer and colleagues refer to as normative affective splitting, represents the typical organization of childhood cognitive structures (Calverley et al., 1994; Fischer & Ayoub, 1993; Fischer & Pipp, 1984). Thus, the mind of the young child naturally fractionates by virtue of its cognitive developmental limitations (Harter, in press; Harter & Whitesell, 1989; Putnam, 1991), compartmentalizing content into positive versus negative. Fischer and colleagues refer to this natural tendency as "passive dissociation."

Trauma caused by chronic abuse, however, leads to active, highly motivated (in Fischer's terminology) dissociative symptoms that represent massive attempts to protect the psyche, by attempts to eliminate the event from consciousness. As such, it represents not only a defensive adaptation but a fundamental reorganization of one's personality (Herman, 1992; Terr, 1991; Putnam, 1991). More specifically, dissociation serves multiple purposes, namely to allow the abuse victim to escape from the punishing constraints of reality, to contain traumatic memories and affects outside of normal conscious awareness, to detach oneself from the traumatic event such that it appears to happen to someone else, and to serve as an analgesic, numbing the physical and psychic pain that is being inflicted (Putnam, 1989). Thus, fully-integrated functioning is seriously compromised as the abuse victim attempts to lessen the pain and anxiety associated with total awareness of the traumatic events (Briere, 1992).

Dissociative symptoms, which represent altered states of consciousness, take several forms. Perhaps the most dramatic is psychogenic amnesia for the abuse itself. Entire segments of one's childhood are lost, repressed, denied (Briere, 1992; Herman, 1992; Putnam, 1993; Terr, 1991). These theorists also identify a number of other mechanisms including attempts at detachment and numbing, invoked to attenuate the intensity of negative affects surrounding abusive assaults. Depersonalization represents another dissociative strategy in which one experiences the self as observing (rather than participating in) the abusive event. Various forms of self-hypnosis, prompted by the desire to become invisible, also add to the dissociative repertoire. In the extreme, dissociative symptomatology leads to multiple personality disorder in which the self becomes so fragmented that different alters are created to bear the burden of contradictory events that defy integration.

SPECIFIC EFFECTS OF ABUSE ON THE I-SELF

Self-awareness. As James (1892) observed, self-awareness is one of the basic functions of the I-self. However, the very mechanisms of dissociation, including psychogenic amnesia, render the abuse victim unaware of events and self-representations that have become inaccessible to consciousness because the content is too terrifying or painful. Westen (1993) refers to a "metacognitive shutdown." Thus, one does not observe the typical processes of introspection, namely the ability to think about one's thoughts and actions that become rampant during adolescence. The cognitive constriction associated with the dissociative symptomatology precludes this type of self-awareness.

Briere (1992) points to another feature of abusing relationships that interferes with the victim's awareness of self. The fact that the child must direct sustained attention to external threats draws energy and focus away from the developmental task of self-awareness. Thus, the hypervigilance to others' reactions, what Briere terms "other-directedness," interferes with the ability to attend to one's own needs, thoughts, and desires. This analysis is consistent with the formulation of Miller (1977) who addresses the impact of the stance that subordinates (e.g., children as well as women in a patriarchal society) must adopt toward dominants. They must attend to the needs and desires of the dominants, and in so doing, they become alienated from, and unaware of, their own needs, thoughts, and emotions. Moreover, the fact that, as children, abuse victims do not share their experiences with others, due to parental prohibitions and codes of secrecy, also contributes to the defensive exclusion of certain experiences from awareness. Recent research findings with children support these contentions in demonstrating that maltreated children report fewer descriptions of inner states and feelings than children with no known history of abuse (Cicchetti, 1989; Cicchetti et al., 1990; Gralinski, Feshbach, Powell, & Derrington, 1993).

Sense of agency. Self-agency involves the sense that one has volition and control over one's actions, thoughts, and emotional experiences, that one is the architect of one's intentions and plans. However, the defense structures driven by abuse will compromise the victim's sense of agency (Briere, 1992; Putnam, 1993). The very fact that abuse victims manifest less self-awareness and attention to internal processes, motives, and intentions, will interfere with a sense of agency (Westen, 1993). Putnam (1993) describes how extreme dissociation will interfere with the development of perceptions of agency on several levels. The person's sense of volition is undermined by "passive influence experiences" in which certain actions (e.g., automatic writing), thoughts, and affects are experienced as if a powerful force outside of the individual's conscious awareness or control is coercing the person to do something against his/her will. Depersonalization, in which the person feels that he/she is observing the self from a detached perspective, also contributes to a lack of a sense of agency. The very fact that one cannot remember, or account for, various actions they have performed also robs the abuse victim of a sense of control.

In the adult survivor of abuse, Westen describes the distortion in one's sense of agency due to the splitting off of sexual impulses that cannot be owned. The tendency to experience overwhelming affects can also prevent a sense of agency, since impulsive, emotion-driven behaviors (e.g., suicidal gestures) may appear to come out of the blue. Westen describes one adult patient who described herself as a sailing ship with no one at the helm. Other theorists (see Briere, 1992; McCann & Pearlman, 1992; Wolfe, 1989) similarly describe how abuse victims lack feelings of efficacy, independence, and control, further eroding their sense of agency.

Cicchetti (1989) brings another perspective to the issue of agency, integrating attachment and Eriksonian perspectives. He notes that autonomy and mastery must build upon a sense of trust in the caregiver's accessibility, one feature of a secure attachment. However, given the interpersonal dynamics in abusive families that lead to insecure attachment, the maltreated child may well not develop the sense of agency that permits him/her to explore and master the environment with confidence. Bukowski (1992) cites another family dynamic that impacts sense of self as agent among child victims of sexual abuse. The fact that the child is forced to be a passive participant in an activity that brings the victim little or no satisfaction is antithetical to the development of a sense of self based upon will and agency.

Sense of self-continuity. A critical "I-self" function is the maintenance of a sense of self-continuity over one's own history. There is now considerable agreement that *autobiographical memory* is a key source of a sense that one is the same person over time (Eder, Gerlach, & Perlmutter, 1987; Stern, 1985). To the extent that the ability to create autobiographical memories hinges upon the early development of a sense of self-agency and self-recognition (Cicchetti et al., 1990; Howe & Courage, 1993), self-continuity will be compromised, since early abuse interferes with a sense of self as causal agent. Moreover, traumatically induced dissociative states and amnesic gaps contribute to a temporally discontinuous sense of self (McCann & Pearlman, 1992; Putnam, 1991; Westen, 1993). That is, the loss of significant childhood and adolescent memories typically encountered with incest victims, in particular (Herman, 1992), deprives the individual of the autobiographical memory upon which one's sense of self

hinges. Building upon Tulving's (1972) distinction between autobiographical or episodic memory and semantic memory, Bowlby (1980) was one of
the first theorists to suggest that child abuse victims repress their autobio-
graphic memory for the traumatic events. Bowlby suggested that they may
retain conscious access only to parental interpretations stored in semantic
memory (Bretherton, 1993).

As Putnam (1993) describes, difficulty in determining whether an event
actually happened or was "incorporated" into memory from other sources
degrades the self-referential qualities of memory and creates doubt about
the reality of what one remembers as his or her life. In addition, among
those with multiple personality disorder, amnesia, loss of time and
memory for the significant events which occurred during such a lost period of time, coupled with more severe dissociative symptoms in the form of
fugue states and switching from one personality to another, seriously
disrupt self-continuity.

Self-coherence and sense of unity. Another I-self function, the maintenance of a coherent, integrated self, is also compromised among abuse
victims. As noted earlier, from a developmental perspective, the self is
initially fragmented, particularly for attributes that can be categorized as
either positive or negative, good or bad. The natural dissociative tendencies of childhood and early adolescence preclude an integrated self-structure (Fischer, 1980; Fischer & Pipp, 1984). However, developing cognitive capabilities toward the end of adolescence provide the necessary
psychological tools to craft a more integrated, coherent self (Harter &
Monsour, 1992).

However, the dissociative symptomatology defensively mobilized by
the abuse victim seriously interferes with the integration of self-attributes
(Briere, 1992; Fischer & Ayoub, 1993; Putnam, 1991, 1993; Westen,
1993). Splitting, fragmentation, compartmentalization, the staples in the
abuse victim's dissociative armamentarium, all, by definition, preclude a
sense of the coherence of the self. As Putnam (1993) observes, depersonalization, and passive influence experiences also undermine a sense of a
unified self.

These tendencies are further exacerbated among multiple personality
disorder (MPD) victims of severe and chronic sexual abuse (Putnam,
1989; 1993). Multiple identities are created to compartmentalize traumatic
memories and affects, and these dissociated alters or personality states
function as separate entities capable of independent volitional activities.
By necessity, they will lead to a fragmented and incoherent self-portrait.
Not only do such patients represent the self as a disjointed collection of
autonomous agents, but often the alters will be in diametric conflict with

each other. For example, a sexually promiscuous alter will be countered by another morally upstanding personality; a self-destructive or persecuting alter will coexist along with a protective alter. Dissociative symptomatology represents a continuum of severity. Level of severity, in turn, will affect the degree to which the self lacks unity and coherence.

DISTURBANCES IN THE ME-SELF

Negative self-evaluations in abuse victims. In addition to disturbances in the I-self, the content of the Me-self is impacted by abuse, leading to a range of negative self-evaluations. There is a growing body of evidence that children experiencing serious forms of maltreatment report greater feelings of inadequacy and incompetence, and manifest lower self-esteem (Briere, 1992: Browne & Finkelhor, 1986; Jehu, 1988; Kaufman & Cicchetti, 1989; Kendall-Tackett, Williams, & Finkelhor, 1993; McCann & Pearlman, 1992; Youngblade & Belsky, 1990). The two broad antecedents of self-esteem identified earlier, perceptions of competence or adequacy in important domains and internalization of the opinions of significant others provide a framework for understanding such negative self-evaluations.

Competence/adequacy in domains of importance. Experts in abuse readily point to the sense of inadequacy that victims feel in a number of domains of their life. At the most basic level of the bodily self, abuse leaves many victims feeling fundamentally damaged (Nash, Hulsey, Sexton, Harralson, & Lambert, 1993; Newberger, 1990; Westen, 1993). Further contributing to their sense of inadequacy and incompetence are early messages from caregivers which communicate that they are generally flawed and ineffective (Briere, 1992; Crittenden & Ainsworth, 1989; McCann & Pearlman, 1992). The assault is not merely upon the physical body but upon the individual's perception of the self as competent and valuable. Cicchetti et al. (1990) report that beginning in middle childhood, maltreated children report that they are less competent and accepted than nonmaltreated peers.

In their efforts to attempt to avoid further abuse and to please punitive parents who set harsh and often unattainable standards, many child victims of abuse strive to be perfect. However, such a strategy may backfire as they develop over-idealized images that they cannot attain (Putnam, 1990). Bleiberg (1994) also observes that abuse can put one at risk for what he terms "narcissistic vulnerability" in which there is a mismatch between the ideal and the real self. Such a mismatch results in part from parents setting conditional and unreachable ideals for their maltreated child. It is this *discrepancy* between one's competence and the importance of success, between one's actual and one's ideal self-image, that contributes to low self-esteem.

Incorporation of the opinions of significant others. Significant others, notably parents in the early years, not only set standards of performance and provide feedback in particular areas of competence, but communicate opinions about their children's overall worth as a person. As described earlier, these more generalized messages have been found to have a powerful impact on children's sense of self-esteem (Harter, 1990). It was observed that maltreating parents not only physically or sexually abuse their children but are likely to engage in many emotionally and psychologically abusive behaviors including rejection, which cause the child to feel unworthy or unacceptable, as well as degradation, criticism, and stigmatization, which further contribute to feelings of inferiority and low self-esteem.

As attachment theorists have informed us, these processes begin during the first year of life, within the context of insecure forms of attachment (Cicchetti et al., 1990; Crittenden & Ainsworth, 1989; Erikson et al., 1990). Although very young children cannot verbalize their sense of low self-esteem, they manifest it in their behavior (Harter, 1990). As Green (1982) observes, the preverbal infant who is repeatedly assaulted acquires an unpleasurable awareness of self which becomes transformed into a devalued self-concept with further cognitive development and the emergence of language. Such children ultimately internalize the contempt that their parents directed toward them, resulting in extreme, self-deprecatory ideation.

It was also noted earlier that *peer* support becomes increasingly critical as one moves into later childhood and adolescence (Harter, 1990). Unfortunately, there are a number of factors associated with child abuse that jeopardize peer support. Abuse experts observe that maltreating parents often deprive the child of social contacts outside the family. Such social isolation removes opportunities for the development of social relationships, social skills, and the potentially buffering effects of peer relationships (Briere, 1992; Cicchetti et al., 1990; Mueller & Silverman, 1989; Wolfe, 1989). Abused children typically develop one of two stances toward peers, either aggression or avoidance, which alienates peers whose approval is a vital source of self-esteem. Many abuse victims provoke personal disapproval, which further erodes feelings of worth initially fostered by parents.

Given potential rejection by one's normative peer group, abused youth may well turn to other sources of support, joining a gang which may also serve as an outlet for their aggression. The support provided through gang membership may, in turn, provide an arena in which one can enhance one's status and self-worth. Such speculation, supported by the higher incidence of abused children and adolescents involved in delinquent behavior (Mallouh & Webb, 1989) as well as in gangs, underscores the importance of understanding the particular *motives* underlying gang membership. Thus, age appropriate needs for approval, esteem, status, power, and outlets for aggression which may be thwarted in one's family and school environment, can be met through gang-related activities.

The abuse victim's sense of inner badness and self-blame. Many experts point out that negative self-evaluations extend beyond mere low self-esteem to include a profound sense of inner badness (Briere, 1992; Caverley et al., 1994; Herman, 1992; McCann & Pearlman, 1992; Westen, 1993). Thus, abuse victims see themselves as fundamentally bad, as "malevolent," in Westen's terms. Moreover, this sense of pervasive badness includes their perceptions that they will bring grief to family members and that others who have contact with them will be harmed, contaminated, or doomed. Moreover, such victims blame themselves for their core badness, making internal, global, and stable attributions about their character flaws.

The *stigmatization* of abuse victims by the abuser, family members, and society contributes to the perception that they are fatally flawed (Briere, 1992; Kendall-Tackett et al., 1993). Victims are often given the message from the abuser or family that "you deserved that," "you asked for it," "you are being punished for being bad." As Briere (1992) notes, our victim-blaming social system condemns the victim after the fact ("you seduced him," "why didn't you just say 'No'," "what must you have done to deserve it?").

From a cognitive-developmental perspective, the young child who is abused will readily blame the self (Herman, 1992; Piaget, 1932; Watson & Fischer, 1993; Westen, 1993). That is, given young children's natural egocentrism, they will take responsibility for events they did not cause or cannot control. Moreover, as Piaget demonstrated, young children focus on the *deed* (e.g., the abusive act) rather than on the intention (e.g., the motives of the perpetrator). As Herman points out, the child must construct some version of reality that justifies continued abuse and inevitably concludes that innate badness is the cause.

Briere (1992) describes the sequential "logic" that governs the abused child's attempt to make meaning of his/her experiences. Given maltreatment at the hands of a parent or family member, the child first surmises that either I am bad or my parents are bad. However, the assumption that adult authority figures are always right leads children to conclude that parental maltreatment must be due to the fact that one was bad or at fault, and that therefore punishment is deserved. When children are repeatedly assaulted, they come to conclude that they must be "very bad," contributing to the sense of fundamental badness at their core.

Paradoxically, many children opt for the attribution of *self*-blame (rather than blaming others) since it offers them some sense of hope and control (Herman, 1992; Westen, 1993). Such a stance may offer some opportunity for atonement. If one has brought this abusive fate upon oneself by being bad, then perhaps one has the power to alter it, by trying to be good. This, in turn, may earn parental forgiveness, as well as the care and protection that has been so desperately lacking.

Fischer and his colleagues (Fischer & Ayoub, 1993; Calverley et al., 1994) document the sense of profound negativity that female adolescent sexual abuse victims experience with regard to their core self. They compared two groups of adolescents, both of whom suffered from depressive/affective disorders; one group were sexual abuse victims with diagnoses of post-traumatic stress disorder, while the second group were not. These investigators built upon Harter and Monsour's (1992) procedure in which adolescents arranged spontaneously-generated self-attributes into a self-portrait in which they identified attributes that were the most important or central, less important, and least important. Adolescents, in Harter and Monsour's normative sample, displayed a positivity bias, placing the majority of favorable attributes at the core of the self, and relegating negative attributes to the periphery of their self-portrait, judging them to be their least important characteristics.

Fischer and colleagues found that adolescent girls with depressive disorders, coupled with a history of sexual abuse, not only reported significantly more negative self-attributes but identified negative characteristics as far more *central* to their self-concepts, namely, the defining features of their core self. The comparison group, with depressive symptomatology but no history of abuse, showed the positivity bias reported in normative samples. These findings provide clear research support for the argument that one outcome of abuse is a sense of the core badness of the self.

Guilt and shame. Closely linked to abuse victims' perceptions of low self-esteem, self-blame, and a sense of inner badness are *emotional* reactions of guilt and shame (Briere, 1992; Herman, 1992; Kendall-Tackett et al., 1993; McCann & Pearlman, 1992; Westen, 1993). Normatively, such self-affects are intimately related to evaluative self-perceptions, both of which result from internalizing the opinions of significant others (Cooley, 1902; Harter, in press). Thus, the blame, stigmatization, condemnation and ostracism which parents, family, and society express toward the abuse victim are not only incorporated into attributions of self-blame but result in powerful negative affects directed toward the self. The sexual abuse victim is made to feel humiliated for his/her role in shameful acts. Moreover, guilt and shame are also fueled by the perception that one's badness *led* to the abuse, rather than that the abuse was the cause of one's negative self-views.

Depression, suicide, and self-destructive behaviors. As noted earlier, negative self-perceptions and low global self-esteem are highly linked to depressive symptomatology. Thus, abusive treatment, coupled with other forms of psychological abuse, not only provoke self-deprecatory ideation but depression, associated with both the loss of a caring significant other as well as loss of the self. This pattern is common among abuse victims who typically manifest a range of depressive reactions, including suicidal behavior (Bagley & McDonald, 1984; Elliot & Briere, 1992; Browne & Finkelhor, 1986; Kendall-Tackett et al., 1993; Putnam, 1989, 1991). Moreover, the single most common presenting symptom in MPD patients, who have a severe history of sexual abuse, is depression (Putnam, 1989). Many are at risk for a major affective disorder as well as suicidal behaviors. Suicidal behaviors among abuse victims typically represent the ultimate avoidance strategy (Briere, 1992). Thus, suicide represents the final out, providing an escape from extreme psychic pain including intolerable memories, as well as "escape from the self" (Baumeister, 1990), depression, and hopelessness (Schneidman, 1985), in the face of other strategies that did not provide relief. Self-injury, in the form of carving or burning parts of the body, is also common among victims of severe sexual abuse. However, abuse experts note that such behaviors are not to be confused with suicidal gestures (Briere, 1992; Herman, 1992). Rather, self-mutilation strategies serve to allow the abuse victim to regulate autonomic arousal and certain internal states. Such behaviors temporarily reduce the psychic tension associated with negative affect, self-deprecatory ideation, guilt, and painfully fragmented thought processes (Briere, 1992). However, such self-injurious strategies lead to only temporary relief.

For some victims, self-mutilating behaviors occur during periods of extreme dissociation and depersonalization, which is often accompanied by profound agitation and a desire to attack the body (Herman, 1992). The mutilating act itself produces feelings of calm and relief, since physical pain is preferable to the severe emotional pain that abuse victims experience. In abuse victims suffering from MPD, self-mutilation may also reflect one persecutor personality who is punishing another alter or the host personality, herself (Putnam, 1989). Thus, self-mutilation serves a variety of functions, each of which represents a defensive strategy to find relief from other symptoms associated with abuse.

False self behavior. Abuse puts one at risk for suppressing one's true self and displaying various forms of unauthentic or false self behavior. Such a process has its origins in childhood, given the parenting that constitutes psychological abuse. Parenting practices such as lack of attunement to the child's needs, empathic failure, lack of validation, threats of harm, coercion, and enforced compliance all cause the true self to go underground (Bleiberg, 1984; Stern, 1985; Winnicott, 1965) and lead to what Sullivan (1953) labelled "not me" experiences.

The emergence of *language* also sets the stage for suppression of the true self. As Stern cogently argues, language is a double-edge sword since it can create a wedge between what is actually experienced from what is verbally represented and shared with others. The failure to share experiences with others, exacerbated by secrecy pacts around sexually abusive interactions, further leads the child to defensively exclude such episodic memories from awareness (Bretherton, 1991). Thus, sexual and physical abuse, coupled with parenting practices that represent psychological abuse, cause the child to split off experiences, either consciously or unconsciously, relegating them to either a private or inaccessible part of the self. The very disavowal and dissociation of one's experiences, coupled with psychogenic amnesia and numbing, as defensive reactions, set the stage for loss of one's true self.

Herman (1992) introduces other dynamics that represent barriers to authenticity among victims of abuse. She notes that the malignant sense of inner badness is often camouflaged by the abused child's persistent attempts to be good. In adopting roles designed to please the parent, to be the perfect child, one comes to experience one's behavior as false or unauthentic (Miller, 1990). Thus, one develops a socially-acceptable false self that conforms to others' demands, in an attempt to obtain their approval. If one's true self, corroded with inner badness were to be revealed, it would be met with scorn and contempt. Therefore, it must be concealed at all costs.

CONCLUSION

Against a backdrop of normative-developmental processes, this article has attempted to demonstrate how traumatic abuse in childhood can lead to profound disturbances in the self. In addition to abusive acts themselves, accompanying psychological abuse at the hands of parents, coupled with dissociative defensive reactions, conspire to disrupt the self-system. With regard to I-self functions, one can observe impairments in self-awareness, sense of agency, sense of self-continuity over time, and sense of a unified self. Disturbances in the Me-self include feelings of incompetence, low self-esteem, a profound sense of inner badness, self-blame, guilt and shame, depression, suicide and other self-destructive behaviors, as well as a sense that the self that one presents to the world is false or unauthentic. The mandate of this article was to describe these painful sequelae of abuse. The larger mandate for the field and for society is to develop our skills in understanding and treating these disorders, as well as ultimately to prevent their occurrence.

REFERENCES

Baumeister, R.F. (1990). Suicide as escape from self. *Psychological Review, 97*, 90-113.

Baumrind, D. (1971). Current patterns of parental authority. *Developmental Psychology Monographs, 4*, 1-102.

Bleiberg, E. (1984). Narcissistic disorders in children. *Bulletin of the Menninger Clinic, 48*, 501-517.

Bowlby, J. (1969). *Attachment and loss. Vol. 1: Attachment*. New York: Basic Books.

Bowlby, J. (1980). *Attachment and loss. Vol. 3: Loss, sadness, and depression*. New York: Basic Books.

Bretherton, I. (1991). Pouring new wine into old bottles: The social self as internal working model. In M. Gunnar & L.A. Sroufe (Eds.), *Self-processes in development*. Minnesota Symposium on child psychology (Vol. 23, pp. 1-41). Hillsdale, NJ: Lawrence Erlbaum Associates.

Briere, J. (1992). *Child abuse trauma: Theory and treatment of the lasting effects*. Newbury Park, London: Sage Publications.

Browne, A., & Finkelhor, D. (1986). Impact of child sexual abuse: A review of the research. *Psychological Bulletin, 99*, 66-77.

Bukowsky, W.M. (1992). Sexual abuse and maladjustment considered from the perspective of normal developmental processes. In W. O'Donohue & J.H. Geer (Eds.), *The sexual abuse of children: Theory and research, Vol. 1* (pp. 261-282). Hillsdale, NJ: Lawrence Erlbaum Associates.

Calverley, R.M., Fischer, K.W., & Ayoub, C. (1994). Complex splitting of self-representations in sexually abused adolescent girls. *Development and Psychopathology, 6*, 195-213.

Cicchetti, D. (1989). How research on child maltreatment has informed the study of child development: Perspectives from developmental psychology. In D. Cicchetti & V. Carlson (Eds.), *Child maltreatment: Theory and research on the causes and consequences of child abuse and neglect*. New York: Cambridge University Press.

Cicchetti, D., Beeghley, M., Carlson, V., & Toth, S. (1990). The emergence of the self in atypical populations. In D. Cicchetti & M. Beeghley (Eds.), *The self in transition: Infancy to childhood*. Chicago: University of Chicago Press.

Cooley, C.H. (1902). *Human nature and the social order.* New York: Charles Scribner's Sons.

Coopersmith, S. (1967). *The antecedents of self-esteem.* San Francisco, CA: W.H. Freeman.

Crittenden, P.M. (1988). Relationships at risk. In J. Belsky & T. Nezworski (Eds.), *Clinical implications of attachment theory.* Hillsdale, NJ: Erlbaum.

Crittenden, P.M., & Ainsworth, M.D.S. (1989). Child maltreatment and attachment theory. In D. Cicchetti & V. Carlson (Eds.), *Child maltreatment: Theory and research on the causes and consequences of child abuse and neglect.* New York: Cambridge University Press.

Damon, W., & Hart, D. (1988). *Self understanding in childhood and adolescence.* New York: Cambridge University Press.

Eder, R.A., Gerlach, S.G., & Perlmutter, M. (1987). In search of children's selves: Development of the specific and general components of the self-concept. *Child Development, 58,* 1044-1050.

Elliot, D.M., & Briere, J. (1992). Sexual abuse trauma among professional women: Validating the Trauma Symptom Checklist (TSC-40). *Child Abuse and Neglect, 16,* 391-398.

Epstein, S. (1980). The stability of behavior: II. Implications for psychological research. *American Psychologist, 35,* 790-806.

Erickson, M.F., Egeland, B., & Pianta, R. (1989). The effects of maltreatment on the development of young children. In D. Cicchetti & V. Carlson (Eds.), *Child maltreatment: Theory and research on the causes and consequences of child abuse and neglect.* New York: Cambridge University Press.

Finkelhor, D. (1984). *Child sexual abuse: New theory and research.* New York: Free Press.

Finkelhor, D., & Browne, A. (1985). The traumatic impact of child sexual abuse: A conceptualization. *American Journal of Orthopsychiatry, 55,* 530-541.

Fischer, K.W. (1980). A theory of cognitive development: The control and construction of hierarchies of skills. *Psychological Review, 87,* 477-531.

Fischer, K.W., & Ayoub, C. (1993). Affective splitting and dissociation in normal and maltreated children: Developmental pathways for self in relationships. In D. Cicchetti & V. Carlson (Eds.), *Child maltreatment: Theory and research on the causes and consequences of child abuse and neglect.* New York: Cambridge University Press.

Fischer, K.W., & Pipp, S.L. (1984). Development of the structures of unconscious thought. In K. Bowers & D. Meichenbaum (Eds.), *The unconscious reconsidered* (pp. 88-148). New York: Wiley.

Gecas, V. (1972). Parental behavior and contextual variations in adolescent self-esteem. *Sociometry, 36,* 332-345.

Gralinsky, J., Fesbach, N.D., Powell, C., & Derrington, T. (1993). *Self-understanding: Meaning and measurement of maltreated children's sense of self,* Paper presented at the meeting of the Society for Research in Child Development, New Orleans, LA.

Green, A.H. (1982). Child abuse. In J. Lachenmeyer & M. Gibbs (Eds.). *Psychopathology in childhood*. New York: Gardner Press.

Hart, D. (1988). The adolescent self-concept in social context. In D.K. Lapsley & F.C. Power (Eds.), *Self, ego, and identity* (pp. 71-90). New York: Springer Verlag.

Hart, S.N., Germain, R., & Brassard, M.R. (1987). The challenge: To better understand and combat the psychological maltreatment of children and youth. In M.R. Brassard, R. Germain, & S.N. Hart (Eds.), *Psychological maltreatment of children and youth* (pp. 3-24). New York: Pergamon.

Harter, S. (1983). Developmental perspectives on the self-system. In E.M. Hetherington (Ed.), *Handbook of child psychology: Vol. 4. Socialization, personality, and social development* (pp. 275-386). New York: Wiley.

Harter, S. (1986). Processes underlying the construction, maintenance, and enhancement of the self-concept in children. In J. Suls & A.G. Greenwald (Eds.), *Psychological perspectives on the self* (Vol. 3, pp. 137-181). Hillsdale, NJ: Lawrence Erlbaum Associates.

Harter, S. (1990). Causes, correlates and the functional role of global self-worth: A life-span perspective. In J. Kolligian & R. Sternberg (Eds.), *Perceptions of competence and incompetence across the life-span* (pp. 67-98). New Haven, CT: Yale University Press.

Harter, S. (1993). Causes and consequences of low self-esteem in children and adolescents. In R.F. Baumeister (Ed.), *Self-esteem: The puzzle of low self-regard*. New York: Plenum.

Harter, S. (In press). The development of self-representations. In N. Eisenberg (Ed.), *Handbook of child psychology: Social and personality development*. New York: Wiley.

Harter, S., Marold, D.B., Whitesell, N.R., & Cobbs, G. (In press). A model of the effects of parent and peer support on adolescent false self behavior. *Child Development*.

Harter, S., & Monsour, A. (1992). Developmental analysis of opposing self-attributes in the adolescent self-portrait. *Developmental Psychology, 28*, 251-260.

Harter, S., & Whitesell, N.R. (1989). Developmental changes in children's understanding of single, multiple, and blended, emotion concept (pp. 37-50). In C. Saarni & P. Harris (Eds.), *Children's understanding of emotion*. New York: Cambridge University Press.

Herman, J. (1992). *Trauma and recovery*. New York: Basic Books.

Howe, M.L., & Courage, M.L. (1993). On resolving the enigma of infantile amnesia. *Psychological Bulletin, 113*, 305-326.

James, W. (1892). *Psychology: The briefer course*. New York: Henry Holt & Co.

Jehu, D. (1988). *Beyond sexual abuse: Therapy with women who were childhood victims*. Chichester, UK: John Wiley.

Kaufman, J., & Cicchetti, D. (1989). Effects of maltreatment on school age children's socio-emotional development: Assessment in a day camp setting. *Developmental Psychology, 25*, 516-524.

Kelly, G.A. (1955). *The psychology of personal constructs*. New York: Norton.

Kendall-Tackett, K.A., Williams, L.M., & Finkelhor, D. (1993). Impact of sexual abuse on children: A review and synthesis of recent empirical studies. *Psychological Bulletin, 113*, 164-180.

Main, M., & Solomon, J. (1990). Procedure for identifying infants as disorganized/disoriented during the Ainsworth Strange Situation. In M. Greenberg, D. Cicchetti, & E.M. Cummings (Eds.), *Attachment during the preschool years: Theory, research, and intervention* (pp. 121-160). Chicago: University of Chicago Press.

Maslow, A.H. (1971). *The farther reaches of human nature*. New York: Viking.

McCann, I.L., & Pearlman, L.A. (1992). *Psychological trauma and the adult survivor*. New York: Brunner/Mazel.

Mead, G.H. (1934). *Mind, self, and society*. Chicago: University of Chicago Press.

Miller, A. (1990). *Thou shalt not be aware*. New York: Meridan.

Miller, J.B. (1977). *Toward a new psychology of women*. Boston: Beacon Press.

Mueller, N., & Silverman, N. (1990). Peer relations in maltreated children. In D. Cicchetti & V. Carlson (Eds.), *Child maltreatment: Theory and research on the causes and consequences of child abuse and neglect*. New York: Cambridge University Press.

Nash, M., Hulsey, T., Sexton, M., Harralson, T., & Lambert, W. (1993). Long-term sequelae of childhood sexual abuse: Perceived family environment, psychopathology, and dissociation. *Journal of Consulting and Clinical Psychology, 61*, 276-283.

Newberger, E.H. (1973). The myth of the battered child syndrome. In R. Bourne & E.H. Newberger (Eds.), *Critical perspectives on child abuse*. Lexington, MA: Lexington Books.

Nikkari, D., & Harter, S. (1994). *Toward a model of the determinants of presented self-esteem in young children*. University of Denver, Unpublished manuscript.

Oosterwegel, A., & Oppenheimer, L. (1993). *The self-system: Developmental changes between and within self-concepts*. Hillsdale, NJ: Lawrence Erlbaum.

Piaget, J. (1932). *The moral judgment of the child*. New York: Harcourt, Brace, & World.

Piaget, J. (1963). *The origins of intelligence in children*. New York: Norton.

Putnam, F.W. (1989). *Diagnosis and treatment of multiple personality disorder*. New York: Guilford Press.

Putnam, F.W. (1990). Disturbances of self in victims of childhood sexual abuse. In R.P. Kluft (Ed.), *Incest-related syndromes of adult psychopathology*. Washington, DC: American Psychiatry Press.

Putnam, F.W. (1991). Recent research on multiple personality disorder. *Psychiatric Clinicals of North America, 14*, 489-502.

Putnam, F.W. (1993). Dissociation and disturbances of the self. In D. Cicchetti & S. Toth (Eds.), *Disorders and dysfunctions of the self: Rochester Symposium on Developmental Psychopathology* (Vol. 5). Rochester, NY: University of Rochester Press.

Rosenberg, M. (1979). *Conceiving the self*. New York: Basic Books.

Sarbin, T.R. (1962). A preface to a psychological analysis of the self. *Psychological Review, 59,* 11-22.

Selman, R. (1980). *The growth of interpersonal understanding.* New York: Academic Press.

Stern, D. (1985). *The interpersonal world of the infant.* New York: Basic Books.

Stipek, D. (1983). A developmental analysis of pride and shame. *Human Development, 26,* 42-54.

Sullivan, H.S. (1953). *The interpersonal theory of psychiatry.* New York: Norton.

Terr, L. (1991). Childhood traumas: An outline and overview. *American Journal of Psychiatry, 148,* 10-20.

Tulving, E. (1972). Episodic and semantic memory. In E. Tulving & W. Donaldson (Eds.), *Organization of memory* (pp. 381-403). New York: Academic Press.

Westen, D. (1993). The impact of sexual abuse on self structure. In D. Cicchetti & S. Toth (Eds.), *Disorders and dysfunctions of the self: Rochester Symposium on Developmental Psychopathology* (Vol. 5). Rochester, NY: University of Rochester Press.

Winnicott, D. (1965). *The maturational processes and the facilitating environment.* New York: International Universities Press.

Wolfe, D. (1989). *Child abuse.* Newbury Park, CA: Sage Publications.

Youngblade, L., & Belsky, J. (1990). The social and emotional consequences of child maltreatment. In R. Ammerman & M. Herssen (Eds.), *Children at risk: An evaluation of factors contributing to child abuse and neglect.* New York: Plenum Press.

Multiple Maltreatment
and the Development
of Self and Emotion Regulation

Penelope K. Trickett

SUMMARY. The impact of multiple victimization on the development of social and emotional regulatory processes is examined. Questions are raised regarding both the quantitative and qualitative impact of singular versus multiple maltreatment. Normal development of self regulation is discussed as well as measures commonly used to assess it. Abuse research findings relevant for considering the development of regulatory processes are reviewed. Finally, the influence of family, individual child, and parenting factors is considered as related to regulation. The recommendation is made for more careful research, guided by developmental theory and using more specific measures of developmental problems and competencies. *[Article copies available for a fee from The Haworth Document Delivery Service: 1-800-342-9678. E-mail address: getinfo@haworth.com]*

The purpose of this article is to examine the impact of multiple forms of maltreatment on the social and emotional development of the child. Specifically, what is examined is how such multiple victimization may affect the development of regulatory processes, that is, processes that allow the

Address correspondence to: Penelope K. Trickett, PhD, Department of Psychology, University of Southern California, Los Angeles, CA 90089-1061.

[Haworth co-indexing entry note]: "Multiple Maltreatment and the Development of Self and Emotion Regulation." Trickett, Penelope K. Co-published simultaneously in *Journal of Aggression, Maltreatment & Trauma* (The Haworth Maltreatment & Trauma Press, an imprint of The Haworth Press, Inc.) Vol. 2, No. 1 (#3), 1998, pp. 171-187; and: *Multiple Victimization of Children: Conceptual, Developmental, Research, and Treatment Issues* (ed: B. B. Robbie Rossman, and Mindy S. Rosenberg) The Haworth Maltreatment & Trauma Press, an imprint of The Haworth Press, Inc., 1998, pp. 171-187. Single or multiple copies of this article are available for a fee from The Haworth Document Delivery Service [1-800-342-9678, 9:00 a.m. - 5:00 p.m. (EST). E-mail address: getinfo@haworth.com].

child to control and modulate his or her own social behavior or emotional expression. These processes, termed self and emotion or affect regulation, are key developmental tasks of early childhood, necessary if the child is to develop the autonomy, independence and social competence required for a successful transition into middle childhood. Stating that the focus of the article is on the impact of multiple maltreatment on self-regulatory processes implies concern with two related questions: First, does experiencing multiple forms of maltreatment result in *more severe problems* or *delays* in children's development of self regulation than would experiencing single forms of maltreatment? Cumulative theories of risk (Sameroff & Seifer, 1983) posit that the number of risk factors, including those associated with maladaptive parenting of different sorts, combine to increase the likelihood and degree of developmental problems in children. It is reasonable to think that different forms of child maltreatment, when experienced in combination, might have a more deleterious effect on the development of self regulation than when experienced singly. The second question is a variant of the first: Does multiple maltreatment victimization result in *different* developmental outcomes than single forms of maltreatment? The answer to this latter question has to depend in part on whether different forms of maltreatment themselves result in different types of developmental problems. For example, if physical abuse results in different maladaptive outcomes than sexual abuse, then experiencing both physical abuse and sexual abuse should result in different types or patterns of developmental problems than experiencing either type of maltreatment alone. Both questions will be considered in this article.

The first section of this article defines self and emotion regulation, and describes normal developmental measures used in child development research, and factors associated with individual differences. The next sections review findings of maltreatment research relevant for understanding of the impact of maltreatment on the development of regulatory processes. The final section turns to the child rearing context in maltreating families.

SELF AND EMOTION REGULATION

Self regulation has been defined as the ability to conform to family and social conventions of acceptable behavior and to inhibit disruptive antisocial behavior (Kopp, 1989). Maccoby and Martin (1983) note that self-regulatory processes include " . . . the ability to start and stop behavior on the basis of situational requirements, to postpone the pursuit of a given goal, and to regulate the intensity of both overt action and affective arousal" (p. 35). They review the decades of research in child development that have been concerned with the development of self regulation, especially in terms of young children's abilities to comply with parental socialization demands and then to internalize parental and societal values. Another emphasis of this research has been on children's disruptive and/or antisocial behavior, such as aggressiveness, and their developing ability to control and inhibit such behaviors (Parke & Slaby, 1983). A more recent emphasis has been on the regulation of emotion or affect, per se (Fox, 1994). Here the focus has been on the modulation of emotional expression and the ability to deal with stressful, distressing, and challenging situations by keeping emotional expression within manageable bounds. Thompson (1994) recently noted that although this has been the emphasis, emotion regulation also may involve maintaining and enhancing emotional arousal, not just inhibiting it, and that a more comprehensive definition of emotion regulation is that it is those processes responsible for "monitoring, evaluating, and modifying emotional reactions, especially their intensive and temporal features, to accomplish one's goals" (pp. 27-28).

Kopp (1989) has outlined the usual developmental progression of these forms of self regulation over the first four years of life. During the first year of life the infant is acquiring the neurophysiological and motor maturation necessary to engage in voluntary motor acts and to modulate, change, or cease such responses. Such maturation is obviously a prerequisite for self-regulatory behavior. During this period, the mother is viewed as providing the emotion regulation for the infant, for example, by calming a distressed infant by holding or rocking (Calkins, 1994). There is also evidence of efforts at emotion *self* regulation in very young infants (e.g., getting fingers to the mouth and sucking or turning away from an aversive stimulus as ways of reducing distress). During the second year of life, in large part due to the rapidly increasing locomotor skills of the child, socialization pressures aimed at controlling the behavior of the child are introduced. Many "do's" and "don'ts," and especially "don'ts," are experienced by the child. Since during this year the language comprehension of the child is growing, it becomes possible for the first time for the child to comply with such verbal commands and the beginnings of self control are seen. During the third and especially the fourth year of life, as the child's language comprehension and expression develops and as there are increases in cognitive abilities, particularly representational thinking and recall memory, self regulation that is based on internalization of values and standards begins to be possible. Thus, the foundation for the development of self and emotion regulation is set during the first four or so years of life. This is not to say that the process is complete at this age. Rather, the preschool and early school-age child continues developing these skills as he or she encounters increasing socialization and maturity demands from family, school and others.

What are the predictors of individual differences in the development of self and emotion regulation? Kopp (Kopp, 1989; Kopp & Wyer, 1994) has emphasized the importance of cognitive and language abilities in the development of regulatory abilities. She notes the importance of representational thinking, recall memory, associative learning, and both receptive and expressive language for both behavioral and emotional regulation. Those children who are more advanced in cognitive and language development than their peers would be capable of more advanced self regulation as well. Kopp (1989) also points out the importance of situations that provide an optimal level of novelty and challenge–optimal in terms of the child's cognitive developmental level. She says, " . . . Planful emotion regulation arises in situations that are novel and not too distressful, in situations where there are strong social sanctions for wrongful behavior and caregivers are not available for helpful reminders, or in situations where personal efficacy is threatened (but not to the point of major discomfort and behavioral disorganization). . . . Situations that markedly overload the child inhibit ability to think in an organized fashion" (p. 345). Others whose research focuses on emotion regulation place more emphasis on temperament and other biological factors when explaining individual differences in children (Fox, 1989), although recent conceptualizations have emphasized the *interaction* of biological processes and socialization (Thompson, 1994).

There are also well-established links between parent-child relationships and child rearing beliefs and practices of parents and the development of regulatory processes. Maccoby and Martin (1983) emphasize the following as being critical: " . . . parental behaviors that antecede secure attachment (sensitivity, cooperation, acceptance, etc.); secure attachment itself; parental emotional bonding and the fostering of trust; high levels of playful, affectively positive interaction with the child; frequent joint task related activity; and the parents' use of non-power-assertive techniques emphasizing the child's individuality" (p. 68). Also, interaction with peers, as well as parents, can play an important role in the development of self regulation. Peers use techniques such as segregating themselves from others who show socially unacceptable levels of distress or aggression, thus providing a powerful incentive to modulate such emotions or behavior (Kopp, 1989).

CHILD MALTREATMENT AND SELF REGULATION

The focus of this article is on the impact of multiple maltreatment victimization on the development of self and emotion regulation in children. Unfortunately there is scant empirical evidence that can be brought to bear on this issue. This is so largely because of two gaps in the body of research knowledge on child maltreatment. First, although there is considerable evidence that different forms of maltreatment often co-occur (Claussen & Crittenden, 1991), there has been little systematic investigation of the impact of multiple forms of victimization on development. Rather most studies (a) compare one form of maltreatment to no maltreatment; (b) compare one form of maltreatment to another form (e.g., neglect vs. physical abuse); or (c) acknowledge that the maltreatment group varies in the nature and types of maltreatment experience but not enter this factor into the design or analysis strategies. In fact, only four studies concerned with the impact of multiple victimization on social and emotional development were identified.

The second reason that so little is known about the connection between multiple forms of maltreatment and self regulation is that few maltreatment studies have been explicitly focussed on self regulation in children. There are, however, many studies, including the four multiple maltreatment studies just noted, that have been concerned with components of self regulation. These studies have examined such developmental outcomes as children's aggressive, disruptive, or other antisocial behavior or level of anger and hostility; children's distress, sadness, depression, or lack of affect; children's compliance or noncompliance with parents; and children's prosocial behavior with peers or socially withdrawn behavior.

First, the studies which explicitly examined the impact of multiple victimization on some of the components of self-regulated behavior noted above will be reviewed. Then, other studies concerned with these same outcomes, but in samples with single forms of maltreatment, will be summarized.

Multiple Victimization and Self Regulation

Four studies compared multiply maltreated children with children who suffered one form of abuse and with a nonmaltreated comparison group of children. In three of these studies, the types of maltreatment examined were physical abuse and witnessing violence. Hughes, Parkinson and Vago (1989) compared 4- to 12-year-old children who had: witnessed domestic violence (N = 44); been physically abused *and* witnessed domestic violence (N = 40); or were not maltreated (N = 66). These groups were compared on parental reports of behavior problems using the Child Behavior Checklist. For the total behavior problem score, the children who had been abused and witnessed domestic violence were significantly more elevated than were the children who had witnessed domestic violence but were not abused, who, in turn, had significantly higher scores than the nonmaltreated comparison children. For the two broad-band scores for internalizing and externalizing problems, the abused witnesses were significantly higher than the comparison group. In these instances, the mean for the nonabused witness group was intermediate to the other two groups and not significantly different from either.

Rossman and her colleagues (Rossman et al., 1991) also examined the Child Behavior Checklist, and other outcome variables in three groups of children: witnesses of domestic violence (N = 10); witnesses who were also physically abused (N = 10); and a nonmaltreated comparison group (N = 23). Subjects were boys and girls between 4 1/2 and 5 1/2 years old. In this study the comparison group had significantly higher perceived competence and verbal IQ and lower behavior problem scores than the maltreated groups. Consistently, the abused witnesses had scores indicating poorer adjustment than the non-abused witnesses but many of these differences were not statistically significant.

Sternberg and her colleagues (Sternberg et al., 1993) compared four groups of 8- to 12-year-old Israeli males and females: children who were physically abused and witnessed domestic violence (N = 30); children who witnessed domestic violence but were not abused (N = 16); children who were physically abused but did not witness domestic violence (N = 33); and a nonmaltreated comparison group (N = 31). These researchers found that the results depended on who the reporter was (child, mother, or father). For child-reported depression, the comparison group scored lower than the three maltreated groups who did not differ from one another. The same was true for internalizing and externalizing scores on the Youth Self Report (the child-report version of the Child Behavior Checklist). When the mothers were the reporters, the abused-witness and witness-only groups were higher on the externalizing scale of the Child Behavior Checklist than were the abused-only and comparison group children. Mothers' reports showed no differences on the internalizing scale of this measure. And when fathers were the reporters, no group differences were found for either the externalizing or internalizing scale. Thus, mothers reported adverse effects of domestic violence on their children only when they themselves were victims of violence, but not when the children alone were victimized (perhaps at the hands of the mother). Fathers (frequently the victimizers in this study) reported no adverse effects of any of the types of maltreatment.

The fourth study which compared multiply maltreated to singly maltreated children was conducted by Kaufman and Cicchetti (1989). These researchers compared 5- to 11-year-old males and females in three groups:

those who had been neglected, emotionally abused *and* physically abused (N = 28); those who had been neglected *or* emotionally abused but not physically abused (N = 28); and a nonmaltreated comparison group (N = 67). This study took place in a summer camp setting and measures included observers' (counselors') ratings of behavior and peer ratings of behavior. Analyses indicated that the comparison group had significantly better adjustment on all measures than the maltreated groups. Only one measure statistically distinguished the maltreated groups: children who were neglected, emotionally abused *and* physically abused were rated more disruptive by peers than those who were neglected or emotionally abused only.

In sum, the results of these four studies of multiple victimization provide only scant support for the "cumulative hypothesis" of more severe impact of multiple victimization than of single type maltreatment. There are hints of this, though. In several instances the multiple maltreatment group had scores indicating the most maladjustment although statistical significance was not attained. For the most part, these studies have small Ns and thus may have insufficient power to detect group differences. These studies are few in number and, with one exception, consider only one type of multiple victimization (co-occurrence of witnessing domestic violence and experiencing physical abuse). Another limitation of these latter studies is that parent report measures predominate. The Sternberg et al. (1993) results show the difficulty of relying solely on data from maltreating or maltreated parents who may have problems with accurate perceptions of their children's behavior and/or vested interests in reporting either few or many child problems.

Thus, it is premature to conclude that multiple victimization has no additional impact on children over and above the impact of single forms of maltreatment. It is also not possible to say anything conclusive based on these few existing research studies about whether different combinations of maltreatment result in different impacts on development.

Since extant research does not allow a conclusive answer to the questions about whether multiple forms of maltreatment lead to more severe or different sorts of problems in the development of self regulatory processes, the remainder of the chapter will consider, in a speculative way, how such processes might be affected. These speculations will be based, first, on research on the impact of single forms of different types of maltreatment on components of self regulation, with an eye toward distinguishing the general effects of maltreatment and effects that may be specific to particular forms of maltreatment. This will be followed by a consideration of how parent-child relationships, child rearing, and family environment might be thought to affect the development of self regulation in children.

Single Forms of Maltreatment and Self Regulation

Research on the psychological impact of child abuse and neglect has proliferated in recent years as a number of recent reviews attest (e.g., Kendall-Tackett, Williams & Finkelhor, 1993; Trickett & McBride-Chang, 1995; Widom, 1989). Despite this proliferation, there are still some glaring gaps in this research. For example, with a very few notable exceptions, research involving samples of children and adolescents has consisted of cross-sectional designs in which short-term or acute impact has been assessed. There are very few longitudinal studies. Instead, long-term impact has been assessed using retrospective designs with adults who report experiencing abuse as children.

There are a number of other limitations of this research, many of which are beyond the scope of this paper. (See Trickett & McBride-Chang, 1995.) One is critical, though, to understanding the selection of research reviewed below. Many child abuse and neglect studies have not included an appropriate control or comparison group. Some have no comparison group at all; others use one that is notably higher in social class than the abuse group. This latter approach is a basic flaw given the clear research evidence that many of the outcome measures of interest are adversely influenced by poverty or low social class. This review only considers studies that have a comparison group comparable to the abuse group in socioeconomic status (SES) or use statistical methods to control for differences.

Sexual Abuse Research. In the area of sexual abuse, cross-sectional studies have been done with samples of children ranging in age from toddlers to adolescents. These studies show considerable evidence of internalization problems, especially depression and anxiety (Trickett & Putnam, 1991; White, Halpin, Strom & Santilli, 1988). There is also consistent evidence of externalizing problems, especially in the form of sexual acting out or the presence of inappropriate sexual behavior even from a very early age (Einbender & Friedrich, 1989; Kolko, Moser & Weldy, 1990). There is no evidence of aggressive acting out at the toddler or preschool age, but from elementary school age on there is evidence of problems with controlling aggression among sexually abused children (Einbender & Friedrich, 1989; Trickett & Putnam, 1991). There is evidence of elevated levels of dissociation (Putnam, Helmers & Trickett, 1993). Dissociation is a psychophysiological process that produces a disturbance or alteration in the normally integrative functions of memory and identity and which may produce attention problems and memory lapses. Elevated dissociation is likely to interfere with adaptive emotion regulation (Cole, Michel & Teti, 1994). There is also some evidence of disregulated cortisol activity among sexually abused girls, a pattern that has been found to be associated with high levels of stress and with major depression and other forms of psychopathology in adults (DeBellis et al., 1993; Putnam & Trickett, 1991). This pattern is similar to that found in studies concerned with the physiological processes and emotional regulation (Stansbury & Gunnar, 1994).

In sexually abused adolescents some related problems appear: suicidal, self-injurious behavior or delinquent behavior (Kendall-Tackett et al., 1993); and promiscuous sexual activity (Wyatt, 1988). Retrospective studies of adults sexually abused as children indicate depression, other affective and anxiety disorders, diagnoses of antisocial personality, and drug and alcohol abuse (e.g., Stein, Golding, Siegel, Burnam & Sorenson, 1988).

Physical Abuse Research. The cross-sectional studies of the impact of physical abuse also indicate the presence of both internalizing and externalizing problems in early and middle childhood (Dodge, Bates & Pettit, 1990; Trickett, 1993; Wodarski, Kurtz, Gaudin & Howing, 1990). There is some evidence that physically abused boys are especially demanding and aggressive and girls are more often withdrawn and wary (Trickett, 1993) but both genders show both types of problems. Physically abused children (boys and girls) are also reported by their parents to be oppositionally noncompliant in disciplinary situations (Trickett & Kuczynski, 1987). They have also been found to be less prosocial with peers (Dodge et al., 1990), including showing low empathy, and to be disliked by peers (Salzinger et al., 1989). Social problem solving skills are also problematic. One study (Trickett, 1993) found that physically abused children were as capable as nonabused children of generating prosocial solutions to hypothetical social problems, but they also generated *more* antisocial solutions. That is, they seemed unable to modulate their aggressive responses even in a verbal, hypothetical situation, but showed no evidence that they had not learned socially acceptable responses.

Studies with physically abused adolescents also indicate internalizing, externalizing and peer problems (e.g., Wodarski et al., 1990). Studies of adults physically abused as children indicate greater and more violent criminal activity (Rivera & Widom, 1990), other antisocial behavior (Pollack et al., 1990), and greater anger and depression (Briere & Runtz, 1990).

Research on Neglect. There are fewer studies of the impact of neglect on children's social and emotional behavior. The studies that do exist, though, show no evidence of aggressive or antisocial behavior in early or middle childhood. Rather, neglected children demonstrate social withdrawal, lack of affect in interaction with peers, and less prosocial behavior (Howes & Eldredge, 1985). There is one study of neglected adolescents in which both internalizing and externalizing problems were elevated as reported by parents but not as reported by teachers (Wodarski et al., 1990). Also, in adulthood, one study indicated more violent criminal offenses among adults neglected as children (Rivera & Widom, 1990). So there is a hint that, while not aggressive or antisocial in childhood, neglected children develop problems in this domain in adolescence or adulthood, but evidence is not conclusive.

"Mixed" Maltreatment Research. There is another category of studies in which more than one type of maltreatment may have been experienced by the child although this is not a feature of the design or analysis. These studies, termed "mixed maltreatment" studies, have samples which have individuals who have experienced more than one form of maltreatment and/or individuals who have experienced different forms of maltreatment. Usually these samples consist of a varying proportion of children who have experienced physical abuse and/or neglect with occasionally a few sexual abuse victims as well. A number of such studies with samples of young and school-aged children indicate problems with both verbal and physical aggression, disruptive behavior, elevated anger and hostility, and peer problems including social withdrawal and maladaptive responses to peer provocation (Kaufman & Cicchetti, 1989). Research with young maltreated children found that they were less likely than nonmaltreated agemates to verbalize internal states like emotions (Cicchetti & Beeghly, 1987). However, Frodi and Smetana (1984) found that, with IQ controlled, there was no difference between school-aged maltreated children and a comparison group in ability to discriminate emotions.

In sum, based on all these studies, the following conclusions seem justified. Maltreatment, whether it be sexual abuse, physical abuse, neglect, or some mixture, seems to have a general adverse impact on children on aspects of their social and emotional development that are related to the development of self and emotion regulation. These have most often been measured in terms of internalizing and externalizing problems that are exhibited in depression or mood disorders, aggressive tendencies, undercontrol in peer situations, and, among adolescents and adults, delinquency and criminality. There are also problems that are apparently specific to different forms of maltreatment. One of the clearest of these is sexual acting out. It is only sexually abused children who have been shown to exhibit this form of acting out behavior. It also seems to be the case that sexually abused and neglected children, especially when young, are most likely to show problems of social withdrawal and isolation. While physically abused children also show these problems as well, problems with aggressive, disruptive interpersonal behavior leading sometimes to peer rejection predominate. What is confounding here, though, is that females predominate in the samples of sexual abuse studies while there are more males in the physical abuse studies. To what degree this apparent type-of-abuse finding reflects instead the tendency for females to develop internalizing problems relative to males is not clear (Zahn-Waxler, 1993). It appears that young neglected children who have not also been abused do not exhibit externalizing problems. However, according to one study (Rivera & Widom, 1990), as adolescents and adults, they do tend to exhibit criminal and especially violent criminal behavior. This is a puzzle. It is possible that this apparent change to more aggressive and violent behavior is a long-term result of inadequate development of self-regulatory skills coupled with a history of poor and scant peer relationships which lead, in adolescence, to being vulnerable to the influence of antisocial peers who offer acceptance, relief from loneliness, and maybe even friendship, to those willing to share in delinquent, criminal, or otherwise antisocial activities.

One other important point about the impact of maltreatment on children's development needs to be made. Consistently, from the earliest ages, physically abused and neglected children show poorer cognitive development and poorer school performance than comparison group children, with neglected children showing the worst delays in cognitive and language development (Culp et al., 1991; Eckenrode, Laird & Doris, 1993; Trickett, 1993; Vondra, Barnett & Cicchetti, 1990; Wodarski et al., 1990). This is so even when SES is carefully controlled. For sexual abuse the findings are less consistent but most studies show this delay as well (e.g., Trickett, McBride-Chang & Putnam, 1993). Given the role of cognitive development in the development of self regulation, this would suggest a possible mediator of importance. If abuse results in developmental delays in such functions as representational thought, receptive and expressive language, and memory, this could impede the development of self regulatory skills.

PARENT-CHILD RELATIONSHIPS, CHILD REARING ENVIRONMENT, AND SELF REGULATION IN MALTREATING FAMILIES

There is another body of maltreatment research that is relevant when speculating about the impact of multiple forms of maltreatment on self-regulatory processes. This has to do with the nature of parent-child relationships and the child rearing environment of maltreating families. Aspects of the child rearing environment have been found to be associated with the development of self regulation in nonmaltreating families. Some of these same characteristics have been found to be problematic in maltreating families. Studies indicate problems with mother-child attachment in physically abusive (Erickson & Egeland, 1987), neglecting (Egeland et al., 1983), and mixed abuse (Carlson, Cicchetti, Barnett & Braunwald, 1989) families. Attachment has not been examined for sexually abused children.

Among physically abusive parents, considerable evidence has now accrued to show that the child rearing beliefs and practices of these parents, as a group, differ in a number of important ways from those of non-abusive parents. Abusive parents are not only more punitive in their disciplinary style, they are less likely to use reasoning and other educative types of discipline; they are less flexible and adaptive in their use of discipline; they are less open to new experiences and less encouraging of the development of autonomy and independence in their children; they report more anger and conflict in the family and in their reaction to the abused child; they express more dissatisfaction with their child and with the parenting role; they report smaller social networks, especially networks that characteristically provide support for child rearing; they report greater isolation from the wider community (Corse, Schmid & Trickett, 1990; Trickett, Aber, Carlson & Cicchetti, 1991; Trickett & Kuczynski, 1986; Trickett & Susman, 1988). Much less is known about the child rearing styles of other types of maltreating parents. Neglecting parents have been shown to be socially isolated (Belsky, 1994), as have parents in sexually abusive families (Helmers, Everett & Trickett, 1991). Mothers in sexually abusive families have not been shown to hold beliefs in harsh punishment or authoritarian control similar to physically abusive parents, but they are similar to physically abusive parents in their greater dissatisfaction with their child than nonmaltreating parents (Trickett, Everett & Putnam, 1995). Little else is known about the child rearing approaches of neglecting parents and mothers in sexually abusive homes although there is a widespread belief that these parents do not provide the active involvement and structure that a child needs optimally in order to develop self-regulatory processes.

There are several other family factors that need to be considered. As Kopp (1989) noted, the child needs an optimal level of novelty and challenge, neither too much nor too little, for self regulation to develop. Clearly, the degree of distress and conflict experienced by children being physically or sexually abused or witnessing domestic violence is likely to be overwhelming and not optimal for such development. A neglecting home may well provide too little novelty and challenge. It may be more like the environments of homes with a depressed parent which have been shown to have a deleterious effect on emotion regulation (Field, 1994). As noted earlier, such homes may also provide too little structure, with appropriate consequences, for the development of self control and other self-regulatory processes.

It is also possible that there are some biological processes related to emotion regulation that are associated with the tendency to become a maltreating parent. Vasta (1982), for example, has argued cogently that physically abusive parents are hyper-reactive and have a "short fuse," which contributes to the likelihood that a specific parent-child interaction will become abusive. This characteristic is very similar to the type of hyper-reactivity that is associated with emotional undercontrol and a heightened tendency to distress in young children and primates (Bolig, Price, O'Neill & Suomi, 1992; Fox, 1989; Calkins, 1994). It is possible that this hyper-reactivity has a genetic component which could contribute to problems with emotion regulation in abused children (especially physically abused children).

In sum, research on the impact of multiple forms of maltreatment on the social and emotional development of children is scant and cannot provide conclusive evidence that multiple maltreatment either has a more deleterious effect on the development of self-regulatory processes or that multiple maltreatment has a distinct impact which differs from the impact of singly experienced forms of maltreatment. There are hints, though, that this may be the case. To proceed beyond this stage of "hinted" effects requires new research that is explicitly designed to compare the impact of different forms of maltreatment including that experienced in various combinations. Such research needs samples large enough that the power problems that plague so much of the existing research are avoided. More critically, such research needs to be guided by developmental theory. In part this means that outcome measures need to be selected that are less oriented toward assessing "global dysfunction" and more oriented toward assessing developmentally relevant problems and competencies. Also researchers need to be careful and explicit in defining and describing the characteristics of maltreatment experienced by research subjects including the age of the child when the maltreatment occurred. This is especially important for research relating to self and emotion regulation because one would expect that maltreatment at an early age would have the most deleterious impact. Finally, more research needs to focus on the family environments, socialization practices, attachment and nurturance of maltreating families of different sorts since these contextual variables surely influence the social and emotional development of children.

The quality of maltreatment research appearing in the literature has shown marked improvement over the last decade or so. Consequently, there is room for optimism that in the next decade we will begin to gain understanding about how multiple forms of maltreatment affect the development of children.

REFERENCES

Bolig, R., Price, C.S., O'Neill, P.L., & Suomi, S.J. (1992). Subjective assessment of reactivity level and personality traits of rhesus monkeys. *International Journal of Primatology, 13*, 287-306.

Briere, J., & Runtz, M. (1988). Multivariate correlates of childhood psychological and physical maltreatment among university women. *Child Abuse and Neglect, 12*, 331-341.

Briere, J., & Runtz, M. (1990). Differential adult symptomatology associated with three types of child abuse histories. *Child Abuse and Neglect, 14*, 357-364.

Burkett, L.P. (1991). Parenting behaviors of women who were sexually abused as children in their families of origin. *Family Processes, 30*, 421-434.

Calkins, S.D. (1994). Origins and outcomes of individual differences in emotion regulation. In N. Fox (Ed.) The development of emotion regulation: Biological and behavioral considerations. *Monograph of the Society for Research in Child Development, Serial No. 240*, 53-72.

Carlson, V., Cicchetti, D., Barnett, D., & Braunwald, K. (1989). Disorganized/disoriented attachment relationships in maltreated infants. *Developmental Psychology, 25*, 525-531.

Cicchetti, D., & Beeghly, S. (Eds.). (1987). *Symbolic development in maltreated children: An organizational perspective* (New Directions in Child Development, No. 36). San Francisco: Jossey-Bass.

Claussen, A. H., & Crittenden, P.M. (1991). Physical and psychological maltreatment: Relations among types of maltreatment. *Child Abuse and Neglect, 15*, 5-18.

Cole, P.M., Michel, M.K., & Teti, L.O. (1994). The development of emotion regulation and dysregulation: A clinical perspective. In N. Fox (Ed.) The development of emotion regulation: Biological and behavioral considerations. *Monograph of the Society for Research in Child Development, Serial No. 240*, 73-100.

Conaway, L.P., & Hansen, D.J. (1989). Social behavior of physically abused and neglected children: A critical review. *Clinical Psychology Review, 9*, 652-687.

Corse, S.A., Schmid, K.D., & Trickett, P.K. (1990). Social network characteristics of abusing and non-abusing mothers and their relationships to parenting beliefs. *Journal of Community Psychology, 18*, 44-54.

Culp, R., Watkins, R.V., Lawrence, H., Letts, D., Kelly, D.J., & Rice, M.L. (1991). Maltreated children's language and speech development: Abused, neglected, and abused and neglected. *First Language, 11*, 377-389.

DeBellis, M.D., Chrousos, G.P., Dorn, L.D., Burke, L., Helmers, K., Kling, M.A., Trickett, P.K., & Putnam, F.W. (1993). Hypothalamic-pituitary-adrenal axis dysregulation in sexually abused girls. *Journal of Clinical Endocrinology and Metabolism, 78*, 249-255.

Dodge, K.A., Bates, J.E., & Pettit, G.S. (1990). Mechanisms in the cycle of violence. *Science, 250*, 1678-1683.

Eckenrode, J., Laird, M., & Doris, J. (1993). School performance and disciplinary problems among abused and neglected children. *Developmental Psychology, 29*, 53-62.

Egeland, B., Sroufe, L.A., & Erickson, M. (1983). The developmental consequences of different patterns of maltreatment. *Child Abuse and Neglect, 7*, 459-469.

Einbender, A.J., & Friedrich, W.N. (1989). Psychological functioning and behavior of sexually abused girls. *Journal of Consulting and Clinical Psychology, 57*, 155-157.

Field, T. (1994). The effects of mothers' physical and emotional unavailability on emotion regulation. In N. Fox (Ed.) The development of emotion regulation: Biological and behavioral considerations. *Monograph of the Society for Research in Child Development, Serial No. 240*, 208-227.

Fox, N.A. (1989). Psychophysiological correlates of emotional reactivity during the first year of life. *Developmental Psychology, 25*, 364-372.

Fox, N.A. (Ed.). (1994). The development of emotion regulation: Biological and behavioral considerations. *Monograph of the Society for Research in Child Development, Serial No, 240*. Chicago: University of Chicago Press.

Frodi, A., & Smetana, J. (1984). Abused, neglected and nonmaltreated preschoolers' ability to discriminate emotions in others: The effects of IQ. *Child Abuse and Neglect, 8*, 459-465.

Helmers, K., Everett, B.A., & Trickett, P.K. (1991). *Social support of sexually abused girls and their mothers*. Paper presented at the Biennial Meetings of the Society for Research in Child Development, Seattle, WA.

Howes, C., & Eldredge, R. (1985). Responses of abused, neglected, and non-maltreated children to the behaviors of their peers. *Journal of Applied Developmental Psychology, 6*, 261-270.

Kaufman, J., & Cicchetti, D. (1989). Effects of maltreatment on school-age children's socioemotional development: Assessment in a day-camp setting. *Developmental Psychology, 25*, 516-524.

Kendall-Tackett, K.A., Williams, L.M., & Finkelhor, D. (1993). Impact of sexual abuse on children: A review and synthesis of recent empirical studies. *Psychological Bulletin, 113*, 164-180.

Kolko, D.J., Moser, J.T., & Weldy, S.R. (1990). Medical/health histories and physical evaluation of physically and sexually abused child psychiatric patients: A controlled study. *Journal of Family Violence, 5*, 249-267.

Kopp, C.B. (1989). Regulation of distress and negative emotions: A developmental view. *Developmental Psychology, 25*, 343-354.

Kopp, C.B., & Wyer, N. (1994). Self-regulation in normal and atypical development. In D. Cicchetti & S. Toth (Eds.) *Disorders and dysfunctions of the self.* Rochester: University of Rochester Press.

Maccoby, E.E., & Martin, J.A. (1983). Socialization in the context of the family: Parent-child interaction. In P.H. Mussen (Series Ed.) and E.M. Hetherington (Vol. Ed.) *Handbook of child psychology, Vol. 4: Socialization, personality, and social development* (pp. 1-102). New York: Wiley.

Parke, R.D., & Slaby, R.G. (1983). The development of aggression. In P.H. Mussen (Series Ed.) and E. M. Hetherington (Vol. Ed.) *Handbook of child psychology, Vol. 4: Socialization, personality, and social development* (pp. 547-642). New York: Wiley.

Pollack, V.E., Briere, J., Schneider, L., Knop, J., Mednick, S.A., & Goodwin, D.W. (1990). Childhood antecedents of antisocial behavior: Parental alcoholism and physical abusiveness. *American Journal of Psychiatry, 147*, 1290-1293.

Putnam, F.W., Helmers, K., & Trickett, P.K. (1993). Development, reliability and validity of a child dissociation scale. *Child Abuse and Neglect, 17*, 731-740.

Putnam, F.W., & Trickett, P.K. (1991). *Cortisol abnormalities in sexually abused girls.* Paper presented at Annual Meetings of the American Psychological Society, Washington, DC.

Rivera, B., & Widom, C.S. (1990). Childhood victimization and violent offending. *Violence and Victims, 5*, 19-35.

Salzinger, S., Rosario, M., Feldman, R.S., Hammer, M., Alvarado, L., Carabello, L., & Ortega, A. (1989). *Social relationships of physically abused preadolescent urban school children.* Paper presented at the Biennial Meeting of the Society for Research in Child Development in Kansas City, MO.

Sameroff, A., & Seifer, R. (1983). Sources of continuity in parent-child relations. In M. Lewis (Chair), *Sociability and change in parent-child interaction in normal and at-risk children.* Symposium conducted at the meeting of the Society for Research in Child Development, Detroit, MI.

Stansbury, K., & Gunnar, M.R. (1994). Adrenocortical activity and emotion regulation. In N. Fox (Ed.) The development of emotion regulation: Biological and behavioral considerations. *Monograph of the Society for Research in Child Development, Serial No. 240*, 108-134.

Stein, J.A., Golding, J.M., Siegel, J.M., Burnam, M.A., & Sorenson, S.B. (1988). Long-term psychological sequelae of child sexual abuse: The Los Angeles Epidemiologic Catchment Area Study. In G.E. Wyatt & G.J. Powell (Eds.) *Lasting effects of child sexual abuse.* Newbury Park, CA: Sage.

Sternberg, K.J., Lamb, M.E., Greenbaum, C., Cicchetti, D., Dawud, S., Cortes, R.M., Krispin, O., & Lorey, F. (1993). Effects of domestic violence on children's behavior problems and depression. *Developmental Psychology, 29*, 44-52.

Thompson, R.A. (1994). Emotion regulation: A theme in search of a definition. In N. Fox (Ed.) The development of emotion regulation: Biological and behavioral considerations. *Monograph of the Society for Research in Child Development, Serial No. 240*, 25-52.

Trickett, P.K. (1993). Maladaptive development of school-aged, physically abused children: Relations with the child rearing context. *Journal of Family Psychology, 7*, 134-147.

Trickett, P.K., Aber, J.L., Carlson, V., & Cicchetti, D. (1991). Relationship of socioeconomic status to the etiology and developmental sequelae of physical child abuse. *Developmental Psychology, 27*, 148-158.

Trickett, P.K., McBride-Chang, C., & Putnam, F.W. (1994). The classroom performance and behavior of sexually abused females. *Development and Psychopathology, 6,* 183-194.

Trickett, P.K., & Kuczynski, L. (1986). Children's misbehaviors and parental discipline strategies in abusive and nonabusive families. *Developmental Psychology, 22*, 115-123.

Trickett, P.K., & Putnam, F.W. (1991). *Patterns of symptoms in prepubertal and pubertal sexually abused girls.* Annual Meeting of the American Psychological Association, San Francisco, CA.

Trickett, P.K., & McBride-Chang, C. (1995). The developmental impact of different forms of child abuse and neglect. *Developmental Review, 15*, 311-337.

Trickett, P.K., & Susman, E.J. (1988). Parental perceptions of child-rearing practices in physically abusive and nonabusive families. *Developmental Psychology, 24*, 270-276.

Vasta, R. (1982). Physical child abuse: A dual-component analysis. *Developmental Review, 2*, 125-149.

Vondra, J., Barnett, D., & Cicchetti, D. (1989). Perceived and actual competence among maltreated and comparison school children. *Development and Psychopathology, 1*, 237-255.

Vondra, J.I., Barnett, D., & Ciccheti, D. (1990). Self-concept, motivation, and competence among preschoolers from maltreating and comparison families. *Child Abuse and Neglect, 14*, 525-540.

White, S., Halpin, B.M., Strom, G.A., & Santilli, G. (1988). Behavioral comparisons of young sexually abused, neglected, and nonreferred children. *Journal of Clinical Child Psychology, 17*, 53-61.

Widom, C.S. (1989). Does violence beget violence? A critical examination of the literature. *Psychological Bulletin, 108*, 3-28.

Wodarski, J.S., Kurtz, P.D., Gaudin, J.M., & Howing, P.T. (1990). Maltreatment and the school-age child: Major academic, socioemotional, and adaptive outcomes. *Social Work, 35*, 506-513.

Wyatt, G.E. (1988). The relationship between child sexual abuse and adolescent sexual functioning in Afro-American and white American women. *Annals of the New York Academy of Sciences*, 111-122.

Zahn-Waxler, C. (1993). Warriors and worriers: Gender and psychopathology. *Development and Psychopathology, 5*, 79-90.

The Effects of Multiple Abuse
in Interpersonal Relationships:
An Attachment Perspective

Holland Cole-Detke
Roger Kobak

SUMMARY. This article reviews attachment theory and research with high-risk maltreated samples. Evidence linking maltreatment to disorganized behavior in the Strange Situation and Adult Attachment Interview is presented. In addition, we review research linking disorganized attachment status in infants and adults to subsequent interpersonal difficulties. Together, research and theory suggest that the experience of abuse leaves victims vulnerable to lapses in organized behavior. These lapses may include violent or frightening experiences that disrupt close interpersonal relationships. Although individuals with disorganized attachment status are capable of organized behavior in most interpersonal contexts, situations involving high levels of interpersonal stress may increase vulnerability to lapses in self-regulation. *[Article copies available for a fee from The Haworth Document Delivery Service: 1-800-342-9678. E-mail address: getinfo@haworth.com]*

During the past two decades, researchers have become increasingly aware of the consequences of childhood abuse for its victims' subsequent relationships. More specifically, studies have pointed to victims' vulnerability to becoming abusive parents (Egeland, Jacobvitz, & Sroufe, 1988)

[Haworth co-indexing entry note]: "The Effects of Multiple Abuse in Interpersonal Relationships: An Attachment Perspective." Cole-Detke, Holland, and Roger Kobak. Co-published simultaneously in *Journal of Aggression, Maltreatment & Trauma* (The Haworth Maltreatment & Trauma Press, an imprint of The Haworth Press, Inc.) Vol. 2, No. 1 (#3), 1998, pp. 189-205; and: *Multiple Victimization of Children: Conceptual, Developmental, Research, and Treatment Issues* (ed: B. B. Robbie Rossman, and Mindy S. Rosenberg) The Haworth Maltreatment & Trauma Press, an imprint of The Haworth Press, Inc., 1998, pp. 189-205. Single or multiple copies of this article are available for a fee from The Haworth Document Delivery Service [1-800-342-9678, 9:00 a.m. - 5:00 p.m. (EST). E-mail address: getinfo@haworth.com].

as well as the effects of abuse on victims' peer (George & Main, 1979) and marital relationships (Holtzworth-Munroe, Hutchinson, & Stuart, 1993). As the consequences of abuse become more clearly documented, new questions are raised about the psychological processes and mechanisms that link victimization to subsequent interpersonal difficulties. Although these questions can be partially addressed with social learning or cognitive theories, Bowlby's (1969, 1980) attachment theory holds particular promise for understanding the motivational and emotional processes associated with victimization. In the following article, we will outline the basic tenets of attachment theory and then consider how abuse and trauma disrupt the individual's capacity for maintaining organized behavior in close relationships. Our general hypothesis is that abuse leaves the individual vulnerable to potential lapses in self-regulation particularly in high-stress parenting, peer, and marital interactions.

ATTACHMENT ORGANIZATION IN NON-ABUSIVE RELATIONSHIPS

Bowlby (1969, 1973, 1980) described attachment as an adaptive, biologically-based system which promotes the proximity of the child to its mother (or primary caregiver) during times of distress. Proximity to a caregiver serves a protective function that increases the child's likelihood of survival. Attachment or proximity seeking behaviors are organized into an attachment system that is regulated through control systems mechanisms (Bowlby, 1969). As the child monitors the attachment figure's availability and responsivity, he or she alters attachment behavior accordingly. Over time, the child develops what Bowlby termed an "internal working model" of the attachment figure that summarizes the child's past experiences with the parent and guides expectations concerning future parental behavior. As a result, working models organize the child's behavior, thoughts, and feelings with regard to attachment.

Several different types of attachment organization have been identified by researchers. Ainsworth (Ainsworth, Blehar, Waters, & Wall, 1978) identified three different categories of infant attachment organization: secure, anxious-avoidant, and anxious-ambivalent on the basis of how infants organized behavior in a laboratory setting called the Strange Situation (Ainsworth & Wittig, 1969). In this paradigm, the infant's attachment organization is inferred from how he or she attempts to reestablish contact with the parent following a brief separation. Infants coded as "secure" (type B) successfully balance attachment and exploration behaviors–gaining comfort from the parent in a way that allows them to return to play and exploration. Infants coded as insecure display two different strategies. "Insecure-avoidant" or (A) infants do not seek comfort from the parent, nor do they display much distress when separated in the Strange Situation. "Insecure-ambivalent" or (C) infants usually seek comfort from the parent but will simultaneously mix contact seeking with anger or excessive passivity.

All three types of infant are assumed to be pursuing an attachment strategy that allows them to maintain organized behavior when faced with a potential disruption of the parent-child relationship. Ainsworth and her colleagues (Ainsworth, Bell, & Stayton, 1971) observed that mothers' behaviors in the home were closely linked to their infants' behavior in the laboratory. Mothers of secure (B) babies were found to be more affectionate, engage in more physical contact, were more effective at soothing their infants, and were more sensitive to their infants' signals. However, mothers of avoidant (A) babies were found to express more controlled anger and to be more rejecting of their infants, while mothers of ambivalent (C) babies were insensitive and inept but not rejecting (Ainsworth, Blehar, Waters, & Wall, 1978). These findings lend support to Bowlby's hypothesis that attachment organization results from the infant's history of interactions with the attachment figure (Bowlby, 1969) and that individuals develop adaptive *strategies* for maintaining the relationship with the parent (Main, 1990; Kobak, Cole, Ferenz-Gillies, Fleming, & Gamble, 1993).

The notion that individuals develop strategies for maintaining attachment organization has recently been extended to assessing adults' "states of mind" in the Adult Attachment Interview (AAI) (George, Kaplan, & Main, 1985). The AAI asks parents to describe and evaluate their experiences with their own parents during childhood. Through detailed reading of interview transcripts, Main and Goldwyn (1985) identified three "states of mind" in parents that paralleled their infants' classifications in the Strange Situation. They found that parents of secure infants most frequently approached interview topics with a "Freedom to Evaluate" attachment. They were able to freely discuss attachment topics and processed attachment information in an objective and coherent way. In contrast, parents of infants classified as insecure-avoidant were most frequently classified as "Dismissing of Attachment." These parents demonstrated difficulty recalling or processing attachment information, particularly if such information was negatively valenced. Finally, parents of infants classified as insecure-ambivalent were more frequently classified as "Preoccupied with Attachment." These parents were so entangled in attachment concerns that they conversed in a confused and overwhelmed manner. They often responded to interview topics with highly detailed, emotional, and run-on sentences that lacked perspective or objectivity about attachment relationships. Subsequent research suggests that pre-natal assessments of parental states of mind in the AAI can prospectively predict infant Strange Situation classifications at 12 months (Fonagy, Steele, & Steele, 1991).

INFANT ATTACHMENT ORGANIZATION IN MALTREATED SAMPLES

Both secure and insecure patterns of attachment can be viewed as ways that individuals organize behavior and feeling in order to maintain a relationship with an attachment figure. These patterns were initially identified in middle-class samples where the caregiver served as a source of protection and safety for the child. However, as attachment researchers considered samples of maltreated children, limitations of previous research became more apparent. For instance, how does a child who has experienced physical or emotional abuse maintain organized behavior toward an attachment figure, if that person has served not only as a source of protection, but also as a threat or source of danger? When the caregiver becomes a source of danger, it is *not* clear that it is in the child's best interest to maintain the relationship with such a parent.

Attachment researchers initially anticipated that abuse and/or neglect would be associated with an increase in insecurity of attachment relationships (Crittenden, 1985; Egeland & Sroufe, 1981; George & Main, 1979; Schneider-Rosen & Cicchetti, 1984). While two thirds of normal middle-class infants were usually classified as secure (Spieker & Booth, 1988), infants from maltreated groups showed substantially higher proportions of insecure attachment, ranging from 64% to 90% insecure (Lyons-Ruth, Connell, Grunebaum, Botein, & Soll, 1984; Lyons-Ruth, Connell, Soll, & Stahl, 1985; Schneider-Rosen, Braunwald, Carlson, & Cicchetti, 1985). These early findings raise a number of methodological and theoretical considerations. Factors such as maternal youth, socioeconomic status, limited resources, limited education, and limited caretaking skills that increase risk for insecure attachment could be confounding the link between maltreatment and insecurity of attachment. In a review of studies using "high risk" samples, Spieker and Booth (1988) reported that when cases of maltreatment and inadequate care were removed from analyses, high-risk samples showed roughly the same proportions of A, B, and C babies as middle-class, low-risk samples (Egeland & Farber, 1984; Lyons-Ruth et al., 1984; Vaughn, Egeland, Sroufe, & Waters, 1979).

Another important issue involves the heterogeneity of children labeled maltreated (Cicchetti & Rizley, 1981). This label can encompass a wide variety of experiences, ranging from neglect to emotional, sexual, or physical abuse to any combination of these. Moreover, there can still be a great deal of heterogeneity within types of abuse. For instance, Gil (1971) identified four subtypes of physical abuse, including uncontrolled anger by the parent toward the child due to perceived misconduct, general rejection of the child, quarrels between caretakers resulting in injury of the child, and leaving the child with inappropriate caretakers who abuse the child (cf. Wissow, 1990). Variables such as severity, chronicity, and pervasiveness of abuse must be considered as well. Other important variables may be the identity of the abuser and his or her importance/meaning in the child's life. And, at least in the case of sexual abuse, age and gender of the abuser may be important as well in terms of the child's experience of the abuse and its subsequent outcome (Finkelhor, 1979; Russell, 1983; cf. Hartman & Burgess, 1989).

Only a few studies have reported the percentages of abuse and the occurrence of multiple abuse. For instance, Cicchetti and Barnett (1991) reported 60% multiple abuse, while other investigators have attempted to differentiate among subtypes (Crittenden, 1985; Egeland & Sroufe, 1981b) and have addressed the issue of multiple abuse via certain combinations of types of abuse (Crittenden, 1985; Egeland & Sroufe, 1981b). In the Minnesota Mother-Child Project study, maltreating mothers were selected from a larger group of 200 mothers of infants who were deemed at "high-risk" for developmental problems (Egeland & Sroufe, 1981b). The investigators observed mother-infant pairs at home over the course of the infants' first year of life, and in the laboratory up to age two. When the children reached two years of age, the mothers were selected into an adequate care control group and a maltreating group consisting of four subgroups: physically abusive, hostile/verbally abusive, psychologically unavailable, and neglecting. Considerable overlap in sub-group membership was reported, with over 90% of the physical abuse group belonging to another subgroup. As expected, the findings indicated that physical abuse was associated with increased risk for insecure attachment. The study also reported systematic differences between maltreatment types. Comparing verbal abuse with and without physical abuse, the investigators found no significant differences at 12 months, but at 18 months 75% of the verbal-abuse-only group could no longer be classified using the A/B/C classification system and was labeled as D ("disorganized"). However, the combination verbal-plus-physical-abuse group showed a more even mix of types, with 15% avoidant, 31% ambivalent, and 8% disorganized. At 12 months, neglect without physical abuse was strongly associated with ambivalence (57% C) while neglect with physical abuse was more associated with avoidance (46% A). However, by 18 months, both groups, neglect with and without physical abuse, showed a predominance of avoidance. Thus, not only were there significant differences in attachment outcomes between different maltreatment subgroups, but also sometimes significant changes in infants' attachment organization between 12 and 18 months.

Crittenden (1985) also attempted to differentiate between types of maltreatment and levels of severity of maltreatment. She found that 70% of the physically abused infants were unclassifiable using the A/B/C categories, while her neglected sample was 55% avoidant, 27% ambivalent, and 18% unclassifiable. A third group, described as "marginally maltreated," showed a distribution of attachment types not significantly different from that of most normal samples, with 50% being secure. Cicchetti and Barnett (1991) also attempted to differentiate between types of maltreatment but found no significant differences. Together these findings highlight the need for further studies to continue examining and clarifying the differences between types of maltreatment in relation to attachment outcomes as well as examining the issue of severity of maltreatment. These studies also pointed to a group of maltreated infants who did not fit the existing attachment classifications and who seemed to lack a traditional attachment strategy.

THE DISCOVERY
OF ATYPICAL/DISORGANIZED ATTACHMENT

Egeland and Sroufe's D's and Crittenden's studies of severe child maltreatment suggested that many abused children displayed behavior that did not fit the existing classifications schemes. This finding led to a reexamination of Ainsworth's classification system and the development of new categories and coding guidelines for describing atypical attachment behavior. The D category, described by Main and Solomon (1986), is assigned to infants who display Disorganized or Disoriented behavior in the Strange Situation. In reviewing the videotapes of 34 infants who were considered "unclassifiable" out of the 368 infants who had been coded in the Strange Situation as part of the Berkeley Social Development Project, Main and Solomon (1986) discovered a new group of infants whose behavior in the Strange Situation was characterized by disorganized and/or disoriented behavior such as freezing all movement, covering the mouth with the hand, approaching the parent backwards, or other signs of extreme fear in the parent's presence.

The disorganized/disoriented behavior observed in the Strange Situation is believed to be indicative of internal conflict between approach and avoidance of the parent (Ainsworth & Eichberg, 1991). While the child needs to seek proximity and gain comfort, the child is also frightened of the parent, either because the parent's behavior is frightening or threatening or because the parent (him- or herself) appears frightened, which in turn is frightening to the child (Main & Hesse, 1990). Disorganized behavior usually only occurred very briefly, often when the parent reentered the room. At such times, the child would freeze or move his hand to his mouth in a sign of fear for a few seconds. These brief episodes appear to represent lapses or temporary disruptions of attachment organization. The child's behavior could otherwise fit into one of the organized attachment categories, A, B, or C. For this reason, infants receiving a D classification also are assigned to one of the standard categories. In this sense, the D category does not really represent a type of attachment organization but instead appears to represent an infant's vulnerability to temporary disorganization of its usual attachment organization.

Crittenden (1988) developed a somewhat different classification for describing atypical infant behavior in the Strange Situation, the A/C classification. Following the startling finding that a number of children who were severely abused were being rated secure, a number of researchers chose to reexamine their data (Crittenden, 1988; Carlson, Cicchetti, Barnett, & Braunwald, 1989). Crittenden (1988) observed that these seemingly secure children had been rated as secure because they had displayed approach behaviors that were typical of secure children. However, approach behavior was mixed with avoidance and resistance, indicating a lack of single organized attachment strategy. She relabelled this group "avoidant-resistant" or "A/C," representing a combination of anxious-avoidant (A) and anxious-ambivalent (C) behaviors. Other researchers were also developing coding guidelines for A/C type infants who had previously been rated as secure or unclassifiable (Spieker & Booth, 1988) and for other types of atypical patterns such as "unstable avoidance" (Lyons-Ruth, Connell, & Zoll, 1989).

Using revised classification schemes, researchers have found a high rate of atypical attachment patterns in maltreated samples (Carlson, Cicchetti, Barnett, & Braunwald, 1989; Cicchetti & Barnett, 1991; Crittenden, 1985; Lyons-Ruth, Connell, Zoll, & Stahl, 1987). Carlson et al. (1989) found that over 80% of their maltreatment sample were disorganized (D), compared to under 20% of their non-maltreatment sample, while Crittenden (1988) found that 50% of her physically abused and 58% of her abused and neglected children were classified as avoidant-resistant (A/C). However, rates of disorganization or atypical attachment have varied from one maltreated sample to another. For instance, Lyons-Ruth et al. (1985)

reported only 30% of their maltreatment sample as being atypical. This variability may be due in part to the issue of stability of attachment classification. Lyons-Ruth, Repacholi, McLeod, and Silva (1991) found that the majority of their infants who were disorganized at 18 months had not been disorganized at 12 months. Cicchetti and Barnett (1991) also addressed the issue of stability. Among maltreated children, atypical patterns of attachment remained relatively stable over time (assessed over a 6- to 18-month period) with insecurity, particularly avoidance, increasing. In contrast, among the non-maltreated children atypical patterns were not as stable, but security of attachment was more stable. Thus, abused children had higher rates of insecurity and atypical patterns of attachment which appeared to increase over time.

Overall, researchers agree that maltreatment samples have a significantly higher percentage of atypical attachment patterns than do non-maltreating low- and high-risk samples (Carlson et al., 1989; Crittenden, 1988; Lyons-Ruth et al., 1989, 1991). Moreover, most data supports the hypothesis that severity and chronicity of abuse are associated with increasingly insecure and probably disorganized or other atypical attachment (Carlson et al., 1989; Cicchetti & Barnett, 1991). Crittenden and Ainsworth (1989) have suggested that multiple abuse may be the most strongly associated with disorganized types of attachment because of the unpredictability of the parenting (for example, passive withdrawal of a neglecting parent combined with sudden periods of violent/abusive involvement). Consequently, the child may be unable to develop a consistent and stable strategy for coping.

More home observation studies are needed to understand what attachment behaviors mean in this context. For instance, Crittenden (1985) found that in three studies of mother-child interaction in maltreating samples, mother and child behaviors usually matched in predictable ways, i.e., the child's behavior appeared to correspond to quality of caregiving. However, in 16 cases, the child's behavior appeared completely discrepant from what would be expected given the mother's level of insensitivity and inappropriate behaviors. These 16 children appeared unusually accommodating and cooperative if not eager to please (behavior which might normally be viewed as secure). Crittenden (1988) hypothesized that these children, who tended to have experienced more severe or pervasive maltreatment than the other children, may have learned that negative or passive behaviors on their part could be extremely dangerous for them. Thus, much more study is necessary to understand how attachment behavior is altered.

Several investigators have examined the sequelae of abuse and atypical attachment. Studies of peer relations have been particularly revealing. Lyons-Ruth et al. (1991) found that children who had been assessed as disorganized in the Strange Situation at 18 months had higher rates of hostile-aggressive behavior toward peers in kindergarten than did children who had consistent, organized patterns of attachment. Other studies have found high rates of physical and verbal aggression among abused children as toddlers (George & Main, 1979), preschoolers (Herrenkohl & Herrenkohl, 1981; Hoffman-Plotkin & Twentyman, 1984) and school-aged children (Salzinger, Feldman, Hammer, & Rosario, 1993). Klimes-Dougan and Kistner (1990) found that abused preschoolers exhibited more inappropriate responses, such as aggression and withdrawal, to peers' distress. George and Main (1979) also reported approach-avoidance behavior with peers and caregivers in daycare settings in addition to "harassing" types of behaviors toward others such as spitting or threatening assault. These behaviors may account for the findings that abused children are less well liked by their peers (Coie, Dodge, & Coppotelli, 1982; Haskett & Kistner, 1991; Salzinger, Feldman, Hammer, & Rosario, 1993) and lend support to the hypothesis that abused children are more likely to become abusive toward others.

UNRESOLVED TRAUMA AS A RISK FACTOR FOR ABUSIVE PARENTING, PSYCHOPATHOLOGY AND MARITAL VIOLENCE

The growing recognition of atypical or disorganized attachment behavior in infants led to an effort to identify similar difficulties in adults' states of mind in the Adult Attachment Interview (AAI). To capture atypical states of mind, Main and Goldwyn (1991) added a new *adult* attachment category, "Unresolved loss or trauma" or "U," to their existing AAI classification system. Unresolved status in the AAI can be seen in lapses in the monitoring of reasoning or discourse while the individual is discussing traumatic events such as the death of an attachment figure or physical or sexual abuse (Main, 1991; Main, Van IJzendoorn, & Hesse, 1993). Such individuals may make statements about a deceased attachment figure indicating a belief that the person is not really dead or other odd beliefs about the death (e.g., "My father died because I forgot to pray for him that night."). Other indications of unresolved status are seen in failures in metacognitive monitoring during the interview such that speech becomes disorganized or disoriented (e.g., slipping into present tense or a child's perspective, odd interjections, or unusually eulogistic speech). These slippages may be something akin to "flashbacks" or instances of dissociation (Main et al., 1993). Thus, AAI transcripts may be classified as Unresolved

(U) even on the basis of a single sentence, just as infants in the Strange Situation may be classified as disorganized (D) based on only a few seconds of frightened behavior. Also, because the U classification is based upon brief lapses in the interview discourse, transcripts receiving a U also receive a second, best-fitting classification using one of the three original categories, Secure, Dismissing, or Preoccupied.

An important first step in understanding the Unresolved pattern will be to consider how such status is linked to parenting and atypical attachment classifications in infants of parents who have lapses in the AAI. Attachment theory provides some specific hypotheses that might link Unresolved status in the AAI to abusive parenting. If a parent is Unresolved with respect to trauma (i.e., the parent experienced traumatic abuse as a child at the hand of an attachment figure), the parent shows lapses in metacognitive monitoring during the interview which calls up memories of the trauma. Such lapses make it impossible for these individuals to attend to the context of the interview. Instead, they appear temporarily to lose touch with the interview context and become absorbed in the memory of the trauma. If such lapses also occur in the home when such memories are triggered, what behaviors might occur? Assuming that the parent has temporarily become absorbed in the memory of past trauma, the parent may display inappropriate or dysregulated affect and behavior. At such moments, as Main and Hesse (1990) hypothesize, the parent is likely to behave in a frightened or frightening manner. This behavior, when witnessed and/or experienced by the child, is in turn extremely frightening and traumatizing to the child. The child is then at risk for displaying atypical frightening or conflicted behaviors in the Strange Situation.

While direct links between atypical adult AAI and infant Strange Situation patterns are lacking, initial studies point to links between atypical AAI status and various indicators of psychopathology or interpersonal aggression and violence. Rosenstein and Horowitz (1993) found that 42% of their dual-diagnosis sample in an adolescent psychiatric hospital were classified as Unresolved. Similarly, Allen, Hauser, and Borman-Spurtell (1993) found that compared to a normal, control sample, their sample of young adults who had been psychiatrically hospitalized during adolescence had over three times as many Unresolved and over twice as many Cannot Classify cases. Thus, atypical AAI patterns may be associated with more severe forms of psychopathology. Given that the U-type mental lapses in the AAI appear to be mini-dissociative experiences, it seems logical to expect that U classification would be common among individuals suffering from Post-traumatic Stress Disorder or various dissociative disorders, particularly given that these types of disorders often result from traumatic experiences (Bliss, 1984; Coons & Milstein, 1986; Putnam, Guroff, Silberman, Barban, & Post, 1986). Dissociative disorders have been associated with abuse, particularly multiple, severe, and/or chronic abuse (Briere & Runtz, 1988; Putnam, 1989; Sandberg & Lynn, 1992; Sanders, McRoberts, & Tollefson, 1989).

Two studies also suggest associations between unresolved status in the AAI and inappropriate or aggressive social behavior. In a study comparing violent to non-violent maritally distressed men, Holtzworth-Munroe and her colleagues found that men who were maritally violent were much more likely to be classified as having an atypical attachment pattern (over 50%) compared to a non-violent, distressed group and a non-violent, non-distressed group (Holtzworth-Munroe, Hutchinson, & Stuart, 1993). Given that maltreatment has been associated with increased levels of atypical attachment patterns in infants and with increased levels of interpersonal aggression, this finding of increased marital violence in men with atypical attachment patterns suggests that a disorganized behavior in the AAI may be linked to violent behavior in adults. Allen et al. (1993) also report that scale scores for Unresolved trauma as a result of abuse by a parent were predictive of criminal behavior. Such a finding is consistent with the extensive literature linking delinquency and criminality with harsh or abusive parenting during childhood (Dodge, Bates, & Pettit, 1990; Garbarino & Plantz, 1986; Salzinger, Feldman, Hammer, & Rosario, 1991) and suggests that Unresolved trauma may mediate such a relationship (Allen et al., 1993).

Together, these studies demonstrate further links between aggressive or maladaptive interpersonal behaviors and atypical attachment patterns. In particular, the Allen et al. (1993) and Holtzworth-Munroe et al. (1993) studies point to processes that may link child maltreatment to atypical attachment and later maladaptive behaviors (criminality and marital violence). Observations from the Strange Situation and Adult Attachment Interview suggest that temporary disorganization in these research paradigms may be linked to failure to develop a consistent and normative strategy for coping with stressors and relating to others. This failure to develop an organized attachment strategy would appear to leave these individuals vulnerable to periods of disorganization which result in inappropriate or aggressive behaviors in stressful interpersonal situations. As children, their peer relationships may be unsatisfactory and rejecting due to their own inappropriate and aggressive responses to others. This may lead to social isolation which places the child at further risk for negative developmental outcomes. Moreover, these disorganized and even bizarre methods of coping and relating, in which the individual strikes out at others, probably due to his or her own insecurity and fear of threat from others, will most likely continue into adulthood where relationships with one's spouse and children are also subject to abusive episodes. Thus, the pattern of abuse and disorganized attachment may be transmitted across generations.

CONCLUSION AND FUTURE DIRECTIONS

The studies described here link child maltreatment to difficulties in maintaining organized attachment-related behavior in the Strange Situation and Adult Attachment Interview, which in turn have been related to difficulties in interpersonal relationships. Lapses in organization in the Strange Situation have been related to violent and aggressive behavior in later peer relations, and lapses in the AAI have been linked to psychopathology, criminal behavior, and marital violence. While these findings suggest that disorganized or atypical attachment patterns may play a mediating role between child maltreatment and later negative outcomes, we should note that directions of effect cannot be determined from these studies. In particular, we should not ignore the possibility that there may be a genetic predisposition for violent behavior that accounts for the reported correlations. Additionally, much more information is needed as to the nature of disorganized attachment patterns. Future studies need to investigate the links between atypical status in the Strange Situation and atypical status in the AAI. Attention should also be given to the different subtypes of atypical attachment, particularly the difference between lapses versus pervasive disorganization. More information is also needed about adults who report trauma but do not show lapses in meta-cognitive monitoring in the AAI. Such studies could inform programs for helping survivors of childhood abuse and trauma.

We suspect that multiple abuse may lead to severe impairment of attachment organization and difficulty forming trusting relationships. While a strategy of playing down attachment feelings and behaviors and maintaining interpersonal distance in relationships would seem viable for a victimized individual, this strategy itself might be prone to breaking down in ways that result in severe disturbances including violent behavior directed toward self and others. Such breakdown may be especially likely to occur in interpersonal contexts in which an individual is faced with or called upon to respond to severe distress. Failure to maintain an organized attachment strategy may manifest itself in several forms of psychopathology. For instance, pervasively disorganized strategies may be associated with the development of Borderline personality features, while acute lapses in organized defensive strategies may result in: (1) severe dissociation, such as multiple personality disorder, (2) temporary psychosis, i.e., complete departure from reality, or (3) violent criminal or suicidal behavior. Therapists working with such individuals must anticipate the possibility for potentially harmful lapses and may use psychiatric hospitalization as a way of assuring clients' safety. Work with such individuals is very likely to require a long-term supportive treatment that initially focuses on reducing symptomatic behavior and gradually moves toward exploring the clients' difficulties and distrust of others. The formation of a secure and stable relationship between the individual and the therapist may provide a corrective experience which may foster the development of an increasingly secure attachment organization.

REFERENCES

Ainsworth, M.D.S., Bell, S.M., & Stayton, D.J. (1971). Individual differences in the development of some attachment behaviors. *Merrill-Palmer Quarterly, 18*, 123-143.

Ainsworth, M.D.S., Blehar, M., Waters, E., & Wall, S. *Patterns of attachment: A psychological study of the strange situation.* Hillsdale, NJ: Erlbaum.

Ainsworth, M.D.S., & Eichberg, C. (1991). Effects on infant-mother attachment of mother's unresolved loss of an attachment figure, or other traumatic experience. In C.M. Parkes, J. Stevenson-Hinde, & P. Marris (Eds.), *Attachment across the life cycle* (pp. 160-183). London: Routledge.

Ainsworth, M.D.S., & Wittig, B. (1969). Attachment and exploratory behavior of one-year-olds in a strange situation. In B. Foss (Ed.), *Determinants of infant behavior (vol. 4).* New York: Wiley.

Allen, J.P., Hauser, S.T., & Borman-Spurrell, E. (1993). Attachment theory as a framework for understanding outcomes of severe adolescent psychopathology: An eleven-year follow-up study. Manuscript submitted for publication.

Bliss, E.L. (1984). A symptom profile of patients with multiple personalities, including MMPI results. *Journal of Nervous and Mental Disease, 1172*, 197-201.

Bowlby, J. (1969). *Attachment and loss. Vol. 1: Attachment.* New York: Basic Books.

Bowlby, J. (1973). *Attachment and loss. Vol. 2: Separation.* New York: Basic Books.

Bowlby, J. (1980). *Attachment and loss. Vol. 3: Loss, sadness and depression.* New York: Basic Books.

Briere, J., & Runtz, M. (1988a). Multivariate correlates of childhood psychological and physical maltreatment among university women. *Child Abuse and Neglect, 12*, 331-341.

Briere, J., & Runtz, M. (1988b). Symptomatology associated with childhood sexual victimization in a nonclinical adult sample. *Child Abuse and Neglect, 12*, 51-59.

Carlson, V., Cicchetti, D., Barnett, D., & Braunwald, K. (1989). Finding order in disorganization: Lessons from research on maltreated infants' attachments to their caregivers. In D. Cicchetti & V. Carlson (Eds.), *Child maltreatment: Theory and research on the causes and consequences of child abuse and neglect* (pp. 494-528). New York: Cambridge University Press.

Cicchetti, D., & Barnett, D. (1991). Attachment organization in maltreated preschoolers. *Development and Psychopathology, 3*, 397-411.

Cicchetti, D., & Rizley, R. (1981). Developmental perspectives on the etiology, intergenerational transmission, and sequelae of child maltreatment. In R. Rizley & D. Cicchetti (Eds.), *Developmental perspectives on child maltreatment. New directions for child development (no. 11)* (pp. 31-55). San Francisco: Jossey-Bass.

Coie, J.D., Dodge, H.A., & Coppotelli, H. (1982). Dimensions and types of social status: A cross-age perspective. *Developmental Psychology, 18*, 557-570.

Coons, P.M., & Milstein, V. (1986). Psychosexual disturbances in multiple personality: Characteristics, etiology, and treatment. *Journal of Clinical Psychiatry, 47*, 106-110.

Crittenden, P.M. (1985). Maltreated infants: Vulnerability and resilience. *Journal of Child Psychology and Psychiatry, 26*, 85-96.

Crittenden, P.M. (1988). Relationships at risk. In J. Belsky & T. Nezworski (Eds.), *Clinical implications of attachment* (pp. 136-174). Hillsdale, NJ: Erlbaum.

Crittenden, P.M., & Ainsworth, M.D.S. (1989). Child maltreatment and attachment theory. In D. Cicchetti & V. Carlson (Eds.), *Child maltreatment: Theory and research on the causes and consequences of child abuse and neglect* (pp. 432-463). New York: Cambridge University Press.

Crowell, J.A., & Feldman, S.S. (1988). Mothers' internal models of relationships and children's behavioral and developmental status: A study of mother-child interaction. *Child Development, 59*, 1273-1285.

Crowell, J.A., & Feldman, S.S. (1991). Mothers' working models of attachment relationships and mother and child behavior during separation and reunion. *Developmental Psychology, 27*, 597-605.

Crowell, J.A., O'Connor, E., Wollmers, G., Sprafkin, J., & Rao, U. (1992). Mothers' conceptualizations of parent-child relationships: Relation to mother-child interaction and child behavior problems. *Development and Psychopathology, 3*, 431-444.

Dodge, K.A., Bates, J.E., & Pettit, G.S. (1990). Mechanisms in the cycle of violence. *Science, 250*, 1678-1683.

Egeland, B., & Farber, E. (1984). Infant-mother attachment: Factors related to its development and changes over time. *Child Development, 55*, 753-771.

Egeland, B., Jacobvitz, D., & Stroufe, L.A. (1988). Breaking the cycle of abuse. *Child Development, 59*, 1080-1088.

Egeland, B., & Sroufe, L.A. (1981a). Attachment and early maltreatment. *Child Development, 52*, 44-52.

Egeland, B., & Sroufe, A. (1981b). Developmental sequelae of maltreatment in infancy. In R. Rizley & D. Cicchetti (Eds.), *Developmental perspectives on child maltreatment. New directions for child development (no. 11)* (pp. 77-92). San Francisco: Jossey-Bass.

Finkelhor, D. (1979). *Sexually victimized children.* New York: Free Press.

Fonagy, P., Steele, H., & Steele, M. (1991). Maternal representations of attachment during pregnancy predict the organization of infant-mother attachment at one year of age. *Child Development, 62*, 891-905.

George, C., Kaplan, N., & Main, M. (1985). *An adult attachment interview: Interview protocol.* Unpublished manuscript, University of California, Berkeley.

George, C., & Main, M. (1979). Social interactions of young abused children: Approach, avoidance, and aggression. *Child Development, 50*, 306-318.

Gil, D. (1971). Violence against children. *Journal of Marriage and Family, 33*, 637-657.

Hartman, C.R., & Burgess, A.W. (1989). Sexual abuse of children: Causes and consequences. In D. Cicchetti & V. Carlson (Eds.), *Child maltreatment: Theory and research on the causes and consequences of child abuse and neglect* (pp. 95-128). New York: Cambridge University Press.

Haskett, M.E., & Kistner, J.A. (1991). Social interactions and peer perceptions of young physically abused children. *Child Development, 62*, 979-990.

Herrenkohl, R.C., & Herrenkohl, E.C. (1981). Some antecedents and developmental consequences of child maltreatment. In R. Rizley & D. Cicchetti (Eds.), *Developmental perspectives on child maltreatment. New directions for child development (no. 11)* (pp. 57-92). San Francisco: Jossey-Bass.

Hoffman-Plotkin, D., & Twentyman, C.T. (1984). A multimodal assessment of behavioral and cognitive deficits in abused and neglected preschoolers. *Child Development, 55*, 794-802.

Holtzworth-Munroe, A., Hutchinson, G., & Stuart, G.L. (1993). Comparing the working models of attachment of violent and nonviolent husbands. Manuscript submitted for publication.

Kobak, R.R., Cole, H.E., Ferenz-Gillies, R., Fleming, W.S., & Gamble, W. (1993). Attachment and emotion regulation during mother-teen problem solving: A control theory analysis. *Child Development, 64*, 231-245.

Lynch, M., & Cicchetti, D. (1991). Patterns of relatedness in maltreated and nonmaltreated children: Connections among multiple representational models. *Development and Psychopathology, 3*, 207-226.

Lyons-Ruth, K., Connell, D., Grunebaum, H., Botein, S., & Zoll, D. (1984). Maternal family history, maternal caretaking and infant attachment in multi-problem families. *Preventive Psychiatry, 2*, 403-425.

Lyons-Ruth, K., Connell, D.B., & Zoll, D. (1989). Patterns of maternal behavior among infants at risk for abuse: Relations with infant attachment behavior and infant development at 12 months of age. In D. Cicchetti & V. Carlson (Eds.),

Child maltreatment: Theory and research on the causes and consequences of child abuse and neglect (pp. 464-493). New York: Cambridge University Press.

Lyons-Ruth, K., Connell, D.B., Zoll, D., & Stahl, J. (1985). *Infants at social risk: Relationships among infant attachment behavior, infant development and maternal behavior at home in maltreated and non-maltreated infants.* Paper presented at the Society for Research in Child Development, Toronto.

Lyons-Ruth, K., Connell, D.B., Zoll, D., & Stahl, J. (1987). Infants at social risk: Relations among infant maltreatment, maternal behavior, and infant attachment behavior. *Developmental Psychology, 23*, 223-232.

Lyons-Ruth, K., Repacholi, B., McLeod, S., & Silva, E. (1991). Disorganized attachment behavior in infancy: Short-term stability, maternal and infant correlates, and risk-related subtypes. *Development and Psychopathology, 3*, 377-396.

Main, M. (1990). Cross-cultural studies of attachment organization: Recent studies, changing methodologies, and the concept of conditional strategies. *Human Development, 33*, 48-61.

Main, M. (1991). Metacognitive knowledge, metacognitive monitoring, and singular (coherent) vs. multiple (incoherent) models of attachment: Findings and directions for future research. In C.M. Parkes, J. Stevenson-Hinde, & P. Marris (Eds.), *Attachment across the life cycle* (pp. 127-159). London: Routledge.

Main, M., & Goldwyn, R. (1984). Predicting rejection of her infant from mother's representation of her own experience: Implications for the abused-abusing intergenerational cycle. *Child Abuse and Neglect, 8*, 203-217.

Main, M., & Goldwyn, R. (1985, 1991, in press). *Adult attachment rating and classification systems.* Unpublished manuscript, Department of Psychology, University of California at Berkeley.

Main, M., & Hesse, E. (1990). Parents' unresolved traumatic experiences are related to infant disorganized attachment status: Is frightened and/or frightening parental behavior the linking mechanism? In M.T. Greenberg, D. Cicchetti, & E.M. Cummings (Eds.), *Attachment in the preschool years* (pp. 161-182). Chicago: University of Chicago Press.

Main, M., Kaplan, N., & Cassidy, J. (1985). Security in infancy, childhood, and adulthood: A move to the level of representation. In I. Bretherton & E. Waters (Eds.), *Growing points of attachment theory and research. Monographs of the Society for Research in Child Development, 50*(1-2, Serial No. 209, pp. 66-104). Chicago: University of Chicago Press.

Main, M., & Solomon, J. (1986). Discovery of a new, insecure-disorganized/disoriented attachment pattern. In M. Yogman & T.B. Brazelton (Eds.), *Affective development in infancy* (pp. 95-124). Norwood, NJ: Ablex.

Main, M., & Solomon, J. (1990). Procedures for identifying infants as disorganized/disoriented during the Ainsworth Strange Situation. In D. Cicchetti & M. Cummings (Eds.), *Attachment in the preschool years* (pp. 121-160), Chicago: University of Chicago Press.

Main, M., Van IJzendoorn, M.H., & Hesse, E. (1993). *Unresolved/unclassifiable responses to the Adult Attachment Interview: Predictable from unresolved states and anomalous beliefs in the Berkeley-Leiden Adult Attachment Ques-*

tionnaire. Paper presented at the Society for Research in Child Development, New Orleans.

Main, M., & Weston, D.R. (1982). Avoidance of the attachment figure in infancy: Descriptions and interpretations. In C. Parkes & J. Stevenson-Hinde (Eds.), *The place of attachment in human behavior* (pp. 31-59). New York: Basic Books.

Putnam, F.W. (1989). *Diagnosis and treatment of multiple personality disorder.* New York: Guilford Press.

Putnam, F.W., Guroff, J.J., Silberman, E.K., Barban, L., & Post, R.M. (1986). The clinical phenomenology of multiple personality disorder: Review of 100 recent cases. *Journal of Clinical Psychiatry, 47*, 285-293.

Rosenstein, D.S., & Horowitz, H.A. (1993). *Working models of attachment in psychiatrically hospitalized adolescents: Relation to psychopathology and personality.* Paper presented at the Society for Research in Child Development, New Orleans.

Russell, D. (1983). The incidence and prevalence of intrafamilial and extrafamilial sexual abuse of female children. *Child Abuse and Neglect, 7*, 133-146.

Salzinger, S., Feldman, R.S., Hammer, M., & Rosario, M. (1993). The effects of physical abuse on children's social relationships. *Child Development, 64*, 169-187.

Salzinger, S., Feldman, R.S., Hammer, M., & Rosario, M. (1991). Risk for physical child abuse and the personal consequences for its victims. *Criminal Justice and Behavior, 18*, 64-81.

Sandberg, D.A., & Lynn, S.J. (1992). Dissociative experiences, psychopathology and adjustment, and child and adolescent maltreatment in female college students. *Journal of Abnormal Psychology, 101*, 717-723.

Sanders, B., McRoberts, K.G., & Tollefson, C. (1989). Childhood stress and dissociation in a college population. *Dissociation, 2*, 17-23.

Schneider-Rosen, K., Braunwald, K., Carlson, V., & Cicchetti, D. (1985). Current perspectives in attachment theory: Illustration from the study of maltreated infants. In I. Bretherton & E. Waters (Eds.), *Growing points in attachment theory and research. Monographs of the Society for Research in Child Development, 50*(1-2, Serial No. 209, pp. 194-210). Chicago: University of Chicago Press.

Schneider-Rosen, K., & Cicchetti, D. (1984). The relationship between affect and cognition in maltreated infants: Quality of attachment and development of visual self-recognition. *Child Development, 55*, 648-658.

Spieker, S.J., & Booth, C.L. (1988). Maternal antecedents of attachment quality. In J. Belsky & T. Nezworski (Eds.), *Clinical implications of attachment* (pp. 135). Hillsdale, NJ: Erlbaum Associates.

Vaughn, B., Egeland, B., Sroufe, L.A., & Waters, E. (1979). Individual differences in infant-mother attachment at twelve and eighteen months: Stability and change in families under stress. *Child Development, 50*, 971-975.

Wissow, L.S. (1990). *Child advocacy for the clinician: An approach to child abuse and neglect.* Baltimore: Williams & Wilkins.

TREATMENT APPROACHES AND ISSUES

Interventions with Young Children Who Have Been Multiply Abused

Jan L. Culbertson
Diane J. Willis

SUMMARY. This article provides an overview of theory-driven interventions for young children who have been multiply abused and their families. The interventions are based primarily upon two theories: (1) Developmental-ecological theory provides a conceptual framework for understanding the *context* of abuse, and for planning effective interventions for the individual, the parents, and the family, and other social contexts; (2) Attachment theory provides a conceptual framework for understanding the disordered parent/child *relationships* that can lead to or result from maltreatment, and can suggest directions for intervention. *[Article copies available for a fee from The Haworth Document Delivery Service: 1-800-342-9678. E-mail address: getinfo@haworth.com]*

Multiple abuse is particularly devastating to young children due to their vulnerability, their dependency upon their caregivers for protection and

[Haworth co-indexing entry note]: "Interventions with Young Children Who Have Been Multiply Abused." Culbertson, Jan L., and Diane J. Willis. Co-published simultaneously in *Journal of Aggression, Maltreatment & Trauma* (The Haworth Maltreatment & Trauma Press, an imprint of The Haworth Press, Inc.) Vol. 2, No. 1 (#3), 1998, pp. 207-232; and: *Multiple Victimization of Children: Conceptual, Developmental, Research, and Treatment Issues* (ed: B. B. Robbie Rossman, and Mindy S. Rosenberg) The Haworth Maltreatment & Trauma Press, an imprint of The Haworth Press, Inc., 1998, pp. 207-232. Single or multiple copies of this article are available for a fee from The Haworth Document Delivery Service [1-800-342-9678, 9:00 a.m. - 5:00 p.m. (EST). E-mail address: getinfo@haworth.com].

207

nurturance, and often the absence of other protective factors in their environment to mitigate the effects of maltreatment. The vulnerability of infants, toddlers, and preschoolers to multiple abuse is exacerbated by their developmental stage, and the importance of the early months and years of life in the formation of stable attachment relationships.

Developmental-ecological theory (Belsky, 1993) is an important organizing construct related both to the etiology and intervention of child maltreatment. Based on the seminal work of Bronfenbrenner (1979), Belsky elaborated a view that child maltreatment is multiply determined by factors operating through transactional processes at different levels of analysis, ranging from the individual, to the family, to the community, and to the culture. These factors create the "context of maltreatment," and are felt to be nested ecologically within one another, so that the interactions among them are more important in the etiology of maltreatment than any single factor operating alone. The implication of the developmental-ecological perspective is that there are a variety of targets of intervention, ranging from the specific caregiving behavior of a parent to the social conditions that make it difficult for parents to be emotionally sensitive or psychologically available to their children (Belsky, 1993).

Attachment theory provides another useful framework for understanding the disordered parent-child relationships that can lead to maltreatment. Most theorists agree that, whether maltreatment occurs in the form of neglect, physical abuse, sexual abuse, or emotional abuse, the common thread for maltreated children is their parents' lack of sensitivity to their emotional needs (Crittenden & Ainsworth, 1989; Erickson & Egeland, 1987). The parents' lack of emotional availability to their child creates a situation of psychological neglect that interrupts the formation of secure attachment relationships with the parents. Children who lack a foundation of secure attachment have been found to be ill equipped in forming new relationships, learning to trust others, adapting successfully to new situations, and dealing with new demands over their life span (Cicchetti, 1987; Crittenden & Ainsworth, 1989; Graziano & Mills, 1992). From the perspective of the child's psychological development, maltreatment not only has an immediate impact, but also a potentially long-range impact based on disruption of the child's critical phases of attachment and development (Cicchetti, 1987). Therefore, attachment theory is also viewed as an important organizing construct through which both the etiology of maltreatment and the treatment of its effects can be understood.

Both developmental-ecological theory and attachment theory provide the theoretical underpinnings for intervention strategies with infants, toddlers, and preschoolers who are victims of multiple forms of maltreatment.

It would be ideal if there were a large empirical literature on the efficacy of interventions with children who have been victims of multiple forms of abuse. Unfortunately, the distinctions between physical abuse, emotional abuse, and neglect are difficult to make in most research. Indeed, most of the literature on child maltreatment is fraught with problems in definition, labeling and identification, and imprecise distinctions based on the severity or chronicity of maltreatment. The lack of precision in the current literature makes it quite difficult to suggest specific interventions that have been proven to work with children of either single types of maltreatment or combined types. Therefore, it is reasonable to start from a theoretical perspective and to propose interventions that are logically based upon currently accepted theory. This chapter uses both developmental-ecological theory and attachment theory as the bases for suggesting interventions for young children who are victims of multiple forms of maltreatment.

Before initiating an intervention program, it is important to assess the child, family, and social context so that an appropriate treatment can be planned. The next section of the article discusses a model for assessment as a prelude to intervention.

ASSESSING THE SOCIAL CONTEXT
IN WHICH ABUSE OCCURS

Assessing the social context in which multiple abuse occurs is an important precursor to planning an effective intervention. The multiple, interacting variables that affect the balance between risk and protective factors in the environment must be understood. Prior to establishing a treatment plan for the multiply victimized child, it is important to incorporate information from a variety of sources to assess the specifics of the abuse situation, the child's current family status, parental goals and attitudes toward treatment, and the developmental impact of the abuse upon the child.

Assessing the Specifics of the Abuse Situation

The first step in assessment, as illustrated in Table 1, involves obtaining objective historical information through a variety of sources and methods. These may involve interviewing the protective services caseworker, and reviewing child protective service records and/or pertinent medical records. The goals of assessment are to determine the specifics of the abuse situation in terms of type (i.e., physical, sexual, emotional, neglect, or

TABLE 1. Assessing the Social Context in Which Abuse Occurs

Goals of Assessment	Methods of Assessment
Assess the Specifics of the Abuse Situation 1. Understand the nature of the abuse (type, severity, chronicity) 2. Assess the child's current living situation with regard to safety, stability, parental availability. 3. Determine the short-term and long-term child protective service plan for the family	Obtain Objective History • Interview caseworker • Review child protective service records • Review medical records
Assess the Family Environment 1. Obtain demographic information about the family of origin and assess their practical needs 2. Assess the family's social support network and the parents' priorities for intervention 3. Determine parental motivation for treatment	Obtain Subjective History and Clinical Impressions • Clinical interview of parents or substitute caregiver • Parenting Stress Index
Assess the Parent-Child Relationship 1. Determine the nature of the parent-child attachment relationship 2. Assess the parents' personal resources and psychopathology	Obtain Observational Data • Observe parent-child interaction • Adult Attachment Interview
Assess the Impact of Abuse on the Child 1. Understand the impact of abuse on the child's cognitive, linguistic, adaptive, social, and behavioral functioning 2. Assess the possible disruptive effects of abuse on the child's development 3. Assess for signs of post-traumatic stress or other emotional reactions in the child	Developmental Assessment of the Child • Naturalistic Observation • Parent-Child Interaction • Standardized testing • Play interview

combined types), severity, and chronicity. It is important to determine the perpetrator, if known, his/her relationship to the child, and any court actions that have been taken with regard to the abusive incident(s). A second major goal is to assess the child's current living situation with regard to safety, stability, and parental availability. With whom is the child living currently? What is the relationship of the current caregiver to the child (biological parent, foster parent, other substitute caregiver)? The third goal is to determine the short-term and long-term child protective service plan for the child and family. What is the current status of parental rights? Is there a plan for family reunification or will parental rights likely be terminated? Will the child likely be in long-term foster care, or is there a plan for adoption? Who will be responsible for bringing the child to treatment?

The answers to these questions influence the short-term and long-term goals of treatment. If the child resides with the perpetrator, or resides with a nonabusive parent in the perpetrator's home, the therapist will want to know if the caregiver has also been abused and whether or not the child feels secure with the caregiver. While assessing the current environment, it is helpful for the therapist to know the type of environment to which the child has been exposed in the past. The child will have more strengths if he/she has been reared in a home where at least one parent was nurturing and available than in a home where both parents/caregivers were emotionally unavailable and/or abusive.

Assessing the Family and Home Environment

While child abuse and neglect occur in families from all economic levels, the risk factors are more likely to outweigh the protective factors in lower socioeconomic status (SES) homes (U.S. Advisory Board on Child Abuse and Neglect, 1991). Selected social and demographic characteristics, such as poor young parents, poor single mothers, and highly stressed poor families, increase the likelihood of severe abuse of young children (Gelles, 1992). Poverty in and of itself can have detrimental effects on the child's cognitive and behavioral development, and can negatively affect family functioning (Duncan, Brooks-Gunn, & Klebanov, 1994). Either from history or interview with the family, the therapist should obtain information such as family income, job status, housing, and supplemental benefits they may receive. It may well be that the first goal of treatment will be to help stabilize the family by facilitating access to services such as stable housing, Women with Infants and Children (WIC) food supplements, Supplemental Security Income (SSI), enrollment in Head Start for their child, school lunch programs, or Aid to Families with Dependent Children (AFDC) benefits.

Along with determining the family's socioeconomic situation, it is important to assess their social network and practical needs. Are there extended family members or friends who can provide respite in child care, economic assistance when needed, or social support during times of stress? Is someone able to act as a buffer for the child when the parent(s) become too stressed to provide adequate care or when they are at risk for becoming abusive? As the therapist assesses family strengths, weaknesses, and needs, and assigns priorities to those needs, it is critical to *ask the parents* what their priority needs might be. The therapist's perspective about what the parents must do or what the parents need may be quite different from the parents' perspective. For example, the therapist's priority might be Family Preservation Services, while the parents' priority is to obtain adequate housing or to get a job. The parents will likely be more receptive to treatment if they feel the therapist is listening to their perspective. A survey such as the Parenting Stress Index (PSI; Abidin, 1990) provides information regarding a variety of sources of child and parental stress, as well as life stresses, and can guide the therapist toward potential areas of intervention.

A third goal is to determine the parents' motivation for participating in treatment. Parental motivation may be influenced by whether the treatment is court ordered vs. voluntary, whether the parent is the perpetrator or the nonmaltreating parent, and the level of social support available to the parent. Understanding and acknowledging the circumstances under which the treatment is being done will be important to establishing rapport with the parents.

Assessing the Parent-Child Relationship

If both the child and parent are available for treatment, it is important to assess the nature of the parent-child attachment relationship. This relationship must be assessed independently for each caregiver in relation to the child, as the child may have a secure relationship with one caregiver but an anxious/avoidant relationship with another, for example. Ainsworth, Blehar, Waters, and Wall (1978) developed the Strange Situation paradigm as an experimental observational tool for assessing the quality and nature of the attachment relationship between infants (12 to 18 months of age) and their parents. Variations of the Strange Situation have been developed for older children as well. However, this paradigm has not been adapted for clinical use, and it is restricted by the age range of the child. More informal observational methods might be substituted by clinicians, with a focus on observing the parent's responsivity to his/her child's social cues, the child's response to brief separation and reunion with the parent, and the child's use of the parent as a base of support in an unfamiliar environment. One can also observe the child's interest versus reticence in exploring the environment. The more securely attached child will be likely to explore the environment while using the parent as a base of support, whereas the insecurely attached child who is avoidant may be unperturbed by separation from the parent and overly involved in object play. The child who has an anxious/ambivalent attachment may alternate between clinging to the parent and rejecting the parent's approaches. A full description of assessment for various types of disordered attachment is beyond the scope of this article. However, the interested reader is referred to Ainsworth et al. (1978), Cassidy (1990), Cassidy and Main (1985), and Main and Cassidy (1987, 1988).

It is also important to assess the parents' personal resources and the presence of psychopathology. A structured interview such as the Adult Attachment Interview (George, Kaplan, & Main, 1985; Main & Hesse, 1990) provides information about the adults' relationship to their own parents during childhood, whether adults have experienced the death of any parental figure or other close family members that were especially important in their life, how they reacted to the loss at the time, how they thought the loss affected their adult personality, and how it may have affected their response to their child. Research by Main and Hesse (1990) has suggested that a parent's unresolved loss is associated with atypical and insecure attachment relationships with their offspring. The assessment of the parent's personal resources may reveal protective factors such as a supportive social network, positive personality attributes, or other factors that will be important in treatment. On the other hand, assessing for presence of psychopathology may reveal clinical symptoms of depression, anxiety, passive dependent personality, impulsivity, cognitive limitations, or antisocial/hostile personality characteristics. This information must be understood when developing a treatment plan.

Assessing the Impact of Abuse on the Child

It is well documented that abuse and neglect can have a negative effect upon child development (U.S. Advisory Board on Child Abuse and Neglect, 1991; Willis, 1992). It is informative to obtain baseline developmental evaluations of the child's cognitive, linguistic, and adaptive functioning prior to treatment, with comparisons made at the end of treatment. Often dramatic gains in development are noted when children are removed from abusive situations and receive treatment while in a more stable and nurturing environment.

Second, it is important to understand the ways in which maltreatment may have disrupted the child's development. The therapist must determine the *age* and *developmental level* of the child at the time of the abuse, and determine if the abuse has been *chronic* or occurred in a *single* episode. This information will help the therapist understand the developmental discontinuities that might have occurred, whether or not the very young child's competence has been compromised, as well as the child's ability to form a secure attachment relationship with a primary caregiver. Also, understanding the type of abuse experienced by the very young child helps in formulating a treatment plan. Abuse caused by physical injury and emotional trauma serious enough to warrant hospitalization will require a different treatment focus than sexual abuse and neglect. The therapist must recognize post-traumatic symptoms presented by the child either through the history or by direct observation. Does the child have nightmares suggestive of post-traumatic stress? Does the child reenact the trauma or demonstrate fears during a diagnostic play interview? Finally, Zeanah (1994) suggests that the therapist will want to take note of the protective factors present in the child's environment that will help the child to cope. For example, does the child have a nurturing and supportive caregiver, and can the child talk about the trauma, or use play as a means of expressing his/her feelings about the abuse?

Once the social context has been assessed, and the therapist has a better understanding of the multiple risk and protective factors at work in the family of the multiply abused child, it is possible to choose among various interventions or combinations of interventions that seem most appropriate to the presenting clinical issues. Although many models for intervention are available, the preferred treatment for very young children and their parents is focused on understanding the disruption in their attachment relationship and facilitating a more secure attachment that may ameliorate the negative effects of maltreatment. The next sections discuss theoretical-ly-based intervention strategies for children who have been maltreated and their caregivers, beginning with treatment of disordered attachment relationships.

ATTACHMENT THEORY AND DEVELOPMENTAL-ECOLOGICAL THEORY AS A BASIS FOR INTERVENTION

Treating Disordered Attachment Relationships

Treating the attachment relationship presumes that the infant or toddler will be seen in conjunction with the caregiver. If the infant has been removed from parental custody, then a nurturing foster parent or other substitute caregiver may play an important role in the treatment. If the child's abusive and/or neglectful parents are involved in treatment, the focus must be upon helping the interactional patterns change in both parties.

Treatment during infancy should focus on enhancement of the caregiver's contingent responsivity to the infant's signals. One goal of treatment is to help the parent understand the infant's need to develop a sense of security and basic trust, and the infant's need to learn that his or her signals will be responded to. This goal may be accomplished via the therapist building a relationship with the parent (e.g., the mother) and developing an understanding of the mother's experience of her child in the context of her own past history and present circumstances (Lieberman & Pawl, 1990). As the therapist supports and understands the parent, it becomes possible to understand the relationship between the mother's individual experience and her perceptions and feelings toward her child. The therapist may help the mother gain insight into her own past experiences and the impact of those experiences on her current behavior; this in turn facilitates a shift in the mother's own working model of attachment. This shift is the first stage to changing the mother's interaction with her child. As the mother's caregiving improves, improvements should be noted concomitantly in the quality of her relationship with her infant (Lieberman & Pawl, 1990). It is important that the infant or toddler be present in these sessions, so that the therapist can assist in identifying the child's signaling behaviors and modeling appropriate responses. As the infant grows into the toddler years, the therapist's role is to help the caregiver support the child's growing autonomy and self-control while recognizing the child's need for security and need to feel protected from danger.

Treating the attachment relationship during the toddler years may present additional challenges as the toddler's behavior changes. Lieberman and Pawl (1990) describe three potential patterns of distortion in the toddler's attachment relationship with the caregiver. These patterns represent qualitatively different adaptations that help the child cope with the issues of protection from danger when the caregiver does not reliably provide such protection. The child in this situation must develop coping strategies to manage both the fear of danger and the anxiety resulting from the caregiver's unavailability as a protector (Lieberman & Pawl, 1990). The first pattern involves recklessness and accident proneness, which is seen as a counterphobic defense against perceived danger. A second pattern involves inhibition of exploratory behavior, which may be interpreted as a phobic flight from danger. The third pattern involves excessive self-reliance, which may be viewed as an advanced sense of competence in self-protection (Lieberman & Pawl, 1990). These patterns evolve in an effort to solve the problem of self-protection when the parent does not provide appropriate support for negotiating environmental risks and developmental tasks.

Toddlers who are reckless and accident prone may present clinically as oppositional or even hyperactive. Although the attachment relationship between the parent and infant should be the focus of treatment, much as was described in the preceding paragraphs, there also may be a need for collateral treatment to assist the parent in managing the child's behavior so as to reduce the risk of danger. The Parent-Child Interaction Therapy approach to treatment, described later in this article, provides a good model for both relationship building and behavior management. Toddlers who display the second pattern involving inhibition of exploratory behavior often are hypervigilant and fearful, and lack an age appropriate range of emotional expression. According to Lieberman and Pawl (1990), some children with this pattern cling to the caregiver and refuse to separate, while others tend to avoid proximity to the caregiver but also avoid exploration. Again, parent-toddler psychotherapy may be used to explore the etiology of this disordered attachment relationship, and help the mother gain insight into the child's developmental needs and the reasons for the inhibition of exploration.

Finally, the pattern of excessive self-reliance often is characterized by a role reversal between mother and child, so that the child engages in protective behaviors ordinarily expected from the mother and is unusually aware of the mother's moods (Lieberman & Pawl, 1990). This interactional pattern is seen when a mother shows inconsistent emotional investment in her toddler, often due to her own depression or tendency to be self-absorbed. Treatment of this pattern of disordered attachment typically involves a multifaceted approach which may include practical assistance to stabilize the mother's life circumstances, developmental guidance around the child's physical and emotional needs, and infant-parent psychotherapy to explore ways in which the mother's own past experiences and current circumstances are now interfering with her emotional availability to her child (Lieberman & Pawl, 1990).

The treatment strategies just described presume a theoretical understanding of the role of attachment in parent-child relationships; knowledge of developmental transitions during the infant, toddler and preschool years; and understanding of the potential impact of disrupted attachment on the child's emotional development. The focus of treatment necessarily is on the relationship, rather than on either the child or parent (or other caregiver) individually. It is felt that treating the attachment relationship should be the preferred treatment whenever possible, but other types of treatment may provide collateral benefits as well. In the sections that follow, the developmental-ecological perspective will be used to illustrate various other interventions at the level of the individual child, individual parent, parent-child interaction, and family. These interventions encompass not only individual characteristics of the child and parent, but also social support needs and practical assistance for the families.

Intervention Programs Focused on the Individual

Therapeutic Day Treatment or Diagnostic Nursery

Multiply abused infants and toddlers often experience developmental delays across a broad spectrum, including cognitive, language, motor, and socialization skills (Culp, Heide, & Richardson, 1987). Treatment programs that teach appropriate socialization and enhance other areas of development in the young child can help to ameliorate some of the adverse effects of maltreatment. A therapeutic day treatment program or therapeutic nursery focuses on nurturing and supportive enhancement of the child's development, and is effective in increasing the self-esteem, confidence, and joy of a child. Groups that provide at least 12 to 30 hours of intervention per week are preferred. In one well-controlled study, Culp et al. (1987) compared 35 maltreated children enrolled in a treatment program six hours per day and five days per week with 35 maltreated children who were not enrolled in the program. Participants were matched on the basis of age, sex, race, and type of abuse. The day treatment program used a cognitive developmental model, with a high adult-to-child ratio (one adult to two children). The treatment program included normal preschool learning activities, but the major focus was on developing strong and therapeutic teacher-child relationships. The teacher worked to build the child's self-esteem, to improve the child's ability to show empathy and to have caring peer relationships, and to help the child express and cope with his/her feelings. A pre- and post-test developmental assessment was administered to all children, with the results indicating that children in the treatment group demonstrated significantly higher performance in five areas of development: fine motor, cognitive, gross motor, social/emotional, and language abilities.

Other treatment outcome studies have supported the finding of Culp et al. (1987) that maltreated children benefit in several areas of development following treatment in a therapeutic nursery. In an unpublished study, Willis (1986) compared pre- and post-test developmental scores of seven severely abused 3- to 6-year-old children enrolled in a therapeutic nursery six hours per week. The children were taught normal preschool activities along with social skills training and enhancement of self-esteem. Post-test scores of the children increased from 10 to 40 IQ points. Culp, Little, Letts, and Lawrence (1991) assessed the effects of a comprehensive treatment program on preschool children's self-concept. Seventeen treatment and 17 control children (all maltreated), enrolled in a therapeutic day treatment program, were administered the Pictorial Scale of Perceived Competence and Social Acceptance (Harter & Pike, 1984) as a pre- and post-treatment measure. The results revealed that the treatment group had developmental gains and enhancement of self-concept compared both to the control group and to their own pretreatment levels.

Intervention in a Hospital Environment

The effects of maltreatment may be so severe at times that it is necessary to hospitalize a youngster. A good example of this occurs in cases of nonorganic failure-to-thrive, where emotional neglect and absence of nurturing caregiving can result in failure to thrive. In this situation, intervention may need to occur in a hospital setting with health care professionals, especially if the parent is unavailable or unwilling to be engaged in treatment. The following case illustrates this type of intervention.

> Amy, an 18-month-old toddler, was admitted to Children's Hospital suffering from abuse and severe neglect. She was dehydrated and had feeding and respiratory problems. After six days on the unit a psychological consult was requested due to Amy's lack of progress. Amy had feeding problems, was not gaining weight, and her sleep-awake cycle was atypical in that she slept fitfully during the day and was awake crying at night.
>
> The psychologist (DJW) designed an intervention to address the effects of the psychosocial neglect experienced by Amy prior to admission. A volunteer, who assumed a nurturing "maternal" caretaking role, was assigned to hold and rock Amy several times a day, and provide the attention and nurturance lacking in the child's previous experience. Amy was taken off the "teaching circuit" of this teaching hospital to prevent her exposure to multiple medical personnel. It was also requested that the same physician follow Amy consistently, and that a specific nurse be assigned to care for her on each shift. Within two days Amy began to eat better, was less fussy, and began sleeping normally. By the third day she cried when her substitute caregiver left and reacted in an excited manner when the

caregiver came on the unit. She became more alert, began to smile, recognize, and play on the lap of her caregiver.

Interventions in a hospital setting may need to incorporate the use of a volunteer, a play nursery, and consistently assigned nurses and physicians to the care of the child who has been neglected or abused. In the present case, Amy's mother never visited the hospital and eventually relinquished her parental rights, so a transition from the substitute caregiver to the prospective foster mother was also done on the ward. Amy continued to thrive after discharge with the nurturance provided by the foster mother.

Individual and Group Psychotherapy for the Child

There is a large literature describing individual play and/or group psychotherapy models for children who are victims of various forms of abuse. Like most of the other literature in the area of child maltreatment, the psychotherapy literature does not often address the treatment of the multiply abused child, and is often imprecise in terms of the type, chronicity, and severity of the abuse experienced by the children. Most therapists agree, however, that therapy must provide corrective and reparative experiences for the child who has been maltreated. Often a psychoeducational model is used to provide young abuse victims education, free-play, and reeducation about the abuse experience (Cohen & Mannarino, 1993; Mandell & Damon, 1989). The treatment of children is often geared to helping them express and explore their feelings, reduce their fears and anxiety, alter their attributions of responsibility, and enhance their relationship (attachment) to a significant other. Several articles/chapters detail more thoroughly the healing power of play (see Gil, 1991; Terr, 1983), and the reader is referred to them for further detail.

Racusin and Moss (1992) provided one of the few reports of an intervention with children who have been multiply abused. They described a psychotherapy group for five preschool victims of multiple abuse that ran for fifty-three 75-minute sessions. The group psychotherapy was structured to begin with a "talking time" for 5-30 minutes where children could share their experiences or verbalize current concerns, followed by a free play period where the children could play by themselves, with others, or with the therapist. This was followed by a more structured play period whereby the children were encouraged and helped to engage in a shared group activity. Snack time and a short talking time concluded the group. Unfortunately, the efficacy of this treatment approach is unknown because the authors presented no pre-post assessment data or control group comparisons.

Damon and Waterman (1986) described a structured group approach to treating young sexually abused children and their mothers in a parallel group treatment format (i.e., in which both the children and the mothers received treatment simultaneously, but within parallel groups). Thirteen treatment modules were used with the children, covering the following issues: (1) The right to say "no"; (2) What happens when you say "no"; (3) Private parts; (4) Who can you tell? (5) Anger and punishment; (6) What happens when you tell? (7) What happened to you? (8) Fault and responsibility; (9) Separation; (10) What happens to the perpetrators? (11) Integration of positive and negative feelings toward the perpetrator; (12) What if the denial is maintained? and (13) Sex education. This treatment format has been used in several studies, as it appears to reduce the child's feelings of guilt, stigmatization, isolation, and betrayal.

In another study, the structured group therapy approach was found to be successful in ameliorating behavioral problems in young sexually abused children (Hall-Marley & Damon, 1993). These investigators provided parallel group treatment to non-offending parents at the same time the children were being seen. Both the Child Behavior Checklist (CBCL; Achenbach & Edelbrock, 1983) and the Child Sexual Behavior Inventory (Friedrich, Grambsch, Broughton, Kuiper, & Beilke, 1991) were substantially lower after the group treatment, suggesting that the behavior disorders and sexual acting out may have decreased as a result of parallel group treatment.

Few empirical studies on treatment of preschool children who have been abused exist. However, Kendall-Tackett, Williams, and Finkelhor (1991) published a meta-analysis of all empirical assessment studies of sexually abused children. This study showed that 68% of the victimized children exhibited symptoms of anxiety; 41% exhibited depressive symptoms; 31% had regressive behaviors; and 36% demonstrated inappropriate sexual behaviors. Treatment of the non-offending caregiver in parallel fashion along with the child (if that caregiver believes and supports the child) appears to offer the best results.

Parent Training Interventions

As discussed in previous sections of this article, children who are victims of multiple abuse may develop feelings of anger, and subsequently display oppositional/defiant behavior. Children in the toddler age range pass through a developmental transition during which negative behaviors, asserting their will, and acting defiantly are expected (Campbell, 1990). In the normal sequence of events, a caring and attentive parent will shape the child's demandingness by setting reasonable boundaries for accepted behavior and by firmly prohibiting the child from crossing these boundaries. However, parents who are neglectful may be inaccessible and overly permissive, so that boundaries are not consistently established. Children whose parents are abusive (either physically, or emotionally, or both) may experience harsh, overly controlling, psychologically damaging reactions to their behavior that results in an exacerbation of anger and oppositional/ defiant behavior. Children whose parents are both neglectful and abusive must incorporate an even more inconsistent, unpredictable and chaotic response to their behavior. In these cases, the child's behavioral problem is not the primary disorder; rather, the parent-child interaction has resulted in development of a behavioral problem and it is the interaction that must be treated.

Parent-Child Interaction Therapy (PCIT; Eyberg, 1988) is a brief intervention method designed for young children (2 to 7 years) and their families. It employs both behavior modification and relationship enhancement approaches to address problems in the parent-child interaction, and to reduce the negative behaviors displayed by the child. PCIT uses the context of a natural play setting between parent and child to facilitate development of a warm, mutually rewarding context for the parent-child interaction. Play is viewed as a primary means through which young children can learn new skills and work through developmental problems, while also providing opportunity for parents to practice various techniques of communication and behavior management necessary to establish a positive influence on their child (Eyberg & Boggs, 1989).

Parent-Child Interaction Therapy consists of two basic phases of treatment. The first phase, Child-Directed Interaction (CDI), focuses on changing the quality of the parent-child relationship by teaching the parents traditional play therapy techniques. These techniques provide a therapeutic interaction that is positive and mutually rewarding to parent and child. Interpersonal factors such as parental warmth, attention directed toward the child, and praise serve as social rewards or incentives that assist the child in developing increased self-control (Robinson, 1985). During CDI, parents are trained to provide differential reinforcement of appropriate child behavior through praise, along with ignoring any undesirable activity. This approach provides a positive form of behavior management through the CDI phase of treatment (Eyberg & Boggs, 1989).

The second phase of treatment is termed Parent-Directed Interaction (PDI). Using techniques based on operant principles of behavior modification, parents are trained to communicate age appropriate instructions clearly to the child, and then to provide consistent positive and negative consequences following the child's obedience or disobedience. During this phase of treatment, parents are also instructed in functional problem solving skills so that they will better understand how a child's behavior is shaped and maintained by the social environment, and how methods of behavior change learned through PCIT can be applied to new problems as they arise (Eyberg & Boggs, 1989). These functional problem solving skills help facilitate the generalization of the parent training learned through PCIT to non-clinic settings (Boggs, Stokes, & Danforth, 1986), and PCIT is one of the few parent-training models with outcome research to indicate low recidivism rates.

However, PCIT is dependent upon the parents' willingness to participate in the training program, to examine their own style of interaction with their child, and the parents' ability to control or modify their negative emotional reactions toward their child. In the case of abusive parents, poor interpersonal skills, feelings of anger and lack of self control, or disinterest in participating in treatment may sabotage the potential positive effects of treatment. Neglectful parents, on the other hand, may have little energy for positive reinforcement of their child's behavior due to their own interpersonal problems or possible psychopathology (e.g., depression). The effectiveness of PCIT is dependent upon the parents' ability to work in the best interest of their child and to be able to apply the techniques for relationship enhancement and behavior modification appropriately. Certainly, the therapist's skill in building rapport with maltreating parents is an important part of the treatment process.

One of the factors that increases the possibility of success for this type of intervention with abusive parents is the therapist's coaching the parent through the different phases of the program. As the parent is being asked to show differential attention to the child's appropriate behavior, and provide praise and warm regard for their child, the therapist is providing similar interventions to the parent through coaching. This supportive and positive approach to parent training often results in a reduction of parental stress, diminishing symptoms of depression, and an improvement in the parents' sense of confidence and competence as parents. For a complete description of PCIT, please refer to a detailed chapter by Eyberg and Boggs (1989).

Other types of parent training programs for abusive parents focus on educating parents about child development, teaching them behavior management strategies, helping them develop better anger control, and facilitating their development of nurturing skills. Parent-training interventions do seem to reduce parental distress, may improve child functioning (Wolfe, Edwards, Manion, & Koverola, 1988), and can reduce out-of-home placement (Szykula & Fleischman, 1985). Teaching parents behavioral management skills and coaching its use with their children can be effective, at least in the clinic setting (Golub, Espinosa, Damon, & Card, 1987). However, there are few studies that demonstrate the efficacy of general parent training programs with abusive parents once the parent and child are dismissed from treatment. Studies on recidivism rates after parent training intervention are needed in this population of abusive parents and their children.

Intervention Programs Focused on the Family

Despite the proven relation of familial risk factors to child abuse and neglect, there are few research studies establishing the efficacy of specific treatment strategies with families (National Academy of Sciences, 1993; Willis, 1992). McCurdy and Daro (1993) found that only 60% of abusive families receive *any* kind of assistance, leaving 40% of the families confirmed as abusive without services. Although abuse is disproportionately high in poor families and lower SES neighborhoods, these are the very neighborhoods that lack resources to support and sustain families. Services for families generally are spread widely over large geographic areas with little coordination and integration. Families who have no reliable transportation and little motivation often find that traversing "the system" is too defeating. Thus, in-home interventions are now gaining support for use with abusive families who have young children (Lutzker & Rice, 1984; 1987). These interventions include Project 12-Ways, Family Preservation Services or Homebuilders (Wells & Biegel, 1991), and Home Visitation (Daro, 1993; Wasik, Bryant, & Lyons, 1990); each of the programs is discussed in the following sections.

Project 12-Ways

Lutzker, Frame, and Rice (1982) developed a university affiliated, eco-behavioral program to treat high-risk or abusive and neglectful parents. Families are provided an in-depth assessment out of which they receive individualized intervention programs, depending upon their needs. Interventions may include one or a combination of the following: stress reduction, anger control, marital therapy, parent-child interaction or behavior management, assertiveness training, assistance with job finding, money management, nutrition and health maintenance, or referral for substance abuse assessment and treatment (Barone, Greene, & Lutzker, 1986). Several case reports have been published demonstrating positive outcomes and lower recidivism rates for program participants compared to controls over a five-year period (Lutzker, 1990; Lutzker, Megson, Dachman, & Webb, 1985; Lutzker & Rice, 1984, 1987). As there is still insufficient independent research on the efficacy of Project 12-Ways, results of this approach must be interpreted cautiously. Indeed, much of the research on Project 12-Ways lacked comparison data and random assignment of participants to the Project intervention. It is possible that the reported treatment gains may not be maintained when compared to a comparison group (Wesch & Lutzker, 1991).

Family Preservation Services

Family Preservation Services (FPS) are widely used in treating families who abuse their children (Wells & Biegel, 1991). Based on the Homebuilders model of intervention (Kinny, Madsen, Fleming, & Haapala, 1977), FPS helps keep children in their own home while ensuring their safety. Families may be assigned a worker 20-30 hours per week for a short period of time (6-8 weeks), and a range of therapeutic services may be instituted depending upon the nature of the family's problems. The family's needs are assessed, and active means of addressing those needs are used. The evaluative research on FPS reports success in preventing foster placement of children and short-term improvement within the family (Bath & Haapala, 1993). The overall effectiveness of FPS at this time, however, is unclear due to methodological problems in the studies published to date (e.g., small sample sizes, nonexperimental designs).

Several researchers note that FPS is cost effective compared to foster placement, as projected state savings are estimated to be $27,000 (Daro, 1988; Rossi, 1992; Wells & Biegel, 1991). If the Family Preservation program can be strengthened by training the personnel who make the home visits, and one can ensure the safety of the child, it offers a potentially less traumatic intervention for the young child who has been multiply abused.

Home Visitation Services

Universal home visitation services have been advocated by the U.S. Advisory Board on Child Abuse and Neglect (1991) as a means of reducing out-of-home placements of children, strengthening the family through support of the parents, and addressing problems at multiple levels of the family system.

In a comprehensive overview of home visitation published by the Center for the Future of Children (1993), a critique of the home visiting program research suggested that programs that "employ professionals (especially nurses) and are based on more comprehensive service models stand a greater chance of influencing qualities of parental caregiving than do narrowly focused programs staffed by paraprofessionals" (p. 79). Of the studies addressing child maltreatment per se, some did find differences in the home visited group in the form of improved parenting, decrease in child abuse and neglect, increase in the number of appropriate play materials, significant reduction in hospitalization for serious injury, and better use of preventive services (Hardy & Streett, 1989; Olds, Henderson, Chamberlin, & Tatelbaum, 1986). The study by Olds et al. (1986) demonstrated a reduction in rates of child abuse reported to the Child Protective System (CPS); only 4% of the home visited, high-risk, unmarried adolescents were reported to CPS for suspected abuse whereas 19% of the comparison sample were reported. While home visitation may not be a panacea, at least some study participants appear to benefit from this approach.

As many abusive parents are socially poor and socially isolated, voluntary home visitation services can reduce the parents' feelings of isolation and alienation, enhance their feelings of self-worth and competence, reduce stress, and help them obtain services they might not otherwise obtain. If the parent is strengthened, this can serve to strengthen the entire family. The following case study provides a brief overview of a multiply abused toddler for whom home visitation services and Parent-Child Interaction Therapy were recommended.

> The early history for 2-year, 5-month-old Laura was fraught with multiple moves and little stability. Since her birth, Laura and her mother have lived with the great grandmother, mother's boyfriend, grandfather, great-grandmother again, another boyfriend, great grandmother, grandfather, and now a cousin. The history provided by the mother suggested disruption of the attachment relationship between daughter and mother, and possible anxious attachment on the part of Laura. The mother reported that Laura screams when left at Day Care, but when mother and Laura are walking someplace, her daughter will reach out for any stranger they pass. The mother described Laura as having "an attitude that aggravates–she hits, acts like a baby, and whines and reaches out for things." Further, the mother reported that when she tries to sit Laura down to teach her to talk, her daughter screams. The mother stated, "When I tell her to come to me, she gives me this 'go to hell look', and when I put her in quiet time and she whines, I spank her butt." "Last night she threw her plate on the floor and I made her pick it up." The mother also

said that she is "to the breaking point now. She (Laura) drives me up the wall."

The mother's description of Laura revealed that she has inappropriate expectations for the behavior of a toddler, and is feeling increasingly frustrated in caring for this child. The mother herself had significant stressors, and reported feeling isolated. She reported that she has had six pregnancies, including two miscarriages, one abortion, one child given up for adoption, and two children at home. The mother also appeared to be borderline to mildly retarded, likely secondary to a reported birth injury.

On the first clinic visit, Laura presented as a timid and quiet, but visually alert toddler who remained cooperative throughout the evaluation. She curiously but cautiously explored her environment. Laura responded to a few verbal directions, but her vocalizations were minimal and appeared limited to grunts. She communicated with facial expressions and gestures. Laura was also observed to reach out for strangers to hold her; when given an option among going to her grandfather, a stranger, or her mother, she chose her grandfather or a stranger. Finally, Laura's affect in play was somber and flat and it took considerable effort to get her to respond even minimally in a spontaneous manner.

Cognitively, Laura was functioning at the 17-month level according to the Mental Scale of the Bayley Scales of Infant Development, with skills ranging from 14 to 20 months. Her performance translated to a Mental Development Index of < 50 when compared with same-age peers. Her overall performance indicated significantly delayed development of cognitive skills with present functioning within the range of Mental Retardation, Unspecified.

In summary, Laura presented with a history of neglect, poor environmental stimulation, lack of a stable home, and harsh punishment and who remains at high risk for abuse and continued developmental problems. She presented with significantly delayed development, flat affect, and anxious attachment to her mother. Laura's mother, who appeared to be mentally handicapped, had little knowledge of child development and little patience for, or understanding of, normal toddler behavior. After individual work with Laura at this Center it was evident that she learned with minimal repetition, and became more spontaneous and joyful during active, intensive play. It was felt that an intensive developmental program over the next year coupled with stability, patience, and nurturance in her environment would likely enhance her overall development. Parent-Child Interaction

Therapy coupled with intensive home visitation services was recommended. The caseworker was notified of our concerns and the mother and child were referred to a home visitation program for high-risk children for developmental stimulation, parent training, and other services as needed. The mother was agreeable with all recommendations and plans.

Most home visitation services are offered on a weekly basis to low-income families or families with children from birth to three years of age. Most programs deliver a variety of services, with 80% offering services to enhance child development and/or parenting skills, and 68-75% delivering services to strengthen parental coping, provide emotional support and information, and/or conduct diagnostic services (Roberts & Wasik, 1990). While home visitation is no panacea there are indications that if it is carried out by personnel who have good interpersonal and communication skills and is comprehensive in scope, it can be successful. Wasik et al. (1990) provide an excellent overview of various home visitation programs across the U.S., including information on visiting families at risk for abuse, and assessment and documentation in home visiting.

Interventions with Substance Abusing Families

While it is not the intent of this article to focus on treatment of substance abusing families, many young children who come to the attention of CPS live in homes with polysubstance abusers. Often these children must be placed in foster care while the parent receives treatment, and often these children have experienced multiple forms of abuse. Infants who have been prenatally exposed to alcohol or drugs may present with very difficult behavior requiring sensitive and specialized care which the infant cannot get from a drug addicted mother (Chasnoff & Griffith, 1989; Scherling, 1994). Parenting stress in mothers of drug exposed infants can lead to child maltreatment due to a combination of infant and caregiver characteristics (Kelley, 1992). Drug exposed infants are easily overstimulated, can be difficult to hold and cuddle, and are often irritable (Dixon, 1989; Griffith, 1988).

Treatment of this rapidly increasing population of multiply abused children requires close cooperation and collaboration among agencies working with the parent and the child. The National Center on Child Abuse and Neglect (NCCAN; 1994) published an excellent manual on protecting children in substance-abusing families that details an assessment/intervention guide for use when working with this population. Sample medical center protocols as well as interagency agreement forms and an overview of drugs, drug paraphernalia, and observable effects of drug use are published in the appendix. Treatment of this group of young children requires specialized care due to unpredictable sleep patterns, feeding difficulties, irritability, atypical social interactions, delayed language development, and increased muscle tone and poor fine motor development (NCCAN, 1994).

Swaddling the infant (with infant's hands exposed) and holding the infant close to one's body helps to soothe the child's irritability. Soothing, quiet talk coupled with consistency and structure helps the infant and toddler to begin to organize their behavior (NCCAN, 1994). If the parent is still using substances, out-of-home placement with relatives or in foster care must be considered to ensure that the child is safe.

In addition to the suggestions provided here, substance abusing families may benefit from the other types of intervention discussed in this article.

CONCLUSION

The young child exposed to multiple forms of abuse begins life precariously and often suffers cognitive, social, emotional, and behavioral consequences throughout life, unless effective and intensive early intervention services are provided. Treatment services for children who have been maltreated and their families currently are fragmented and difficult to coordinate. It is imperative, given the multiplicity of problems that may exist, to have comprehensive, coordinated, and integrated services for this population. The various forms of intervention discussed in this article are grounded in theory, and reflect the growing body of research in the child maltreatment field. Yet, they often lack empirical support from well-controlled studies to prove their efficacy. Much work remains to be done, but the field is ready to embark on such studies. It is hoped that this article will serve a heuristic effect to stimulate further research, and will serve the clinician who must provide interventions to young victims of multiple abuse in the interim.

REFERENCES

Abidin, R.R. (1990). *Parenting Stress Index manual* (3rd ed.). Charlottesville, VA: Pediatric Psychology Press.

Achenbach, T.M., & Edelbrock, C. (1983). *Manual for the Child Behavior Checklist*. Burlington, VT: Queen City Printers.

Ainsworth, M.D., Blehar, M.C., Waters, E., & Wall, S. (1978). *Patterns of attachment: A psychological study of the strange situation*. Hillsdale, NJ: Erlbaum.

Barone, V.J., Greene, B.F., & Lutzker, J.R. (1986). Home safety with families being treated for child abuse and neglect. *Behavior Modification, 10*, 93-114.

Bath, H.I., & Haapala, D.A. (1993). Intensive family preservation services with abused and neglected children: An examination of group differences. *Child Abuse & Neglect, 17*, 213-225.

Belsky, J. (1993). Etiology of child maltreatment: A developmental-ecological analysis. *Psychological Bulletin, 114(3)*, 413-434.

Boggs, S.R., Stokes, T.F., & Danforth, J. (1986, August). Functional problem-solving skills: Increasing the generality of parent training. Paper presented at the annual meeting of the American Psychological Association, Washington, DC.

Bronfenbrenner, U. (1979). *The ecology of human development.* Cambridge, MA: Harvard University Press.

Campbell, S.B. (1990). *Behavior problems in preschool children.* New York: Guilford.

Cassidy, J. (1990). Theoretical and methodological considerations in the study of attachment and the self in young children. In M.T. Greenberg, D. Cicchetti, & E.M. Cummings (Eds.), *Attachment in the preschool years* (pp. 87-119). Chicago: The University of Chicago Press.

Cassidy, J., & Main, M. (1985). The relationship between infant-parent attachment and the ability to tolerate brief separation at six years. In R. Tyson & E. Galenson (Eds.), *Frontiers of infant psychiatry* (vol. 2, pp. 132-136). New York: Basic Books.

Center for the Future of Children (1993). *The future of children: Home visiting.* Los Angeles, CA: David & Lucille Packard Foundation.

Chasnoff, I.J., & Griffith, D.R. (1989). Cocaine: Clinical studies of pregnancy and the newborn. In D.E. Hutchings (Ed.), *Prenatal abuse of licit and illicit drugs* (pp. 42-55). New York: New York Academy of Sciences.

Cicchetti, D. (1987). Developmental psychopathology in infancy. Illustrations from the study of maltreated youngsters. *Journal of Consulting and Clinical Psychology, 55*, 837-845.

Cohen, J., & Mannarino, A. (1993). A treatment model for sexually abused preschoolers. *Journal of Interpersonal Violence, 8*, 115-131.

Crittenden, P.M., & Ainsworth, M.D.S. (1989). Child maltreatment and attachment theory. In D. Cicchetti & V. Carlson (Eds.), *Child maltreatment: Theory and research on the causes and consequences of child abuse and neglect* (pp. 432-463). New York: Cambridge University Press.

Culp, R.E., Heide, J., & Richardson, M.T. (1987). Maltreated childrens' developmental scores: Treatment versus nontreatment. *Child Abuse & Neglect, 11*, 29-34.

Culp, R.E., Little, V., Letts, D., & Lawrence, H. (1991). Maltreated children's self-concept: Effects of a comprehensive treatment program. *Journal of Orthopsychiatry, 61*, 114-121.

Damon, L., & Waterman, J. (1986). Parallel group therapy treatment of children and their mothers. In K. MacFarlane & J. Waterman (Eds.), *Sexual abuse of young children.* New York: Guilford.

Daro, D. (1988). *Confronting child abuse: Research for effective program design.* New York: Free Press.

Daro, D. (1993). Home visitation and preventing child abuse. *The APSAC Advisor, 6,* 1, 4.

Dixon, S.D. (1989). Effects of transplacental exposure to cocaine and methamphetamine on the neonate. *Western Journal of Medicine, 150,* 436-442.

Duncan, G.J., Brooks-Gunn, J., & Klebanov, P.K. (1994). Economic deprivation and early childhood development. *Child Development, 65,* 296-318.

Erickson, M.F., & Egeland, B. (1987). A developmental view of the consequences of maltreatment. *School Psychology Review, 16,* 156-168.

Eyberg, S.M. (1988). Parent-Child Interaction Therapy: Integration of traditional and behavioral concerns. *Child and Family Behavioral Therapy, 10,* 33-46.

Eyberg, S.M., & Boggs, S.R. (1989). Parent training for oppositional-defiant preschoolers. In C.E. Schaefer & J.M. Briesmeister (Eds.), *Handbook of parent training: Parents as co-therapists for children's behavior problems* (pp. 105-132). New York: Wiley.

Friedrich, W.N., Grambsch, P., Broughton, D., Kuiper, J., & Beilke, R.L. (1991). Normative sexual behavior in children. *Pediatrics, 88,* 456-464.

Gelles, R.J. (1992). Poverty and violence toward children. *American Behavioral Scientist, 35,* 258-274.

George, C., Kaplan, N., & Main, M. (1985). Adult Attachment Interview. Unpublished doctoral dissertation, University of California, Berkeley.

Gil, E. (1991). *The healing power of play* (pp. 37-82). New York: Guilford Press.

Golub, J.S., Espinosa, M., Damon, L., & Card, J. (1987). A video-tape parent education program for abusive parents. *Child Abuse & Neglect, 11,* 255-265.

Graziano, A.M., & Mills, J.R. (1992). Treatment for abused children: When is a partial solution acceptable? *Child Abuse & Neglect, 16,* 217-228.

Griffith, D.R. (1988). The effects of prenatal cocaine exposure on infant neurobehavior and early maternal-infant interactions. In I.J. Chasnoff (Ed.), *Drugs, alcohol, pregnancy, and parenting* (pp. 105-113). Boston, MA: Kluwer Academic Publishers.

Hall-Marley, S.E., & Damon, L. (1993). Impact of structured group therapy on young victims of sexual abuse. *Journal of Child and Adolescent Group Therapy, 3,* 41-48.

Hardy, J.B., & Streett, R. (1989). Family support and parenting education in the home: An effective extension of clinic-based preventive health care services for poor children. *Journal of Pediatrics, 115,* 927-931.

Harter, S., & Pike, R. (1984). The pictorial scale of perceived competence and social acceptance for young children. *Child Development, 55,* 1969-1982.

Kelley, S.J. (1992). Parenting stress and child maltreatment in drug exposed children. *Child Abuse & Neglect, 16,* 317-328.

Kendall-Tackett, K.A., Williams, L.M., & Finkelhor, D. (1991). The impact of sexual abuse on children: A review of recent empirical studies. Presented at the San Diego Conference on Responding to Child Maltreatment, San Diego, CA.

Kinny, J.M., Madsen, B., Fleming, T., & Haapala, D. (1977). Homebuilders: Keeping families together. *Journal of Consulting and Clinical Psychology, 45*, 667-673.

Lieberman, A.F., & Pawl, J.H. (1990). Disorders of attachment and secure base behavior in the second year of life. In M.T. Greenberg, D. Cicchetti, & E.M. Cummings (Eds.), *Attachment in the preschool years* (pp. 375-397). Chicago: The University of Chicago Press.

Lutzker, J.R. (1990). Behavioral treatment of child neglect. *Behavior Modification, 14*, 301-315.

Lutzker, J.R., Frame, R.E., & Rice, J.M. (1982). Project 12-Ways: An ecobehavioral approach to the treatment and prevention of child abuse and neglect. *Education and Treatment of Children, 7*, 141-155.

Lutzker, J.R., Megson, D.A., Dachman, R., & Webb, M.E. (1985). Validating and training adult-child interaction skills to professionals and to parents indicated for child abuse and neglect. *Journal of Child & Adolescent Psychotherapy, 2*, 91-104.

Lutzker, J.R., & Rice, J.M. (1984). Project 12-Ways: Measuring outcome of a large-scale in-home service for the treatment and prevention of child abuse and neglect. *Child Abuse & Neglect, 8*, 519-524.

Lutzker, J.R., & Rice, J.M. (1987). Using recidivism data to evaluate Project 12-Ways: An ecobehavioral approach to the treatment and prevention of child abuse and neglect. *Journal of Family Violence, 2*, 283-290.

Main, M., & Cassidy, J. (1987). Reunion-based classifications of child-parent attachment organization at six years of age. Unpublished scoring manual, University of California, Berkeley.

Main, M., & Cassidy, J. (1988). Categories of response to reunion with the parent at age six: Predictable from infant attachment classifications and stable over a one-month period. *Developmental Psychology, 24*, 415-426.

Main, M., & Hesse, E. (1990). Parents' unresolved traumatic experiences are related to infant disorganized status: Is frightened and/or frightening parental behavior the linking mechanism? In M.T. Greenberg, D. Cicchetti, & E.P. Cummings (Eds.), *Attachment in the preschool years* (pp. 161-182). Chicago: The University of Chicago Press.

Mandell, J.G., & Damon, L. (1989). *Group treatment for sexually abused children*. New York: Guilford.

McCurdy, K., & Daro, D. (1993). *Current trends in child abuse reporting and fatalities: The results of the 1992 annual 50-state survey*. Chicago: National Committee to Prevent Child Abuse.

National Academy of Sciences Panel on Research on Child Abuse and Neglect (1993). *Understanding child abuse and neglect*. Washington, DC: National Academy Press.

National Center on Child Abuse and Neglect (1994). *Protecting children in substance-abusing families*. Washington, DC: Clearinghouse on Child Abuse and Neglect Information.

Olds, D.L., Henderson, C.R., Chamberlin, R., & Tatelbaum, R. (1986). Preventing child abuse and neglect: A randomized trial of nurse home visitation. *Pediatrics, 78*, 65-78.

Racusin, G.R., & Moss, N.E. (1992). Rational work and basic assumption life in a psychotherapy group for preschool victims of abuse: A case study. *Journal of Child and Adolescent Group Therapy, 2*, 3-15.

Roberts, R.N., & Wasik, B.H. (1990). Home visiting programs for families with children birth to three: Results of a national survey. *Journal of Early Intervention, 14*, 274-284.

Rossi, P.H. (1992). Assessing family preservation programs. *Children and Youth Services Review, 14*, 75-95.

Scherling, D. (1994). Prenatal cocaine exposure and childhood psychopathology: A developmental analysis. *American Journal of Orthopsychiatry, 64*, 9-19.

Szykula, S.A., & Fleishman, M.J. (1985). Reducing out-of-home placement and abused children: Two controlled studies. *Child Abuse and Neglect, 11*, 421-432.

Terr, L. (1983). Play therapy and psychic trauma: A preliminary report. In C. Schaefer & K. O'Conner (Eds.), *Handbook of play therapy*. Boston: John Wiley & Sons, 308-319.

U.S. Advisory Board on Child Abuse and Neglect (1991). *Creating caring committees: Blueprint for an effective federal policy on child abuse and neglect.* Washington, DC: U.S. Government Printing Office.

Wasik, B.H., Bryant, D.M., & Lyons, C.M. (1990). *Home visiting: Procedures for helping families.* Newbury Park, CA: Sage Publications.

Wells, K., & Biegel, D.E. (Eds.). (1991). *Family preservation services: Research and evaluation.* Newbury Park, CA: Sage.

Wesch, D., & Lutzker, J.R. (1991). A comprehensive 5-year plan for evaluating Project 12-Ways: An ecobehavioral approach for treating and preventing child abuse and neglect. *Journal of Family Violence, 6*, 17-35.

Willis, D.J. (1986). Unpublished data. Child Study Center, 1100 N.E. 13th Street, Oklahoma City, OK 73117.

Willis, D.J. (1992). Child abuse and neglect. Testimony before the Panel on Research on Child Abuse and Neglect, National Research Council, National Academy of Sciences, Washington, DC.

Wolfe, D.A., Edwards, B., Manion, I., & Koverola, C. (1988). Early intervention for child abuse and neglect: A preliminary investigation. *Journal of Consulting and Clinical Psychology, 56*, 40-47.

Zeanah, C.H. (1994). The assessment and treatment of infants and toddlers exposed to violence. In J.D. Osofsky & E. Fenichel (Eds.), *Caring for infants and toddlers in violent environments: Hurt, healing, and hope.* National Center for Clinical Infant Programs, Washington, DC.

Multiple Victimization
and the Process and Outcome
of Child Psychotherapy

Stephen R. Shirk
Michael Eltz

SUMMARY. Maltreated youngsters present a complex picture of treatment needs. This is nicely illustrated by a review of the treatment outcome research with abused children. Prominent among their treatment issues are relationship problems and poor emotion regulation strategies. The treatment relationship and process variables in psychotheraphy are of particular concern with maltreated children. Concepts and research in these areas are reviewed. Finally, the recommendation is made that multiply victimized children need a comprehensive, multi-component approach to treatment. *[Article copies available for a fee from The Haworth Document Delivery Service: 1-800-342-9678. E-mail address: getinfo@haworth.com]*

There is emerging evidence in both the adult and child treatment literatures that individuals with co-morbid conditions may be more severely disturbed (Strauss, Last, Hersen, & Kazdin, 1988), more difficult to treat (Shea, Widiger, & Klein, 1992), and less likely to benefit from intervention (Shea et al., 1992; Hinshaw, 1992) than individuals with a single

Address correspondence to: Stephen R. Shirk, PhD, Department of Psychology, University of Denver, Denver, CO 80208.

[Haworth co-indexing entry note]: "Multiple Victimization and the Process and Outcome of Child Psychotherapy." Shirk, Stephen R., and Michael Eltz. Co-published simultaneously in *Journal of Aggression, Maltreatment & Trauma* (The Haworth Maltreatment & Trauma Press, an imprint of The Haworth Press, Inc.) Vol. 2, No. 1 (#3), 1998, pp. 233-251; and: *Multiple Victimization of Children: Conceptual, Developmental, Research, and Treatment Issues* (ed: B. B. Robbie Rossman, and Mindy S. Rosenberg) The Haworth Maltreatment & Trauma Press, an imprint of The Haworth Press, Inc., 1998, pp. 233-251. Single or multiple copies of this article are available for a fee from The Haworth Document Delivery Service [1-800-342-9678, 9:00 a.m. - 5:00 p.m. (EST). E-mail address: getinfo@haworth.com].

disorder. If we transpose these observations to the domain of child maltreatment, where there is increasing recognition of the "co-morbidity" of abuse experiences, a number of questions immediately come to mind. First, what are the effects of multiple forms of victimization on the child's capacity to benefit from therapy? Second, how might the experience of multiple victimization affect the *process* of child therapy? And finally, what are the implications of multiple victimization for the design of child treatment interventions? In this article we will attempt to address these questions by combing the child psychotherapy outcome literature, especially child-focused outcome research with abused children, for potential answers. Our emphasis will be on psychotherapy with school-age children, though some relevant studies with adolescents will be included. Given the limited scope of the controlled treatment outcome literature with abused children, our goal will be twofold: first, to highlight what we know, and second, to draw attention to what we need to learn.

TREATMENT OUTCOMES WITH ABUSED CHILDREN

Despite its obvious importance, very few empirical studies have addressed the effectiveness of psychotherapy with maltreated children. Much of the existing treatment literature focuses on proposed treatments, but rarely are these treatments systematically evaluated. Those that do typically focus on one type of maltreatment (e.g., physical abuse, sexual abuse, or neglect), or no distinction is made among types of maltreatment. However, in order to provide a current assessment of the empirical literature on psychotherapy outcome with maltreated children, a computer search was conducted with a set of key words (e.g., treatment outcome, abuse, neglect, etc.) which yielded a small sample of published studies. In an effort to extend the search, the references of all studies produced by the computer search were examined. This process resulted in a sample of thirteen studies of *child-focused* treatments that met the minimal conditions of adequate sample size (not N of one) and some form of pre-post assessment. Studies without controls were included because of the small number of published studies. In an effort to describe this research, studies will be reviewed separately by type of maltreatment.

Sexual Abuse. Several studies have been conducted regarding the effectiveness of treatment with sexually abused children (Verleur, Hughes, & de Rios, 1986; Corder, Haizlip, & DeBoer, 1990; and Deblinger, McLeer, & Henry, 1990). Unfortunately, O'Donohue and Elliott (1992) in their review of this outcome literature reported that many of the studies in this area are fraught with methodological problems and that, as yet, there has been no definitive demonstration of the efficacy of any treatment approach.

Examination of some of the studies reveals many of the characteristic problems. For example, the study by Corder et al. (1990) examined eight 6 to 9 year-old females in time-limited group therapy, and reported an abatement of symptomatology. The abuse experienced was described as short-term sexual abuse without severe physical violence. No other information was given regarding co-occurrence of abuse types or about other maltreatment classifications (e.g., severity, duration, etc.). A very detailed treatment protocol was presented, but in addition to its small sample size and no control group, this study also used only anecdotal assessments with no statistical analyses of outcome as opposed to any standardized assessment techniques (O'Donohue & Elliott, 1992).

Verleur et al. (1986) examined differential group-therapy outcome among thirty female adolescents in a residential treatment setting, fifteen of whom received group therapy and fifteen who did not. All subjects were victims of intrafamilial incest; however, no other information was given regarding either co-occurrence of abuse types or about other maltreatment classifications (e.g., severity, duration). The treatment approach was not explicitly described; and since all subjects were exposed to other elements of the residential treatment setting, the authors were unable to control for the effects of collateral treatments. It was not surprising, then, that both groups showed similar outcomes on various measures of self-concept.

Downing, Jenkins, and Fisher (1988) compared psychodynamic and reinforcement treatments in a group of twenty-two sexually abused elementary school children. While the authors report that 90% of these children were abused by a non-biological relative, they otherwise report no information was given regarding either co-occurrence of abuse types or about other maltreatment classifications (e.g., severity, duration, etc.). While results show numerical improvements on several areas of symptomatology, such as sleep disturbances and sexual play, as resulting from both treatments, no statistical comparisons were performed on the outcome data.

Deblinger et al. (1990) showed that of nineteen female children suffering from Post Traumatic Stress Disorder symptomatology, subsequent to sexual abuse, all showed statistically significant improvement. Perpetrator, duration of abuse, age when abuse occurred, and severity of abuse were reported, with severity classified by the specific nature of sexual victimization, i.e., genital-oral contact, penile penetration, genital touching, etc. Treatment involved structured individual cognitive-behavioral therapy for twelve sessions, combined with parent training designed to teach parents how to therapeutically intervene with their children. Results indicated significant pre/post reductions in PTSD symptomatology, Child Behavior Checklist internalizing and externalizing symptomatology, and self-reported measures of depression and anxiety. While this study had the virtue of including reliable assessment instruments, there was no control group, and outcome measures focused on self-report and interview data of the children and parents, with no objective behavioral assessments (O'Donohue & Elliott, 1992).

Finally, Gomes-Schwartz, Horowitz, Cardarelli and Sauzier (1990) examined the emotional and behavioral functioning of sexually abused children when they entered treatment and compared this to their level of functioning at an 18-months follow-up. Fifty-five percent of this sample showed improvement in their emotional and behavioral functioning regardless of whether they participated in treatment, although those who did participate in treatment tended to show greater gains. Because this was not a traditional treatment outcome study, method of treatment was not specified, nor was there any reported classification of multiple maltreatment.

Most of these studies suggest the potential usefulness of therapy for treating victims of sexual abuse. Unfortunately, the prevalent, and serious, methodological and statistical problems cloud the validity of any conclusions based on this research. Additionally, most studies did not report information on the specific nature of the sexual maltreatment, and of relevance to the issue of multiple victimization, no study reported the possible co-occurrence of maltreatment types.

Physical Abuse. Nicol, Smith, Kay, Hall, Barlow, and Williams (1988) examined differential outcome among families with physically-abused children, comparing a focused casework intervention with a structured play therapy intervention. In all cases, documented evidence of child physical abuse was obtained from social services. It was reported that there were no cases with known involvement of sexual abuse, but there was no evidence regarding neglect nor any classification of other maltreatment variables (e.g., severity, duration, etc.). Their results showed a statistically significant treatment advantage for the focused casework management, as assessed by improvement in family interactions. The casework approach involved an in-home supportive parent education approach, while the play therapy approach involved individual play therapy with the children, combined with parental contact by a social worker who "maintained a supportive role with the family" (Nicol et al., 1988, p. 705). Unfortunately, the descriptions of the treatment methods were inadequate for replication, and no control group was included in the design. However,

Fantuzzo (1990) suggested that the play therapy condition may have been used simply as a placebo control. Several methodological problems were found with this study: there was a 45% dropout rate in this study; no control for any demographic factors; and no standardized assessment measures. Consequently, the utility of this study is unclear. All other published studies of treatment effectiveness with physically-abused children have been parent- rather than child-focused (Azar & Wolfe, 1989).

Again, the physical abuse literature provided no empirical evidence for the treatment of children who have experienced multiple forms of victimization. As reflected in the Nicol et al. (1988) study, the emphasis of existing research has been on identifying single (pure) forms of maltreatment, but with limited assessment of possible co-morbid abuse experiences.

Physical Abuse and Neglect. Fantuzzo and his colleagues conducted two studies on the role of peer-based social interventions in therapeutic pre-schools with neglected children. In the first study (Fantuzzo, Stovall, Schachtel, Goins, & Hall, 1987) which examined only four children, results suggested an improvement in prosocial behaviors of two maltreated children following prosocial peer intervention by a child confederate who was trained to positively initiate and interact with the neglected child in comparison to the prosocial behaviors of two control children who were also neglected.

The second study (Fantuzzo, Jurecic, Stovall, Hightower, Goins, & Schachtel, 1988) replicated and extended the first study with a sample of thirty-six abused preschool children: nine with documented histories of physical abuse, eighteen with histories of neglect, and twelve considered at high-risk, all as determined by social service. No information was given regarding co-occurrence of abuse types or about other maltreatment parameters (e.g., severity, duration, etc.). These children were then randomly assigned into peer-treatment, adult-treatment, and control groups. Treatment in the experimental conditions involved the initiation of social interaction by a peer or adult who was trained in two social initiation strategies–play organization and sharing–for thirty minutes of their day in the pre-school. Results demonstrated improvements and increased generalization of prosocial behaviors in maltreated children through peer-based intervention. Also, children in the peer-based treatment remained stable or showed slight decreases in problematic behaviors over time, while the other two groups showed increases. While this study also does not fully assess the nature of the maltreatment experienced by these children, it otherwise represents one of the best studies conducted in this area from a methodological standpoint.

One additional study was found which compared seventeen maltreated children who received treatment with seventeen maltreated children who did not receive treatment (Culp, Little, Letts, & Lawrence, 1991). Maltreatment history was established by social services' documentation of physical abuse or neglect as perpetrated by the child's mother. Twenty children experienced neglect without physical abuse, while the other fourteen experienced physical abuse. It was not stated whether any of the physically-abused children also experienced neglect or whether any of the children in either group experienced sexual abuse. There was no classification of other maltreatment variables (e.g., severity, duration). The treatment group was admitted to a therapeutic day treatment program staffed by certified preschool teachers with experience working with maltreated children. The milieu experience of the children, which encompassed the majority of their six-hour day, focused on facilitating the emotional expression of the children, as well as developing strong teacher-child and peer relationships. The children received individual play therapy, family therapy, speech therapy, and physical therapy. In essence, children received a multi-component treatment package. Parents of the maltreated children also were provided with individual therapy, parent education, support counseling, and emergency aid. This study demonstrated gains in cognitive competence, peer acceptance, and maternal acceptance, as reported both by self and teacher reports. Unfortunately, there was no evidence that subjects were randomly assigned into treatment or control groups, suggesting the possibility of baseline differences which may account for the outcome effects.

Maltreatment, Unspecified. Gabel and his colleagues looked at differences among disturbed populations of children, including an abused group, regarding their need for post-treatment placement in three separate studies. In all studies, maltreated children, ranging in age from four to twelve, who had participated in treatment at a psychiatric hospital, were compared as to whether they were discharged to their homes or to out-of-home placements. The results across the three studies (Gabel, Finn, & Ahmad, 1988; Gabel, Swanson, & Shindledecker, 1990; Gabel & Shindledecker, 1990) tended to show that maltreated children, along with children in all three other groups (e.g., children who were suicidal, assaultive, or had parents with substance abuse problems), were significantly more likely to be placed out-of-home following treatment as compared to a sample with none of those preadmission characteristics. Although this set of studies considered multiple risk factors in relation to placement outcome (an important form of treatment outcome), the lack of systematic maltreatment classification or description of the treatment approach limits the usefulness of the findings.

Conclusions. As this review reveals, further research into the effectiveness of psychotherapy with maltreated children is desperately needed. As yet, there is little evidence for the effectiveness of child-focused treatment methods with maltreated children, even though there is some *suggestion* in this literature that treatment is useful. As a number of reviewers (Ammerman, 1989; Gonzales-Ramos & Goldstein, 1989; Fantuzzo, 1990; and O'Donohue & Elliott, 1992) have observed, many of the outcome studies have significant methodological problems which make it difficult to draw clear conclusions about the usefulness of various interventions. For example, outcome studies with maltreated children often have used single-subject designs, inadequate operationalization of maltreatment status, inadequate specification of treatment methods, or insufficient monitoring of treatment progress. While these problems are often found in child psychotherapy outcome studies (Shirk & Russell, 1992), they appear to be particularly problematic in the maltreatment literature, perhaps owing to the lack of any accepted maltreatment assessment strategy or treatment protocol. Often studies do not include information on pre-abuse status, maltreatment severity, chronicity, duration, or perpetrator, and, in some cases, even type of maltreatment.

Essentially, there is no compelling empirical evidence for the utility of treatment with children who have experienced multiple forms of victimization. Most studies have attempted to isolate one specific type of abuse, e.g., sexual vs. physical, but have often failed to consider important characteristics such as the severity, duration, or perpetrator of the maltreatment. It is not clear whether investigators have systematically evaluated children for the co-occurrence of other forms of maltreatment. Consequently, it is possible that many of the existing studies contain subsets of children who have experienced multiple forms of victimization. It is striking that chronicity of maltreatment, a potential proxy for multiple victimization, has rarely been assessed as a moderator of treatment responsiveness. On the other hand, research on child psychotherapy, in general, has tended to neglect salient child characteristics, such as developmental level, that could affect treatment outcome (Kazdin, Bass, Ayers, & Rodgers, 1990). Similarly, early research on child psychotherapy often did not use reliable assessment procedures for patient inclusion and exclusion, and only recently have child therapy investigators begun to consider the problem of co-morbidity. Hopefully, researchers who evaluate the effectiveness of treatments with victimized children will not continue to replicate some of the notable problems of the early child therapy literature.

Of particular importance, researchers must attend to child characteristics that could moderate treatment effectiveness. One of the most critical, it seems, is the severity and "co-morbidity" of maltreatment experiences. Although many children may experience one form of abuse only, it is likely that a subset of children have been exposed to multiple forms of victimization, including collateral inter-parental violence. The inclusion of these types of children in a single maltreatment category is likely to obscure the effects of treatment programs. Rectification of this problem may require the development of a standardized maltreatment interview that fully assesses the nature, severity, and duration of maltreatment, and provides a method for assessing the co-occurrence of multiple forms of victimization. Second, there is clearly a need for greater specification of treatment approaches or protocols. This problem must be addressed in order that effective treatments, once identified, can be replicated in clinical practice.

In the absence of data, it is tempting to speculate about the effectiveness of therapy for children who have experienced multiple forms of victimization. By analogy, one might argue that each added form of victimization constitutes another risk factor for psychopathology. Research by Rutter (1987) has indicated that as risk factors mount, so does the probability for serious psychopathology. Thus, children who have experienced multiple forms of victimization may evidence more serious forms of psychopathology or greater adaptive deficits than children who have experienced only one form of maltreatment. If this is the case, then such children may be less likely to benefit from child psychotherapy. Research on predictors of treatment effectiveness has consistently shown that pretreatment level of functioning is a significant predictor of treatment benefit (Luborsky, Diguer, Luborsky, McLellan, Woody, & Alexander, 1993). Thus, if multiply-victimized children are more seriously disturbed than children who have experienced one type of maltreatment, psychotherapy might be expected to produce smaller beneficial effects. However, this hypothesis has yet to be tested, and a reasonable argument could be made that chronicity, context (intra- vs. extra-familial abuse), and developmental timing of maltreatment could exert equally deleterious effects on pretreatment level of functioning as do multiple forms of victimization.

MULTIPLE VICTIMIZATION AND CHILD THERAPY PROCESS

Although outcome studies are sorely needed by child clinicians, the exclusive focus on therapeutic procedures or technique ignores other dimensions of therapy process that have been shown to be related to treatment outcome (Orlinsky & Howard, 1986). Perhaps the most remarkable victim of neglect by child clinical researchers has been the therapeutic relationship (Shirk & Saiz, 1992). As Strupp (1986) has maintained, "Psychotherapy is the use of a human relationship to effect enduring changes" (p. 513); and all psychotherapy, be it nondirective play therapy or cognitive skill-training, occurs in the context of a therapeutic relationship. Of equal importance, relationship processes, specifically therapeutic alliance variables, have been shown to be among the most consistent predictors of treatment outcome with adult patients across types of treatments, problems, and outcome measures (Horvath & Luborsky, 1993). For children who have been maltreated, especially those who have experienced multiple forms of victimization, the formation of a therapeutic relationship or alliance could be uniquely challenging, and thus represents a critical dimension of child therapy process with abused children.

Bowlby (1988) and other interpersonal theorists (cf. Safran, 1990) have proposed that children develop internal representations of relationships–working models–through recurrent interactions with early caregivers. These representations contain core information about the worthiness of the self and the responsiveness and dependability of others (Main, Kaplan, & Cassidy, 1985). Such representations are not static images of self and other, but instead are functional schema that exert an influence over the processing of social information, the regulation of emotion, and the direction of interpersonal behavior (Baldwin, 1992). There is growing evidence that these early models are incorporated into generalized schema of relationships (Crittendon, 1990) which are readily elicited under conditions of ambiguity or high emotional arousal (Collins & Read, in press). In this context, it is interesting to consider the impact of victimization on the development of working models.

Research has shown that maltreated children are more likely to have insecure attachments with primary caregivers than nonmaltreated children (Egeland & Sroufe, 1981). In fact, Carlson, Cicchetti, Barnett, and Braunwald (1989) found that a very high percentage of maltreated infants (over 80%) showed a disorganized pattern of approach mixed with high levels of apprehension in relation to caregivers. As Carlson et al. (1989) point out, this type of disorganization in the attachment relationship is likely to be a function of inconsistent care and fear associated with maltreatment. From the perspective of working models, such children may develop problematic expectations that others, especially others in a caregiving role, are not only unreliable, but dangerous as well. In support of this perspective, Lynch and Cicchetti (1991) found that maltreated children's "relatedness"–a combination of the child's perception of the emotional quality of relationships and their level of psychological proximity-seeking–was more likely to reflect a "confused" pattern than nonmaltreated agemates who showed more optimal patterns. Equally important, these representations were not circumscribed to primary caregivers, but appeared to generalize to other significant relationships as well.

It is likely that victimized children will transfer expectations derived from early care-receiving interactions to the caregiving context of psychotherapy. If such children have developed working models that predict that caregivers are not just unreliable and unresponsive, but potentially dangerous as well, then the formation of a therapeutic alliance could be especially problematic for maltreated children. As Collins and Read (in press) have suggested, core working models are likely to exert a strong influence on interpersonal perceptions and behavior during the early stages of relationship formation when ambiguity is high. That is, victimized children are likely to be highly sensitized to issues of safety that would not be a focal concern for other clinic-referred children.

In our own research (Eltz, Shirk, & Sarlin, in press), we examined alliance formation in a sample of maltreated and nonmaltreated adolescents who were admitted to an inpatient psychiatry unit. The maltreated group included both physically and sexually-abused teens. The two groups of adolescents were comparable in age, gender, and severity of psychopathology. Alliance quality was assessed independently from both the adolescents' and therapists' perspectives with the Penn Helping Alliance Scales (Luborsky, Crits-Christoph, Alexander, Margolis, & Cohen, 1983) approximately one week after admission and one week before discharge. These measures provided an index of the degree to which teen and therapist experienced the relationship as supportive and their work as collaborative. Results indicated that maltreatment status, chronicity of maltreatment, and type of perpetrator were all predictive of alliance difficulties at the beginning of treatment. Even after carefully controlling for severity of psychopathology, maltreated teens evinced greater difficulty engaging with their therapist than did their nonmaltreated peers. Comparisons of teens who had experienced multiple forms of victimization with teens who had experienced one type of abuse failed to reveal significant effects. However, such analyses were compromised by very limited sample size, and thus, by low power to detect differences. Moreover, some of the adolescents who had experienced one form of victimization had been abused chronically. Consequently, it is unclear whether chronicity of abuse or multiple forms of abuse have a greater impact on severity of maltreatment experience. It is possible that adolescents who have experienced multiple forms of victimization, particularly at the hands of multiple perpetrators, will develop more "generalized" expectations of danger and exploitation in close relationships. Such generalized expectations could make alliance formation acutely problematic for the multiply-victimized, though such a hypothesis remains to be tested.

Nevertheless, the results clearly indicated that the experience of maltreatment constituted an obstacle to alliance formation. Fortunately, over the course of therapy, maltreated teens developed comparable alliances as their nonmaltreated counterparts. This finding suggests that the treatment of victimized children is likely to require a longer initial phase of alliance-building than is typically needed for most clinic-referred children. Unfortunately, the study did not examine therapist behaviors that enabled maltreated teens to overcome their initial difficulties with alliance formation. However, informal interviews with clinicians on this unit suggested that these therapists were highly attuned to issues of safety and coercion. For example, initial sessions with some maltreated teens were conducted in "quasi-public" places in order to offset fears that might be associated with isolation with a caregiver. In addition, teens were given some degree of control over the time and location of therapy sessions.

The results of this study are highly consistent with clinical perspectives on the treatment of abused children; namely, that the development of a treatment alliance is a formidable task with children who have experienced maltreatment at the hands of caregivers (Herman, 1992). The parallels between parental and therapeutic roles, particularly with young maltreated children, are likely to elicit core conflicts around nurturance and safety. Consequently, one might expect an oscillating or disorganized pattern of alliance formation with such children that resembles the approach-avoidance conflicts evinced by maltreated children in attachment situations. Although the results of our research require replication with broader samples, including younger and non-hospitalized children, they do suggest that maltreated children are capable of establishing a productive relationship with their therapist over time. However, time may be the essential element in that maltreated children appear to show greater difficulty with entry into therapy than their nonmaltreated peers.

A number of other factors could influence the process of therapy with multiply-victimized children. However, the case for such factors requires inferential reasoning from studies of child psychotherapy that did not explicitly include an abuse sample. One potential factor is the child's recognition or awareness of their own problems. Anna Freud (1965) has maintained that children's lack of insight into their own problems undermines their motivation for treatment. That is, without the recognition or acknowledgment of problems, "they do not develop the same wish to get well and the same type of treatment alliance" as adults (A. Freud, 1965; p. 28). In fact, our research (Shirk, Saiz, & Sarlin, 1993) showed that problem acknowledgement, rather than symptomatology, was a significant predictor of alliance formation among psychiatrically-hospitalized children. Children who acknowledged difficulties and a need for personal change at admission evinced more positive working alliances with their therapists three weeks into treatment than children who minimized their problems or the necessity of change. Although the minimization of problems is typical of many clinic-referred children, one might expect this tendency to be amplified among victims of multiple forms of abuse.

According to Terr (1991), one of the features that characterizes children who have been exposed to chronic or multiple forms of trauma is denial or psychic numbing. As she has noted, "Massive attempts to protect the psyche and to preserve the self are put into gear" (p. 15), including the use of massive denial, repression, and dissociation. Thus, children who have experienced multiple forms of victimization are likely to rely on defensive operations that limit their ability to acknowledge problems. For such children, these strategies undoubtedly protect vulnerabilities in their sense of self-worth. However, to the degree that problem acknowledgement is a catalyst for active participation in psychotherapy, children who rely on denial as a coping strategy may be more difficult to engage in the process of treatment.

A second factor involves maltreated children's perceptions of control. According to Finkelhor and Browne (1985), one of the major consequences of victimization is disempowerment. As they point out, "The dynamic of rendering the victim powerless refers to the process in which the child's will, desires, and sense of self-efficacy are continually contravened" (p. 532). Although their focus was on child sexual abuse, it is not difficult to extend this perspective to children who have experienced multiple forms of maltreatment. The lack of control over maltreatment episodes is likely to engender assumptions about the uncontrollability of events, and to foster beliefs in an external locus of control. In one study with abused children, Barahal, Waterman, and Martin (1981) found that abused children, compared with matched controls, were more likely to feel that outcomes were determined primarily by external factors. Although no attempt was made to assess the relationship between control beliefs and severity or multiplicity of victimization, it seems reasonable to hypothesize that multiple forms and episodes of victimization would reinforce assumptions about the uncontrollability of events and outcomes.

The assumption of the uncontrollability of events and outcomes could have a profound impact on victimized children's ability to engage in and benefit from child psychotherapy. Weisz (1986) hypothesized that children's control-related beliefs would be an important predictor of treatment gains. According to Weisz, children who believe that outcomes, such as problem resolution, are not controllable, are likely to show less effective problem-solving activity in therapy, compared to children who perceive their problems as controllable. Thus, differences in control beliefs should predict differential rates of change because "children invest levels of energy in the therapeutic process commensurate with their beliefs about control" (p. 789). In a study with eight to seventeen year olds referred for outpatient therapy, Weisz (1986) found that control-related beliefs, measured prior to the start of treatment, accounted for a significant portion (29%) of outcome variance. That is, children who viewed problem resolution as contingent on their efforts and who believed that desired outcomes were controllable showed larger treatment benefits than children who held the opposite assumptions. Thus, if abused children, particularly those who have experienced multiple forms of victimization, assume a lack of control over events and outcomes, it is likely that they will attain smaller gains in therapy. Of course, for many victimized children, especially those who face continuing threats of maltreatment, the "true" locus of their problem is, in fact, external to the self. Consequently, enhancing victimized children's use of therapy by modifying their control-related beliefs is not a simple matter. There is even some evidence to suggest that abused children are overly inclined to attribute negative events to the self (Barahal et al., 1981). The task for the child therapist, then, is to help the victimized child differentiate controllable from non-controllable events, and to recognize the areas in which problem resolution is contingent on the child's own efforts.

In sum, a number of factors could exert a disruptive influence on the process of psychotherapy with children who have experienced multiple victimization. Of central importance is the relationship between the experience of multiple victimization and alliance formation. Here several factors may conspire to obstruct the formation of a positive therapeutic relationship, including expectations of danger in caregiving interactions, denial or minimization of problems, and assumptions about the uncontrollability of outcomes. To the degree that a positive alliance is essential for treatment progress, then, therapists will need to address these potential obstacles to relationship formation. Obviously, research is needed on the association between these potential obstacles and alliance formation among victimized children, and on the facilitating behaviors by therapists that enable maltreated children to overcome obstacles to the treatment process.

IMPLICATIONS FOR TREATMENT

Although child victims of maltreatment represent a significant portion of referrals to clinics and hospitals (O'Donohue & Elliot, 1992), there appears to be a substantial gap between clinical practice and empirical evidence for the effectiveness of specific treatment programs. For example, in the case of child sexual abuse treatment, O'Donohue and Elliot (1992) concluded that, "It should be apparent from this review that to date there has been no study demonstrating definitively the efficacy of any treatment method" (p. 225). Our review indicates that a similar, perhaps even stronger, conclusion can be reached concerning the treatment of children who have experienced multiple forms of maltreatment. Not only is there an absence of definitive evidence for treatment effectiveness with multiply-victimized children, no study has even targeted this group for investigation. Even a potential proxy for multiple victimization–severity or chronicity of abuse–is rarely treated as a child characteristic that could moderate the effectiveness of therapy. Consequently, the current empirical literature provides a very weak foundation for the construction of treatment programs for children with maltreatment "co-morbidity."

However, if we take Terr's (1991) observations of children who have experienced multiple or chronic forms of trauma (Type 2) as a starting point for the treatment of multiply-victimized children, then attention must be directed toward the child's emotional experience and capacity for emotion regulation. According to Terr (1991), one of the most prominent characteristics of such children involves the use of coping and defensive processes that isolate them from their emotions and potentially distort their experience of reality. Problems with emotion regulation are reflected in both numbing of emotional experience and in unmodulated expressions of rage and fear (Terr, 1991).

For some child clinicians, the revival of the trauma model has entailed the resurrection of early methods for treating trauma (Shirk, 1988). Historically, when trauma was central to Freud's etiological formulations, the goals of treatment were to uncover past traumatic events and to release the associated repressed affect. In essence, uncovering and abreaction were viewed as the necessary and sufficient conditions for resolving the sequelae of traumatic experiences. The operating assumption, derived from this perspective, is that current problems reflect a repetition of past trauma, and can be relieved by uncovering memories and discharging emotions associated with the traumatic experience. Viewed from this perspective, expressive play therapy would appear to be the treatment of choice for school-aged children.

There are two problems with this prescription. First, expressive play therapy, as a treatment procedure, typically does not address significant deficits in social competence that characterize many abused children (Shirk, 1988). That is, the experience of maltreatment may be directly linked to maladjustment through unexpressed memories and feelings, but past trauma is also indirectly connected to maladjustment through its disruption of early developmental tasks. For example, physical abuse of toddlers can interfere with their early social relations (George & Main, 1979), which in turn may lead to significant social skill or social problem-solving deficits through isolation from the peer group. Uncovering traumatic episodes and releasing the associated affect will not, by itself, remediate deficits that were incurred by early disruptions in normal developmental processes. It is interesting to note that many of the current treatments for child sexual abuse are based on a skill-remediation model (O'Donohue & Elliott, 1992).

Second, and of equal importance, the process of uncovering and releasing traumatic memories and emotions can be extremely disorganizing for a child who is in the midst of developing adaptive coping strategies. Although the expression and reworking of emotions associated with victimization represent an important component of treatment, an exclusive emphasis on uncovering and discharge ignores the fragility of severely traumatized children's capacity for affect regulation. Thus, an essential component of treatment is the development of adaptive emotion-regulation strategies. Only when such strategies are in place should the therapist attempt to uncover potentially disorganizing memories and feelings (Herman, 1992).

A recent case illustrates this point. A nine-year-old child who had witnessed severe inter-parental violence and had been verbally abused by her father was referred for child psychotherapy. In the early phase of treatment, the therapist adopted a nondirective play therapy approach, and provided a rich array of play materials including dolls, action figures, a play house, and a small toy gun. The child who had witnessed the use of a gun between her parents was overwhelmed by its mere presence in the therapy room. Though the therapist had made no direct effort to engage the child in play that included the toy gun, the child became extremely disorganized, covered her eyes, and refused to participate in the session. It was evident that she lacked the internal resources to process–even through the indirect medium of symbolic play–the traumatic episodes she had witnessed. The goal of therapy, then, shifted to "scaffolding" the child's capacity for affect regulation through a series of activities that involved graded experiences around current emotional situations, e.g., keeping a feelings checklist for the week, answering one feelings question per session. Over the course of therapy the child demonstrated an increased capacity to tolerate strong affect, as reflected in her willingness to talk about upsetting events, and eventually the therapist, with the help of the mother, began to address some of the child's early traumatic experiences.

The main point of this brief case vignette is to emphasize the role of emotion regulation in the treatment of victimized children. Although reworking emotions associated with early trauma is an important component of treatment, successful reworking depends on the existence of adequate emotion regulation strategies. Though it is interesting to note the rise of skill-oriented approaches to the treatment of victimized children, most of these programs appear to focus on social, social problem-solving, or communication skills, rather than on coping skills or emotion regulation strategies. It is our contention that the latter represent an indispensable part of the treatment of victimized children. Thus, an integrated approach to the treatment of multiply-victimized children would involve several phases: first, the establishment of a safe relationship; second, the development of the child's coping and emotion regulation resources; third, the uncovering or expression of traumatic material; and finally, the facilitation of adaptive interpersonal skills. Approaches that focus on only one of these components, e.g., the development of social skills, are likely to be insufficiently powerful interventions.

Multiple victimization is a complex phenomenon, which will undoubtedly require a complex, multi-component approach to treatment. As such, therapists who treat multiply-victimized children may need to disavow allegiances to specific treatment orientations and be willing to embrace a comprehensive treatment program that incorporates techniques from both behavioral and nonbehavioral traditions.

REFERENCES

Achenbach, T. (1985). *Assessment and taxonomy of child and adolescent psychopathology.* Beverly Hills, CA: Sage.

Ammerman, R.T. (1989). Child abuse and neglect. In M. Hersen (Ed.), *Innovations in child behavior therapy.* New York: Springer Publishing Company.

Azar, S.T. (1988). Methodological considerations in treatment outcome research in child maltreatment. In G.T. Hotaling, D. Finkelhor, J.T. Kirkpatrick, & M.A. Straus (Eds.), *Coping with family violence.* Newbury Park, CA: Sage.

Baldwin, A. (1992). Relational schemas and the processing of social information. *Psychological Bulletin, 112,* 461-484.

Barahal, R., Waterman, J., & Martin, H. (1981). The social cognitive development of abused children. *Journal of Consulting and Clinical Psychology, 49,* 508-516.

Beutler, L., & Clarkin, J. (1990). *Systematic treatment selection: Toward targeted therapeutic interventions.* New York: Brunner/Mazel.

Bowlby, J. (1988). *A secure base*. New York: Basic Books.

Carlson, V., Cicchetti, D., Barnett, D., & Braunwald, K. (1989). Disorganized/dis-oriented attachment relationships in maltreated infants. *Developmental Psychology*, *25*, 525-531.

Cohen, J.A., & Mannarino, A.P. (1993). A treatment model for sexually abused preschoolers. *Journal of Interpersonal Violence*, *8*(1), 115-131.

Cohn, A.H., & DeGraaf, B. (1982). Assessing case management in the child abuse field. *Journal of Social Service Research*, *5*, 29-43.

Collins, N., & Read, S. (in press). Cognitive representations of attachment: The structure and function of working models. In D. Perlman & K. Bartholomew (Eds.), *Advances in personal relationships*, *Vol. 5: Attachment processes in adulthood*. London: Jessica Kingley.

Corder, B.F., Haizlip, T., & DeBoer, P. (1990). A pilot study for a structured time-limited therapy group for sexually abused pre-adolescent children. *Child Abuse and Neglect*, *14*, 243-251.

Crittendon, P. (1990). Internal representational models of attachment relation-ships. *Infant Mental Health Journal*, *11*, 259-277.

Culp, R.E., Little, V., Letts, D., & Lawrence, H. (1991). Maltreated children's self concept: Effects of a comprehensive treatment program. *American Journal of Orthopsychiatry*, *61*(1), 114-121.

Deblinger, E., McLeer, S.V., & Henry, D. (1990). Cognitive behavioral treatment for sexually abused children suffering post-traumatic stress: Preliminary find-ings. *Journal of the American Academy of Child and Adolescent Psychiatry*, *29*, 747-752.

Egeland, B., & Sroufe, A. (1981). Developmental sequelae of maltreatment in infan-cy. In R. Rizley & D. Cicchetti (Eds.), *New directions in child development: Developmental perspectives on child maltreatment*. San Francisco: Jossey-Bass.

Eltz, M., Shirk, S., & Sarlin, N. (in press). Alliance formation and treatment outcome among maltreated adolescents. *Child Abuse and Neglect*.

Fantuzzo, J.W. (1990). Behavioral treatment of the victims of child abuse and neglect. *Behavior Modification*, *14*(3), 316-339.

Fantuzzo, J.W., Jurecic, L., Stovall, A., Hightower, A.D., Goins, C., & Schachtel, D. (1988). Effects of adult and peer social initiations on the social behavior of withdrawn, maltreated preschool children. *Journal of Consulting and Clinical Psychology*, *56*, 34-39.

Fantuzzo, J.W., Stovall, A., Schachtel, D., Goins, C., & Hall, R. (1987). The effects of adult and peer social initiations on the social behavior of withdrawn maltreated preschool children. *Journal of Behavioral Therapy and Experimen-tal Psychiatry*, *18*, 357-363.

Finkelhor, D., & Browne, A. (1985). The traumatic impact of child sexual abuse. *American Journal of Orthopsychiatry*, *55*, 530-539.

Freud, A. (1965). *Normality and pathology in childhood: Assessments of develop-ment*. New York: International Universities Press.

Friedrich, W.N., & Reams, R.A. (1987). Course of psychological symptoms in sexually abused young children. *Psychotherapy*, *24*, 160-170.

Gabel, S., Finn, M., & Ahmad, A. (1988). Day treatment outcome with severely disturbed children. *Journal of the American Academy of Child and Adolescent Psychiatry, 27*(4), 479-482.

Gabel, S., & Shindledecker, R. (1990). Parental substance abuse and suspected child abuse/maltreatment predict outcome in children's inpatient treatment. *Journal of the American Academy of Child and Adolescent Psychiatry, 29*(6), 919-924.

Gabel, S., Swanson, A.J., & Shindledecker, R. (1990). Aggressive children in a day treatment program: Changed outcome and possible explanations. *Child Abuse and Neglect, 14,* 515-523.

Gomes-Schwartz, B., Horowitz, J.M., Cardarelli, A.P., & Sauzier, M. (1990). The aftermath of child sexual abuse: 18 months later. In B. Gomes-Schwartz, J.M. Horowitz, & A. P. Cardarelli (Eds.), *Child sexual abuse: The initial effects* (pp. 132-152). Newbury Park, CA: Sage.

Gonzales-Ramos, G., & Goldstein, E.G. (1989). Child maltreatment: An overview. In S.M. Ehrenkranz, E.G. Goldstein, L. Goodman, & J. Seinfeld (Eds.), *Clinical social work with maltreated children and their families: An introduction to practice.* New York: New York University Press.

Healy, K., Kennedy, R., & Sinclair, J. (1991). Child physical abuse observed: Comparison of families with and without history of child abuse treated in an in-patient family unit. *British Journal of Psychiatry, 158,* 234-237.

Herman, J. (1992). *Trauma and recovery.* New York: Basic Books.

Hinshaw, S. (1992). Academic underachievement, attention deficits, and aggression: Comorbidity and implications for intervention. *Journal of Consulting and Clinical Psychology, 60,* 893-903.

Horvath, A., & Luborsky, L. (1993). The role of the therapeutic alliance in psychotherapy. *Journal of Consulting and Clinical Psychology, 61,* 561-573.

Kazdin, A., Bass, D., Ayers, W., & Rodgers, A. (1990). Empirical and clinical focus of child and adolescent psychotherapy research. *Journal of Consulting and Clinical Psychology, 58,* 729-740.

Kendall, P., & Clarkin, J. (1992). Introduction to special section: Comorbidity and treatment implications. *Journal of Consulting and Clinical Psychology, 60,* 833-834.

Luborsky, L., Crits-Christoph, P., Alexander, L., Margolis, M., & Cohen, M. (1983). Two helping alliance methods for predicting outcomes of psychotherapy. *Journal of Nervous and Mental Disorders, 171,* 480-492.

Luborsky, L., Diguer, L., Luborsky, E., McLellan, A., Woody, G. & Alexander, L. (1993). Psychological health-sickness (PHS) as a predictor of outcomes in dynamic and other psychotherapies. *Journal of Consulting and Clinical Psychology, 61,* 542-548.

Lynch, M., & Cicchetti, D. (1991). Patterns of relatedness in maltreated and nonmaltreated children: Connections among multiple representational models. *Development and Psychopathology, 3,* 207-226.

Main, M., Kaplan, N., & Cassidy, J. (1985). Security in infancy, childhood, and adulthood: A move to the level of representation. In I. Bretherton & E. Waters

(Eds.), *Growing points of attachment theory and research. Monographs of the Society for Research in Child Development, 50* (1-2, Serial No. 209).

Newberger, C.M., & Gremy, I.M. (1993). *The role of interventions in children's recovery from sexual abuse.* Paper presented at the biennial meeting of the Society for Research in Child Development, New Orleans, LA.

Nicol, A.R., Smith, J., Kay, B., Hall, D., Barlow, J., & Williams, B. (1988). A focused casework approach to the treatment of child abuse: A controlled comparison. *Journal of Child Psychology and Psychiatry, 29,* 703-711.

O'Donohue, W.T., & Elliott, A.N. (1992). Treatment of the sexually abused child: A review. *Journal of Clinical Child Psychology, 21*(3), 218-228.

Orlinsky, D., & Howard, K. (1986). Process and outcome in psychotherapy. In S. Garfield & A. Bergin (Eds.), *Handbook of psychotherapy and behavior change.* New York: Wiley.

Rutter, M. (1987). Psychosocial resilience and protective mechanisms. *American Journal of Orthopsychiatry, 57,* 316-331.

Safran, J. (1990). Towards a refinement of cognitive therapy in light of interpersonal theory. *Clinical Psychology Review, 10,* 87-105.

Shea, M., Widiger, T., & Klein, M. (1992). Comorbidity of personality disorders and depression: Implications for treatment. *Journal of Consulting and Clinical Psychology, 60,* 857-868.

Shirk, S. (1988). The interpersonal legacy of physical abuse of children. In M. Straus (Ed.), *Abuse and victimization across the lifespan* (pp. 57-81). Baltimore, MD: Johns Hopkins Press.

Shirk, S., & Russell, R. (1992). A reevaluation of estimates of child therapy effectiveness. *Journal of the American Academy of Child and Adolescent Psychiatry, 31,* 703-709.

Shirk, S., & Saiz, C. (1992). Clinical, empirical, and developmental perspectives on the therapeutic relationship in child psychotherapy. *Development and Psychopathology, 4,* 713-728.

Shirk, S., Saiz, C., & Sarlin, N. (1993). *The therapeutic alliance in child and adolescent treatment: Preliminary studies with inpatients.* Paper presented at meeting of Society for Psychotherapy Research, Pittsburgh, PA.

Strauss, C., Last, C., Hersen, M., & Kazdin, A. (1988). Association between anxiety and depression in children and adolescents with anxiety disorders. *Journal of Abnormal Child Psychology, 16,* 57-68.

Strupp, H. (1986). The nonspecific hypothesis of therapeutic effectiveness: A current assessment. *American Journal of Orthopsychiatry, 56,* 513-520.

Terr, L. (1991). Childhood traumas: An outline and overview. *American Journal of Psychiatry, 148,* 10-20.

Verleur, D., Hughes, R.E., & de Rios, M.D. (1986). Enhancement of self-esteem among female adolescent incest victims: A controlled comparison. *Adolescence, 21,* 843-854.

Weisz, J. (1986). Contingency and control beliefs as predictors of psychotherapy outcomes among children and adolescents. *Journal of Consulting and Clinical Psychology, 54,* 789-795.

Into the Haunted House of Mirrors: The Treatment of Multiply Traumatized Adolescents

Donna B. Marold

SUMMARY. The treatment of youth with histories of multiple victimization is discussed. A developmental treatment approach is presented based on Eriksonian theory that highlights particular difficulties abuse presents for a child's successful movement through different developmental stages. Interventions addressing these difficulties are also discussed with many case examples. Finally, the issue is raised concerning which multiple abuse victims can be helped by the therapeutic process. *[Article copies available for a fee from The Haworth Document Delivery Service: 1-800-342-9678. E-mail address: getinfo@haworth.com]*

Children are born into our society totally helpless and dependent upon caregivers for their physical and emotional well-being. Fortunately, the preponderance of caregivers, including the majority of adults who were abused as children (Gil, 1970), are able to protect their offspring and guide them through the challenges inherent in growing to adulthood. However,

---

Address correspondence to: Donna B. Marold, PhD, 50 South Steel Street, Denver, CO 80209.

The author wishes to dedicate this article to her clients, who have taught her that the human spirit can heal in the context of trusting relationships.

[Haworth co-indexing entry note]: "Into the Haunted House of Mirrors: The Treatment of Multiply Traumatized Adolescents." Marold, Donna B. Co-published simultaneously in *Journal of Aggression, Maltreatment & Trauma* (The Haworth Maltreatment & Trauma Press, an imprint of The Haworth Press, Inc.) Vol. 2, No. 1 (#3), 1998, pp. 253-272; and: *Multiple Victimization of Children: Conceptual, Developmental, Research, and Treatment Issues* (ed: B. B. Robbie Rossman, and Mindy S. Rosenberg) The Haworth Maltreatment & Trauma Press, an imprint of The Haworth Press, Inc., 1998, pp. 253-272. Single or multiple copies of this article are available for a fee from The Haworth Document Delivery Service [1-800-342-9678, 9:00 a.m. - 5:00 p.m. (EST). E-mail address: getinfo@haworth.com].

253

human history is marked by child abuse and neglect in all cultures (De-mause, 1990) and is an all too common phenomenon in the United States (Coh, 1983).

Despite the recognition and documentation of child abuse, our society continues to condone violence and minimizes the impact of abuse (Belsky, 1993; Gil, 1970). There are only a few longitudinal studies of the impact of abuse on the developmental trajectory of children (Cicchetti & Carlson, 1988; Putnam & Trickett, 1994). More studies are needed to both document and educate the public regarding the impact of abuse, as well as to guide clinicians in the treatment of this population. In addition, research has typically been conducted in separate areas, such as sexual abuse (Finkelhor & Dziuba-Leatherman, 1994), and often does not take into account the chronicity or duration of the abuse. However, common sense and clinical experience tell us that a child who is abused in one way is at high risk of other forms of victimization, and will probably require some form of mental health intervention in his/her lifetime. This article will address treatment issues for a challenging population of clients-adolescents who have a history of multiple victimization.

Multiple victimization occurs when a child is abused in a variety of ways, and may involve abuse by more than one perpetrator, abuse over long periods of time, and actions done to the child which are sadistic and cruel. Abused children are neglected children. They suffer from the violence, and from not having the emotional support a child requires to reach their full potential (Finkelhor & Dziuba-Leatherman, 1994).

The psychological scars from chronic abuse appear to be indelibly laid down for life, and the therapeutic treatment of these young people is a challenge for the most experienced therapist. Treatment of severely maltreated youth requires that the therapist suspend all notions based on logic and travel with the young person through a world of haunted house mirrors, in which good becomes bad and bad becomes good, trust is earned primarily by actions, not words, and emotions vacillate between non-existence and extreme expression. Most importantly, successful treatment requires that the therapist have a philosophical stance that people can change for the better, and that symptoms have served a functional purpose as reactions to the person's experience. Clinicians need to have the patience to nurture, in an always tested relationship, so that the client can learn to put words with feelings, and ultimately give up self-defeating symptoms. Therapy must provide a safe context in which the adolescent can form a "good enough" sense of identity in order to go forward in life.

Treatment of adolescents who have suffered multiple abuse requires knowledge in the areas of developmental psychopathology, trauma, family systems, and adolescent development. Clinical work with traumatized individuals is difficult to do in a vacuum, and is best carried out within the context and support of other professionals with a similar philosophy and expertise. Finally, given the political and economic atmosphere at the end of the twentieth century in which health care change is ongoing and pressure is mounting for cost effective treatment, it is imperative that the therapist utilize the supportive resources available to the adolescent, and discover and create those resources when none exist.

The words of a 17 year old provide a window into the world of the severely abused:

> I don't remember being a child, Carol says with her eyes cast to the floor. Dressing up for a porn film was the closest I got to having fun. Yeah, it wasn't great to have sex with strangers at age seven, but at least I made money to feed the family. Playing court was the worst. The father made us spy on each other. He would pick the one we were closest to, and we would have to "narc" on each other. At the end of the week, during court, we had a choice of snitching or being beaten. If we didn't tell we were beaten anyway, so we usually told. My father almost drowned my younger brother in the toilet bowl because I told that he wore his hair different from the father one day. I also forced my sister to sleep on the outside of the bed so she would be chosen for sex, not me. I tried to help the younger ones, but sometimes I just had to take care of myself. I would rather die than remember anymore. I am evil and made all the bad things happen.

A discussion of the core symptoms secondary to different forms of abuse and a brief review of trauma theory will provide the background from which to address the primary goal of the article: to take the reader through theoretically based guidelines for the treatment of the psychologically compromised adolescent. The psycho-social theory of Eric Erikson will be utilized as a framework to conceptualize the developmental nature of the impact of abuse, and as a rationale for the identification and inclusion of key treatment goals. The final section will address clinical issues unique to this special population. Clinical vignettes, based on composite information from my clients, are used to illustrate theory and interventions.

NORMATIVE DEVELOPMENT

The conceptualization of adolescence as a unique developmental stage between childhood and adulthood is relatively recent (Hall, 1904). It is a period of often rapid change in all areas, both intra- and interpersonally. Adolescents must cope with the onset of puberty and adult sexuality. Advanced cognitive skills bring the ability to understand the world in an abstract way, but also promote self-absorption and the return to egocentrism (Inhelder & Piaget, 1955). The adolescent's relationships outside of the family increase both in number and importance, and autonomy and self-determination are driving forces in all domains. Yet of all the changes occurring in this developmental period, the most profound and important in charting the life course is that of identity formation (Erikson, 1959). Thus, the normative challenges of adolescence pose unique and complicated demands on healthy, nonabused adolescents who, presumably, have families that provide at least minimal support.

For the adolescent with past and often continuing victimization, protecting one's self from injury or death at the hands of a family member and defending against emotional annihilation are the primary goals. All other developmental tasks are subsumed and impacted by a basic drive for survival. Adaptation, both psychological and physical, is shaped by a home environment, and often a social milieu, which offers little in the way of support and where violence is a way of life. The following section highlights the work of several theorists, and addresses the specific areas of development that are affected by chronic abuse.

CONCEPTUALIZATIONS OF MALTREATMENT EFFECTS

There are several existing paradigms and descriptions of consequences of trauma that illuminate the impact of abuse on adolescents. Working from a trauma approach, Lenore Terr (1991) has described two types of trauma in children: Type I trauma is essentially a single traumatic episode that potentially results in repeated visualizations of the trauma, symbolic reenactments of the traumatic event, a chronic state of fear, and the sense of futurelessness. Type II trauma is the exposure to ongoing experiences of trauma which can result in denial and psychic numbing, and extremes in affect, including rage and unremitting sadness. Terr also points out that children can experience a mixture of symptoms of both Type I and II trauma, especially children who grow up in violent families. Although Terr's work is primarily based on her work with pre-adolescent children, this typology is applicable in understanding the adolescent client.

Symptoms of Type I trauma are similar to those noted in models which examine child abuse from a post-traumatic stress perspective (van der Kolk, 1889; Herman, 1992), emphasizing alternating periods of denial and intrusive thoughts, as well as the tendency for the individual to recreate the traumatic event. Terr's description of a Type II trauma response provides the clinician with a framework to understand that the symptoms of ongoing abuse allow the person to cope with events that cannot be controlled. This pattern of response becomes a style of coping in all situations and relationships. Clinical intervention with chronically abused adolescents involves treatment of post-traumatic symptoms and altering a personality style based on defending against chronic trauma. Dave's story illustrates the symptoms Terr describes, including psychic numbing, extreme experiences of affect, reenactment of the violence through harming himself and attacking his mother, and the reexperiencing of the abuse in night terrors. Dave, age 15, never knew his father, and was raised by his mother and five stepfathers. He was physically abused by three of them and sexually abused by an older stepbrother. Dave watched his mother being battered, and was once beaten up when he tried to intervene. Starting at age 12, he was placed in foster homes and physically abused in two of them. He made several impulsive suicide attempts, and once struck his mother during a home visit. Dave described himself as not caring about anyone, and said, "I can't remember the last time I cried. It's as if someone sewed my tear ducts shut. I'm jinxed. I can't sleep at night, and red demons haunt me."

Focusing more specifically on abuse, maltreatment histories have often been associated with symptoms characterizing borderline personality disorder, dissociative disorders, and eating disorders. Putnam (1990) has identified the following symptom clusters as common across these diagnostic categories: impairment in regulation of affect, including difficulty in using, or use of primitive, self-soothing behaviors; disturbances in the development of the self, including fragmentation, identity diffusion, low self-worth, aggression towards the self, disturbed body image, and a disturbance in integration of self; and, difficulties in socialization, including tumultuous relationships, fear of abandonment, disturbances in sexual behavior, and struggles for control in the relationship.

Impairment occurs not only from the failure to develop adequate emotional regulation, positive self-worth, and the ability to enter into and maintain healthy relationships, but also from maladaptive attempts at satisfying the underlying need. For example, an adolescent who has not developed the ability to self-soothe is at risk for using mind altering substances in an attempt to manage intense feelings. Attempting to satisfy intimacy needs, the abused adolescent often goes through a series of unhealthy relationships which may recapitulate the patterns of the familial structure. Joining gangs, with their unique signature rituals and dress, may be a maladaptive way to achieve a sense of identity. Steve's story illuminates Putnam's observations of symptom clusters. Steve, age 17, came to the attention of the mental health center when he was found underneath a bridge with both arms slit open. He claimed not to remember what happened. Steve had been involved in prostitution since age 14, and expressed confusion as to his identity as a male. "I just can't seem to make it in a relationship with anyone, male or female. I fall for someone, and they walk out on me, just like my parents. I hurt so much inside, and the only thing that seems to help is a six-pack."

Finkelhor and Brown (1985) describe sequelae of sexual molestation in childhood, including: traumatic sexualization; betrayal and a violation of trust; stigmatization which results in the development of shame and lower self-worth; and, a sense of powerlessness and defenselessness. Sexual molestation, especially when repeated, undermines the trust that is the essence of healthy relationships. The young child who has been sexualized often thinks that all relationships have to be sexualized, and when older, has difficulty forming nonsexualized close relationships. This propensity to engage in indiscriminate sexual activity is in painful juxtaposition to the core sense of shame about one's sexuality that usually develops with childhood sexual abuse. Due to normal egocentrism, often accompanied by perpetrators putting responsibility for sexual contact on the child, abused children often develop a self-image of worthlessness and may blame themselves for having caused the sexual abuse (Hornstein & Putnam, 1992). When faced with normal adolescent sexual drives and feelings, abused adolescents are caught in the bind of a compulsion to be in sexualized relationships accompanied by reactivation of betrayal, shame and a negative sense of self.

Dora exemplifies these consequences of sexual abuse. Dora, age 14, grew up in two worlds, one a black middle-class family dominated by her sexually, physically, and emotionally abusive grandfather, and the second a gifted and talented program where she was only one of three minority students. Despite her intellectual acuity, she had little capacity for self-empathy, blaming herself for a series of victimizations, including rape by a white male teacher. When asked about the abuse by her family and others, Dora matter-of-factly stated, "I am evil inside. No one will be able to love me, and I can never love anyone."

From his studies of adolescent girls and women diagnosed with borderline personality disorder, Westin (1993) noted several aspects of the impact of sexual abuse on the self-structure: confused and distorted sense of bodily experiences; disruption of episodic or autobiographical memory; denial of self-representations related to the abuse that can not be understood or are too frightening to acknowledge, and which can contribute to the denial of the abuse; cognitive constrictions regarding introspection about one's thoughts and behavior, a process Westin labels "metacognitive shutdown"; and, disruption in normative developmental processes, such as the integration of more abstract, differentiated self-representations. Westin's observations contribute to the understanding of developmental processes that are thwarted by abuse, especially in the development of a cohesive identity, the primary task of adolescence. Amy, age 13, typifies these patterns. Amy was referred to therapy by her family physician who diagnosed an eating disorder. She reported low self-esteem, depression, and suicidal thinking. Her parents were surprised to learn that Amy's perception of her appearance was very negative, since they saw her as the most attractive of all their children. Amy admitted to carving on her arms to "know I'm alive." She had been abused over several years by a Sunday School teacher, which her parents minimized.

An additional complexity in thinking about the effects of maltreatment is introduced by the work of Eth and Pynoos (1985). They examined the interaction between trauma in childhood and experience of the normal grieving process. They pointed out that trauma and loss can occur in the same event, such as witnessing the violent death of a parent. This may result in impaired ego and emotional functioning, guilt over surviving, stigma within the community, and reunion fantasies. Pynoos and Nader (1990) also noted that abuse may constrict the grieving process, thus impairing emotional development. For the adolescent who has not had appropriate role models for grieving, and/or has been discouraged from expression of affect, unresolved issues around loss can be monumental. These losses may be of people or pets, through death or abandonment, and symbolic or real.

THE ROLE OF TRAUMA THEORY

Social scientists have renewed interest in the impact of trauma on behavior (Horowitz, 1978; Lindemann, 1944). Post traumatic stress disorder (PTSD), as defined in the Diagnostic and Statistical Manual, Fourth Edition (DSM-IV) (American Psychiatric Association, 1994), is the development of characteristic symptoms after experiencing, observing, or hearing about disaster, death, injury, or the threat of harm. In PTSD two groups of symptoms are noted, persisting for at least one month and causing significant impairment in functioning: one group includes intrusions, such as flashbacks and nightmares; the second group are of a numbing or exclusionary nature. The traumatized individual rides an emotional rollercoaster. Intrusive trauma thoughts and affect bombard the senses at unexpected times, disrupting the ability to be in the present, and propelling the mind to the traumatic past. In contrast, there are periods in which perceptions and affects are dissociated and/or distorted and the individual feels emotionally numb and disconnected from the self and the world (Chu & Dill, 1990).

Another key aspect of trauma theory is that of replay or recapitulation of the trauma (Chu, 1992; van der Kolk, 1990). The reenactment may take many forms, and the person is not aware of the significance of their behavior. Unlike intrusive flashbacks and nightmares which occur in the person's mind, recapitulation of the trauma is the creation of behaviors and situations that approximate the themes of the abuse. For example, when Steve talks about "falling for people who walk out on me, just like my parents," this is a classic reenactment. It has been suggested that early childhood abuse may be encoded in the sensorimotor system, and acted out behaviorally, even without conscious knowledge of the abuse (van der Kolk, 1989). A person caught in this black hole of "traumatized thinking" (Cole, 1993), lives in a world dominated by repeating the same self-defeating themes of trauma and victimization, especially in relationships.

For the young child who has been abused, traumatic play takes the form of making dolls hit each other, running trucks into walls, or other symbolic acts of anger and destruction (Terr, 1990). Unlike children, who have limited resources to realistically act their trauma, the adolescent has both the physical and cognitive resources to engage in traumatic play using the world as a playground. Sexually abused children have a high rate of sexualized activity extending into adolescence (Kendall-Tackett, Williams, & Finkelhor, 1994) with promiscuity reflected in higher rates of teen pregnancy, prostitution, or acts of violent sexual behavior towards others (Burgess, 1987; Rosenthal, 1988).

Adolescents who have witnessed and experienced violence now also have the physical strength to act out their anger in more organized violence such as gang activity, or individual acts against parents, siblings or peers (Lewis, Mallouh & Webb, 1989). Abused teens also turn their anger and anguish towards themselves. From 1970 to 1980, reported rates of adolescent suicide rose 66% (Pardes, 1985). Precursors of suicidal behaviors are many and complex, but researchers have demonstrated a strong link between child abuse and suicidality in adolescents (van der Kolk, Perry & Herman, 1991).

Adolescence may also foster other clusters of symptoms which represent an attempt to cope with psychic stress. For example, drug and alcohol abuse by maltreated teens may be attempts to self-medicate the wide range of affects, and post-traumatic responses secondary to the abuse (Cavaiola &

Schiff, 1988). Eating disorders, which have been shown to have a high correlation with child abuse (Hibbard, Ingersoll & Orr, 1990), may also surface in adolescence as the young person attempts to control a distorted body image.

The paradox in trauma reactions is that, while adolescents may continuously reenact traumas they have experienced, both as victim and perpetrator, there is also a high rate of discounting the abuse and a lack of insight into the subsequent behavior. A poignant example of this can be found in interviews of adolescents who were identified by emergency room personnel as having suffered significant abuse, and who later became part of the DSM IV trials for PTSD. When asked about the abuse they had suffered, most made light of what happened or totally denied the abuse (van der Kolk, 1994).

GENERAL TREATMENT MODELS

Faced with the multifaceted responses and symptoms of multiply traumatized teens, even the most experienced clinician is often at a loss regarding how to proceed. In addition to the lack of outcome research or consensus about the efficacy of therapy with traumatized adolescents (Weisz & Weisf, 1993), there exists no proven paradigm for successful treatment. Models are emerging that address the issues identified above, and offer guidance in providing service for this population. These models differ from the more traditional psychodynamic model of therapy, which emphasizes the dominance of the therapist in the therapeutic relationship and tends to pathologize symptoms. These newer models are different in that they view therapy as a collaborative process, place the major locus of control and responsibility for change on the client, and view the client's symptoms as understandable responses to maltreatment.

These newer models have several points in common. First, the therapy is predicated on the belief that symptoms are a predictable and adaptive response to having been traumatized in ways outside the normal range of childhood experience (Briere, 1992; Courtois, 1988; Herman, 1991; Miller, 1990). Second, the therapeutic relationship must be a collaborative effort which provides a safe arena in which corrective changes can occur (Briere, 1992; Herman, 1991; Jorden, 1993). Third, these models acknowledge the role of trauma theory in understanding client behaviors and symptoms, especially the client's reenactments in the context of the therapeutic and other relationships (Chou, 1992; Sanders & Arnold, 1991; van der Kolk, 1994). Fourth, these models draw upon psycho-educational tools, such as teaching relaxation strategies, to help the client understand

and achieve mastery over his/her symptoms (Briere, 1992; Herman, 1992). Fifth, there is a focus on helping clients identify traumatic events and understand the ways they have impacted their lives. In recent years, the means to achieve this last goal of treatment have become more controversial, with major disagreements over how important the actual reexperiencing of the trauma is to successful recovery (van der Hart & Brown, 1992).

Several researchers/clinicians who address treatment issues (Briere, 1992; Herman, 1992) refer to the importance of the inclusion of non-verbal and expressive arts therapies in the treatment of chronic abuse victims. However, little has been written about the integration of these therapies, or the collaborative relationship between the primary clinician and adjunctive therapists. Rationale for and examples of such treatment techniques are described next.

A DEVELOPMENTAL TREATMENT APPROACH

The psycho-social theory of Erikson (1963) provides a framework to assess the sequelae of multiple victimization reviewed above, and systematically identify essential treatment goals (Bryant, Kessler & Shirar, 1992). Each developmental stage has potentially been impacted by the abuse, and the clinician needs to understand the type and level of impairment for each client. In assessing the client, it is best to inquire about which areas of his/her life are most problematic, and to ascertain the reasons for the difficulties. It is possible and pragmatic to understand the client's behavior and formulate treatment interventions from all stages, but it behooves the clinician to pay attention to earlier stages if the treatment does not appear to be going well. For example, a clinician may too quickly expect the adolescent to follow through on a homework assignment that theoretically would promote mastery, whereas the client could be having difficulty with trust issues with the therapist and/or may lack the ability to believe that completion of the assignment is feasible. Instead of viewing non-compliance as negative, it can be viewed as the opportunity to work on the underlying developmental difficulty that prevents the client from following through on an assignment or being able to tell the therapist that the assignment was not helpful, which requires trust in the relationship.

Trust and Hope

Erikson's first stage of development, trust vs. mistrust, occurs primarily at the sensori-motor level (Piaget, 1936). The caregiver must respond to an infant's basic needs and the young infant must learn to reach out to the environment and connect to the caregiver, thereby satisfying physical needs, as well as establishing the beginning of relational interaction (Critendon & Ainsworth, 1989). A healthy attachment lays the foundation for trusting oneself and others, as well as the development of an appropriate sense of mistrust. When this basic foundation is not fostered by the infant's environment, the abused child grows up with a maladaptive mistrust of self and other. For the child who has been abused, relationships are a source of physical and emotional pain rather than of comfort. This failure to develop a predominant sense of trust curtails the emergence of hope at later stages (Erikson, 1963).

The first therapeutic task is to establish a trusting relationship with the adolescent through doing activities together, and by striving to have actions consistent with words, thus meeting the client at the sensori-motor level, rather than through cognitive interactions and interpretations. Over time, the second therapeutic goal is to engender a sense of hope about one's self and the world. Activities such as sharing food and drink, making up jokes together, taking a walk, playing games, listening to the client's favorite CD, as well as having an office that feels safe, all facilitate these goals.

Returning to consistency, the therapist should not promise what he/she cannot deliver, and should let the adolescent know that the therapist is human and will make mistakes. Set the ground rule that the adolescent must learn to verbalize when something is not going right in the relationship. Too many well meaning therapists have made promises that the client hears concretely, then uses to prove the insincerity of the therapist. For example, "I'll always be there for you" is a phrase that will come back to haunt the therapist. The client may interpret absence due to vacation or illness as the breaking of a promise and yet another abandonment by an adult. In a similar fashion, consistency around the parameters of therapy is essential. If a therapist promises a phone call, the call should be made. Being on time for sessions and not having a double standard about lateness is important. If a promise to read a poem is made, the poem should be read by the next session. When the therapist makes a mistake, taking responsibility for the mistake and rectifying it in some way is crucial.

Carol, the 17 year old presented earlier, had seen several therapists, and had become very attached to the last person, who had encouraged an overly dependent relationship. When that therapist closed her practice and left town, Carol was convinced that it was her "badness" that drove the therapist away. After three years in her present therapy, Carol still believes that the therapist will leave her, but is beginning to verbalize that it does not have to be her fault when the therapeutic relationship ends. Vacations are difficult for her, and it does not matter if the therapist travels or she does for it is the separation that she has difficulty tolerating. In addition to talking about her feelings, including past feelings of abandonment which are triggered by breaks in therapy, her breaks are structured as one would with a young child. It is preferable to tell the client the general whereabouts of the therapist, while maintaining clear boundaries and not promoting an excessively dependent connection. Most importantly, for clinical and ethical reasons, one must have an on-call therapist, preferably one who is familiar with the client, to respond to emergencies.

Once the safety of the relationship has been established at an acceptable level, then and only then can clients begin to verbalize their inner thoughts and feelings. It is important to inquire about what was negative in the young person's life, but also to identify positive experiences, adults who were helpful, and positive coping strategies used by the client. My own experience has been that many children cope with abuse and the lack of adult nurturing by turning to animals. Alice, in the movie *Wildflower,* offers a poignant example. Banished to live in a shed because she is partly deaf and cannot speak, initially Alice's sole companion is a possum which she carries around her neck. I keep pictures of my animals in the office, and a conversation about a first pet can often help the client see the therapist as an "O.K. person." Unfortunately, a teen's grief may be embedded in stories about animals, including parents who injure or get rid of pets, and one must be alert for signs to stop talking about a pet until the ability to talk about intense feelings is established.

Establishing a trusting relationship was a central issue for Steve, the 17-year-old male prostitute discussed earlier who was ordered to undergo therapy as a condition of probation. He did not want to have anything to do with therapy and feared being used in therapy the way the street pimps used him. Much to his surprise, he was not "hassled," but therapy focused on our mutual interests in music. It was also arranged that the courts receive minimal information about Steve's therapy, and following through on this agreement meant making sure that he saw and approved of all written information. When we started to explore Steve's abuse history, he forcefully stated he could not talk about his feelings. Steve's interest in and knowledge of computers were used to provide him a safe format to explore the abuse. The computer became both a means and a metaphor for affect regulation. He kept his disks between sessions, and ultimately was able to work at home on "hot issues assignments." He had the control to decide if or when to show me what he was writing. For half of the session he would "turn on the computer" and "allow himself access to his feelings." He set up different files for various emotional states and would go to a chosen file to write about the different abuses that he endured. Later in treatment he was able to label and understand that he had several feelings for different events in his life, and he rearranged his files and stories to reflect his new level of awareness. In the final stages of treatment he wrote a narrative story about both the positive and negative events in his childhood, and with the wisdom of someone much older, was able to begin to ascribe positive outcomes to his ability to survive. In Steve's words "you're not too bad for a Doc. . . . maybe I been able to trust you. . . . maybe I can make something out of my life after all."

Autonomy and Regulation

The second psychosocial task is being able to act upon one's environment in such a way as to gain a sense of autonomy and self-confidence, while also learning to control one's actions. In Erikson's words, "will is the unbroken determination to exercise free choice as well as self-restraint" (1963, p. 119). This process is stymied when caregivers punish the child for no reason, or when the child's behavior fails to produce results (i.e., the child can not stop violence between parents). Development is also thwarted by a lack of positive responses to the child's attempt to achieve mastery over the environment. Developmentally, the young child needs to acquire a sense of control over his/her actions, and to begin to adapt to societal norms. However, the norms of an abusive family are usually organized around the rightness of the parents and the wrongness of the children. Therefore, the child grows up with a core sense of shame, rather than a healthy sense of autonomy. This phenomenon was empirically demonstrated in a recent study of psychiatrically hospitalized adolescent girls where Calverly, Fischer and Ayoub (1994) found that abused subjects reported a large number of negative characteristics central to their core self, as compared to the nonabused subjects who reported fewer negative characteristics which were not central to the core self. Interestingly, Calverly et al. (1994) found that the abused group also showed a slightly higher level of complexity in cognitive development than the nonabused subjects, suggesting that symptom formation may arise from a difference in rather than a failure in development.

While young children need to acquire the skill of being able to both control and express emotions in a family context, adults in abusive families impulsively act out their emotions towards children while the child is often punished for expressing feelings. Lack of modeling and scaffolding in affect regulation impacts children differently, with some children attempting to master their environment through passivity, and others seeking to protect themselves through violent acting out behavior. For most children there is a mixture of extremes of passivity and acting out behaviors.

One major therapeutic task is to challenge shame-based behaviors. It is important to provide safe environments in which the adolescent can develop a heathy sense of agency or free will, and the ability to be an actor upon the world, rather than be acted upon as victim as described by Terr (1991). It is also critical to give permission and provide structure so that the adolescent can begin to identify and express intense affect, including emotions related to the abuse. The expressive therapies, including art, movement, and journaling provide the adolescent with nonverbal means to express feelings and descriptors of abuse that cannot be verbally expressed. These therapies also provide a means to help the client face intense feelings in a controlled manner, rather than being overwhelmed by affect and flashbacks to the abuse. For example, Dave, who was presented earlier, was incapacitated by nightmares at the beginning of therapy, but was taught in his day treatment program to draw his dreams in the middle of the night when he woke in fear. The art therapist then encouraged him to draw how he wanted his dreams to be. Dave quickly turned the red demons into playful trolls and saw himself playing with them. Drawing and journaling provided a first step for Dave to identify and express his feelings, and in Dave's words "taking the stitches out of my tear ducts."

Initiative and Risk Taking

In the initiative/guilt stage of development, children become creators. In a supportive environment they are builders, artists, actors and scholars all in the same day. In contrast, young children who lack support and/or are given negative messages about their behavior learn that it is not O.K. to be spontaneous or to take appropriate risks. Behavior that is inherently good is labeled bad, and the child internalizes a global sense of guilt.

The first therapeutic task is to awaken creativity by providing a safe place and permission for the adolescent to find a medium to express his/her self. A second task is to challenge excessive guilt, and help the adolescent to form a balanced internalized feed-back system regarding risk taking and creativity. A therapist can reward appropriate risk taking, both verbally and in concrete ways such as presenting a certificate of achievement. Even independent, seemingly aloof adolescents want to be praised.

Amy, who developed an eating disorder at age 13, showed symptoms related to initiative that were typical of an adolescent's response to abuse in the environment. Amy was often given "no win double messages" from her parents. Sometimes she was told to eat chicken with a knife and fork, and other times she was told that she was stupid because everyone knew that chicken is a finger food. Her mother, who was an artist, would rip up Amy's paintings because they were not good enough, and would physically punish her by hitting her with art tools. When first given permission to finger paint in a therapy session, Amy refused because her mother would be upset if she got paint on her clothes. After being reassured that the therapist would be meeting with her parents and making suggestions to them about their parenting styles, Amy gradually began a long process of reclaiming her innate ability to express herself through art. And, responding to her self-perception of being unattractive, we worked on strategies for improving her appearance, such as looking through magazines and inventing new combinations of outfits from her existing clothes.

Mastery and Productivity

The next stage of development, industry versus inferiority, brings the opportunity for cognitive and social skill development. In our society, school provides the framework for learning, making friends and developing a sense of competency in various areas. For the chronically abused child, school may bring welcome relief in the form of a supportive teacher and avenues to develop a positive sense of identity outside the abusive family. For children who are already severely psychologically compromised, the challenges of this stage may increase existing feelings of inferiority.

The major therapeutic task is to assess the educational strengths and weaknesses of the adolescent. The therapist needs to work with the school system, and find ways to help the adolescent live up to his/her academic potential. If there is not an adult in the home who can help the adolescent with his or her work and act as an advocate with the school, someone in the community should be found to fill this role, drawing upon resources such as the Big Sisters. The therapist needs to identify potential areas of competence, helping the adolescent feel a sense of pride and accomplishment in doing something. This can be roller bladeing, Karate, computer games, reading or whatever they choose to pursue. It is useful to encourage one area of interest that involves other teens, in order that the adolescent can learn teamwork and build a peer support system.

Dora, the sexual and physical abuse victim discussed earlier who was in a gifted and talented program, lacked the spontaneity of a person with her talent. She criticized everything she did, and had already used self-mutilation in an attempt to ease the tension she experienced and to punish herself for being bad. While letting Dora know that her cutting was not appropriate, the therapist did not overreact or criticize her when she did cut. Substitute behaviors were introduced, and she learned to write on her arms with a red marker rather than cutting with a razor blade. Imagery was also used to help her with the strong images she had about her badness. For example, drawing upon the metaphor of the Black Spiritual "Wading in the Waters," the therapist would suggest that Dora walk through a cool river as a means to help with adverse physical sensations she experienced during flashbacks, and help symbolically "wash away her badness." The therapist also helped Dora find a multi-racial theater company that had a special program to teach acting to community youth.

Identity Formation and Individuation

The adolescent's primary task, according to Erikson, is the establishment of ego identity, a sense of self in a social order. The young person continues to build on past competencies and develops new ones, such as self as worker or romantic other. For the child who reaches adolescence with a legacy of abuse, deficits from prior developmental levels impede the formation of a coherent sense of self (see Harter in this volume). In cases where the abuse has been severe and other factors are present, the adolescent may have developed dissociative identity disorder (D.I.D.), previously known as multiple personality disorder (M.P.D.). This is a condition in which an individual has two or more distinct selves which take control of the person's behavior.

The major therapeutic task at this stage is to identify and address past developmental deficits and provide support in the separation/individuation process. Properly identifying the etiology of the presenting symptoms, especially differentiating between behaviors that are normative in adolescence and those that may indicate developmental psychopathology, is critical. For example, a normal process in adolescence is "trying on different social roles," as a means to identity formation (Harter & Monsour, 1992), not to be confused with D.I.D. A second therapeutic task is to help clients identify important relationships in their lives, including parents and parent figures, with an emphasis on negotiating family rules that support increased autonomy, while maintaining responsible decision making.

Steve, the young male prostitute, showed the identity confusion that may be inherent in chronic abuse. After several months of therapy, Steve was diagnosed with D.I.D., and six ego states were eventually identified. The first clues to D.I.D. emerged when Steve asked the therapist to read some short stories he had written during the past years. After inquiring why the stories were typed, he gave a response about bad handwriting. The therapist then made a very general comment normalizing different alter states. The next day a folder with the original stories, each in a very different handwriting, was slipped under my office door. In addition, a complete history which incorporated school, medical and legal records, revealed a pattern of symptoms, including loss of memory, which substantiated the diagnosis, and proper treatment was initiated.

CONCLUSION

Working with adolescents who have a history of multiple trauma is tedious and demanding and requires knowledge and experience in several mental health specialties. Most importantly, clinical work in this area is best conducted by people who are committed to self-knowledge and growth. Due to the reenactment phenomenon inherent in working with traumatized adolescents, the clinician must walk a narrow tightrope, balancing the use of acting out behaviors that occur as grist for therapy, while not allowing the client to be abusive toward the therapist.

Not all children who are abused can be helped by the therapeutic process. Unfortunately, the price that abuse extracts from the human psyche can lead to humans harming others without a sense of remorse about their actions. This article addresses treatment of those children who still have the capacity to engage in a healthy relationship, and who can mend the internal developmental scars that interfere with full engagement in the process of human development. Too many young people who have been abused have been misdiagnosed and not given the advantage of proper treatment. The rewards are many for the therapist who is able to look past the armor that the abused clients bring to therapy, and to help them discover and repair their natural course of development. The greatest satisfaction for the clinician is being a factor in helping to curb and repair the epidemic of human pain and violence which plagues our society.

REFERENCES

American Psychiatric Association. (1994). *Diagnostic and statistical manual of mental disorders* (4th ed.). Washington, DC: Author.

Belsky, J. (1993). Etiology of child maltreatment: A developmental-ecological analysis. *Psychological Bulletin, 114*, 413-434.

Briere, J. (1992). *Child abuse trauma: Theory and treatment of the lasting effects.* Newbury Park, London: Sage Publications.

Bryant, D., Kessler, J., & Shirar, L. (1992). *The family inside—working with the multiple.* New York: W.W. Norton and Company.

Burgess, A., Hartman, C., & McCormack, A. (1987). Abused to abuser: Antecedents of socially deviant behaviors. *American Journal of Psychiatry, 144*, 1431-1436.

Calverly, R.M., Fischer, K.W., & Ayoub, C. (1994). Complex splitting of self-representations in sexually abused adolescent girls. *Development and Psychopathology, 6*, 195-213.

Cavaiola, A., & Schiff, M. (1988). Behavioral sequelae of physical and/or sexual abuse in adolescents. *Child Abuse and Neglect, 12*, 181-188.

Chu, J. (1991). The repetition compulsion revisited: reliving dissociated trauma. *Psychotherapy, 28*, 327-332.

Chu, J., & Dill, D. (1990). Dissociative symptoms in relation to childhood physical and sexual abuse. *American Journal of Psychiatry, 147*, 887-892.

Cicchetti, D. (1989). How research on child maltreatment has informed the study of child development: Perspectives from developmental psychology. In D. Cicchetti & V. Carlson (Eds.), *Child maltreatment: Theory and research on the causes and consequences of child abuse and neglect*. New York: Cambridge University Press.

Coh, A.H. (1983). *An approach to preventing child abuse*. Chicago: National Committee for the Prevention of Child Abuse.

Cole, N. (1991). The theory of traumatic thinking. *Proceedings of the 8th Annual International Conference on Multiple Personality and Dissociative States*.

Courtois, C.A. (1988). *Healing the incest wound: Adult survivors in therapy*. New York: W.W. Norton & Company.

Crittenden, P.M., & Ainsworth, M.D.S. (1989). Child maltreatment and attachment theory. In D. Cicchetti & V. Carlson (Eds.), *Child maltreatment: Theory and research on the causes and consequences of child abuse and neglect*. New York: Cambridge University Press.

Dell, P., & Eisenhower, J. (1990). Adolescent multiple personality disorder: A preliminary study of eleven cases. *Journal of the American Academy of Child and Adolescent Psychiatry, 29*, 359-366.

Demause, L. (1990). The history of child assault. *Journal of Psychohistory, 18*, 1-29.

Erikson, E.H. (1963). *Childhood and society* (2nd ed.). New York: Norton.

Eth, S., & Pynoos, R. (1985). Interaction of trauma and grief in childhood. In S. Eth & R. Pynoos (Eds.), *Post-traumatic stress disorder in children* (pp. 171-186). Washington, DC: American Psychiatric Press.

Finkelhor, D., & Brown, A. (1985). The traumatic impact of child sexual abuse: A conceptualization. *American Journal of Orthopsychiatry, 55*, 530-541.

Finkelhor, D., & Dziuba-Leatherman, J. (1994). Victimization of children. *American Psychologist, 49*, 173-183.

Gil, D. (1970). *Violence against children: Physical abuse in the United States*. Cambridge, MA.: Harvard University Press.

Hall, G.S. (1904). *Adolescence* (Vols. 1-2). New York and London: Appleton.

Harter, S., & Monsour, A. (1992). Developmental analysis of conflict caused by opposing attributes in the adolescent self-portrait. *Developmental Psychology, 28*, 251-260.

Herman, J.L. (1992). *Trauma and recovery*. New York: Basic Books.

Hibbard, R., Ingersoll, G., & Orr, D. (1990). Behavioral risk, emotional risk, and child abuse among adolescents in a nonclinical setting. *Pediatrics, 86*, 896-901.

Hornstein, N., & Putnam, F. (1992). Clinical phenomenology of child and adolescence: Dissociative disorders. *Journal of the American Academy of Child and Adolescent Psychiatry, 31*, 1077-1085.

Horowitz, M. (1978). *Stress-response syndromes* (2nd ed.). New York: Jason Aronson.

Inhelder, B., & Piaget, J. (1955). *The growth of logical thinking from childhood to adolescence* (A. Parson & S. Megram, Trans.). New York: Basic Books.

Jorden, J. (1993). The relational self: Implications for adolescent development. In S. Feinstein (Ed.), *Adolescent psychiatry–developmental and clinical studies* (pp. 228-239). Chicago: The University of Chicago Press.

Kendall-Tackett, K.A., Williams, L.M., & Finkelhor, D. (1993). Impact of sexual abuse on children: A review and synthesis of recent empirical studies. *Psychological Bulletin, 113*, 164-180.

Kluft, R. (1984). Treatment of multiple personality disorder–A study of 33 cases. *Psychiatric Clinics of North America, 7*, 9-23.

Kluft, R. (1986). Treating children who have multiple personality disorder. In B.G. Braun (Ed.), *Treatment of multiple personality disorder*. Washington, DC: American Psychiatric Press.

Lewis, D., Mallouh, C., & Webb, V. (1989). Child abuse, delinquency, and violent criminality. In D. Cicchetti & V. Carlson (Eds.), *Child maltreatment: Theory and research on the causes and consequences of child abuse and neglect* (pp. 707-721). New York: Cambridge University Press.

Lindemann, E. (1942). Symptomatology and management of acute grief. *American Journal of Psychiatry, 101*, 141-148.

Miller, A. (1990). *Thou shalt not be aware*. New York: Meridian.

Pardes, H. (1985). *Youth studies*. New York: Springer.

Piaget, J. (1936). *The construction of reality in the child* (M. Cook, Trans.). New York: International Universities Press, 1974.

Putnam, F.W. (1990). Disturbances of self in victims of childhood sexual abuse. In R.P. Kluft (Ed.), *Incest-related syndromes of adult psychopathology*. Washington, DC: American Psychiatry Press.

Putnam, F.W. (1991). Recent research on multiple personality disorder. *Psychiatric Clinics of North America, 14*, 489-502.

Putnam, F.W. (1993). Dissociation and disturbances of the self. In. D. Cicchetti & S. Toth (Eds.), *Disorders and dysfunctions of the self: Rochester Symposium on Developmental Psychopathology* (Vol. 5). Rochester, NY: University of Rochester Press.

Pynoos, R., & Nader, K. (1990). Children's exposure to violence and traumatic death. *Psychiatric Annals, 20,* 334-344.

Rosenthal, J. (1988). Patterns of reported child abuse and neglect. *Child Abuse and Neglect, 12,* 263-271.

Saunders, E., & Arnold, F. (1993). A critique of conceptual and treatment approaches to borderline psychopathology in light of findings about child abuse. *Psychiatry, 56,* 188-203.

Terr, L.C. (1991). Childhood traumas: An outline and overview. *American Journal of Psychiatry, 148,* 1, 10-20.

van der Hart, O., & Brown, P. (1992). Abreaction re-evaluated. *Dissociation, 5,* 127-140.

van der Kolk, B. (1987). *Psychological trauma.* Washington, DC: American Psychiatric Press.

van der Kolk, B. (1994). *Memory and trauma–Part II* [Videotape]. California: Cavacade Productions.

van der Kolk, B., Perry, J., & Herman, J. (1991). Childhood origins of self-destructive behavior. *American Journal of Psychiatry, 148,* 1665-1671.

van der Kolk, B., & van der Hart, O. (1989). Pierre Janet and the breakdown of adaption in psychological trauma. *American Journal of Psychiatry, 146,* 1530-1540.

Weisz, J., & Weisf, B. (1993). *Effects of psychotherapy with children and adolescents.* New York: Sage.

Westin, D. (1993). The impact of sexual abuse on self structure. In D. Cicchetti & S. Toth (Eds.), *Disorders and dysfunctions of the self: Rochester Symposium on Developmental Psychopathology* (Vol. 5). Rochester, NY: University of Rochester Press.

SPECIAL ISSUES

Correlates of Multiple Forms of Victimization in Religion-Related Child Abuse Cases

Gail S. Goodman
Bette L. Bottoms
Allison Redlich
Phillip R. Shaver
Kathleen R. Diviak

SUMMARY. Abuse perpetrated under the guise of religion is a devastating form of child maltreatment that often involves multiple types of victimization. In a large-scale survey of clinicians, we investigated the nature and emotional sequelae of religion-related child sexual abuse cases. We predicted that there would be marked differences between cases involving multiple forms of abuse and

---

Address correspondence to: Gail S. Goodman, PhD, Department of Psychology, University of California, Davis, CA 95616.

[Haworth co-indexing entry note]: "Correlates of Multiple Forms of Victimization in Religion-Related Child Abuse Cases." Goodman, Gail S. et al. Co-published simultaneously in *Journal of Aggression, Maltreatment & Trauma* (The Haworth Maltreatment & Trauma Press, an imprint of The Haworth Press, Inc.) Vol. 2, No. 1 (#3), 1998, pp. 273-295; and: *Multiple Victimization of Children: Conceptual, Developmental, Research, and Treatment Issues* (ed: B. B. Robbie Rossman, and Mindy S. Rosenberg) The Haworth Maltreatment & Trauma Press, an imprint of The Haworth Press, Inc., 1998, pp. 273-295. Single or multiple copies of this article are available for a fee from The Haworth Document Delivery Service [1-800-342-9678, 9:00 a.m. - 5:00 p.m. (EST). E-mail address: getinfo@haworth.com].

those involving only sexual abuse. Our results indicate that as the number of abuses increases, so does the severity of the abusive experience and the seriousness of psychological consequences for the victim. Thus, religion-related abuse is best understood in light of the specific types and combinations of abuses suffered by victims. *[Article copies available for a fee from The Haworth Document Delivery Service: 1-800-342-9678. E-mail address: getinfo@haworth.com]*

INTRODUCTION

Abuse perpetrated under the guise of religion is a devastating form of child maltreatment that has been virtually ignored in the professional and scientific literatures (Bottoms, Shaver, Goodman, & Qin, 1995; Capps, 1992; Greven, 1991). Religious overtones may add an additional layer of complexity to child abuse, further inhibiting a child's ability to cope with the trauma of maltreatment. For example, sexual abuse at the hands of trusted religious officials may be particularly damaging for children who have been raised to fear God and revere the Church and its leaders (Berry, 1992). They may believe that the abuse is parentally, socially, or supernaturally sanctioned, or is a punishment for their own sins (Greven, 1991). Withholding of medical care for religious reasons is another form of religion-related maltreatment that may have severe consequences for children (Bullis, 1991; Skolnick, 1994). Consider, for example, the following case description from Bottoms et al. (1995): "Child's tumor was untreated. Needed amputation was not allowed. Father believed child was being punished for sins and could be cured only through prayer." As a final example, some religions teach that a child's "willfulness" or misbehavior is the result of sin, evil, or the activity of devils who literally possess the child. Adults with such beliefs sometimes consider it their duty to "beat the devil" out of the child, which can cause severe emotional and psychological damage.

Of particular concern for the present discussion, religious beliefs can contribute to single or multiple forms of child abuse. In certain religious sects or cults, for example, children suffer physical abuse as well as emotional abuse and sexual violations. It is believed that some children in the Branch Davidian cult in Waco, Texas, suffered all three kinds of abuse as a consequence of leader David Koresh's religious delusions. Abuse allegations were responsible, in part, for authorities storming the cult's compound, spurring Koresh to start the conflagration that killed many of the children that the government sought to rescue. Of course, it is not just in isolated cults or small religious sects that religion-related ideology can lead to multiple forms of child abuse. More mainstream religious followers may also justify a variety of forms of child abuse in the name of religion (Greven, 1991).

In this article, we examine the nature and emotional correlates of multiple forms of religion-related child victimization. Given that religion-related abuse may be associated with multiple forms of maltreatment and may be particularly detrimental to children's well being, it is surprising that little research has been conducted to explore its characteristics or consequences. To address this important need, we conducted a large nationwide survey study of American clinicians' experiences with cases involving religion-related child abuse. The findings we detail in this article are based on the reports of clinicians who responded to our questionnaire and described cases they encountered in their practices. All of the cases we discuss involved allegations of child sexual abuse, but many of the cases involved other forms of abuse as well. This afforded us an opportunity to compare correlates of sexual abuse alone with correlates of sexual abuse combined with other types of abuse.

Having outlined several ways in which religion may be involved in child abuse, we next consider the prevalence, in general, of the multiple victimization of children. We then review research on the emotional effects of multiple abuse in comparison to the emotional effects of child sexual abuse alone, and formulate predictions we tested in our data set. Finally, we present the findings of our study and discuss their implications for understanding religion-related abuse and the effects of multiple victimization.

How Often Are Children Multiply Abused?

It is difficult to determine with any precision how often children suffer multiple forms of maltreatment. Official abuse statistics are often presented in the form of tallies for specific kinds of abuse totaled across all child abuse cases reported to state social service agencies, without regard for whether a child was the victim of different forms of abuse (e.g., NCCAN, 1994). In addition, some kinds of child abuse (e.g., sexual abuse, emotional abuse) often go unreported to authorities (Finkelhor, 1984; Russell, 1983), making official statistics problematic in any case.

A few researchers have attempted to determine the prevalence rates for multiple victimization by surveying nonclinical samples. For example, Riggs, Alario, and McHorney (1990) report that 2.7% of 600 children in grades 9 to 12 had suffered both physical and sexual abuse. Moeller, Bachmann, and Moeller (1993) asked 668 middle-class women at a gynecology clinic whether they had experienced sexual, physical, and/or emotional abuse as children. Approximately 53% reported childhood abuse, with 28.9% reporting one type of abuse, 18.7% reporting two types, and 5.4% reporting all three types. In one of the more methodologically sound studies to date, Finkelhor and Dziuba-Leatherman (1994) investigated whether some children are more at risk of multiple abuse than others. In a telephone survey of a nationally representative sample of 2,000 10- to 16-year-olds, a quarter of the children reported a completed victimization experience in the previous year, and over half of the children reported a completed or attempted victimization at some time in their lives. Finkelhor and Dziuba-Leatherman (1994) noted that "children who experienced one form of victimization were more likely to have experienced another form as well. For example, victims of sexual assault were 2.67 times more likely . . . than other children to have experienced an additional form of victimization" (p. 415).

Researchers have also investigated the prevalence of multiple forms of abuse in clinical samples, arriving at varying prevalence estimates. For example, Brown and Anderson (1991) found that 18% of 947 adult psychiatric inpatients suffered some form of physical or sexual abuse as children, with 3% (more women than men) reporting a combination of physical and sexual abuse. Hobbs and Wynne (1990) report that of 769 children diagnosed with physical abuse, approximately 17% were also sexually abused, and out of 949 diagnosed with sexual abuse, nearly 14% were also physically abused. Somewhat higher rates of multiple victimization were found by Kiser, Millsap, and Heston (1992) in a sample of 241 child and adolescent psychiatric day patients: 60% reported a history of physical and/or sexual abuse, 26% of whom reported both types of abuse. Finally, dramatically higher rates were reported by Ney, Fung, and Wickett (1994) in a study of children's self-reported physical abuse, physical neglect, verbal abuse, emotional neglect, and sexual abuse. Fewer than 5% of the 167 abused children they studied had suffered only one form of abuse, a rate that probably results from the researchers' inclusion of emotional and verbal abuse as maltreatment categories.

In summary, although there is wide variability in prevalence estimates due to differences in samples, sources of report (e.g., self-report versus parental report), definitions of abuse, types of maltreatment investigated, etc., all studies indicate that children who experience sexual abuse not infrequently experience other forms of abuse as well.

Effects of Child Sexual Abuse Alone Compared with Effects of Multiple Forms of Abuse

We were primarily concerned with the emotional correlates of child sexual abuse alone compared with the emotional correlates of child sexual abuse occurring in conjunction with other abuses. First, it is important to consider what is currently known about the emotional sequelae of childhood sexual abuse. A number of short- and long-term emotional effects have been linked to childhood sexual violations, including (but not limited to) sexualized behavior, symptoms of PTSD, depression, fear, anxiety, aggression, anger, feelings of isolation, and suicidal ideation (Briere & Elliott, 1994; Browne & Finkelhor, 1986). The first of these–sexual acting out–is the most consistently reported consequence of childhood sexual abuse, although symptoms of PTSD are also relatively common (Deblinger, McLeer, Atkins, Ralphe, & Fox, 1989; Kendall-Tackett, Williams, & Finkelhor, 1993). Researchers have also uncovered a significant relation between dissociative symptoms and a history of abuse (Chu & Dill, 1990; Swett & Halpert, 1993). When abuse is particularly severe, it has been proposed that multiple personality disorder (MPD; also known as dissociative identity disorder) may develop (e.g., Coons, 1986; Putnam, Post, Guroff, Silberman, & Barban, 1983), although this diagnosis remains controversial (Spanos, 1994).

For child sexual abuse victims, what are the psychological consequences of additional types of abuse? Most researchers have examined this question within clinical samples. In Brown and Anderson's (1991) study (see above), suicidal tendencies were particularly common in patients with a history of combined childhood abuse, and substance abuse was also prevalent. In a study of 51 inpatient adolescents at a state psychiatric hospital, Hart, Mader, Griffith, and deMendonca (1989) found that child victims of both sexual and physical abuse reported more symptoms than did nonabused children or children who had suffered only one of these two kinds of abuse. In contrast, Kiser et al. (1992) concluded that victims of child sexual abuse reported higher levels of internalizing behaviors than victims of physical abuse or of both physical and sexual abuse. In that study, however, compared to mothers of non-abused children or of children who had experienced only one form of abuse, mothers of children who had been both physically and sexually abused reported the greatest concerns about their children's psychosis, delinquency, hyperactivity, and somatic complaints. They reported the fewest concerns about withdrawal, family functioning, depression, and anxiety. Finally, in one of the few studies of a nonclinical sample (women gynecology clinic patients), Moeller et al. (1993) found that the more kinds of childhood abuse reported by a patient, the more likely she was to have poorer health and to have been revictimized as an adult. In general, then, these studies suggest that multiple victimization is associated with more severe symptoms than single-abuse experiences.

In interpreting these results, however, it is important to consider the overlap between different forms of abuse. It has recently been argued, for example, that all forms of child abuse involve psychological maltreatment (Brassard, Germain, & Hart, 1987; Claussen & Crittenden, 1991; Garbarino, 1980). In fact, Garbarino and Vondra (1987) contend that psychological maltreatment is the concept that unifies all forms of child maltreatment. To the extent that this is true, it is difficult to differentiate emotional abuse from sexual abuse, physical abuse, and neglect. Even so, the magnitude or significance of psychological maltreatment may vary. If a child is classified by authorities as emotionally abused or views him or herself as having suffered emotional abuse in addition to sexual or physical abuse, the psychological abuse may have been particularly salient or severe. In a number of studies, distinguishing between sexual abuse and emotional abuse has been useful. For example, Bagley, Wood, and Young (1994) surveyed 750 males in Canada about unwanted sexual contacts before the age of 17 years. About 16% reported experiencing one or more unwanted sexual contacts. The combination of emotional abuse (as measured by a standardized scale consisting of questions such as "Could you seek comfort from your parents if you were sad?") with multiple incidents of sexual abuse was a significant predictor of poor mental health in adulthood and sexual interest in or sexual contact with children. These findings led Bagley et al. (1994) to conclude that the combination of emotional and sexual abuse in childhood is a risk factor for adult mental health problems. Thus, the classification of children as having suffered emotional abuse in addition to sexual abuse proved important.

These findings are consistent with research on cumulative effects of stressful life experiences ("risk factors") in childhood (e.g., Garbarino, Dubrow, Kostelny, & Pardo, 1992; Sameroff, Siefer, Barocas, Zax, & Greenspan, 1987). Such research indicates that the experience of multiple stressful events places children at risk for emotional and cognitive deficits, particularly in the absence of sufficient compensatory factors (e.g., social support, secure attachment) (Garmezy & Rutter, 1983; Rutter, 1979).

Predictions

A set of predictions emerges from the literature concerning the emotional effects of child sexual abuse and multiple victimization. A primary prediction is that, compared to individuals who experience sexual abuse only, individuals who experience sexual abuse in combination with other forms of abuse will be more likely to evidence psychological disturbance (e.g., more likely to report certain kinds of symptoms when seeking therapy and to be diagnosed with certain disorders). Clinical symptoms that should be particularly elevated include sexualized behavior, depression, social withdrawal, excessive fears and phobias, suicidal ideation, MPD, PTSD, and other dissociative disorders. Further, these symptoms and disorders should increase as does number of forms of abuse, because, as the studies mentioned above indicate, experiencing child sexual abuse in combination with other kinds of abuse is likely to be more stressful and traumatic than experiencing any one form of abuse alone.

Regarding the sequelae of specific combinations of forms of child abuse, one might make several predictions. One possibility is that there will be negative effects of abuse regardless of the type of abuse suffered, but somewhat different emotional outcomes of specific types of victimization. For example, if sexual abuse is associated with later sexual problems, and physical abuse is associated with later violence and aggression, and both are associated with PTSD, a child who experiences both sexual and physical abuse may eventually evidence symptoms of PTSD, sexual problems, and inappropriate aggression. In other words, the emotional effects of specific combinations of abuse may be the sum of the effects of each form considered separately.

Alternatively, multiple forms of victimization might result in a set of psychological symptoms not necessarily predictable from the individual components, and certain combinations might be particularly devastating. One of the few studies to explore this possibility was the previously mentioned study by Ney et al. (1994). Although methodological limitations make interpretation difficult, Ney et al. concluded that the worst combination of abuse was physical abuse, physical neglect, and verbal abuse (which we would classify as a form of emotional abuse). Experiencing these three forms of abuse was associated with decreased enjoyment of living and a lack of hope for the future. When sexual abuse was involved, the worst combination included verbal abuse and physical neglect. This combination was associated with decreased enjoyment in life and negative expectations about the future of the world and the future of one's own parenting prospects.

In our research, we examined whether specific combinations of abuse are associated with a greater likelihood of certain presenting symptoms or clinical diagnoses in our sample of religion-related child abuse cases.

An Overview of the Present Research

Although religion makes many positive contributions to society, it can also contribute to, and be used to justify, multiple forms of child abuse. As mentioned earlier, because virtually no empirical studies of religion-related child abuse exist, we felt it was important to begin to collect data on such cases (see Bottoms et al., 1995; and Bottoms, Shaver, & Goodman, 1996, for further discussion of our investigations into this issue). We concentrated on the following specific kinds of religion-related maltreatment: abuse perpetrated by religious authorities, abuse related to attempts to rid a child of "evil spirits," abuse committed in religious settings, and the withholding of medical care for religious reasons. Our data allowed us to compare the characteristics and psychological outcomes of religion-related cases involving one form of abuse (child sexual abuse) with cases involving multiple forms of abuse.

All cases were encountered by mental health professionals (clinical psychologists, psychiatrists, and clinical social workers) who responded to a nationwide survey concerning religion-related child abuse in the United States. For each case, the clinician/respondent indicated the type(s) of childhood abuse a particular client had experienced: sexual, physical, emotional, and/or neglect. For present purposes, we examined the subset of religion-related cases that involved child sexual abuse, as indicated by the clinicians' reports and case descriptions. We created three case categories, those including sexual abuse only, sexual abuse plus one additional kind of abuse ("sexual abuse plus one"), and sexual abuse plus two or more additional kinds of abuse ("sexual abuse plus two or more"). For example, the following case was categorized by a respondent as "sexual abuse plus two or more" (sexual, physical, and emotional): "Father was abused as a child; father quoted scriptures [demeaning the child] and whipped child; also sexually molested her from ages 13-16." In contrast, another clinician described a sexual-abuse-only case in which a woman had been sexually abused from age 5 to 8 in a parochial school by someone in a position of trust. We sought to determine the nature and correlates of such cases, and to see whether such cases differed from cases involving only sexual abuse.

METHOD

The study was conducted in two phases: (a) a postcard survey to identify clinicians who had encountered relevant cases in their clinical practice, and (b) a detailed survey to obtain more complete information about the cases (see Bottoms et al., 1995, and Bottoms et al., 1996, for more detail about our methods). In the first phase, 19,272 postcard surveys were mailed to members of the American Psychological Association, the American Psychiatric Association, and social workers who were members of the National Association of Social Workers. Each clinician received a cover letter explaining that we were interested in child abuse allegations involving religious or ritualistic practices. ("Ritualistic" child abuse is multi-victim, multi-perpetrator sexual abuse said to involve allegations of quasi-religious satanic rituals and unspeakable acts of torture, murder, and cannibalism—but rarely substantiated by conclusive evidence. Because discussion of the ritualistic abuse cases is beyond the scope of this paper, we refer the reader to Bottoms et al., 1996, for details.) Respondents were asked to report the number of such cases they had encountered during the 1980s on a return postcard.

After accounting for inappropriately targeted individuals (people who had retired, etc.), our response rate was approximately 37%, of whom 2,136 (31%) reported that they had encountered at least one religion-related *or* ritualistic abuse case. In the follow-up survey, each of the 2,136 clinicians was asked to provide detailed information about up to eight typical religion-related or ritualistic cases he or she had encountered. The main issues covered by the detailed questionnaire included case features, victim and perpetrator characteristics (including victim's psychological symptomatology), abuse types and settings, and information about case adjudication and outcome. Of these questionnaires, a little more than 37% were returned. After eliminating 77 respondents because they or we decided that they had not actually encountered any relevant cases, there were 720 valid respondents: 297 clinical psychologists, 200 psychiatrists, and 223 social workers. They provided information about a total of 1,548 cases in which a client claimed to have been the victim of religion-related or ritualistic child abuse. Of these, there were 405 religion-related (non-ritualistic) cases: 171 reported to our clinician/respondents by child clients, and 234 reported by adult survivors (i.e., adults who reported abuse that they had experienced as children). Finally, we eliminated cases in which the clinician/respondent failed to indicate the specific form of abuse suffered by the client-victim.

In the remaining cases, sexual abuse was the most commonly reported form of abuse, occurring in 243 cases. Physical abuse was allegedly involved in 130 cases, emotional or psychological abuse in 174 cases, and neglect in 84 cases. (Cases could include more than one kind of abuse.) As previously noted, we chose to focus specifically on the religion-related sexual abuse cases (N = 243). Among them, there were 129 cases involving only sexual abuse (45 reported by children and 84 by adults), 50 cases of sexual abuse plus one other type of abuse (19 reported by children and 31 by adults), and 61 cases of sexual abuse plus two or more additional types of abuse (18 reported by children and 43 by adults). In three cases it was impossible to determine whether the victim was a child or an adult; hence, the sample size was 240 for certain analyses. The specific forms of abuse involved in the excluded non-sexual abuse cases were diverse: emotional abuse only ($N = 32$), neglect only ($N = 12$), physical abuse only ($N = 21$), neglect and emotional abuse ($N = 13$), neglect and physical abuse ($N = 3$), physical and emotional abuse ($N = 22$), and neglect and physical and emotional abuse ($N = 16$).

RESULTS

We begin with a discussion of the general characteristics and legal outcomes of the cases. We then provide details concerning the psychological sequelae of various forms of abuse, testing the predictions outlined earlier. Whenever respondents provided enough information, we performed 2 (victim type: child or adult survivor) × 3 (number of abuses: sexual only, sexual plus one, sexual plus two or more) analyses of variance (ANOVAs). When missing data or numerous cells with means of zero would not permit this kind of analysis, we conducted one-way ANOVAs comparing the three number-of-abuse categories, collapsing across victim type. Main effects of number of abuses were followed by Tukey tests (pairwise comparisons of means), as recommended by Keppel (1982). For present purposes, we report only significant effects, placing special emphasis on findings concerning the number-of-abuses variable.

Case Characteristics

First, we conducted analyses to determine whether there were differences in general case characteristics (i.e., victim age, relationship between victim and perpetrator, number and gender of victims and perpetrators, and setting of the abuse). Our 2 (victim type) × 3 (number of abuses) ANOVAs revealed few significant effects of victim type for these variables. For the sake of brevity in our text and Table 1 (where all means for this section are shown), we have chosen to discuss only the results of one-way ANOVAs investigating effects associated with the number of abuses.

Victim age. As shown in Table 1, victim age when abuse ended and when it was discovered did not differ significantly as a function of the number of abuses suffered. But multiple forms of abuse had a significantly earlier onset than sexual abuse alone. Thus, cases involving multiple forms of abuse are particularly serious not only in terms of the number of abuses suffered but also in terms of the young age at which the abuse purportedly begins.

TABLE 1. Case Characteristics

	Case Type			Significance	
	Sexual only	S + 1	S + 2 or more	Degrees of freedom	F
Age of victim (years) when abuse:					
Began	10.58_a	7.97_b	5.67_c	(2,211)	29.97**
Ended	12.12	11.90	11.81	(2,189)	.09
Was discovered	23.65	20.74	24.04	(2,190)	.80
Relationship of perpetrators to victims (proportions)					
Parent or step-parent	$.10_a$	$.40_b$	$.78_c$	(2,228)	66.43**
Trusted person (e.g., teacher, priest)	$.87_a$	$.58_b$	$.33_c$	(2,228)	35.00**
Number of victims (mean per case)					
Both genders	$1.76^{\#}_a$	2.21_{ab}	2.96_b	(2,200)	3.06*
Male	$.96^{\#}$	1.08	1.70	(2,191)	1.20
Female	$.81_a$	1.45_a	2.68_b	(2,194)	13.59**
Number of perpetrators (mean per case)					
Both genders	1.30_a	2.12_a	3.69_b	(2,213)	18.29**
Male	1.09_a	1.27_a	2.67_b	(2,206)	12.01**
Female	$.14_a$	$.46_a$	2.00_b	(2,207)	21.53**
Settings of abuse (proportions)					
Daycare or schools	.11	.16	.05	(2,218)	1.75
Parent's/relative's home	$.26_a$	$.39_a$	$.64_b$	(2,218)	12.49**
Religious setting	$.46_a$	$.29_{ab}$	$.10_b$	(2,218)	12.19**

NOTE. Sexual only = sexual abuse only; S + 1 = sexual abuse plus one additional type of abuse; S + 2 or more = sexual abuse plus two or more additional types of abuse. The gender totals ("both genders") are not simple summations of separate male and female totals because some respondents provided only a total number of victims or perpetrators, without specifying gender. Each case may have included more than one type of perpetrator or setting. Means within a row that differ in their subscripts are statistically different at $p < .05$.

* $p < .05$. ** $p < .001$.

Excludes two cases involving 100 male victims. Including these outliers results in a sexual-only total mean of 3.58 and a sexual-only male-victim mean of 2.88.

Relationship of victim and perpetrator. As is true in most child abuse cases, perpetrators in virtually all cases were people the children knew and trusted. When multiple abuses were committed, the perpetrator was especially likely to be a parent or step-parent. In cases involving only sexual abuse, the perpetrator was most often another trusted person, reflecting the fact that many cases in this category involved abuse committed by a person with religious authority. There were virtually no cases in which the perpetrator was a stranger (< 1% of cases) and relatively few in which the perpetrator was an acquaintance (6% of cases).

Number and gender of victims and perpetrators. There were significantly more victims, especially girl victims, in the cases involving multiple abuses than in cases involving only sexual abuse. Further, as might be expected, the greater the number of abuses suffered by the children, the greater the number of perpetrators (male and female) involved in the cases. These findings again point to the more extreme nature of purported multiple abuse cases: They are more likely than single-abuse cases to involve multiple victims and perpetrators.

Setting of the abuse. In most cases, the abuse took place either in parents' or other relatives' homes or in religious settings such as a church or church summer camp. Consistent with our finding that multiple abuse was usually intrafamilial, multiple abuse cases were more likely to occur in the home than in daycare centers, schools, or religious settings. Cases involving only sexual abuse were more likely to occur in religious settings than in the home or daycare settings. Again, this probably reflects the large number of sexual-abuse-only cases involving religious authorities as perpetrators. The results suggest that parents were inflicting worse levels of abuse on their children than were non-familial perpetrators such as priests or ministers. Of course, as we discuss later, even single forms of abuse can have serious consequences for a child victim.

Investigation and Adjudication of Cases

Significant effects of both victim type and abuse type were revealed by 2 (victim type) × 3 (number of abuses) ANOVAs exploring case investigation and outcome variables (see Table 2). First, most cases (70%) were not even investigated by any legal authority or social service agency. This was more likely to be true for adult survivor cases (89%) than for child cases (32%), $F(1, 221) = 118.96$, $p < .001$, which reflects changes over time in the societal recognition of child abuse. That is, when the adults experienced their abuse decades ago, the social climate was less hospitable towards abuse reporting or investigation.

Table 2 also shows the proportion of cases investigated by specific

TABLE 2. Case Investigation and Adjudication (Proportion of Cases)

| | Case type | | | |
	Sexual only	S + 1	S + 2 or more	Mean
Type of investigation				
Social services[1,2]				
Child	.36	.63	.61	.47
Adult	.04	.10	.07	.06
Mean	.15	.28	.23	.20
Police[2]				
Child	.48	.38	.39	.43
Adult	.04	.07	.07	.05
Mean	.19	.17	.16	.18
District attorney[1,2]				
Child	.10	.44	.11	.17
Adult	.00	.07	.00	.01
Mean	.03$_a$	.20$_b$	.03$_a$	.07
Case outcome				
Social services substantiated[1,2]				
Child	.22	.39	.28	.28
Adult	.00	.10	.00	.02
Mean	.07$_a$	.22$_b$	.07$_{ab}$	.11
Arrest[2]				
Child	.38	.50	.39	.41
Adult	.06	.00	.05	.05
Mean	.17	.18	.16	.17
Trial[2]				
Child	.28	.44	.22	.30
Adult	.03	.03	.00	.02
Mean	.11	.18	.07	.12
Conviction[2]				
Child	.25	.22	.22	.24
Adult	.03	.00	.00	.01
Mean	.10	.08	.07	.09

NOTE. Sexual only = sexual abuse only; S + 1 = sexual abuse plus one additional type of abuse; S + 2 or more = sexual abuse plus two or more additional types of abuse. Means within a row that differ in their subscripts are statistically different at $p < .05$.
[1]Significant main effect of number of abuses, Fs$(2, \geq 219) \geq 3.23$, ps $< .05$.
[2]Significant main effect of victim type, Fs$(1, \geq 219) \geq 24.29$, ps $< .001$.

agencies. Child cases were significantly more likely than adult cases to be investigated by police, social services, and district attorneys. There were no reliable differences in police investigation as a function of the number of abuses in cases, but social service workers were more likely to investigate multiple abuse cases than cases involving sexual abuse only. District attorney investigations were more likely in cases involving sexual abuse plus one other form of abuse.

We also examined the outcomes of cases that were investigated (see Table 2). Legal action (e.g., arrest, trial, conviction) and social service substantiation were more likely in child than adult survivor cases. However, the likelihood of legal action did not generally increase as a function of the number of abuses. The one significant difference associated with the number of abuses concerned social service substantiation. Social service agencies were more likely to substantiate sex-plus-one cases than either of the other two types of cases. It is possible that when a child experiences sexual abuse plus another form of maltreatment, there may be more evidence than when a child is experiencing sexual abuse only. Thus, the abuse claims can be more easily substantiated. Moreover, social services may intervene before the number of abuses increases further. It is less clear why cases involving three or more abuses were not as likely to be substantiated. Perhaps some of these cases involve false reports or exaggeration (see Bottoms et al., 1996).

Psychological Sequelae of Abuse

The main goal of our research was to understand the psychological correlates of religion-related abuse. Thus, we examined the relations between the forms of abuse experienced by the victims and (a) the symptoms for which they originally sought therapy and (b) their Diagnostic and Statistical Manual III-R (DSM III-R) diagnoses (made by our clinician/respondents). We performed 2 (victim type) × 3 (number of abuses) analyses of variance on the proportion of cases involving the various symptoms and diagnoses. In addition, because preliminary correlational analyses indicated that the number of abuses suffered was significantly related to the perpetrator being the child's parent or step-parent ($r = .61, p < .01$), we conducted analyses of covariance with perpetrator relationship serving as the covariate.

Presenting symptoms. As predicted, compared to clients who experienced only child sexual abuse, clients who experienced multiple forms of abuse were more likely to complain of a variety of psychological symptoms. As revealed in Table 3, the number-of-abuses variable was significantly related to depression, insomnia, somatic complaints, excessive fears

TABLE 3. Presenting Psychological Symptoms (Proportion of Cases)

	Case type			
	Sexual only	S + 1	S + 2 or more	Mean
Depression[1,2]				
Child	.38	.53	.63	.48
Adult	.63	.67	.83	.70
Mean	.54$_a$	.65$_{ab}$	.78$_b$	.63
Insomnia[1,2]				
Child	.00	.05	.25	.07
Adult	.11	.15	.45	.21
Mean	.07$_a$	.11$_a$	.40$_b$	.17
Somatic complaints[1]				
Child	.09	.05	.31	.13
Adult	.13	.19	.45	.23
Mean	.12$_a$	.13$_a$	.41$_b$	.20
Excessive fears and phobias[1]				
Child	.12	.32	.31	.22
Adult	.17	.33	.40	.27
Mean	.15$_a$	.33$_b$	.38$_b$	.25
Suicidal ideation[1,2]				
Child	.03	.37	.31	.19
Adult	.26	.44	.55	.38
Mean	.19$_a$	.41$_b$	.48$_b$	.32
Social withdrawal[1]				
Child	.15	.26	.50	.26
Adult	.13	.19	.31	.19
Mean	.14$_a$	.22$_{ab}$	.36$_b$	.21
Inappropriate aggression[1,2]				
Child	.24	.16	.38	.25
Adult	.07	.04	.31	.13
Mean	.12$_a$	.09$_a$	.33$_b$	.17

NOTE. Sexual only = sexual abuse only; S + 1 = sexual abuse plus one additional type of abuse; S + 2 or more = sexual abuse plus two or more additional types of abuse. Means within a row that differ in their subscripts are statistically different at $p < .05$.

[1]Significant main effect of number of abuses, Fs(2, 208) $\geq$ 3.94, $ps < .05$.

[2]Significant main effect of victim type, Fs(1, 208) $\geq$ 6.18, $ps < .05$.

and phobias, substance abuse, social withdrawal, and inappropriate aggression. It was also significantly related to less frequently mentioned symptoms that are not included in the table, including inappropriate toilet behavior (in 5% of cases), obsessive compulsiveness (in 10% of cases), and substance abuse (in 17% of cases), all Fs (2, 208) $\geq$ 3.63, ps < .05. With the exception of substance abuse, these main effects were all still significant (or closely approached significance in the case of depression) when perpetrator relationship was statistically controlled in the analyses of covariance. For each of the symptom categories, victims who had experienced two or more types of abuse in addition to sexual abuse were significantly more likely to have reported the symptom than victims who alleged only sexual abuse. Moreover, for insomnia, somatic complaints, inappropriate toilet behavior, and inappropriate aggression, having experienced two types of abuse in addition to sexual abuse was associated with more symptoms than having experienced sexual abuse plus one other form of abuse. Finally, victims who experienced sexual abuse plus one other type of abuse presented clinically with more fears and phobias than those who experienced only sexual abuse.

Among children, sexual acting out is one of the most consistent indicators of child sexual abuse (Finkelhor & Browne, 1986; Kendall-Tackett, Williams, & Finkelhor, 1992). Victims in 19% of our cases (23% child and 17% adult) began therapy with sexual behavior problems. Although there were no significant main effects of either victim type or number of abuses, a significant interaction revealed that child cases involving sexual abuse plus one (37%) or two or more (31%) forms of abuse were more likely to result in sexual acting out than cases involving only sexual abuse (12%), $F(2, 208)$ = 3.19, p < .05. This predicted pattern did not emerge for adults.

DSM III-R diagnoses. We also examined the DSM III-R diagnoses that the clinician/respondents gave to their clients (see Table 4). Several diagnoses are of particular interest for child sexual abuse cases, including PTSD, MPD, and other dissociative disorders. Victims were diagnosed with PTSD in 24% of cases, with MPD in 15% of cases, and (not shown in the table) with other dissociative disorders in 6% of cases. Because of missing data in some cells, we performed one-way ANOVAs to test for effects of number of abuses for each diagnosis. Significant main effects of number of abuses emerged for all three. However, when relationship to perpetrator was covaried, the main effect of number of abuses remained significant for other dissociative disorders, $F(2, 152)$ = 3.08, p < .05, and closely approached significance for MPD, $F(2, 152)$ = 2.41, p < .10. Clients who experienced sexual abuse plus two other types of abuse were more likely to be diagnosed with MPD, other dissociative disorders, and

TABLE 4. DSM III-R Diagnoses (Proportion of Cases)

	Case type			
	Sexual only	S + 1	S + 2 or more	Mean
Alcohol/drug problems				
Child	.06	.15	.10	.10
Adult	.08	.12	.00	.06
Mean	.07	.13	.02	.07
Affective disorders				
Child	.19	.38	.00	.21
Adult	.27	.27	.16	.24
Mean	.26	.31	.12	.23
Multiple personality disorder[1]				
Child	.00	.15	.20	.10
Adult	.11	.12	.31	.16
Mean	$.09_a$	$.13_{ab}$	$.29_b$	.15
Post-traumatic stress disorder[1]				
Child	.25	.15	.40	.26
Adult	.14	.31	.38	.23
Mean	$.16_a$	$.26_{ab}$	$.38_b$	.24
Personality disorders				
Child	.13	.08	.10	.10
Adult	.23	.27	.19	.23
Mean	.21	.21	.17	.20
Sexual disorders				
Child	.06	.00	.00	.03
Adult	.08	.00	.03	.05
Mean	.07	.00	.02	.04
Adjustment disorders				
Child	.19	.08	.10	.13
Adult	.15	.12	.03	.11
Mean	.16	.10	.05	.12

NOTE. Sexual only = sexual abuse only; S + 1 = sexual abuse plus one additional type of abuse; S + 2 or more = sexual abuse plus two or more additional types of abuse. Other diagnoses were mentioned infrequently: organic disorders, schizophrenic disorders, somatoform disorders, and eating disorders in 1% of cases, and impulse control problems in 2% of cases. Childhood disorders were noted only in child cases: 25% of sexual only cases, 8% in S + 1 cases, and 10% of S + 2 or more cases. Means within a row that differ in their subscripts are statistically different at $p < .05$.
[1]Significant main effect of number of abuses, $Fs(2, 157) \geq 3.88$, $ps < .05$.

PTSD than clients who experienced sexual abuse only or sexual abuse plus one additional type of abuse.

As would be expected, a variety of other diagnoses were given to victims in the cases, including affective and personality disorders. Interestingly, eating disorders characterized less than 1% of cases, even though such disorders are often thought to be prevalent among survivors of sexual abuse (see Ofshe & Watters, 1994, for a discussion).

Psychological correlates of specific combinations of abuse. Finally, we were interested in victims' psychological symptomatology and diagnoses as a function of the exact combinations of abuse characterizing the cases. In Table 5, we present the proportion of cases (broken down into catego-

TABLE 5. Presenting Symptoms and DSM III-R Diagnoses as a Function of Specific Combinations of Abuse (Proportion of Cases)

		Case type: Combinations of abuse						
		S	S/E	S/N	S/P	S/N/E	S/P/E	S/P/E/N
Symptoms:	N =	113	29	3	14	3	26	26
Depression		.55	.69	1.00	.50	.67	.77	.81
Insomnia		.07	.10	.67	.00	.33	.54	.31
Somatic complaints		.11	.17	.33	.07	.00	.58	.31
Excessive fear/phobias		.16	.34	.33	.21	.33	.42	.38
Sexual acting out		.16	.17	.33	.36	.67	.35	.00
Obsessive/compulsive		.07	.03	.00	.07	.33	.38	.00
Suicidal ideation		.20	.38	1.00	.36	.33	.50	.50
Substance abuse		.11	.10	.33	.29	.00	.35	.27
Social withdrawal		.13	.28	.33	.14	.33	.50	.23
Inappropriate aggression		.11	.07	.00	.21	.00	.42	.27
DSM III-R diagnoses:	N =	84	27	3	10	1	15	23
Alcohol/drugs		.07	.07	.00	.30	.00	.00	.04
Affective disorders		.25	.33	.67	.10	.00	.20	.09
MPD		.08	.15	.00	.10	.00	.40	.26
PTSD		.15	.30	.00	.40	1.00	.33	.35
Personality disorders		.20	.19	.33	.30	.00	.07	.22
Sexual disorders		.07	.00	.00	.00	.00	.07	.00
Adjustment disorder		.15	.07	.00	.20	.00	.00	.09

NOTE. S = sexual abuse only; S/E = sexual and emotional abuse; S/N = sexual abuse and neglect; S/P = sexual and physical abuse; S/N/E - sexual abuse, neglect, and emotional abuse; S/P/E = sexual, physical, and emotional abuse; S/P/E/N = sexual, physical, and emotional abuse, and neglect.

ries of every possible combination of abuse) involving various presenting symptoms and diagnoses. Because the number of cases in some of the categories is quite low, statistical analyses were not performed. However, the breakdown is still interesting and suggestive of future lines of research. For example, the means indicate that, predictably, the presenting symptom of aggression is primarily associated with sexual abuse in combination with physical abuse. Examining DSM III-R diagnoses reveals that MPD was particularly likely to be diagnosed if sexual, physical, and emotional abuse were all alleged to have occurred. Additionally, the table reveals that our sample included more cases involving certain combinations of abuse (i.e., sexual abuse, physical abuse, and emotional abuse) rather than others (i.e., sexual abuse, neglect, and emotional abuse). These trends deserve to be examined in future studies.

DISCUSSION

As expected, the data revealed that, compared to victims who experienced only sexual abuse, clients who experienced multiple forms of abuse were significantly more likely to exhibit psychological symptoms such as depression, suicidal ideation, and phobias, and were more likely to be diagnosed by clinicians with serious conditions such as PTSD, MPD, and other dissociative disorders. In children, sexual acting out was more likely to occur among sexual abuse victims who were also abused in other ways. These results are consistent with previous research on the effects of multiple forms of abuse (e.g., Hart et al., 1989) and with research on the effects of accumulated risk factors (e.g., Garmezy & Rutter, 1983; Rutter, 1979). According to earlier studies and our own findings, children who experience multiple forms of abuse are especially likely to suffer adverse psychological consequences.

However, we did not find a significant increase across the three levels of abuse in the presenting symptoms of substance abuse and inappropriate aggression, or in DSM III-R diagnoses of substance-abuse addictions and impulse control. The occurrence of such symptoms and diagnoses would not be expected to differ significantly if substance abuse and aggression are associated with all of the kinds of religion-related abuse we studied, including child sexual abuse only. It is still surprising that the symptoms and diagnoses did not increase as the number of abuses increased.

Ney et al. (1994) reported that, in child sexual abuse cases, the worst combination of additional abuses is verbal (i.e., emotional) abuse and physical neglect. Unfortunately, very few ($n = 3$) of the cases in our sample fell into this category. However, for those few, there did not seem to be an increase in presenting symptoms compared, for instance, to cases involving the combination of sexual, physical, and emotional abuse.

It is important to keep in mind that our findings are restricted to religion-related child abuse cases involving allegations of sexual abuse. Although we suspect that the pattern of our results will generalize to other samples, further research is necessary. Religion-related abuse may involve additional stressors not normally included in abuse cases lacking a religious component. Consider, for example, that in many sexual abuse cases the trusted abuser gives contradictory messages—taking sexual advantage of a child while saying, "This is how Daddy shows his love for you." Consider further that religion-related abuse may create an additional "double bind" for children. Many of the victims in our study were abused by parents who communicated, in effect, that "God wants me to do this" or by religious authorities who indicated, for example, that "You can trust me, I'm a priest." Thus, like a daughter who is sexually abused by her father and simultaneously told that he is doing it for her own good, religion-related abuse victims may be abused by someone who uses religion as a means of creating, or adding to, a child's emotional confusion.

Finally, because our findings are correlational, causal relations cannot be confidently inferred. There may be confounding variables about which we are unaware. First, for example, clinicians' theories about the emotional sequelae of abuse may have affected their diagnoses. Second, although we statistically controlled for perpetrator relationship in our central analyses, the effects of multiple victimization associated with intra- versus extrafamilial abuse should be disentangled further in future studies. Third, we did not examine how compensatory factors within or outside the family might have affected clients' outcomes. Fourth, we had no measure of abuse severity, independent of the number of kinds of abuses suffered. It therefore remains unknown whether excessive abuse of one type is more damaging than the combined force of several types of abuse that are less serious or long-lasting. Moreover, a child may have suffered multiple forms of abuse even though only one form could be documented with confidence, and different definitions of abuse may have been used by different clinicians. Finally, it is possible that some of the reports of abuse were false; clinicians are generally not in a position to verify reported abuse. Especially when extreme forms of abuse were described and MPD was diagnosed, there is a possibility that highly suggestible, disturbed clients exaggerated or confabulated some of their abuse experiences (Spanos, 1994).

Obviously, random assignment to single versus multiple abuse groups is not, and never will be, feasible. Hence, even correlational results such as ours are helpful in providing insight into the issue of multiple forms of abuse. As far as we know, ours are the first empirical findings on the correlates of multiple forms of abuse in religion-related abuse cases. We have found that adherence to certain religious ideologies and practices can contribute to single or multiple forms of child maltreatment, and that the psychological sequelae of religion-related abuse are best understood in light of the specific types and combinations of abuses suffered by victims. We hope that our findings will be of benefit to practitioners encountering cases involving multiple abuses and religious ideology, and to future researchers who may address important issues that remain unanswered in the study of religion-related, multi-form child abuse.

AUTHOR NOTE

The research reported in this article was funded by the National Center on Child Abuse and Neglect (Department of Health and Human Services) and conducted in collaboration with Alexis Thompson and with the assistance of Jim Brandt, Kathy Cavanaugh, Eugene Colucci, Maureen Coughlin, Leslie Dreblat, Brian Flaherty, Erica Howard, Noelle Kardos, Todd Karl, Wendy Landman, Anne Orgren, Kimberly Packard, Steve Pawlowski, Chowdry Pinnamaneni, Jianjian Qin, Susan Reisch, Chris Rhoadhouse, Karleen Robinson, Julie Rothbard, Tracey Schneider, and Kimberly Tyda. Tina Goodman-Brown and Michael Raulin kindly consulted on the use of Diagnostic and Statistical Manual III-R diagnostic categories. We extend special thanks to all of the professionals who completed our survey.

REFERENCES

Bagley, C., Wood, M., & Young, L. (1994). Victim to abuser: Mental health and behavioral sequels to child sexual abuse in a community survey of young adult males. *Child Abuse and Neglect, 8,* 683-697.

Berry, J. (1992). *Lead us not into temptation: Catholic priests and the sexual abuse of children.* New York: Doubleday.

Bottoms, B.L., Shaver, P.R., & Goodman, G.S. (1996). An analysis of ritualistic and religion-related child abuse allegations. *Law and Human Behavior, 20,* 1-34.

Bottoms, B.L., Shaver, P.R., Goodman, G.S., & Qin, J. (1995). In the name of God: A profile of religion-related child abuse. *Journal of Social Issues, 51,* 85-111.

Brassard, M., Germain, R., & Hart, S. (1987). *Psychological maltreatment of children and youth.* New York: Pergamon.

Briere, J.N., & Elliott, D.M. (Summer/Fall 1994). Immediate and long-term impacts of child sexual abuse. In R.E. Behrman (Ed.), *The future of children:*

Sexual abuse of children (Vol. 4, pp. 54-69). Los Altos, CA: Center for the Future of Children, The David and Lucile Packard Foundation.

Brown, G.R., & Anderson, B. (1991). Psychiatric morbidity in adult inpatients with childhood histories of sexual and physical abuse. *American Journal of Psychiatry, 148*, 55-61.

Browne, A., & Finkelhor, D. (1986). Impact of sexual abuse: A review of the research. *Psychological Bulletin, 99*, 66-77.

Bullis, R.K. (1991). The spiritual healing "defense" in criminal prosecutions for crimes against children. *Child Welfare, 30*, 541-555.

Capps, D. (1992). Religion and child abuse: Perfect together. *Journal for the Scientific Study of Religion, 31*, 1-14.

Chu, J.A., & Dill, D.L. (1990). Dissociative symptoms in relation to childhood physical and sexual abuse. *American Journal of Psychiatry, 147*, 887-892.

Claussen, A.H., & Crittenden, P.M. (1991). Physical and psychological maltreatment: Relations among types of maltreatment. *Child Abuse and Neglect, 15*, 5-18.

Coons, P.M. (1986). Child abuse and multiple personality disorder: Review of the literature and suggestions for treatment. *Child Abuse and Neglect, 10*, 455-462.

Deblinger, E., McLeer, S.V., Atkins, M.S., Ralphe, D., & Fox, E. (1989). Post-traumatic stress in sexually abused, physically abused, and nonabused children. *Child Abuse and Neglect, 13*, 403-408.

Finkelhor, D. (1984). *Child sexual abuse.* New York: Free Press.

Finkelhor, D., & Dziuba-Leatherman, J. (1994). Children as victims of violence: A national survey. *Pediatrics, 94*, 413-420.

Finkelhor, D., Williams, L.M., & Burns, N. (1988). *Nursery crimes.* Newbury Park, CA: Sage.

Garbarino, J. (1980). Defining emotional maltreatment: The message is the meaning. *Journal of Psychiatric Treatment and Evaluation, 2*, 105-110.

Garbarino, J., Dubrow, N., Kostelny, K., & Pardo, C. (1992). *Children in danger: Coping with the consequences of community violence.* San Francisco, CA: Jossey-Bass.

Garbarino, J., & Vondra, J. (1987). Psychological maltreatment: Issues and perspectives. In M. Brassard, R. Germain, & S. Hart (Eds.), *Psychological maltreatment of children and youth* (pp. 25-44). New York: Pergamon.

Garmezy, N., & Rutter, M. (1983). *Stress, coping, and development in children.* New York: McGraw-Hill.

Greven, P. (1991). *Spare the child: The religious roots of punishment and the psychological impact of physical abuse.* New York: Knopf.

Hart, L.E., Mader, L., Griffith, K., & deMendonca, M. (1989). Effects of sexual and physical abuse: A comparison of adolescent inpatients. *Child Psychiatry and Human Development, 20*, 49-57.

Hobbs, C.J., & Wynne, J.M. (1990). Sexually abused battered child. *Archives of Diseases in Childhood, 65*, 423-427.

Kendall-Tackett, K.A., Williams, L., & Finkelhor, D. (1992). Impact of sexual abuse on children: A review and synthesis of recent empirical findings. *Psychological Bulletin, 113,* 164-180.

Keppel, G. (1982). *Design and analysis.* New York: Prentice Hall.

Kiser, L., Millsap, P., & Heston, J.D. (1992). A clinical description of victims of psychical and sexual abuse in a day treatment population. *International Journal of Partial Hospitalization, 8,* 89-96.

Moeller, T., Bachmann, G.A., & Moeller, J.R. (1993). The combined effects of physical, sexual, and emotional abuse during childhood: Long-term health consequences for women. *Child Abuse and Neglect, 17,* 623-640.

NCCAN (1994). *Child maltreatment 1992: Reports from the States to the National Center on Child Abuse and Neglect.* Washington, DC: U.S. Department of Health and Human Services.

Ney, P.G., Fung, T., & Wickett, A.D. (1994). The worst combinations of child abuse and neglect. *Child Abuse and Neglect, 18,* 705-714.

Ofshe, R., & Watters, E. (1994). *Making monsters: False memories, psychotherapy, and sexual hysteria.* New York: Scribners.

Putnam, F.W., Post, R.M., Guroff, J., Silberman, M.D., & Barban, L. (1983). 100 cases of multiple personality disorder. *New Research Abstract #77.* Washington, DC: American Psychiatric Association.

Riggs, S., Alario, A.J., & McHorney, C. (1990). Health risk behaviors and attempted suicide in adolescents who report prior maltreatment. *Journal of Paediatrics, 116,* 815-821.

Russell, D. (1983). The incidence and prevalence of intrafamilial and extrafamilial sexual abuse of female children. *Child Abuse and Neglect, 7,* 133-146.

Rutter, M. (1979). Protective factors in children's responses to stress and disadvantage. In M.W. Kent & J.E. Rolf (Eds.), *Primary prevention of psychopathology,* Vol. 3. Hanover, NH: University Press of New England.

Sameroff, A., Siefer, R., Barocas, R., Zax, M., & Greenspan, S. (1987). Intelligence quotient scores of 4-year-old children: Social-environmental risk factors. *Pediatrics, 79,* 343-350.

Skolnick, A.A. (1994). Massachusetts' new child abuse and neglect felony law repeals religious exemption. *Journal of the American Medical Association, 271* (7), 489-491.

Spanos, N. (1994). Multiple identity enactments and multiple personality disorder: A sociocognitive perspective. *Psychological Bulletin, 116,* 143-165.

Swett, C., & Halpert, M. (1993). Reported history of physical and sexual abuse in relation to dissociation and other symptomatology in women psychiatric patients. *Journal of Interpersonal Violence, 8,* 545-555.

Legal and Ethical Issues
in the Treatment
of Multiply Victimized Children

Daniel J. Sonkin
Douglas S. Liebert

SUMMARY. The article discusses several common legal and ethical issues faced by clinicians when treating families where singular and multiple child victimization is an issue. The authors differentiate between legal requirements and ethical mandates, explore factors affecting reporting decisions, how dual relationships compromise treatment process, and clinicians' scope of competence and professional knowledge in child maltreatment cases. Each issue is addressed within the context of responding to cases where a child(ren) has been multiply victimized. *[Article copies available for a fee from The Haworth Document Delivery Service: 1-800-342-9678. E-mail address: getinfo@haworth.com]*

The problem of child maltreatment has reached epidemic proportions, with nearly 1.9 million reports received for investigation on approximately 2.9 million alleged abused and neglected children (US Department of Health and Human Services, 1992). These figures may well represent the "tip of the iceberg" as many cases are never detected, including situations of marginal physical abuse, psychological maltreatment and neglect. Since

Address correspondence to: Daniel J. Sonkin, PhD, 1505 Bridgeway, Sausalito, CA 94965.

[Haworth co-indexing entry note]: "Legal and Ethical Issues in the Treatment of Multiply Victimized Children." Sonkin, Daniel J. and Douglas S. Liebert. Co-published simultaneously in *Journal of Aggression, Maltreatment & Trauma* (The Haworth Maltreatment & Trauma Press, an imprint of The Haworth Press, Inc.) Vol. 2, No. 1 (#3), 1998, pp. 297-316; and: *Multiple Victimization of Children: Conceptual, Developmental, Research, and Treatment Issues* (ed: B. B. Robbie Rossman, and Mindy S. Rosenberg) The Haworth Maltreatment & Trauma Press, an imprint of The Haworth Press, Inc., 1998, pp. 297-316. Single or multiple copies of this article are available for a fee from The Haworth Document Delivery Service [1-800-342-9678, 9:00 a.m. - 5:00 p.m. (EST). E-mail address: getinfo@haworth.com].

Congress passed the Child Abuse Prevention and Treatment Act in 1974, every state in the union has passed compulsory reporting laws for various professionals who are likely to detect child abuse during the course of their work. Many reports are made by mental health professionals who are identified as mandated reporters (i.e., psychiatrists, clinical psychologists, marriage, family and child counselors and licensed clinical social workers) who must respond and alert protective institutions (e.g., Child Protective Services) to minimize harm and protect victims. Given the prevalence of this devastating problem, it is the unusual clinician who has not made a child abuse report at some time in their career or has not encountered a former victim of child maltreatment.

Since the initial description of "Battered Child Syndrome" was introduced in 1962 (Kempe, Silverman, Steele, Droegmueller & Silver, 1962), the literature on the subject has evolved to include numerous journals dedicated to the study of violence within the family and thousands of articles and books. However, it is curious that little has been written to address legal and ethical issues relating to the treatment of victims, perpetrators and their family members. The only apparent exception are those researchers interested in clinicians' reports of suspected child abuse (e.g., Brosig & Kalichman, 1992). Aside from this one important, but limited area, legal and ethical issues are rarely discussed in the research or clinical literature even though many clinicians frequently confront these issues when treating clients with maltreatment related concerns.

As forensic consultants and members of a state-wide ethics committee representing over 22,000 mental health professionals, we have found that many complaints filed with the ethics committee, the courts and licensing authorities frequently pertain to issues involving child abuse treatment. Unfortunately, traditional mental health training does not typically prepare clinicians to face thorny situations that require thoughtful consideration of legal and ethical issues within the context of treatment. Thus, without adequate training, clinicians can become overwhelmed or confused by the intricacies of treating abuse victims. In this article, we discuss a number of the most common legal and ethical issues faced by clinicians when treating families where child maltreatment is a significant consideration. Specifically, we will differentiate between what constitutes a legal requirement as opposed to an ethical mandate, explore factors that affect the decision to report or not report child abuse, discuss how dual roles can compromise the treatment process, and how a clinician's scope of competence and professional knowledge is critical to respond effectively to the clinical needs of abused children and their families. Each of these issues will be discussed within the context of responding to cases where a child(ren) has been multiply victimized.

LEGAL VERSUS ETHICAL REQUIREMENTS

Mental health practitioners, like many health providers, must adhere to legal reporting requirements related to the performance of their work. Mandates exist in many states to report elder abuse, spouse abuse and dangerous threats and behaviors. These legal requirements are mandatory and in many states, a practitioner can be charged with a crime if they fail to report. Ethical issues, on the other hand, reflect standards of performance and practice that are usually identified by professional organizations and often provide guidance to licensing bodies. Failure to adhere to those standards can result in loss of license and/or expulsion from a professional organization. Standard of practice is the minimal national criteria recognized among similar specialists, rather than a local community based standard (Liebert & Foster, 1994). This standard often becomes the benchmark used by ethics committees and licensing authorities when trying to assess if a practitioner has followed an appropriate course of action and standard of care. Common areas of difficulty include the handling of dual relationships, practicing within the scope of his or her competence, and psychotherapist-patient privilege and confidentiality. In either case, laws and ethical standards are presumably set forth with the directive of "primum non nocere": do not harm anyone, thus reminding therapists of their responsibility to protect.

In an ideal world, one expects legal and ethical practice requirements to be clear; however, the opposite appears to be the case. Not only are there inconsistencies between states, but there are also inconsistencies intra-jurisdiction, within each state. For example, child abuse reporting is a statutory requirement in every state. In Massachusetts, the standard for reporting is ". . . reasonable cause to believe . . . ," whereas in Mississippi, the standard is ". . . that a child brought to him or coming before him . . . " Thus, the standard can vary from reasonable suspicion to actually seeing the abused child. Similarly, it has been the authors' experience that the same set of circumstances was interpreted differently between child protective service workers within and across California counties (e.g., whether a formal abuse report should be filed).

There are similar discrepancies with ethical issues. For example, prior to recently revised ethical standards that prohibit sexual relations with a "former" client for up to two years after termination, the California Association of Marriage and Family Therapists (CAMFT) Ethics Committee would not act upon a client's complaint of sexual exploitation by their "former" therapist when the sexual act took place after a "proper termination" (i.e., "proper termination" being generally defined as termination not occurring for the express or implied purpose of becoming sexually intimate). In apparent contrast, the California Board of Behavioral Science Examiners, who have statutory authority to administer and monitor the Marriage, Family and Child Counselor license, would routinely pursue and prosecute cases of therapists having sex with "former" clients. Similar differences in enforcement exist when discussing the controversial and often vague issue of dual relationships.

Experience shows us that not only are there differences in specific laws and ethical standards but there are also differences in their interpretation across individuals. Legal and ethical standards can appear, at best, ambiguous and open to interpretation guided by such vagaries as the "unique aspects of the case," personal and professional experience, theoretical bias, and other such issues, yet statutes and the teleological basis underlying most ethics codes assume a decision rule based on predictable outcome.

LEGAL ISSUES:
MANDATORY REPORTING OF CHILD MALTREATMENT

One of the most common dilemmas addressed in the child abuse literature relates to the violation of privilege and/or confidentiality. Privilege is a legal term referring to the clients' statutory right that varies by jurisdiction, while confidentiality is a legal and ethical concept that implies a responsibility assumed by the clinician to reveal nothing learned during the course of treatment except what may be mandated by law or agreed to by the client. When surveyed, psychologists indicated that this mandate was the most typical confidentiality issue confronted in the course of their work (Pope & Vetter, 1992). The findings of numerous studies have indicated that a significant number of clinicians have complied inconsistently with the legal mandate to report abuse (Pope & Bajt, 1988). While there has been speculation that underreporting results from professional responsibility and clinical judgement being subordinated to clinicians' serving a policing function (Ansell & Ross, 1990) and concern for the clients' welfare (Wright, 1984), others believe that underreporting, in part, stems from differences in the interpretation of the child abuse laws as well as situational and therapist characteristics (Barksdale, 1989; Brosig & Kalichman, 1992; Kalichman & Craig, 1991; Kalichman, Craig & Follingstad, 1990, 1989; Weinstock & Weinstock, 1989; Zellman, 1990). The problem of reporting is critical in cases of multiple child maltreatment since treatment decisions will be made based on the types of abuse occurring within the family. Moreover, additional acts of abuse are frequently detected and/or perpetrated after the commencement of treatment.

Because the standard for reporting child abuse can vary from state to state, it is impractical for this article to set forth specific reporting criteria for clinicians. We recommend that mental health practitioners become familiar with the threshold criteria in their state by reading the law and contacting the proper reporting authorities. Instead, we will describe a number of decision-making strategies that have been found effective in the reporting of child maltreatment and what factors enter into a decision whether or not to report.

The decision to report maltreatment is complex where the interests of the individual, the family, the profession, and the community potentially conflict (Lippitt, 1985). Although most would agree that child abuse is appalling, disagreements arise regarding the actions taken to protect victimized children and those at risk for further abuse. The fact that many therapists do not report abuse in spite of potential legal and ethical consequences is evidence that legislation is not a panacea for this complex social phenomenon. Researchers have identified a variety of factors that influence clinicians' decision-making process. These factors include responsibility for the abuse (Kalichman, Craig & Follingstad, 1990), abuse history (Zellman, 1992), abuse severity (Zellman, 1990, 1992), recantation (Zellman, 1992), perception of the therapist's role (Ansell & Ross, 1990; Fox 1984), abuse type (Kalichman & Craig, 1991; Williams, Osborne & Rappaport, 1987), socioeconomic status of patient and professional license (Williams, Osborne & Rappaport, 1987), years of practice (Barksdale, 1989), clinicians' expectation of reporting consequences on the individual or family (Zellman, 1990; Kalichman, Craig & Follingstad, 1989), the perpetrators' admission or denial of abuse (Kalichman, Craig & Follingstad, 1989), sex of therapist and alleged perpetrator (Kalichman, Craig & Follingstad, 1990), age of child (Kalichman & Craig, 1991), behavior of alleged victim (Kalichman & Craig, 1991), therapists' history of reporting (Kalichman & Craig, 1991; Zellman, 1991), child's age (Kalichman & Craig, 1991), perpetrators' relationship to child (Kalichman & Craig, 1991), therapists' knowledge of law (Swoboda, Elwork, Sales & Levine, 1978), and clarity of legal requirements (Kalichman & Craig, 1991; Besharov, 1991; Brosig & Kalichman, 1992). Given the large number of variables identified, it remains unclear how any unique variable combination may affect reporting decisions in specific circumstances. It is the authors' belief that both statute and clinical training need to provide greater direction to enhance optimal decision making and thus, outcome. While a number of criteria should be considered for inclusion, one simple example of threshold criteria would be the greater the severity of abuse and the younger the child, the sooner the reporting threshold should be met.

Child Abuse Decision Making: A Model for Clinicians

In their review of the reporting literature, Brosig and Kalichman (1992) propose a three tiered approach to decision making in child abuse reports. They suggest that legal factors, clinician characteristics, and situational factors appear to interact synergistically to influence whether a clinician chooses to report.

Legal factors. Common legal factors affecting child abuse reporting decisions include: the clinicians' knowledge of child abuse laws, the wording of the law itself and the legal requirements of the law. Although reporting has increased since the passage of child abuse reporting laws (Andrew & Lamond, 1989), studies indicate that, as a rule, clinicians' compliance with the law does not increase with increased knowledge of the law (Kalichman, Craig & Follingstad, 1989). However, some clinicians are more inclined to make informed decisions because of the importance of adhering to the law. For these individuals, knowledge of the reporting law does seem to facilitate reporting (Brosig & Kalichman, 1992; Haas, Malouf & Mayerson, 1988; Wilson & Gettinger, 1989).

Similarly, the clarity of the specific child abuse statutes also affects the reporting probability (Zellman, 1990). Laws that fail to adequately define child abuse and/or are unclear about the reporting procedure may affect the therapists' tendency to report or not.

As previously discussed, states that require a "reasonable cause to believe" versus other states that require that a "child be brought to him or coming before him" (i.e., the professional) often result in different outcomes for the same types of cases. The more narrowly defined statutes, such as the latter standard, result in underreporting whereas the more broadly defined laws, i.e., reasonable suspicion standard, increase the probability of reporting (Brosig & Kalichman, 1992).

Clinician characteristics. Typical clinician characteristics identified in the research literature that appear to affect the probability of reporting child abuse include years of experience, training, attitudes and experience making child abuse reports (Brosig & Kalichman, 1992). However, the data is inconsistent. For example, there is research to indicate that experienced clinicians may report more than less experienced clinicians (Barksdale, 1989; Nightingale & Walker, 1986) whereas other studies found the converse to be the case (Haas, Malouf & Mayerson, 1988). There is also data to suggest that some clinicians have had prior negative experiences with the child protective system or believe that not reporting may be the better way of protecting the child (Ansell & Ross, 1990). As with years of experience, training in child abuse issues may increase the probability of reporting (Nightingale & Walker, 1986) as well as the clinicians' previous experience filing child abuse reports (Kalichman, Craig & Follingstad, 1989; Kalichman & Craig, 1991).

From a social policy and ethical standpoint, many clinicians remain concerned about the current degree of legislating human behavior, with child abuse and duty to protect laws being only two examples (Ansell & Ross, 1990). They maintain that confidentiality is the cornerstone of the therapeutic relationship and that legislating, a breach of confidentiality, undermines the therapist's ability to do his or her job. However, research on the impact of the client-therapist relationship after a report indicates that there is either no change or a change for the positive (Watson & Levine, 1989). We would argue that trust, not confidentiality, is the cornerstone of our profession (McNeil, 1987; Sonkin, 1986) and that clients trust that we will act in ways that have their best interest in mind, even if the immediate consequences of their actions may result in pain or discomfort. Certainly the discomfort and embarrassment of the child social services investigation pales in comparison to unnecessary child trauma, or criminal charges and a trial resulting from a child's serious injury or death.

Situational factors. Brosig and Kalichman (1992) describe a number of situational factors that also influence clinicians' decision making on child abuse reporting. These factors include victim attributes, type of abuse, severity of abuse and availability of evidence. Children's age appears to be an important variable in reporting child abuse. Current data infers that clinicians are more likely to report younger children than adolescent victims (Brosig & Kalichman, 1992; Kalichman & Craig, 1991). Similarly, race has been identified as a variable in child abuse reporting (Newberger, 1983), such that families of color are more likely to be reported than Caucasian families. This situation is consistent with data regarding other forms of domestic violence (Walker, 1985).

For a variety of psychological and social reasons, many clinicians believe sexual abuse is more serious than physical or psychological abuse or neglect, and as a result, are more inclined to report these types of cases (Nightingale & Walker, 1986; Zellman, 1990). Similarly, abuse severity is also a factor in reporting rates. The literature suggests that clinicians are more likely to report abuse that is currently happening than past abuse (Wilson & Gettinger, 1989). However, reliance on the treating therapist's perception and clinical acumen remains potentially problematic in high-risk families, especially if the therapist is ill trained, inexperienced or unfamiliar with literature indicating that all forms of family violence tend to be chronic in nature, therefore resulting in increased victim vulnerability over time (Sonkin, 1986; Sonkin & Elison, 1986).

One of the most difficult areas for clinicians is the amount of clinical data or "evidence" necessary to meet the threshold level of reasonable suspicion. Increased "evidence" leads to a greater degree of certainty (Watson & Levine, 1989), which results in a greater probability of reporting (Kalichman, Craig & Follingstad, 1990). Many reports are not ultimately made because clinicians either do not have enough "evidence" to support a reasonable suspicion or do not know the "reasonable suspicion" standard for their community.

The term "evidence" is parenthasized to refer to the physical and psychological indicators of child abuse, as opposed to the evidence that is used in criminal proceedings to prove guilt beyond a reasonable doubt to a "trier of fact." Later in this chapter, we will discuss the ethical issue of clinicians taking on dual roles of therapist and investigator or social advocate (Melton & Limber, 1989).

Deciding to Report

Given the information discussed above, what can clinicians do to better respond to child maltreatment cases? Although in many states, the law indicates that a therapist must contact social services immediately and follow-up with a written report within thirty-six hours once the threshold standard has been met, consultation with colleagues remains an important adjunct to the clinician's decision. In fact, consultation has been found to be correlated positively with child abuse reporting (Brosig & Kalichman, 1992). This may not always be possible, and in those situations when an immediate decision must be made, a clinician may call the appropriate agency and describe the relevant case facts to the on-call intake worker without initially revealing the parties' names. The intake worker may be helpful in the questions asked or will inform the clinician whether the reporting threshold has been met. Similarly, it is important for mental health professionals to meet with law enforcement and child protective service personnel in their community to discuss interpretations of the current statutes as well as reporting policies and procedures and case follow-up. Clinicians are frequently unaware of the outcome of their reports to child protective services. Therefore, building a relationship with these professionals tends to enrich both the clinical community as well as social service personnel.

Continuing education in the identification and treatment of child abuse will not only increase the clinician's ability to recognize the threshold standard, which assists in more accurate reporting, but also find more effective methods of treating families experiencing this problem. The literature in the field is rapidly expanding to such an extent that even the most experienced clinician needs to take the time to review the latest advances in treatment and research findings. Unfortunately, it is often all too easy for seasoned clinicians to get into a rut by continuing to rely on old research data and treatment methodologies, compromising optimal treatment planning for clients.

In order to minimize the trauma experienced by the family as a result of a child abuse report, many specialists suggest that the clinician make the report (i.e., call protective services) while the client(s) are in the office or ask the client(s) to make the call from the office (the latter being most effective when the treatment is with the perpetrator). Similarly, a therapist may also attend meetings with police or protective services as a support to their client(s) should their presence be desired and appropriate. In general, it remains important for the clinician to understand that the potential consequences of the report can be quite devastating to the client(s) and the therapist should be available for continued support and assistance during the investigation and evaluation process.

Feelings of betrayal are likely to be experienced by the client and/or family members towards the therapist for initiating a report to protective services. Therefore, the therapist needs to be prepared for handling anger, pain, and other negative affect when providing appropriate boundaries, with the goal of positive resolution in mind. However, many clients may not be able to overcome these deep feelings of resentment and lack of trust in the clinician. If this occurs, the therapist needs to seek consultation to evaluate whether a referral is appropriate and participate in an orderly transition, if needed.

Reporting Child Maltreatment in Cases of Multiple Victimization

The legal issues of reporting child maltreatment are particularly significant in cases of multiple victimization. Therapists may be reluctant to describe all forms of abuse occurring within the family for fear that the consequences may be even greater to the client. This is most frequently seen with child sexual abuse or physical abuse reports. In both physical and sexual abuse, emotional abuse also occurs concurrently, but is often omitted in reports. Neglect may also be omitted from reports. It is critical that the clinician describe all forms of maltreatment when following through with reporting. If the full breadth of pathology is not adequately assessed, the treatment plan developed may not address appropriately the needs of the family. For example, a family where a father has sexually abused his oldest daughter seeks treatment with a therapist who ultimately reports the abuse to protective services. The report fails to mention that the father is also physically abusing his youngest child and that the mother frequently becomes intoxicated during the day and neglects her newborn child. If the therapist only identifies the sexual abuse to authorities, the treatment plan may ultimately ignore other critical family needs. This can become especially problematic in situations where the court system may mandate the scope of intervention required as a condition of probation. If multiple forms of abuse and neglect are unreported, they may go untreated.

It is also important to identify all forms of maltreatment within the family so that social services workers and law enforcement personnel can become more aware of the different forms abuse may take and the diverse consequences to various family members. Sexual abuse has received so much attention in the past decade even though other forms of maltreatment are equally devastating (Navarre, 1987), that the net result can be minimizing or ignoring other types of maltreatment.

Another important reason for thoroughly documenting child abuse is maintaining statistics. The Department of Social Services keeps statistics on the types and extent of child abuse in the community. This information is ultimately used by the Department of Justice for the compilation of state and national statistics and becomes a basis for programs to pursue funding for services, and research on the problem.

A controversial issue that frequently arises in the treatment of child abuse cases, and particularly in instances of multiple victimization, is what to do when the therapist becomes aware of an additional act of maltreatment that either differs from the type initially reported, falls into the category of a repeated offense, or is a similar or different victimization by or to another person. The therapist is faced with the dilemma of whether to report and initiate another investigation with charges filed or additional sanctions levied against their client. Examples of this would include the discovery of physical maltreatment or neglect (i.e., such as a parent refusing a child's breadth of care needs) while treating an individual or family for child sexual abuse.

Research on child abuse, and other forms of interpersonal family violence (i.e., marital violence), indicates it follows a chronic pattern and that perpetrators are prone to relapse under stress, even while in psychological treatment. In California, state law requires therapists to formally report additional acts of child abuse in situations of physical and sexual abuse, and neglect. In cases of emotional abuse, the therapist has the latitude for discretion (California Penal Code Section 11172). If this is the case in your state, we recommend using a similar decision-making model proposed earlier in determining whether there is a legal and/or ethical duty to report. If your state law is not clear regarding this issue, it is important to discuss with your local social services how they treat multiple offenses and their expectations from mental health professionals.

ETHICAL ISSUES: AN OVERVIEW

National and state associations that represent the various mental health professions have developed and continue to refine ethical standards in an attempt to create a model code of conduct to ensure the protection of clients' rights. Ethical standards are promulgated in part to provide guidance, and help prevent client exploitation and impairment of therapists' judgement.

Ethical codes are frequently adopted or used to provide guidance by state licensing boards to set forth minimum standards of practice in their regulation of various professions. Although there are some idiosyncratic and philosophical differences between the various ethical codes of mental health professions, there is generally greater consistency. For example, in California, the psychology, social work and marriage, family and child counselor code of ethics all prohibit certain dual relationships that are likely to result in client exploitation or impaired therapist judgement. Similarly, each profession's code also dictates that licensees not practice beyond the scope of competence. The breach of ethical principles may result in dismissal from or conditions placed upon membership of their professional organization.

Violations of the licensing law can also result in loss of licensure or other remedial sanctions imposed by the state licensing board. Ethical violations may also lead to punitive damages from a malpractice lawsuit against the therapist and many malpractice carriers consider an ethics violation in their underwriting criteria.

As mentioned earlier, ethical principles range from clear to nebulous. For example, few would argue today that having a sexual relationship with a current client is unethical behavior. However, there has been disagreement about the ethics of having sexual relations with a "former" client. Recently, the ethical standards of many state and national organizations have amended their code to include sex with former clients for a specified period of time subsequent to an appropriate termination. However, the language lacked specificity until the 1992 revision of the American Psychological Association ethics, Standard 4.07, which states:

> Because sexual intimacies with a former therapy patient or client are so frequently harmful to the patient or client, and because such intimacies undermine public confidence in the psychology profession and thereby deter the public's use of needed services, psychologists do not engage in sexual intimacies with former therapy patients and clients even after a two-year interval except in the most unusual circumstances. The psychologist who engages in such activities after the two years following cessation or termination bears the burden of demonstrating that there has been no exploitation, in light of all relevant factors, including (1) amount of time that has passed since therapy terminated, (2) the nature and duration of the therapy, (3) the circumstances of termination, (4) the patient's or client's personal history, (5) the patient's or client's current mental status, (6) the likelihood of adverse impact on the patient or client and others, and (7) any statements or actions made by the therapist during the course of therapy suggesting or inviting the possibility of a posttermination sexual or romantic relationship with the patient or client.

However, there continues to be discussion and debate on this issue. Is it ever acceptable to have sex with former clients? Does placing a two-year limit implicitly mean that having sex after two years is permitted? Other ethical standards remain even less clear in behavioral terms. For example, scope of competence issues are more prone to interpretation as they are typically addressed in vague aspirational language, such as, "Marriage and Family Therapists are dedicated to maintaining high standards of professional competence and integrity." While an advantage to ethical codes remaining vague and aspirational in scope is allowing committees the flexibility to be sensitive to the merits and idiosyncratic nature of each case, the disadvantage remains a lack of clear guidance for the practitioner.

Dual Relationships in the Treatment of Child Maltreatment

In their article, "Psychologists' involvement in cases of child maltreatment: Limits of role and expertise," Melton and Limber (1989) discuss a range of ethical and legal issues that mental health practitioners confront when evaluating victims and perpetrators of child abuse and their families. With increasing numbers of professionals specializing in this clinical area, the police and social service professionals in many communities are requesting that psychologists and other practitioners serve an investigative role in collecting evidence for the prosecution. Similarly, many clinicians are also being asked to serve as an expert witness in trials for the defense or prosecution testifying as to whether or not a particular witness was a victim of abuse or a particular defendant is guilty of hurting the alleged victim. Additionally, experts are also testifying in sentencing hearings suggesting whether or not a particular defendant should be incarcerated or mandated into a rehabilitation program.

A dual relationship exists when a therapist and his or her client engage in a separate and distinct relationship either simultaneously during the therapeutic relationship, or before a reasonable period of time has past following the termination of the therapeutic relationship. The most clearly unethical dual relationships include sexual relationships, friendships or business partnerships. On the other hand, there are relationships that may be categorized as dual in nature, involve a boundary violation, do not necessarily enjoy clear, explicit concrete definition, but nevertheless can be potentially harmful.

For example, when a therapist is treating a child victim, non-offending parent or perpetrator, and files a mandatory child abuse report, he or she may be asked by authorities or volunteers to collect investigative information that will assist in the development of the legal case. When a therapist takes on this investigative role, no matter how cooperative the client may appear in the process, they are stepping outside their role as therapist. Some argue that this dual role of therapist and investigator can be exploitive to the client and impair the therapist's judgement (Weithorn, 1987). For example, a therapist who is treating an alleged perpetrator of abuse cannot protect their client's right to privacy and act as an arm of the justice system at the same time without obvious conflicts.

Additionally, exploitation is likely to occur because the client may believe that the therapist is acting on his or her behalf, when in fact the therapist is acting as an agent of the state. Melton and Limber (1989) argue, "A particularly egregious example of mixture of roles in a manner that violates fidelity and privacy is when psychotherapy is used as a prosecutorial investigative tool." Similarly, victims of abuse may also put their trust in a therapist who ultimately places them in a position to pursue legal action when in fact they may not be emotionally ready for such a step. When a therapist acts as both therapist and investigator, we believe this constitutes a dual relationship that is potentially harmful for the client as well as family members. Therapists must attempt to keep these roles separate by taking on one or the other but refusing to act as both. There is nothing to prevent a therapist from taking on this investigative function in communities where the authorities lack the skills to adequately make child abuse determinations. But because this is a different and distinct role from providing therapeutic treatment to an individual or family, the boundary, by definition should be respected. Thus, taking on any single role, whether it be treater, evaluator or investigator may preclude any other role. Ethical guidance is clear: "Psychologists must always be sensitive to the potential harmful effects of other contacts on their work and on those persons with whom they deal" (American Psychological Association, Standard 1.17 Multiple Relationships, 1992).

Sexual Exploitation of Abuse Victims

Studies have suggested that individuals with a history of childhood sexual victimization are more likely to be victimized by therapists who become sexually involved with their patients (Armsworth, 1990). Kluft (1990) coined the term, "sitting duck syndrome" in discussing the phenomena of incest victims being vulnerable to revictimization. Marvasti (1993) suggests that therapists who are incest survivors are increasingly vulnerable to boundary difficulties, perhaps due in part to repetition compulsion and identification with the aggressor. Kroll (1988) suggests that countertransference issues exist ". . . on a continuum of sexual exploitation, but that never manifest themselves beyond subtleties . . . " (p. 203) and raises concern that these behaviors may occur beyond the conscious awareness of the therapist and thus acted out without consideration of the impact or implication to the client. Our experience as forensic consultants and state ethics committee members has been that therapists who are inadequately trained, experienced or supervised are more prone to act out when presented with extremely dependent clients or those with erotic transference, and these clients are frequently ones who were victims of child sexual abuse. Frequently, these therapists were treating their clients for abuse-related issues when they became sexually involved with their clients.

Some adolescents, young adults and older adults who were sexually abused as children may have a pattern of relating to persons in a position of authority in a seductive manner. They may also be prone to submitting to the control of authority figures (Armsworth, 1990), thus being an easy target for therapists who, for a variety of reasons, are susceptible to acting out in this way. Therefore, it is vital for the mental health professional to be aware of potential transference and countertransference reactions they are likely to encounter when working with this client population. Special favors and treatment needs are likely to be misinterpreted by these clients and have the potential of being misinterpreted and not adequately understood by clinicians. A number of authors speculate that many sexual abuse survivors become highly eroticized (Yates, 1987; Carnes, 1983; Brunne-graber, 1986; Russell, 1986) and unfortunately, all too often victimized during the course of treatment (Bouhoutsos et al., 1983; Herman et al., 1987).

Scope of Competence in Responding to Child Maltreatment

As discussed previously, issues relating to therapists' scope of competence are difficult to measure and evaluate. Ultimately, clinicians are often left to identify their own weaknesses, which may not emerge as a problem until a violation is alleged. Appropriate clinical training, mandatory continuing education, and a commitment to clinical consultation are factors that can mitigate concerns of competence. However, there is no guarantee that the clinician will either learn the specific material or apply it appropriately in the clinical setting. Nevertheless, advertisements of continuing education in the assessment and treatment of child abuse can be found in practically every professional newsletter, magazine and journal today. Opportunities abound for expanding one's knowledge and skill in this area of mental health treatment. Yet, do these workshops ensure that clinicians will practice solely within their scope of competence? Additionally, clinicians can procure any one of a number of child abuse screening instruments or tools (such as sexually anatomically correct dolls) and incorporate their use in a clinical practice with little or no formal training.

Frequently, mental health providers who become involved with forensic evaluations lack familiarity with the appropriate legal standards and procedures that need to be integrated into psychological assessment. Clinicians should not practice outside the scope of their license, or misuse tools, techniques or psychometric tests to misdiagnose child abuse (Grisso, 1986; Weithorn, 1987). To date there remains no error-free behavioral test or technique for identifying child abuse (Melton & Limber, 1989), e.g., hypnosis, eye movement desensitization and reprocessing (EMDR), sexually anatomically correct dolls, child abuse behavioral inventory. False positive and negatives remain problematic and can vary as a result of test administration, technique, or results interpretation (Goodman & Aman, 1987; Milner, Gold, Ayoub & Jacewitz, 1984). In addition, there are several techniques whose application may vary greatly (e.g., EMDR and hypnosis), which have not been empirically tested sufficiently to support or refute their efficacy in assessing and treating child abuse. Therefore, clinicians must exercise extreme caution when interviewing clients and account for the multiple levels of data that either support or refute the existence of child abuse (Faller, Froning & Lipovsky, 1991).

Therapists who become involved in forensic practice need to have a working familiarity with legal standards in order to relate appropriately the relevant psychological data and concepts. Not all practitioners have the interest, understanding or ability to integrate these two disparate disciplines and therefore, should resist getting involved beyond providing treatment so as not to practice beyond their scope of competence (Monahan, 1981). The interested reader is referred to the extensive literature regarding training in the forensic subspecialty since several clinical professional organizations have attempted to elucidate the necessary background to become involved with child abuse evaluations, either at the criminal or civil level (Weithorn, 1987).

Limit of Professional Knowledge

Mental health providers typically form opinions based in degrees of possibility or probability. It is not possible to know whether or not a particular child or adult was abused unless the clinician witnessed the abuse. Instead, clinicians talk about degrees of certainty based on factors observed or evaluated. Therefore, clinicians need to be cautious about statements made to clients, other professionals, law enforcement personnel and in court regarding the level of certainty about a particular individual's abuse assessment. Because an individual says they were abused does not necessarily mean they were abused, or if they were, by the person they say committed the abuse.

Similarly, decisions about a particular person's guilt of abuse must be clearly left in the hands of the judicial process and not with mental health professionals or child abuse advocates. While an attorney may advocate for a particular position and may attempt to convince, trick or cajole the mental health professional to testify to "the ultimate issue," this may well be an invitation to exceed the boundary of the expert's specialized knowledge. As such, the mental health professional has an opportunity and responsibility to educate the "trier of fact" (i.e., the judge or jury) about the bounds of their competence and points of uncertainty.

In the past five years, there has been a plethora of pop-psychology books on child maltreatment that are not grounded in the literature, but grew out of clinical experience of both professionals and paraprofessionals. Relying on this material may result in erroneous assumptions about the characteristics of victims and perpetrators. For example, many of these books offer a laundry list of characteristics that could be symptoms of any one of a number of problems, but are attributed to child abuse (Loftus, 1993). Professionals are cautioned not to form their conclusions based on superficial observations of clinical characteristics that by definition can be transient, but rather, to form the basis of their evaluation of child abuse on sound, broad-based clinical data that is supported by the literature.

Not all children demonstrate observable reactions to child abuse (Browne & Finkelhor, 1986). Similarly, many symptoms attributed to child abuse (e.g., bedwetting) may also be symptoms related to other family problems, or may simply be a reflection of a wide range of normal developmental patterns. If a clinician relies too heavily on these "typical" characteristics, the possibility greatly increases that he or she is going to misdiagnose child abuse when it hasn't occurred. Relying on nonscientific material can result in unethical misrepresentation of psychological knowledge and techniques (Weithorn & Grisso, 1987).

CONCLUSION

In many ways, the legal and ethical issues clinicians confront in treating patients involved in child maltreatment are similar whether the abuse is singular or in multiple forms. The clinician needs to maintain an awareness of the issues of reporting requirements, confidentiality, boundary issues including dual relationships, and scope of practice and competence in order to meet the individual or family's treatment needs, while at the same time practicing within legal and ethical professional standards. Because laws and ethical standards have been created to protect both the consumer and society at large, decisions in this regard must be taken seriously.

The most obvious area in which multiple abuse differs from singular victimization is in the legal mandate to report. Therapists may not report singular instances of abuse and/or multiple forms of abuse for unconscious reasons, or may be reluctant to report child abuse for both deliberate and unintentional purposes. The authors discuss a model proposed by Brosig and Kalichman (1992), who describe a three tiered model for reporting child maltreatment, which is equally applicable for singular and multiple cases of victimization. Given the complexity of child maltreatment cases, we recommend that clinicians receive either legal or professional consultation when confronted with all cases of child maltreatment or other situations that involve a legal mandate to report.

Many clients, abused or not, pull for the clinician to cross over ethical boundaries. This is particularly strong with the most wounded clients who are frequently in therapy to develop healthier relationships with others. There is often a strong pull for the therapist to meet the client at the client's level which can, in the case of an unconscious professional, lead to the blurring of professional boundaries. Even the most highly skilled clinician may lose sight of his or her ethical obligations. Therefore, the authors strongly recommend that clinicians become involved with regular peer or professional supervision/consultation and not only when situations become difficult.

REFERENCES

American Psychological Association (1992). Ethical principles of psychologists and code of conduct. *American Psychologists, 47*, 1597-1628.

Ansell, C. & Ross, H.L. (1990). "When laws and values conflict: A dilemma for psychologists": Reply. *American Psychologist, 45*, 399.

Armsworth, M.W. (1990). A qualitative analysis of adult incest survivors' responses to sexual involvement with therapists. *Child Abuse and Neglect, 14*, 541-54.

Barksdale, C. (1989). Child abuse reporting: A clinical dilemma. *Smith College Studies in Social Work, 59*, 170-182.

Besharov, D. (1991). Reducing unfounded reports. *Journal of Interpersonal Violence, 6*, 112-114.

Bouhoutsos, J., Holroyd, J., Lerman, H., Forer, B., & Greenberg, M. (1983). Sexual intimacy between psychotherapists and patients. *Professional Psychology, 14*, 185-196.

Brosig, C.L. & Kalichman, S.C. (1992). Clinicians' reporting of suspected child abuse: A review of the empirical literature. *Clinical Psychology Review, 12*, 155-168.

Browne, A. & Finkelhor, D. (1986). Impact of child sexual abuse: A review of the literature. *Psychological Bulletin, 99*, 66-77.

Brunngraber, L. (1986). Father-daughter incest: Immediate and long term effects of sexual abuse. *Advances in Nursing Science, 4*, 15-35.

California Association of Marriage and Family Therapists. *Ethical standards for marriage and family therapists.* San Diego: CAMFT.

Carnes, P. (1983). *Out of the shadows.* Minneapolis, MN: Compcare Publishers.

Faller, K.C., Froning, M.L. & Lipovsky, J. (1991). The parent-child interview: Use in evaluating child allegations of sexual abuse by the parent. *American Journal of Orthopsychiatry, 61*, 552-557.

Fox, J.R. (1984). Social work ethics and children: Protection versus empowerment. Special Issue: Hostility of adults to children and youth: Social and psychological sources and institutional forms. *Children & Youth Services Review, 6*, 319-328.

Goodman, G. & Aman, C. (1987). *Children's use of anatomically correct dolls to report an event.* Paper presented at the meeting of the Society of Research in Child Development, Baltimore, MD.

Grisso, T. (1986). *Evaluating competencies: Forensic assessments and instruments.* New York: Plenum.

Haas, L., Malouf, J. & Mayerson, N. (1988). Personal and professional character-istics as factors in psychologists' ethical decision making. *Professional Psychology: Research and Practice, 19,* 35-42.

Herman, J.L., Gartrell, N., Olarte, S., Feldstein, M. & Localio, R. (1987). Psychia-trist-patient sexual contact: Results of a national survey, II: Psychiatrists' attitudes. *American Journal of Psychiatry, 127,* 1141-1146.

Kalichman, S.C. & Craig, M.E. (1991). Professional psychologists' decisions to report suspected child abuse: Clinician and situation influences. *Professional Psychology: Research & Practice, 22,* 84-89.

Kalichman, S.C., Craig, M.E. & Follingstad, D.R. (1990). Professionals' adher-ence to mandatory child abuse reporting laws: Effects of responsibility attribu-tion, confidence ratings, and situational factors. *Child Abuse & Neglect, 14,* 69-77.

Kalichman, S.C., Craig, M.E. & Follingstad, D.R. (1989). Factors influencing the reporting of father-child sexual abuse: Study of licensed practicing psycholo-gists. *Professional Psychology: Research & Practice, 20,* 84-89.

Kempe, C., Silverman, F., Steele, B., Droegmueller, W. & Silver, H. (1962). The battered child syndrome. *Journal of the American Medical Association, 181,* 17-24.

Kluft, R.P. (1990). "Sitting duck" incest victims vulnerable to repeat abuse. *The Psychiatric Times,* Feb., *15.*

Kroll, J. (1988). *The challenge of the borderline patient: Competency in diagnosis and treatment.* New York: W.W. Norton & Company.

Liebert, D.S. & Foster, D.V. (1994). Mental health evaluations: Standard of prac-tice in capital cases. *The American Journal of Forensic Psychiatry, 15,* 43-64.

Lippitt, D.N. (1985). The ethical task in family therapy. *Family Therapy, 12,* 297-301.

Loftus, E. (1993). The reality of repressed memories. *American Psychologist, 48,* 518-537.

Marvasti, J.A. (1993). Psychopathology in adult survivors of incest. *American Journal of Forensic Psychiatry, 14,* 61-73.

Melton, G.B. & Limber, S. (1991). Caution in child maltreatment cases. *American Psychologist, 46,* 82-84.

Milner, J.S., Gold, R.G., Ayoub, C. & Jacewitz, M.M. (1984). Predictive validity of Child Abuse Potential Inventory. *Journal of Consulting and Clinical Psychology, 52,* 879-884.

Monahan, J. (Ed). (1981). *Who is the client? The ethics of psychological interven-tion in the criminal justice system.* Washington, DC: American Psychological Association.

Navarre, E.L. (1987). Psychological maltreatment: The core component of child abuse. In Brassard, M.R., Germain, R., & Hart, S.N. (Eds.). *Psychological maltreatment of children and youth.* New York: Pergamon Press.

Newberger, E. (1983). The helping hand strikes again: Unintentional conse-quences of child abuse reporting. *Journal of Clinical Child Psychology, 12,* 307-311.

Nightingale, N. & Walker, E. (1986). Identification and reporting of child mal-treatment by Head Start personnel: Attitudes and experiences. *Child Abuse and Neglect, 10,* 191-199.

Pope, K.S. & Bajt, T.R. (1988). When laws and values conflict: A dilemma for psychologists. *American Psychologist, 43,* 828-829.

Pope K. & Vetter, V. (1992). Ethical dilemmas encountered by members of the American Psychological Association: A national survey. *American Psychologist, 47,* 397-411.

Russell, D. (1986). *The secret trauma: Incest in the lives of girls and women.* New York: Basic Books.

Sonkin, D.J. & Ellison, J. (1986). The therapist's duty to protect victims of domestic violence: Where we have been and where we are going. *Violence and Victims, 1,* 205-214.

Sonkin, D.J. (1986). Clairvoyant vs. common sense: Therapist's duty to warn and protect. *Violence and Victims, 1,* 7-22.

Swoboda, J., Elwork, A., Sales, B. & Levine, D. (1978). Knowledge and com-pliance with privileged communication and child abuse reporting laws. *Professional Psychology, 9,* 448-457.

U.S. Department of Health and Human Services (1994). *Child maltreatment 1992: Reports from the States to the National Center on Child Abuse and Neglect.* Washington, DC: U.S. Government Printing Office.

Walker, L.E. (1984). *The battered woman syndrome.* New York: Springer Publishing.

Watson, H. & Levine, M. (1989). Psychotherapy and mandated reporting of child abuse. *American Journal of Orthopsychiatry, 59,* 246-256.

Weinstock, R. & Weinstock, D. (1989). Clinical flexibility and confidentiality: Effects of reporting laws. *Psychiatric Quarterly, 60,* 195-214.

Weithorn, L.A. (1987). Psychological consultation in divorce custody litigation: Ethical considerations. In Weithorn, L.A. (Ed.), *Psychology and child custody determinations: Knowledge, roles and expertise.* Lincoln, NE: University of Nebraska Press.

Weithorn, L.A. & Grisso, T. (1987). Psychological evaluations in divorce custody: Problems, principles and procedures. In Weithorn, L.A. (Ed.), *Psychology and child custody determinations: Knowledge, roles and expertise.* Lincoln, NE: University of Nebraska Press.

Williams, H.S., Osborne, Y.H. & Rappaport, N.B. (1987). Child abuse reporting law: Professionals' knowledge and compliance. *Southern Psychologist, 3,* 20-24.

Wilson, C. & Gettinger, M. (1989). Determinants of child abuse reporting among Wisconsin school psychologists. *Professional School Psychology, 4,* 91-102.

Wright, R.H. (1984). They did it again. *Psychotherapy in Private Practice, 2,* 89-95.

Yates, A. (1987). Psychological damage associated with extreme eroticism in young children. *Psychiatric Annals, 17,* 257-261.

Zellman, G.L. (1990). Report decision-making patterns among mandated child abuse reporters. *Child Abuse and Neglect, 14,* 25-336.

Zellman G.L. (1992). The impact of case characteristics on child abuse reporting decisions. *Child Abuse and Neglect, 16,* 57-74.

CONCLUSION

Multiple Victimization of Children: Remaining Issues

Mindy S. Rosenberg
B. B. Robbie Rossman

SUMMARY. The authors identify three areas of empirical and clinical scholarship that need further attention in the area of multiple victimization of children. These include assessment of multiple victimization, assessment of additional sources of adversity in the child's environment, and the creation and use of developmentally appropriate, theoretically driven measures of child outcome. This is the last article in an edited book on multiple victimization of children that focuses on research and treatment issues from a developmental perspective. *[Article copies available for a fee from The Haworth Document Delivery Service: 1-800-342-9678. E-mail address: getinfo@haworth.com]*

Address correspondence to: Mindy S. Rosenberg, PhD, 505 Bridgeway, Suite 105, Sausalito, CA 94965.

[Haworth co-indexing entry note]: "Multiple Victimization of Children: Remaining Issues." Rosenberg, Mindy S., and B. B. Robbie Rossman. Co-published simultaneously in *Journal of Aggression, Maltreatment & Trauma* (The Haworth Maltreatment & Trauma Press, an imprint of The Haworth Press, Inc.) Vol. 2, No. 1 (#3), 1998, pp. 317-322; and: *Multiple Victimization of Children: Conceptual, Developmental, Research, and Treatment Issues* (ed: B. B. Robbie Rossman, and Mindy S. Rosenberg) The Haworth Maltreatment & Trauma Press, an imprint of The Haworth Press, Inc., 1998, pp. 317-322. Single or multiple copies of this article are available for a fee from The Haworth Document Delivery Service [1-800-342-9678, 9:00 a.m. - 5:00 p.m. (EST). E-mail address: getinfo@haworth.com].

317

This volume was organized with the goal of bringing together current theory, research and clinical practice on the psychological effects and treatment of multiple victimization. It was our hope that this integration could stimulate research, clinical, educational and legal efforts that would benefit those children who experience more than one form of maltreatment, often from more than one perpetrator, and often in an environmentally adverse context. What our authors found, however, was that with a few exceptions, the child maltreatment literature has not grappled with the issue of multiple victimization. Nonetheless, the authors' contributions represent an important initial step toward addressing developmental, research, conceptual, clinical, legal and ethical issues for multiply maltreated children. They provide us with the most current thinking and knowledge in this neglected area, orient us toward developing appropriate methodology and interventions, and detail the implications of experiencing such trauma. In reviewing the volume's articles, we identified three areas of empirical and clinical scholarship that needed further attention: (1) the assessment and consideration of multiple victimization; (2) the assessment and consideration of additional sources of adversity in the child's environment; and (3) the creation and use of developmentally appropriate, theoretically driven measures of shorter-term outcome and longer-term adaptation for multiply victimized children. Each of these areas will be discussed briefly as follows.

ASSESSMENT FOR MULTIPLE VICTIMIZATION

One consistent theme expressed by authors of this volume is the limited attention paid to assessing for multiple aspects of child victimization, including intensity, frequency, and nature of the various acts. At the present time, very few researchers evaluate for more than one type of maltreatment so that sample populations and study results may be unknowingly contaminated. Although mental health clients have made clinicians aware that traumatic experiences are not contained in discrete categories, it is the rare researcher who has recognized and incorporated that information into interview protocols and study designs.

The neglect in assessing for multiple victimization may be due, in part, to the difficult issues raised by such assessments for researchers and clinicians alike. The institutional contexts from which clients and research participants come, the disclosure abilities of individual families, and the current dearth of multiple victimization assessment procedures provide obstacles to detecting multiple abuse. First, the thoroughness of assessment instruments available to, or used by, different community agencies will vary. Unfortunately, researchers have needed to rely on referrals for research participants from various governmental and service agencies that have either specialized in treating a particular type of child maltreatment (e.g., sexual or physical child abuse programs) or have focused on one or two types of maltreatment to the exclusion of others. However, researchers may also have been reluctant to corroborate independently the identified maltreatment or assess for other forms of maltreatment. At times, clinicians and other professionals may hesitate to provide multiple reports on the same family, especially when families are already involved in treatment and maintaining a treatment relationship is critical. In addition, they may be misinformed about their legal responsibilities for reporting multiple incidents or new forms of maltreatment for previously identified families (see Sonkin and Liebert, this volume). Furthermore, procedures for assessing some types of maltreatment, such as psychological abuse, are not widely available. Thus, agency data, which provide the basis for assignment to either research or ongoing treatment groups intended for singular types of abuse, may be incomplete.

A second obstacle to gathering accurate information is the willingness and/or ability (e.g., whether memories are available consciously or whether certain behaviors would be recognized as emotionally abusive) of family members or the child to disclose the complete picture of victimization. The emotional and legal (i.e., reporting mandate) consequences of disclosing the intimate and painful material can certainly interfere with family members' desire to provide this type of information. They may be able, over a protracted period of time in a trusting relationship with a clinician, to disclose more information. For an individual in crisis (e.g., upon entry into a battered woman's shelter or abuse treatment program for parents), more complete disclosure for a child or parent may be too overwhelming. In addition, the parent may not be fully aware of the extent of maltreatment that her child or youth has experienced, since the child may not have revealed the extent of abuse and/or psychologically protective processes (e.g., denial, minimization, dissociation) may be operating for the parent. Given both the system and family obstacles to obtaining information about multiple victimization, it seems critical to attempt to obtain data from as many different sources as possible.

Finally, most existing maltreatment assessment instruments have been developed to focus on one specific form of child maltreatment: sexual abuse (e.g., Child Sexual Abuse Inventory; Friedrich, Grambsch, Damon, Hewitt, Koverola, Lang, Wolfe, & Broughton, 1992); adult to child violence or modified format to include witnessing of domestic violence (e.g., Conflict Tactics Scale; Straus, 1979); psychological maltreatment (e.g.,

Brassard, Hart, & Hardy, 1993); or potential for physical child abuse (e.g., Child Abuse Potential Inventory; Milner, 1986). These instruments could be used together in attempts to assess multiple maltreatment. Unfortunately, since they were developed and validated for specific types of abuse, it is not clear if these psychometric properties might change were they to be used together. At least one instrument, A Record of Maltreatment Experiences (McGee, Wolfe, & Wilson, 1990; McGee, Wolfe, Yuen, & Carnochan, 1991), is being developed to assess multiple forms of maltreatment for older children and youth. It includes subsets of questions regarding psychological maltreatment, exposure to parental violence, physical abuse and neglect, and sexual abuse. Initial data based on concordance among information from children aged 11-17 years, their social worker, and records on file suggest that this instrument may provide a needed tool in evaluating multiple victimization. A similar device to be used with younger children is needed. In addition, since there may be some perpetrator behaviors that occur across different types of victimization, it would be important for researchers working with multiple abuse assessment to devote energy to identifying behaviors that are both unique and common to different forms of abuse. This would be similar to the development strategy utilized for the Child Behavior Checklist (Achenbach, 1991), and could aid in the understanding of how developmental processes and domains may be affected by multiple victimization.

COMPLEXITY OF ENVIRONMENTAL CONTEXT: MULTIPLE SOURCES OF ADVERSITY

A second theme that emerged across articles in this volume is the need to pay attention to the complexity of the child's total context of adversity and to consider the potential traumatic features of a child's environment in addition to his/her experiences of specific abusive incidents. Positive features of the child and his/her environment that could buffer the child need to be a part of this contextual picture as well. Generally, the authors do not speculate about the form of impact aggregated adverse factors might have (e.g., whether additive, interactive or something else), but the data suggest that greater adversity is likely to be associated with greater developmental interference. Such interference may lead to immediate or future psychological impairment, especially in the absence of compensatory or resiliency factors.

Authors in this volume have outlined several different conceptual models to map the terrain of multiple sources of adversity. Probably the most comprehensive conceptual consideration of such issues is outlined in the article by Masten and Wright (this volume). Their explanations of multi-system cumulative risk and protection models of child maltreatment and adversity provide researchers and clinicians with a guide to identifying factors within, as well as beyond the child and their family, that may contribute to the child's distress and/or well-being.

DEVELOPMENTALLY APPROPRIATE OUTCOME CRITERIA

By inviting developmental theorists to offer their perspectives on the effects of multiple victimization, we were hoping to make accessible in-depth information about the different domains affected by such experiences (e.g., cognition, the self system, emotion regulation, interpersonal relationships). Our developmentalists have provided much food for thought to stimulate further research and clinical scholarship on the multitude of unanswered questions they identified. In the past, developmental issues have too frequently been considered superficially in child maltreatment studies. For example, age has typically been used as the only variable reflective of development in creating groups or reporting relationships with other variables. In part, this is a function of lack of, or ambiguity about, more sensitive indices that could be used. However, it is time to use measures in addition to chronological age to reflect developmental position and to create outcome indices that are more developmentally sensitive and theoretically driven. Without a strong theoretical developmental base to unify findings and measures, the results of future research will continue to resemble a laundry list of differences and non-differences between victimized and comparison groups. Sadly, this litany of findings seems unlikely to deepen our understanding of how and in what way children's developmental processes become impaired as a result of multiple victimization experiences.

CONCLUSION

What is evident from the material presented throughout this book is that child maltreatment is an extremely complex psychosocial phenomenon. Although historically, various forms of abuse and neglect were studied individually and gave rise to separate literatures, it is now time to change our conceptual direction and find ways to understand the interaction between multiple forms of victimization, the larger environment of adversity, and the resulting psychological consequences from those experiences.

Continuing dialogue between researchers and clinicians becomes all the more important, as both groups find ways to identify the subtleties of maltreatment experiences that add richness and complexity to our conceptual models, research questions, and treatment interventions. As we develop and refine our various theoretical perspectives, we come closer to approximating a child's reality of multiple victimization, including both similarities across groups of children, and understanding unique individual differences. Hopefully, the current book is a beginning foundation for pursuing this new direction in child maltreatment thought and practice.

REFERENCES

Achenbach, T.M. (1991). *Integrative guide for the 1991 CBC/4-18, YSR, and TRF profiles.* Burlington, VT: University of Vermont Department of Psychiatry.

Brassard, M.R, Hart, S.N., & Hardy, D.B. (1993). The psychological maltreatment rating scales. *Child Abuse and Neglect, 17,* 715-729.

Friedrich, W.N., Grambsch, P., Damon, L., Hewitt, S., Koverola, C., Lang, R.A., Wolfe, V., & Broughton, D. (1992). Child sexual behavior inventory: Normative and clinical comparisons. *Psychological Assessment, 4,* 303-311.

McGee, R.A., Wolfe, D.A., & Wilson, S.K. (1990). *A record of maltreatment experiences.* Unpublished instrument. University of Western Ontario, London, Ontario.

McGee, R.A., Wolfe, D., Yuen, S., & Carnochan, J. (1991). *The measurement of child maltreatment: A comparison of approaches.* Paper presented at the Meeting of the Society for Research in Child Development, Seattle, WA.

Milner, J.S. (1986). *The Child Abuse Potential Inventory: Manual* (second edition). Webster, NC: Psytec Corporation.

Straus, M.A. (1979). Measuring intrafamily conflict and violence: The conflict tactics scales. *Journal of Marriage and the Family, 41,* 75-88.

Index

Academic achievement, 267
Accommodation
  biological function and
    adaptation, 136-137
  in infants, 138
Achenbach Child Behavior
  Checklist, 80
Acute Stress Disorder, 54
Adjustment disorders, in
  religion-related abuse
  cases, 288-291
Adolescents
  cognitive development, biological
    basis and treatment
    methods, 142-143
  literature on maltreatment,
    107-129
  delinquency, 108-109
  developmental tasks and,
    107-108,110-117
  dysfunctional family patterns,
    108
  incidence, 109-110
  methodological issues, 109
  multiple maltreatment,
    117-124
  parricide, 119-124
  posttraumatic stress disorder,
    54-61
  prevalence of multiple
    victimization, 276
  self regulation in, 179,180
  self-systems
    false self behavior, 152
    integration of selves, 151-152
    peer opinions in, 160-161
    self-blame, 162
  treatment, 253-272

developmental
  approach/issues, 142-143,
    255-256,262-269
  factors in, 254-255
  psychotherapy, 242-243
  societal issues, 253-254
  trauma theory in, 256-262
Adult Attachment Interview, 191,
  197-200,213
Adults abused as children,
  posttraumatic stress
  disorder in, 57-58. *See also*
  Parenting/parents
Affect. *See* Emotional regulation;
  Emotions
Affective communications, in young
  children, 72
Affective disorders, in
  religion-related abuse
  cases, 288-291
Affective splitting, 155
Age, in response to victimization, 70
Agency, effects of abuse on, 156-157
Aggression. *See* Behavior problems;
  Violence/aggression
Alcohol abuse. *See* Substance abuse
Amnesia, psychogenic, 155,156
Anger
  in marital conflict, impact on
    children, 37,38-41,45
  parental, school-age children
    response to, 100
Animals in therapy, 264
Antisocial behavior. *See* Behavior
  problems; Social interaction
Anxiety, in school-age children, 99.
  See also Fears and phobias

    323

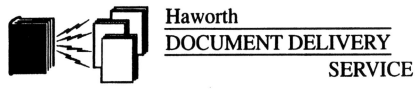

Haworth
DOCUMENT DELIVERY
SERVICE

This valuable service provides a single-article order form for any article from a Haworth journal.

- *Time Saving:* No running around from library to library to find a specific article.
- *Cost Effective:* All costs are kept down to a minimum.
- *Fast Delivery:* Choose from several options, including same-day FAX.
- *No Copyright Hassles:* You will be supplied by the original publisher.
- *Easy Payment:* Choose from several easy payment methods.

Open Accounts Welcome for . . .
- Library Interlibrary Loan Departments
- Library Network/Consortia Wishing to Provide Single-Article Services
- Indexing/Abstracting Services with Single Article Provision Services
- Document Provision Brokers and Freelance Information Service Providers

---

MAIL or *FAX* THIS ENTIRE ORDER FORM TO:

Haworth Document Delivery Service
The Haworth Press, Inc.
10 Alice Street
Binghamton, NY 13904-1580

or FAX: 1-800-895-0582
or CALL: 1-800-342-9678
9am-5pm EST

PLEASE SEND ME PHOTOCOPIES OF THE FOLLOWING SINGLE ARTICLES:

1) Journal Title: _____
   Vol/Issue/Year:_____Starting & Ending Pages:_____
   Article Title:_____
   _____

2) Journal Title: _____
   Vol/Issue/Year:_____Starting & Ending Pages:_____
   Article Title:_____
   _____

3) Journal Title: _____
   Vol/Issue/Year:_____Starting & Ending Pages:_____
   Article Title:_____
   _____

4) Journal Title: _____
   Vol/Issue/Year:_____Starting & Ending Pages:_____
   Article Title:_____
   _____

(See other side for Costs and Payment Information)

COSTS: Please figure your cost to order quality copies of an article.

1. Set-up charge per article: $8.00
   ($8.00 × number of separate articles) _____

2. Photocopying charge for each article:
   1-10 pages: $1.00 _____

   11-19 pages: $3.00 _____

   20-29 pages: $5.00 _____

   30+ pages: $2.00/10 pages _____

3. Flexicover (optional): $2.00/article _____

4. Postage & Handling: US: $1.00 for the first article/
   $.50 each additional article _____

   Federal Express: $25.00 _____

   Outside US: $2.00 for first article/
   $.50 each additional article _____

5. Same-day FAX service: $.35 per page _____

GRAND TOTAL: _____

___

METHOD OF PAYMENT: (please check one)

❏ Check enclosed   ❏ Please ship and bill. PO # _____
(sorry we can ship and bill to bookstores only! All others must pre-pay)

❏ Charge to my credit card: ❏ Visa; ❏ MasterCard; ❏ Discover;
❏ American Express;

Account Number:_____ Expiration date:_____

Signature: *X*_____

Name: _____ Institution: _____

Address: _____

_____

City: _____ State:_____ Zip:_____

Phone Number: _____ FAX Number: _____

___

MAIL or *FAX* THIS ENTIRE ORDER FORM TO:

Haworth Document Delivery Service	**or FAX:** 1-800-895-0582
The Haworth Press, Inc.	**or CALL:** 1-800-342-9678
10 Alice Street	9am-5pm EST)
Binghamton, NY 13904-1580	